BRITANNIA'S REALM

In Support of the State: 1763–1815

A HISTORY OF THE BRITISH MERCHANT NAVY
VOLUME TWO

BRITANNIA'S REALM

In Support of the State: 1763–1815

RICHARD WOODMAN

The History Press

'With Freedom's lion-banner

Britannia rules the waves.'

Thomas Campbell

First published 2009

The History Press
The Mill, Brimscombe Port
Stroud, Gloucestershire, GL5 2QG
www.thehistorypress.co.uk

British Library Cataloguing in Publication Data.
A catalogue record for this book is available from the British Library.

ISBN 978 0 7524 4819 0

Typesetting and origination by The History Press
Printed in Great Britain

CONTENTS

A 300-ton British merchantman typical of many general trading vessels of her day and capable of going anywhere. Plain headed and ship-rigged, she appears to have temporarily raised sides, probably to protect her cargo. She has her anchor catted at the bow as she comes into an open road to anchor. From the drawing by Baugean. (Private Collection)

INTRODUCTION

The first book in this five-volume work was furnished with a long introduction in which I set down both my reasons for attempting this project and the means by which I hoped to accomplish it. To this I added a note containing an explanation of my method, in particular pointing out my reasons for dislocating the chronology in order to bring one story to its conclusion. This was principally true of the slave-trade, the narrative of which insofar as it was carried out in British ships was brought to a conclusion with the abolition of the traffic in 1807, but also to certain aspects of the activities of British shipping in the Far East. The dangers to Great Britain's valuable eastern trade were touched upon in the closing chapter of the first volume of this work, *Neptune's Trident*, with an account of the loss of the Honourable East India Company's ship the *Earl of Abergavenny* in 1805. Thereafter, some account was rendered of the hydrographic surveying undertaken by the East India Company to mitigate the dangers to their ships. Thus *Neptune's Trident* over-ran that break-point of 1763 so beloved by naval, military and constitutional historians but to which trade pays no attention. Apart from these chronological projections the main narrative terminated with the Treaty of Paris ending the Seven Years War in 1763, at which point Britain emerges on the world stage as a serious threat to France and the possessor of a widely dispersed maritime empire.

The present volume is more constrained in its time-frame, firstly dealing with the plight of British shipping in the Atlantic and Arctic Oceans during the reversal of fortune that followed their rebellion, and culminated in the loss of the Thirteen Colonies which, in 1783, became the United States of America. This is followed until the eve of the war of the French Revolution in 1793. Consideration is then given to British shipping in the Far East and the Pacific where the important trade with China is of particular significance, before dealing with the dangers of navigation to and from those remote destinations.

The second part of this volume is entirely taken up with what, before 1914, was known as 'the Great War' with France. It is a story almost untold in its entirety, inevitably being subordinated to the history of the Royal Navy. This fact, in which Nelson's victory at Trafalgar is too often regarded as a battle of annihilation which defeated Napoleonic ambitions of invasion, misses the point. In fact Trafalgar neither annihilated the enemy's naval might, nor prevented invasion, the threat of which had passed weeks earlier and the means of which were no longer deployed on the Channel coast but were in central Europe at Ulm. It is too often forgotten that between Nelson's death in 1805 and Napoleon's final defeat in 1815 lay a decade of hard fighting on land and sea during which, though French fleets rarely got to sea, their flying squadrons of frigates and their swarms of corsairs did so continuously. The effects of their attacks on British trade compromised Britain's ability to wage war, for she filled her war-chest from the proceeds of trade and indeed waged economic warfare on the First French Empire by out-flanking Napoleon's Continental System by trafficking with those parts of the enemy alliance that were in need of embargoed goods and commodities. That these included a Kingdom of Holland, ruled over by Napoleon's younger brother Louis, speaks for itself. Furthermore, as the diplomatic tide turned against Paris, it was British gold that subsidised the armies of Russia, Prussia and Austria; British gold that was itself a product of British trade. At the same time British merchant shipping busied itself supplying the painstaking and intermittent offensives of the future Duke of Wellington in the long slog of the Peninsular War. Thus, as Wellington knew well, the decade that followed Trafalgar was one in which Britain exerted all her sea-power – that of *both* her sea-services – to achieve final victory.

The all-too-frequent eclipse of this important point obscures the true achievement of Trafalgar which was of much more enduring consequence than a temporary access of power, discommoding an enemy who was capable of – and almost achieved – a rebuilding of his naval forces. Trafalgar was a victory of enablement; Britannia did not rule the waves in its immediate tumbling aftermath, but in its longer wake.

The cost of this was immense, not least in the wrecked lives of the nation's seafarers and I make no apology for the lengths to which I have addressed the incidents surrounding the activities of the Admiralty's Impress Service and the often illegal actions of the notorious press-gangs. Too often the depredations of these naval bullies have been rendered romantic whereas, in truth, it was despotic and roused its victims to a fury that was not always impotent and in its turbulence mirrored the social unrest fomented by the Luddites and all those opposed to the illiberal impositions of industrialisation. Such then, is the background to these momentous years.

Richard Woodman
Harwich, 2009

ACKNOWLEDGEMENTS

A considerable number of people have helped in the preparation of this volume and I wish to thank them all for their kindness and generosity. Some have assisted with information or advice, giving of their expertise and time; others have furnished documentary material from their family archives while yet more have given permission to use illustrations from their collections free of charge and I am most grateful. The names of several appear in the list of acknowledgements in the first of this five-volume work, *Neptune's Trident*, but since their aid was necessary in the writing of the present volume it would be churlish to exclude them on those grounds. My thanks therefore to Sir Michael Bibby; Captain Aris Finiefs; Rob Gardiner; Captain Joshua Garner; The Lord Greenway; Michael Grey; Mr R.G. Hart; John Keay; M. Philippe Petout of St Malo.

Especial thanks must go to Michael Charles, owner of the British Mercantile Marine Memorial Collection; to Richard Joslin of the N.R.Omell Gallery, and Richard Green and Susan Morris of the Richard Green Gallery for their wonderful help and generosity in sourcing some of the illustrations; similarly Paul Ridgway and John Robinson have been most helpful in their advice over early drafts of the text. My thanks also go to Rear Admiral Jeremy de Halpert and Mr Peter Galloway, respectively the Deputy Master and Secretary of the Corporation of Trinity House, for permission to use paintings in the Corporation's possession, and to Captain Graham Pepper and the Master and Wardens of the Honourable Company of Master Mariners.

My thanks for their professional help to Chris Rawlings at the British Library, Nathaniel Pendlebury at National Museums on Merseyside, Melissa Atkinson at the National Portrait Gallery and Doug McCarthy at the National Maritime Museum. Thanks also to the Master, Wardens and Brethren of the Hull Trinity House. I am, as always, indebted to my agent, Barbara Levy.

NOTE: For appropriate maps, the reader is referred to *Neptune's Trident*.

PART ONE

'Britannia Contra Mundum'

The Plight of Merchant Shipping 1763–1816

ONE

'TO THE NO SMALL SATISFACTION OF THE CAPTORS'

Peace and War in the Atlantic and Arctic Oceans, 1763–1792

The Treaty of Paris which ended the Seven Years War in 1763 found Great Britain in possession of an empire almost by default. Her military successes in Canada had destroyed the French in North America, thereby securing her American colonies, and so reduced French influence in India that the sub-continent was to fall increasingly under British influence in the years to come. Moreover she had increased her plantations in the West Indies while the necessary expansion of her navy had raised that service to new heights. Thus a war that had started over a provocative British attack on French merchant shipping and in backwoods scraps between colonial rivals and their native American allies, left the British with unrivalled global opportunities for trade, not least because the Imperial Government in London insisted in colonial enterprise being self-financing. Within a dozen years this imposition, exacerbated by the enormous costs of the war, which had almost doubled the national debt to £133 million sterling, prompted ministers to attempt to recoup these costs and in doing so provoked British-American citizens to rebel against such coercion. Despite this, the independence of the Thirteen Colonies produced no dire consequences for Great Britain for almost two centuries. True the new United States of America was to become a maritime competitor and to challenge British sea-power, but it might be argued that this competition was healthy and, as we shall see, benefited British ship design after 1815. In the short-term reconciliation with the former colonies was swift and the resumption of trade profitable to both parties. This circumstance was to the further advantage of the Americans when, with much of the British merchant fleet committed to military transportation in support of the Napoleonic War in general and the Peninsular Campaign in particular, American bottoms picked up the short-fall in world tonnage. That this brought them into direct conflict with the Royal Navy and a short, sharp war (that of 1812-1814) proved an irony in direct conflict with the material well-being of both countries.

Nor was the post-1763 expansion of British trade due solely to new markets and the opportunistic energies of her merchants and seafarers; it was also partly attributable to the sudden access to new sources of ship-building timber occasioned by victory. Just when the native English woodlands were approaching a state of exhaustion and American yards were building for their own flag, Malabar teak became available in greater quantities from India, and mahogany was supplied from the West Indies; moreover, supplies of soft-wood and mast-timber from Canada seemed limitless. To these fortuitous new sources of raw materials for the construction of ships themselves has to be added the impact of the two great dynamic changes that were to power an astonishing increase in the British economy: first the Agrarian and then the Industrial Revolutions. The most obvious consequences of the latter of these events for shipping were, in due course, the development of the steam-ship and the adoption of iron and then steel for ship-building, subjects covered in the third volume of this history.

Such a sweeping period of change was unprecedented. Some idea of its impact on shipping may be had from a brief look at the town of Swansea in South Wales. Then the pre-eminent port and civic centre in Wales, Swansea's trade built rapidly. Timber was imported from Canada, the West Indies and India and exports of coal from local mines rivalled that of the ports of the Tyne and Wear. Unlike Geordie coal, much of which went directly to London, Swansea's output was for export, in part to smelt copper-ore in South America but also, in due course, to provide excellent fuel for world-wide merchant shipping and the coal depots of the Royal Navy during the following century. In time it proved cheaper to bring copper-ore to smelting works in the Swansea valley in a fleet of pretty barques, making Swansea the centre of copper production responsible for 65 per cent of the world's output during the nineteenth century.

Such success was based on the proximity of huge reserves of coal and this was replicated elsewhere, where a local commodity provided the basis for a specific industry and a local river the site for a port from which it was carried by fleets of coasters. China clay, alum, iron and copper-ore, all provided the foundation for a variety of ports, while others grew up round centres of manufacturing and hence population, which in turn created demand not just for raw materials but for food, manufactured goods and luxuries. All these factors created opportunities for the carrying trades; inland by road, canal and – eventually – rail, but elsewhere by sea and only by sea in a vast number of small coasting craft. Indeed, during the nineteenth century such were the delays and congestion inherent in land transport, and so eager were the railway companies to reward the greed of their shareholders that even in a small island such as Great Britain, an already thriving coasting trade prospered and expanded. This was possible wherever a river-estuary provided a quay and, where it did not, a hard sand-bank with a tidal range such as would leave a ship conveniently high and dry at low-water. Here cargo could be worked in and out of horse-drawn carts, and yet allow the discharged vessel to refloat at high tide. Such sand-banks were often misleadingly known as 'wharfs'.

Rivalling the stage and mail coaches, passenger-and-mail-packet sailings operated not only between Dover and Calais, Harwich and Helvoetsluis, or Liverpool and Dun Laoghaire, but on the north/south axis between London and Edinburgh by means of heavily sparred, uncomfortable and hard-driven 'Leith Smacks', and between Liverpool and Glasgow by both passenger and mail-packets.

Some of this is to anticipate. Whilst such expansion is obvious in hindsight, there were other influences at work in the wake of the Seven Years War, an awakening of more than mere commercial instincts. A second, intellectual impetus was added to the first visceral British desire to trade, compounding national effort, uniting disparate societal parts and building a species of patriotism that blazoned its way across the world in the succeeding century and a half, opening British eyes to the additional possibilities of exploration. In this sense trade *did* follow the flag. After the discomfiting of Spain and The Netherlands in previous centuries, the recent victory over France seemed – after the early débâcle of the war – to hint at divine approbation. With India and Canada in the bag, thoughts turned once more to the Pacific, or the Great South Sea; 'South', because from Dairen it appeared to lie south of the east-west axis of the Panamanian isthmus. The flag had been advanced upon its waters in the years 1740–1744, after which Richard Walker's account of Anson's voyage became a best-seller. Other works followed: a reprint of *Harris's Voyages* contained Dr John Campbell's exhortation to 'maintain Trade, and there is no doubt that Trade will maintain us. Let our past Mistakes teach us to be wise, let our present Wants and Difficulties revive our ancient industry.'

One outcome of an independent United States for Great Britain was the need for a new colony, not least as a repository for felons hitherto sent to America. A suitable territory lay, so everyone thought, somewhere south of the Moluccas: its coast had been glimpsed by the Dutch, by Dampier, Torres and De Quiros; a British ship – the *Tryal* – had been lost on its outer reefs, although Abel Tasman had missed its mainland, striking islands off its adumbrated coastline. *Terra australis incognita* had to be there, the cosmographers asserted, to balance the vast land-mass in the north. Despite their defeat, the French were stirring, sending out Bougainville to recoup the losses he personally had had a hand in, in north America; and Spain – still maintaining its mercantile galleons between Acapulco and Manila – again grew nervous. Britain had early probed the northern gateway to the Pacific, and found the North West Passage impassable. In the year following the war's end Lord Egmont, First Lord of the Admiralty, secured the southern gateway, sending Commodore The Hon. John Byron to take possession of the so-called Falkland Islands in the *Dolphin* and the *Tamar* and any other places 'within Latitudes convenient for navigation and in the Climates adapted to the Produce of Commodities usefull(sic) in Commerce'.[1] This done he was to pass into the Pacific where, during his tempestuous passage Byron acquired the soubriquet 'Foul-Weather Jack'. He did not tarry long in the Pacific, compelling Egmont to repeat the experiment in his final year of office, 1766, when he despatched Captain Samuel Wallis in the battered *Dolphin* to find what was then best described as a 'Land or Islands of Great extent…between Cape Horn and New Zeeland' (sic).

In the end it was James Cook, at the other end of the social spectrum to Byron, a man raised in the bluff-bowed mercantile cats of Whitby and in the English east-coast coal and Baltic trades in which they were employed, who best succeeded. It had been an army officer who had first pried open Cook's skills as a surveyor on the damp and foggy shores of Nova Scotia and Newfoundland, while it took another Yorkshireman, John Harrison, to make the break-through in the design of a marine chronometer capable of solving the 'longitude problem'. As mentioned in *Neptune's Trident*, the accurate timepiece – Cook's was actually made by Larcom – along with John Hadley's new sextant, and the 'Nautical Almanac' introduced by Neville Maskelyne, the Astronomer Royal, in 1767 from which daily ephemeris were derived, provided Cook with the grander tools of his new trade, adding to the rod and chain, the bunting pendants and the plane table of local triangulation.

This was all hitched to the international attempt to measure the diameter of the earth and calculate the distance of the sun, occasioned by the forthcoming Transit of Venus. A previous and recent attempt had failed, a second opportunity was to present itself in 1769, after which years would have to elapse before another occurred. Then Joseph Banks weighed in, adding the naturalist's cause to that of exploration and astronomy and Cook was off in his Whitby cat, the modified *Earl of Pembroke*, renamed *Endeavour*, hoisting a naval ensign to match his naval commission as lieutenant. Cook sailed on the first of his three great voyages in August 1768.

Within a short period it was not only the Acapulco galleons of the Spanish who flaunted European flags in the Pacific. Following the naval exploration vessels of Cook's successors, British and French, came the whalers of Britain and the new United States, as we shall presently see, but the southern whale fishery of the Pacific had its predecessor in the more accessible polar seas of the Arctic.

Largely from their east coast ports, the British had long since followed the Dutch north into the waters round Spitsbergen (Svalbard) and later west of Greenland into the Davis Strait in search of the docile and relatively easily harpooned Northern Right Whale, but after an initial flowering, this Arctic fishery had gone into decline. However, it enjoyed a revival around 1750 when a company was floated in Newcastle on the initiative of Captain John Blagdon, a master with interests in the American trade. Two years later the Newcastle Whale Fishing Company was established, founding an industry which lasted with varying success until the beginning of the twentieth century. Following Blagdon's initiative, Newcastle despatched three vessels, the *Swallow*, *Resolution* and *Dolphin* in 1753 – Hull, London, Leith, Dundee and Whitby also joined the quest. Whitby's fortunes throve on the new 'Greenland fishery' and it became the first town in Britain to have its streets lit by oil. Although the *Golden Lyon* had sailed north in 1752, Merseyside's first purpose-built whaler was fitted-out on 1775, Liverpool's whalers peaking later at twenty-three vessels, the Scoresbys' famous *Baffin* among them. To support this fleet a blubber-processing works was added to the increasing maritime infrastructure growing on the banks of the river.[2]

Initially a lack of native expertise required the employment of a few Dutch and Danish harpooners, but these were either quickly dispensed with or subsumed – like so many other 'foreigners' in British ships. However, a more enduring practice was introduced in the closing years of the American War of Independence after arguments between the ship-owners and the Government following the reduction in the Government's tonnage-bounty and the chronic shortage of seamen for the navy, of which more later. Having reduced the bounty, Lord North's cash-strapped ministry threatened to abolish it altogether, but a petition from Hull forced the Government to give way and restore the bounty to its pre-war rate of £2 per ton. As for the man-power problem, whalers from English and Scottish ports were permitted to augment their crews with Shetlanders. The whalers were accustomed to top-up water and stores at Lerwick before proceeding north and the attraction of the port was now doubled, for the Shetland seamen were not only hardy, but driven to sea by lack of alternative work and were willing to accept the system of voyage-shares in lieu of the full regular pay expected by ordinary merchant seamen. However, their reputation for seamanship made them attractive to naval officers short of man-power and while whaler-men, or 'Greenlanders', were theoretically protected from the press, it was not uncommon for them to be forced to defend their liberties with a ferocity that cost lives. After a fracas with the seamen of HMS *Vengeance* during the American War, the *Golden Lyon*'s crew had marched to the

The dangers and perils of the Northern Whale fishery are depicted here. Normally a relatively easy prey, the Northern Right Whale occasionally fought back and the privations endured by Arctic whalers were often frightful. (Author's Collection)

Liverpool Custom-House to secure certificates to this effect, in order that they could safely seek employment 'in the colliery or coasting trade, without being liable to be impressed during the time of the year that they were not employed in the [whale] fishery'. It was not to be an isolated incident.

Due to their specialised nature, both in terms of hull strength and equipment, whalers were expensive, something in the order of £2,200 being required for a second-hand vessel of 300–400 tons burthen, with further capitalisation for each annual 'expedition'. Though at this period few ships were specially built for the trade, the Bounty Acts passed by Parliament to encourage the fishery, and from which owners derived their only income if a whaler returned 'clean', required staunch ships. This was achieved by 'fortifying' or doubling the outer plank-ing to absorb ice-damage and, later on, often included iron bow plating. Along with a name for oily smelliness, whalers acquired a reputation for longevity. Best known was the *Truelove* of Hull, which was actually built in Philadelphia in 1764, made seventy-four voyages to the Arctic and was the last pure sailing whaler at the time of her final voyage in 1868. Other long-lived whalers included the *John* of Newcastle which went a-whaling between 1766 and 1808, and the two Whitby ships *Volunteer* and *Henrietta*, which between them made over 100 voyages into the north polar seas.

Although the Right Whale was, at least relative to the Sperm Whale, a docile animal, boats were often lost in their pursuit and the valuable Arctic fishery was sustained on relatively small numbers of whales caught. The *Swallow*'s maiden voyage was declared an 'uncommon good success,' according to the *Newcastle Courant*, yet she brought in only four whales which nevertheless adduced 'to the general satisfaction of the whole town…which was demonstrated by the ringing of bells'.[3] However, this represented a satisfactory return on the investment of principals. Among early bonanzas was that of the *Resolution* whose slaughter of fifteen whales in 1756 realised a dividend of 20 per cent for her share-holders, but it was a risky and uncertain business. As Tony Barrow points out, there were voyages when the ships returned 'clean' and of the fifteen voyages made by the *Swallow* only seven were actually profitable.

> Between 1750 and 1760, for example, 34 of the 127, Scottish whaling voyages were 'clean', about 25 per cent. The first of the Edinburgh ships *Tryall* appears to have been a financial disaster, with eight 'clean' voyages in eleven, and a total catch of only nine whales.

To the risks of the hunt has to be added the inhospitable nature of the Arctic Ocean. In 1758 the *Resolution* and her Newcastle-registered sister *Phoenix*, together with the *Leviathan* of Whitby, were lost in the ice. The Newcastle company suffered the loss of the *Dolphin* in 1763 and the *Swallow* three years later, causing it to cease trading shortly afterwards, and for a few years Whitby abandoned the fishery. While the Scots companies continued to own whalers, the English adopted the practice of sole-ownership, John Baker & Co. being the most prominent Newcastle merchant involved.

The general expansion of the Tyne required the construction of a large graving dock there, an enterprise undertaken by Francis Hurry who had moved north from Great Yarmouth. His dock at Howdon-on-Tyne was among the first of many on that river and he built both merchant and warships. Hurry also took an interest in whaling, with baleen, bone-cleaning and blubber-processing plant rising on land adjacent to his dock. His first whaler, the 340-ton *Newcastle*, purchased from Baker who had acquired her as a replacement for the *Phoenix*, failed to kill a single whale in three of her first four voyages and then, whilst lying in the Tyne, she caught fire. Undaunted, Hurry and his partner and father-in-law, Thomas Airey, bought an American-built vessel, the *John and Margaret*, which, in Barrow's words, 'became one of the stalwarts of the Tyne whaling fleet for almost half a century'. Other ships joined the fleet, but danger was never far away and one, the *Annabella*, was crushed in the ice on her fourth voyage in May 1768 while the *Royal Exchange* was wrecked in 1773. This vessel had, in the same year the *Annabella* was lost, returned triumphantly with a haul of twelve whales and 2,300 seals, but these successes could not rival those of Whitby.

Whitby merchants had returned to the Arctic in 1767 and the following year, that of the *Royal Exchange*'s record voyage, almost matched it with the *Jenny*, which came home with nine whales, 570 seals and four polar bear-skins. Whitby-built ships were not only suitable for voyages of exploration, as advocated by James Cook, but ideal for whaling. One such was the *Volunteer*, mentioned above, built for Richard Moorsom at Whitby in 1756, and manned by forty men whose lives are outlined in an account written by William Kidd, her surgeon. Leaving Whitby in late March 1772 in company with the *Jenny* and three other whalers, she was prevented from entering Lerwick on 9 April.

> All on a sudden, about four o'clock in the morning, we were seized with a sudden gale from the north…which put us in the greatest extremity, it being impossible for any man to handle a sail; we continued in this deplorable condition until twelve o'clock, when the storm abated a little, then we got our foresail reeved [reefed] and our mainsail smothered; in this condition we continued until the 10th, when this severe gale had pretty much abated…but the sea desperately high and a very intense frost with showers of snow at intervals…[4]

The *Volunteer* finally reached the fishing grounds and the main body of whalers off the west coast of Spitsbergen on 3 May. Disaster dogged them that year with the *Porpoise* and the *Volunteer* still clean and surrounded by loose pack-ice. They had sighted a few whales but caught none, seeing nothing between 14 and 29 June and entertaining 'no hopes of getting into the ice…and the season far spent'. Then on Monday 6 July:

> At 2 o'clock in the morning, we let fall all our boats and in about half an hour after Richard Grice got fast to a fish [as the whalers called their quarry] and was soon seconded by all our boats with four boats from the *Dolphin* (of Liverpool) who was very neighbourly in assisting us. We killed it in about an hour…[and three days later, again at] About 2 o'clock in the morning we saw some fish and instantly lowered down two boats and came up with a fish that was just dying. Jacob Grimes struck a harpoon into it which secured it as our property the *Dolphin*'s boat was not a hundred yards off it…

The *Volunteer* then made for Maklina Bay on the east Greenland coast and 'Here we begun to put our blubber into casks, which employed all hands.

It is the hardest work belonging to the Greenland fishery'. Grice harpooned another whale as they stood out to sea again, and they took two more before setting sail for home, the last of which repaid their earlier frustration, proving 'more superior than any of the former four [having] 15 inches and a half thick of fat or blubber'. Once ashore, the proceeds of these five whales rendered down to '65 tuns' of oil with three tons of baleen 'whalebone', amounting to a value of £2,200 to which was added the Government bounty for the five months' voyage. As owner Moorsom – who appears to have been the master – made about £1,250, Matthew Smith, the mate made £40, and Grice received about £32.

In addition to Greenland whaling, there was also the hunt for the Sperm Whale in which British vessels took part. For example the *Seacombe*, Captain Pagan, of Liverpool took five Sperm Whales between the Azores and Canaries in the summer of 1781, but it was the Americans who were to achieve fame in the hunt for the Sperm Whale, or Cachalot, *Physeter macrocephalus*, and in this context it must be remembered that the famous Nantucket whalers were originally British, albeit colonial British, and their early hunting grounds lay at first in the temperate waters of the mid-latitudes of the North Atlantic, stretching from New England down to the Azores. In 1715 it was Nantucket ships that first ventured offshore with ship-board try-works for processing catches at sea, instead of bringing the blubber home in cask for rendering – or 'trying-out' – at home. The provision of try-works on board enabled a whaler to remain at sea for longer periods in order to fill her casks and this in turn, combined with the greater profits to be made from sperm oil, spermaceti and occasional 'finds' of ambergris, led both the British-American and native British whaling ships into the South Atlantic and the Pacific. The ultimate superiority of sperm oil threatened the Arctic fishery until baleen, or so-called 'whale-bone', became a vital fashion-item in the nineteenth century.

After American independence there was an emigration of Loyalists from Massachusetts to, among other places, Nova Scotia, and in 1784 a new whaling industry was founded at Halifax. Six years later the British naval officer Graham Moore visited Nova Scotia and reported that:

> The trade of Halifax consists entirely of salt fish and whale oil... The Whale Oil is the produce of the Southern Fishery (i.e. that of the South Atlantic and Pacific Oceans) which I learn is by far the most lucrative...it is carried on in vessels of various denominations, and bulk according to the finances of the adventurer to whom they belong. These vessels commonly touch at the Cape Verde Islands for livestock, they then proceed to the southward towards the coast of Brazil where they meet the Spermaceti whales many of which are worth five hundred

pounds. The crews of these vessels are interested in the success of the voyage as they all go on shares… They are seldom out longer than eleven months.'

– a perception that the whaler had it easy compared to the naval man.

Other Loyalists moved to Milford Haven in Pembrokeshire, from where ships joined those from London in seeking the Sperm Whale in the Southern Ocean and thence into the Pacific, as we shall presently see.

During the Seven Years War, Arctic whalers sailed in company for mutual defence against the pernicious French corsairs. Having been 'fitted with great guns and small arms' the several Tyneside masters agreed 'to act in concert with Mr Brown as commodore'.[5]

Towards the end of the Seven Years War the growing trade with North America for mast and ship-building timber provided an alternative to the vulnerable trade with the Baltic and was widely welcomed. Many London companies were involved, ship-owners often acquiring ex-East Indiamen for the trade. The fourth Company ship to be named *London* was bought for the purpose by Messrs Woodman & Co. in 1762 and was sent to Canada for timber. The *Lord Macartney* was sold to Hunter of London in 1792 to take up a regular lumber-run to Halifax, as was the *Tavistock*. Notwithstanding the apparently infinite supply of wood from the softwood forests of North America, trade with north-west Europe remained important, by way of both the Baltic and the White Sea. Men like the ship-owner, financier and Lloyd's under-writer John Julius Angerstein, who owned the former Honourable Company's Ship *Lord Camden*, now renamed the *Juliana*, sent their ships to Archangel.[6]

Indeed the relatively short life of an Indiaman in John Company's service provided a steady supply of redundant second-hand vessels for other commercial uses. Several went into the West African slave-trade, such as the Bombay-built HCS *Syren* which made only one voyage to India and in 1778 went slaving as the *African Queen*; others were bought-up for use as West Indiamen. Among the ship-owners exploiting connections with the East India Company to fill gaps in the regular sailings, was the shrewd Anthony Calvert whom we encountered in *Neptune's Trident*. He acquired second-hand vessels, including former East India Extra-ships, to put into the sugar, rum and molasses trade with the Antilles and for re-use as Extra-ships trading to India. Some of these vessels are of interest and show Calvert's eye for a solid vessel. The Extra-ship *Union* had been built by Barnard at Harwich in 1759 as the bomb vessel *Terror* for the Royal Navy. Such craft were incredibly strongly constructed and used after the Napoleonic War for Arctic exploration. Sold out of naval service to J. Montgomery of London in 1774, the *Terror* was renamed *Union* and refitted for the West Indies trade. Two years later Calvert acquired her, commissioned her as an Extra-ship which, commanded by Richard Owen, was sent back to Calcutta. Another of his acquisitions was the *Albemarle* which had been built in France and was captured in late 1779 by HMS *Albion* while serving as a military transport conveying part of Rochambeau's force to America. Condemned as lawful prize by the Prize Court in Barbados, she was brought home and purchased by Calvert in 1780. Fitted out for the West Indian trade, the 520-ton vessel was renamed *Albemarle* and placed under the command of Captain James Boulton. Ironically she was retaken by a French privateer early in 1793 as we shall see in a later chapter.

Mention of Le Comte de Rochambeau's passage to America recalls the fact that, in part through the assistance of the count's expeditionary force, the north American colonies had ceased to be British following their rebellion. Civil disobedience in the early 1770s had deteriorated into civil war. Armed rebellion and the establishment of a congress with its defiant declaration of independence soon provoked a global war. Insofar as this War of Independence affected the British merchant fleet, its first consequence was to reduce it drastically in size, by removing all vessels owned in the thirteen rebellious colonies from the British flag. Next, it established a new mercantile marine in competition with that of the former mother-country, a fact that would have increasing impact as the United States' merchant fleet expanded and improved the quality of its ships and the standard of service offered to its shippers. Thirdly, it loosed upon the Seven Seas a fleet of fast privateers even more familiar with British trade-routes than the French, and fourthly an additional if less powerful maritime force was raised first by the separate 'states' and then the Continental Navy – the forerunner of the United States Navy – established by an act of Congress in 1775. Finally, of course, all this was of material aid to Britain's enemies which, by the end of the war, included not only the American rebels, but all the maritime states of Europe, most especially the French, Spanish and Dutch, all of whom were commercial as well as military and naval rivals.[7] In her alliance with France, America not only acquired a decisive military partner, but a source of men-of-war, an additional further pack of helpful *loups de mer*, and a geographically convenient refuge, base and market for the British merchantmen seized in European waters by her own privateers, a state of *Britannia contra mundum*.

At a day-to-day level matters for British merchantmen ran much as they had done in the Seven Years War and afterwards. The Royal Navy shamelessly and often illegally abducted merchant seamen, while the French – even before they declared war on Great Britain after their recognition of the new nation of the United States of America in 1778 – were despatching hundreds of privateers of all sizes into every navigable sea upon which they might encounter a British merchant ship. Here they were joined by their new – and dangerously republican – allies, the Yankee rebels.[8] Joining this private commercial form of warfare were a number of Irish renegades or rebels, according to your political colour, the combined effects of all of which drove up the price of insurance and added huge and costly burdens to the ship-owner.

The crisis of the war on trade came on 9 August 1780 when the outward-bound East and West India fleets were abandoned by their naval escort and fell into enemy hands, as is presently described. The crisis of the naval war itself came in October 1781 when De Grasse defeated Graves off the Chesapeake and Cornwallis's army was abandoned at Yorktown. Although New York remained in British hands until the Peace of Versailles was signed in September 1783, the war in North America was effectively over when Cornwallis surrendered and the British army at Yorktown laid down its arms before Washington and Rochambeau in October 1781.

Four months prior to the opening shots of the war – fired across Lexington Green on 19 April 1775 – a meeting of merchants trading to North America gathered from all over the kingdom to meet at the King's Tavern, Cornhill, the venue chosen years earlier by their elders setting up The Marine Society. At the same time the West India merchants assembled in the London Tavern not far away. Clearly seeing the inevitable outcome of the British Government's coercive legislation upon their fellow traders on the far side of the Atlantic, these two groups of sober and anxious gentlemen protested the folly of the Government's policies and petitioned that all such measures enacted against the colonists be repealed.

Their pleas fell upon deaf ears and 'within a month...8,000 tons of shipping', some 400 vessels, 'had to return from America without cargoes, the blockade not allowing them to land'. By September the Liverpool *General Advertiser* invited its readers to:

> Survey our docks; count there the gallant ships laid up and useless. When will they again be refitted? What become of the sailor, the tradesman, the poor labourer, during the approaching winter?

It was no better in London where, two months later, 600 vessels formerly employed in the American trade were idle in the Thames, while the following February a mere six ships were entered inwards at the London Customs House. The only real beneficiary in all this – the American economy itself suffering considerable damage from this suspension of commerce – was the Royal Navy which, in mobilising, had no trouble picking up unemployed seamen.

However, the Americans were not slow in finding alternative employment for many of their faster ships. By the summer of 1776 they had near 180 privateers cruising against British trade which, among a number of prizes, had taken twenty-three West Indiamen. Sent in to Virginian ports, the valuation of their combined cargoes of plate, sugar, rum, old Maderia, pimento, ginger, hides, cocoa, fustic and tortoise-shell was said to be 22,420 Spanish dollars. With each privateer commander receiving £5,000 and every sailor £500, their crews were made men.

Until the war degenerated into another general European conflict, rumours circulated that deals were being done: American rebels were soliciting for certain manufactures unobtainable except from Britain, and these were being supplied by complicit merchants while the bottoms carrying them surrendered to American privateers for the sake of appearances, and on the surety of indemnities or compensation of one sort or another. Some of this seems to have substance and there was reluctance on the part of both the ship-owners and the Admiralty to commission private ships of war to interfere. Certainly many people recognised that family and business connections united the two combatant nations, while the large number of Loyalists, amounting to about a third of the New England population at the commencement of the rebellion, was at that time a significant and influential minority. Eventually, however, on 11 April 1777, Their Lordships gave notice of their readiness to issue Letters-of-Marque-and-Reprisal to British ship-owners.

While the stupidity – both politically and militarily – of the British response to the colonists' defiance rapidly eroded much loyal sentiment on the far side of the Atlantic, the transformation of the war by the entry of first France and then Spain, kindled that patriotism best exemplified by a recognition of commercial opportunity. Once their shipping was being seized and plundered as it had been in the previous war, the British ship-owner took up numerous Letters-of-Marque. The most suitable ships that could be rapidly converted into privateers were the armed and idle slavers, and between August 1778 and the following April London and Liverpool between them sent out some 200, mounting about 2,000 guns and manned by roughly 10,000 men.

> This formidable armament proved a considerable annoyance to the hostile powers, and captured several French ships from the East and West Indies, of such immense value, as enabled the merchants of Liverpool not only to restore their credit and extend their commerce, but to trade upon real capital.

This was only part of the picture, but it ameliorated to some extent the exorbitant insurance rates and paucity of markets the rebellion had created.

One measure to improve matters was the increasingly strict regime ruling the conduct of convoys, which the Admiralty were now compelled to take seriously. Of particular importance was the prohibition against masters of fast ships running ahead of a convoy. Another was the offer of civic bounties in addition to that of the Government to seamen willing to enter the Royal Navy. By this means it was hoped to better regulate recruitment into the navy and prevent the kind of civil disorders that had occurred ashore in the previous war. Unfortunately, in the event, neither of these measures had much impact.

For those at sea the uncertainties were grim and fortune as capricious as ever. The 10-gun *Sally* of Rhode Island, well manned with 103 men and commanded by Captain Munro, was a typical American privateer. In the winter of 1776, having taken a ship from Bristol and another from London, Munro captured the *Union* of Liverpool, Captain Wilson, from West Africa with Malageta pepper and ivory. Taking out all her papers, letters and clearances, along with her cargo, Munro put aboard the *Union* two dozen prisoners from his earlier captures, with some provisions. He then let her go, but two days later the *Union* was boarded by a party from another Rhode Islander under a Captain Field, who found her too much trouble to detain. Finally a third rebel ship, the 14-gun brig *Cabot* 'belonging to the Congress', that is to say a unit of the Continental Navy, detained her. Captain Elisha Hinman searched his prize and ordered her to stand away to the north-west until, to Wilson's relief, British men-of-war hove in sight.

Meanwhile, on 3 October, the *Cabot* went on to seize the brig *Watson* on her way home to Liverpool from Jamaica. Captain Francis Brison was accompanied by the brig's owner, James Bier, who was carried on board the *Cabot* where Hinman at first refused to allow him to return to the *Watson* but then relented. Writing from Dundalk on 3 December, Bier related how he resolved to turn the tables on his enemy.

They took all my men except the captain, one boy and a passenger, putting eight of their own people on board. We were to proceed to New London or Rhode Island. In about three weeks we got into soundings off Boston, but that night I had determined to retake her, having brought over to my party two of their people, by promising them £100. Accordingly, at 8 o'clock, they sent me a pistol by the boy, on which I immediately jumped on deck, clap'd it to the prize-master's breast, and demanded him to surrender the vessel which he instantly complied with. We then secured all the hatches, till I got all the arms, which compleated the business. I bore away for Halifax, but the wind being fair stood on for Newfoundland. The wind still being favourable, stood on for Ireland, where I struck soundings in 27 days. We had but two barrels of beef when I bore away, but fortunately had two turtles about 600 lb. weight, which served us three weeks. We ran in here [Dundalk] in a hard gale of wind, where we lie in safety having (thank God) received no damage, except one boat washed overboard, with studden-sails(sic) and some spare ropes. Our fire and candles were entirely exhausted.

Bier and, presumably Brison, proved both resourceful and courageous seamen, as did others. Captain Ashburn of the Hunter was only taken by the rebel privateer *Pallas* after a two and a half hour action in which the Hunter lost four killed and sixteen wounded and so crippled the Pallas that she was obliged to abort her cruise and seek shelter with her prize.

The new American Continental Navy, which soon amounted to twenty-seven vessels, enjoyed several successes. In 1776, writing from Nantes after being himself captured with his ship, the *Leghorn Galley*, which was one of the private packets established by Mr Thomas Earle of Liverpool, Captain Alexander M'Daniel reported he had been taken by:

the *Enterprize*, Captain Weeks…mounting 16 six-pounders, 24 swivels, and 130 men. She brought over [to France] Dr Franklin, one of the Congress, who is gone to the court of Versailles. She took a brig belonging to Cork from Bordeaux, one Cod, master, and a brig from [La] Rochelle bound to Hull, one Fetchett master…and has sold both vessels and cargoes to the French. Here is also a privateer belonging to Charles Town, South Carolina, commanded by one Cockran, mounting 12 four-pounders, and 80 men, besides four other vessels belonging to the Congress, all taking in naval and military stores, and are arming them all.

This letter reveals both the fact that even before their declaration of war, the French were very materially assisting the American rebellion, and also that such correspondence gave much information in the way of intelligence, an important but largely unacknowledged contribution to naval warfare in this and, more significantly, the greater conflict to come.

In November the Continental cruiser *Independence*, John Young commander, seized the *Sam*, Captain Richardson, on her way from Barbados to Liverpool with a cargo consisting chiefly of two tons of ivory and 20,000 in silver Mexican dollars. The *Sam* was sent in to Philadelphia with her surgeon, mate, and crew; her master and boatswain were landed in Martinique and the remainder of her people 'entered on board' the *Independence*. Richardson's exact fate is unknown but he escaped with his life, which was not always the case. Captain Frith of the *Sarah*, in company with the *Thomas* in January 1777, was attacked near Barbados by an American privateer, the *Revenge*, Captain Joseph Sheffield. The *Thomas* was taken but the *Sarah* escaped, only

to be attacked again two days later. Frith's men put up a stout resistance, the
vessel was damaged, her master and mate wounded, but the enemy were
beaten off. Putting in to Carlisle Bay, Frith's wounds proved mortal. As for
the *Thomas*, her second mate, James Barton, wrote to his owners from Rhode
Island informing them that all but he, a boy and the boatswain had been put
aboard a French vessel bound for Martinique. Barton and his occupying
prize-crew proceeded in company with the *Revenge* until the appearance
of HM Frigate *Unicorn*, Captain John Ford, upon which Sheffield fled and
the *Thomas*, unable to sail so fast, capitulated. Once released and landed
at still friendly Rhode Island, Barton tended the wounded boatswain. He
appears to have been promoted master of the *Thomas*, for in 1779, again in
company with the *Sarah*, now commanded by a Captain Hooton, the two
took a prize of their own. The *Sarah* was subsequently lost on Anguilla, but
the *Thomas* took a further prize, a tobacco-laden schooner, and sent her
into St Kitt's. Both vessels appear to have belonged to the same owner and
sailed in company for mutual support, carrying Letters-of-Marque enabling
them to legitimately acquire prizes if the opportunity offered, but were not
fitted out with the intention of acting as aggressive privateers. The danger
in such a policy lay in depleting one's own ship's company by sending away
prize-crews, for these ships did not carry the large complements required in
a fully commissioned privateer. Nevertheless, it became a common practice
and was exercised by Woodville of the *Hero*, Naylor of the *Valiant* and White
of the *Laurel* – all Liverpool ships – among many others. Likewise Captain
Dawson of the *Marlborough*, who in June 1777 took the American merchantman *Three Brothers*, Captain Bentley, in the North Atlantic laden with rice,
barrel-staves and indigo. On her way towards Liverpool, Bentley attempted
to kill Dawson's prize-master, but thanks to the vigilance of a ship's boy he
was frustrated. Dawson took another prize in 1778 but was himself captured
when the *Marlborough* was seized and sent in to Bordeaux.

As is clear from the foregoing, many merchant ships resisted attempted
seizure, fighting off their assailants, but the results were often dire. On 2 June
1777 the *Elizabeth*, outward-bound to Jamaica, was boarded by the crew of
the 14-gun privateer *Fly*, whose 104 man crew swarmed aboard and 'cut and
mangled' Captain Byrne and his men 'in a shocking manner'. Three seamen
were killed and thirteen wounded. The *Johnson*, Captain Jones, put up a stiff
but useless resistance against three privateers, whereas the *Gregson*, Captain
Wotherspoon, the *Fanny*, Captain Wignall, the *Fancy*, Captain Allanson, and the
Will, Captain James Collinson, were among those surviving their encounters.[9]
Captain Maddock of the 16-gun *Pole* was successful the following month when,
with only forty people – passengers included – he beat off the well-armed and
manned privateer *Tartar* commanded 'by one Davies, a Welshman'. One of his

passengers was 'an elderly woman belonging to Liverpool, but who had been twenty-seven years in America, handed the cartridges to the men':

> Captain Maddock had two mates and a passenger wounded, and supposes that near one half of the people belonging to the privateer must be killed or wounded, he having cleared their forecastle of men three different times, and says he heard dreadful cries among them.

Maddock must have been something of a tartar himself, for on his next voyage he took the *Friendship*, bound to Boston from Bordeaux, though she was afterwards retaken by an American privateer, and in 1778 the *Pole* engaged and took the American schooner *Hannah* and a richly laden brig, the *Prince and Liberty*. The next year Maddock captured the *Salisbury*, from Maryland to Nantes, and the *Hector*, Martinique to France with sugar, coffee and cotton, before himself being overwhelmed by two Continental cruisers, the *Boston* and the *Confederacy*.

In December 1777 Captain James Wiseman of the *Isabella* also encountered a squadron of the Continental Navy consisting of the *General Sullivan*, the *Resistance* and the *Rambler* which he fought fiercely for four hours. Notwithstanding heavy casualties and being vastly outnumbered, he beat off his assailants. On his arrival at St Vincent a few days later, Wiseman learned of the surrender of General Burgoyne at Saratoga in October.

As this, the first real disaster of the war, approached, the British Government resorted to a somewhat desperate exigency. Asserting – as it was to do for many years and thereby provoke a further war with the Americans in 1812 – that anyone born under British rule in the Thirteen Colonies was therefore 'British', a declaration was published inviting the crews of American vessels to mutiny and seize them from their officers. They would be rewarded by 'two-thirds of what such ships and cargoes shall be sold for (and for three years be exempted from being impressed)...' What guarantees came with either statement, especially the latter, is uncertain, but *Williamson's Advertiser* in which this notice appeared on 18 July 1777, cheerfully expected the consequences to yield up 'many a valuable ship and cargo into England, which would otherwise go to the French ports'. The ploy worked only insofar as a few British born seamen who had been forcibly entered into American ships objected to their fate, and on 11 January 1778 the Virginian ship *Oxford* entered the Mersey loaded with '412 hogsheads of sugar and staves'. She had been taken during a passage to Nantes on the 11th by four of the ship's crew who had overwhelmed the remaining eight. Originally a Glaswegian vessel, the *Oxford* had been a British military transport captured earlier by the Americans; she now became a *droit du roi*. Whether or not King George III repaid the 'four resolute, brave men' who had seized her is unclear, but doubtful.

The men who brought in the tobacco-laden *Aurora*, part of a polyglot crew of Americans, French and Englishmen, were granted a reward. Each of the eight Englishmen were rewarded to the tune of £1,828, the Americans helping them receiving £914. However, actual receipt of these monies is uncertain, for on their arrival the Americans were immediately seized and 'impressed on board his Majesty's tender'. Other such seizures were brought into the Clyde and disposed of in Glasgow, so the extent to which the Government kept its promises must remain dubious.

The Admiralty took more practical steps that same month, in stationing cruisers in the Irish Sea, St George's Channel, off Cork and Scilly, at Campbelltown in Scotland and Carrickfergus in Ulster. This was also the month that the *General Mifflin*, formerly the Liverpool privateer *Isaac*, appeared in the Irish Sea under the command of Walter Day. Day took a string of prizes: the *James* from Oporto to Liverpool; the *Rebecca*, Liverpool to Limerick; the *Mary and Betty*, Liverpool to Ballyshannon and the *Priscilla*, Sligo to Liverpool. In another cruise between the Shetlands and Norway, under Daniel McNeil, the *General Mifflin* fought a severe engagement with and took a British privateer, and seized a number of prizes. These – according to Captain Symerson of one of them, the *Dick* of Liverpool, which was captured with 740 barrels of tar, 1,000 masts and a quantity of other marine supplies – consisted of the *Chatham*, *George* and *Lion*, which were plundered and burnt; the *Archangel Packet* with tar and masts, out of which McNeil took all her crew but two; the *Dispatch*, from London to Onega which he kept as a tender; and the *Sally*, on her way from Hull to Archangel in which he stored his plunder. McNeil sent his prizes to France and those British seamen unwilling to sign-on the *General Mifflin* – allegedly forty-three out of seventy – he released in the *Dispatch* at the end of his cruise.

Some enemy privateers like the *General Mifflin* acquired fearsome reputations. The provocatively republican-named *Oliver Cromwell*, described as a 'great frigate' was one such, taking three prizes in a single week, 'one a Guineaman with 300 slaves, one a ship from London…' It was to get worse. Suspicion, even paranoia, was rife. From St Vincent on 5 May 1777 it was said that:

we have numbers of privateers that are [at the time illegally] manned with French; some have only an American, and that perhaps a landsman, just to cloak their piratical proceedings. It is said (and I believe founded on truth) that Mons. Le Compte (sic) D'Argout, present governor of Martinique, is concerned with Bingham, the agent to the Congress, in nine privateers. There are now about 20 sail of [captured] English ships in Martinique. Negroes are cheaper there than in Africa, and provisions than in Ireland.

Among the captured slavers flooding the market were the *Sisters*, Captain Graham, taken with 163 slaves on board; the *Diana*, Captain Colley, taken off Tobago with 378 slaves by the rebel privateers *General Moutrey* and the *Fair American*; the *Greenwood*, taken outwards for Guinea from Africa by the French frigate *Vengeance*; the *Tom*, Captain Davis, the *Hereford*, Captain Harrison; the *Juno*, Captain Beaver.[10]

The paranoia was not confined to the West Indies. A report from Ireland in May 1779 – at the height of the war on trade – spoke of:

> five rebel privateers off Cape Clear and Kinsale, waiting, it is imagined, for the Newfoundland fleet from hence, and transports from Cork. The convoy [escort] is only a sloop of 14 guns. They take our ships in our channel…Where it will end I know not'.

That month losses among the West India ships were estimated at 'upwards of £400,000 sterling'. Other correspondence revealed similar, widespread anxieties. Letters from Dumfries told of two American privateers anchored in the Solway Firth; others spoke of privateers off the Mull of Kintyre; from Jersey came intelligence that they were lying between that island and Guernsey and removed themselves to St Malo on the slightest sign of a British cruiser. All spoke of the numbers of prizes taken, burnt, sent to France. In the West Indies, too, Martinique was reviled as a 'nest of damned piratical scoundrels' where 'the Americans are so much protected' – a benefit derived from their long association with the French islands trading for sugar in defiance of the Navigation Acts.

After the declaration of war by the French, matters grew worse, increasing the losses of ship-owners, freighters and consignees. The *Lydia*, Captain Dean, from Jamaica to Liverpool, serves as an example, for she was seized, taken to Maryland and sold with her cargo for £20,400. British privateers were also captured, as we shall see, but typical was the capture of Warren & Co.'s *Dragon* which, under Captain Briggs, had herself seized a number of rebel American and French ships. One of the latter, taken in February 1779 was *La Modeste* and she had been secured by members of the *Dragon*'s crew swimming across to her to take possession, since the sea was running too high to launch a boat. The *Dragon* did equally well under Captain Reed the following year but in September 1781, Captain Gardner was obliged to strike her colours to a French frigate and submit to being taken in to Brest.

French frigates were particularly dangerous, often sailing as fast as a privateer, particularly as wind and sea rose, and usually of far greater fire-power. The 32-gun British frigate *Minerva*, having been captured and commissioned by the French in 1778, fell in with the *Belcour* of Liverpool, Captain Moore, in May 1779.[11] Moore bore a Letter-of-Marque and had the previous year taken a schooner worth £1,000 and a French brig valued at £2,500. Now, on a passage from Halifax to Jamaica, the tables were turned and Moore found himself fighting for his life:

> We engaged…[the *Minerva*] full two hours and a half, the furthest distance she was off was not more than pistol shot, a great part of the time yard arm and yard arm, as we term it, but that you may better understand it, her sides and ours touched each other, so that sometimes we could not [with]draw our rammers. The French, I assure you, we drove twice from their quarters, but unluckily their wadds set us on fire in several places, and then we were obliged to strike. You may consider our condition, our ship on fire, our sails, masts and rigging being all cut to pieces, several of our men severely mangled. The French seeing our ship on fire, would not come to our assistance for fear of the ship blowing up, as soon as the fire reached the magazine, which it did five minutes after I was out of her. The sight was dreadful, as there was many poor souls on board. You will be anxious to know how we that were saved got out of her. We hove the small boat overboard in a shattered condition…and made two or three trips on board the frigate before she [the *Belcour*] blew up. The next morning, we picked up four men that were on pieces of the wreck…

Moore goes on to list the dead: the third mate, the surgeon and his mate, eleven seamen, 'three Negroes and a child, passengers'.

Another successful French frigate was the 28-gun *L'Aigle* which, in the spring of 1780 took the Liverpool privateer *Tartar*, Captain Butler, 'after a chase of eight hours and an engagement on one hour and a quarter'. In three weeks *L'Aigle* seized nine prizes, a fact lamented by Butler from prison in Bayonne in a letter to his ship's owners. A heavier French cruiser, the *Fripon* of 44 guns, took the privateer *Patsey* off the Hebrides on 31 May 1781. During a fight lasting ninety minutes before her colours came down, Captain Dooling, his sailing master and six of the *Patsey*'s crew were killed and a number wounded. That October a French 44-gun frigate engaged the merchantman *Quaker* off Newfoundland. Despite her pacifist name, the *Quaker*'s master, Captain Evans, had furnished her with a Letter-of-Marque and in the autumn of 1781 she had arrived at Halifax with a 13-gun American privateer as her prize. Early the following year she took in to Antigua three prizes where they realised £21,000 and it was while returning north that, again on the Grand Banks, she fell in with the French frigate in a fog. Undaunted, Evans exchanged a broadside – in which one of the ship's boys was killed and another wounded – then made all sail. After a chase of twelve hours Evans threw his pursuer off and got clear away and in the new year of 1783 he took another prize, a Letter-of-Marque brig from Martinique to France with a cargo of sugar, coffee and cocoa worth £10,000. Such men were redoubtable and one of the most renowned was Nehemiah Holland.

In July 1777 Captain Nehemiah Holland of the *Sarah Goulburn*, who had distinguished himself in the previous war, took the *Sally* of Charleston, South Carolina, when on her way to Nantes with rice and indigo. Throughout the war the trade between the rice plantations in North America and France was a rich hunting-ground for British privateers, capitalising on the rebel necessity to establish new markets for their produce. Tea, silk and wine went the other way and several privateers would form an *ex officio* squadron, agreeing to share prize money. In the winter of 1778/9 the Liverpool privateers *Molly*, Captain Woods, the *Wasp*, Captain Byrne, and the *Bess* took a number of prizes, though the *Molly* was, long afterwards, captured by a brace of French frigates. Captain Ash of the 20-gun *Terrible* took two valuable prizes on a single day that spring, and also recaptured the *Leinster Packet*, which had been taken by the American privateer *Rocket* the previous day when bound from Bristol to Galway. A few days later, on 28 February, Captain Grimshaw, in command of Hall & Co.'s 14-gun *Griffin*, entered the Mersey with a French prize, *Le Comte de St Germain* which he had taken after a spirited running action lasting eight hours. The two vessels had been evenly matched in fire-power, though the Frenchman carried a smaller complement. The prize contained a cargo of tortoise-shell, indigo, sugar, molasses, coffee, cotton and cocoa. Other privateers profiting from this trade route were Wagner & Co.'s *Dreadnought*, Davenport's *Sturdy Beggar*, and Captain Allanson's aptly named *Vulture*.[12] However, success itself ran its own risk, as Captain Leigh of the *Mary Ann* discovered. Having taken thirteen prizes valued at £10,000, the *Mary Ann* was homeward-bound when she struck the Tusker Rock off the east coast of Ireland. Fortunately most of Leigh's cargo of indigo was salved and all his crew saved.

Many privateers, like the *Griffin*, performed a useful service in retaking captured vessels from the enemy. On 10 December 1778 the privateer *Atalanta*, 16 guns, Captain Collinson, recaptured the brig *Eagle* from Newfoundland to Cadiz with fish, and the following winter the *Rawlinson* and *Clarendon*, lying off Land's End, retook the *Weymouth Packet* 'which had sailed from Jamaica without convoy and had been taken by the *General Sullivan* privateer, of Portsmouth, New England'. The importance of recovering such a vessel, with mails, bills of exchange, currency and so forth is self-evident. Later, in May 1781, the 10-gun *Ferret*, Captain Archer, having been seized by a French corsair, was retaken by the privateer *Vulture* from Jersey. A few prizes were recovered by their own people, such as the *Grace*, Captain Wardley, seized in the Irish Sea by the privateer *Lexington* but carried to Torbay instead of France; and the *Lively*, which is related later. Such exertions were often risky.

When in April 1781 the *Balgrove* was captured by a French corsair a prize-crew of sixteen men were put on board, but her mate was unwilling to submit and, with only four men to help him, overpowered the prize-crew and took the *Balgrove* into the Cove of Cork.

Nor had the Royal Navy's cruisers been idle; taking 203 American merchantmen between 11 July 1777 and 1 January 1778, and recapturing fifteen British vessels in rebel hands. Privateers from several British ports had also done their utmost to counter the enemy, but the anxieties and losses drove insurance rates inexorably upwards, a state of affairs only exacerbated by the entry of France – with her swarms of corsairs – and after her the other European maritime states. The American privateers, 'though of limited naval value, certainly contributed to the Revolutionary cause, striking at the British merchant class, who, in turn, ventilated their opposition in Parliament'. This is a naval view, disparaging to the effort and effect of America's private war on trade. The function of a nation's maritime force, howsoever composed, is to destroy the enemy, attack his commerce and thereby ruin his economy. This was a view current at the time, for Thomas Jefferson considered that privateering was a national blessing 'when a Country such as America then was, was at war with a commercial nation'. American analysis concludes that the 676 privateers commissioned under the new ensign of thirteen red stripes took 'over 1,600' British merchantmen.[13] This, of course, excludes captures by the small but efficient Continental Navy and the very much greater impact of French corsairs, and of French men-of-war after 1778.

Such was the alarm in high places that all British merchant vessels were ordered to sail under convoy, though this was no guarantee of safety. When HMS *Falcon*, the escort to a West India convoy, became separated from her charges, two of the merchant ship-masters, Captains William Buddecome and George Ross, undertook the defence, for which they received gifts of silver plate, but convoy, when carried out efficiently, proved its value.

> In the third week in September, 1778, it was announced that all the principal fleets had arrived safely, namely, The Jamaica fleet at Liverpool and Bristol; the Leeward Islands fleet at Plymouth, and the Lisbon and Spanish fleets in the Downs. The arrivals that week were the largest that had been known for many years. In October the London underwriters calculated that the losses sustained by the French since the proclamation of reprisals amounted to upwards of £1,200,000.

When the outward-bound West India fleet sailed in March 1779 it did so under the not inconsiderable escort of two 74-gun line-of-battle-ships, a 50-gun ship and two frigates. This was not the case in August the following year when, as will shortly be related in relation to the East India Company, the combined convoys bound to the East and West Indies were abandoned by their naval escort commanded by Captain John Moutray and captured by Admiral Cordoba's squadron. Significant among the fifty-two vessels taken by the Spanish were the Government-chartered victuallers and store-ships, four of which – the *Lord Sandwich*, *Eliza*, *Friendship* and *Brilliant* – carried stores for the army in the Leeward Islands; eleven of which – the *Sisters*, *Nereus*, *John*, *Susannah*, *Jupiter*, *Lord North*, *Eagle*, *Hambro' Merchant*, *Charming Sally*, *Charlotte* and *James and Jane* – bore provisions for the naval squadrons in the West Indies, while the *Arwin Galley* and *Hercules* were loaded with 'camp equipage and naval stores'. Excepting the five Indiamen captured by Cordoba and mentioned in Chapter Two, the remaining twenty-nine of his prizes consisted of 'the trade'.

What made the commander of the escort's conduct so reprehensible was that shortly before falling in with Cordoba, Captain Moutray had met a north-bound convoy under Captain George Johnstone in HMS *Romney*. Johnstone commanded a heavy escort covering 'forty sail, carrying 10,463 pipes of wine' homeward from Oporto and it seems he warned Moutray of the activity of enemy squadrons. Even when he was apprised of enemy ships in the offing on the 8th, Moutray dismissed them as 'nothing but Dutchmen'. However, in mitigation, it should be noted that when Moutray belatedly discovered his error and hoisted the signal for the convoy to tack and stand to the north-ward, most of the merchantmen failed to see or to obey the order and only those that did, the *British Queen*, the brig *Rodney* 'and two others', escaped. However, nightfall and a hazy dawn combined with light winds probably pre-vented most of the convoy from being aware of Moutray's signals, an opinion given in evidence at Moutray's court-martial by Captain William Garnier of HM Frigate *Southampton*. Damningly, however, Moutray did not send either of his two frigates to recall the convoy, standing away to the north as disaster overtook his charges.

Indeed, between the spring of 1779 and the late summer of 1780, the enemy struck at British merchantmen with near-catastrophic results. 'It was,' according to Gibb in his official history of Lloyd's, 'the heaviest blow that British commerce had received in living memory, the downfall of many respectable firms and the direct cause of half the underwriters in Lloyd's Coffee-House failing to meet their obligations', a summation Gibb attributes to one of them, John Walter, who afterwards founded *The Times* newspaper. A consequence of this turmoil on the insurance market was that the underwriters, of whom there were then less than 100 and who now owned Lloyd's Coffee House and had formed the Society of Lloyd's, revised their standard marine insurance policy which with three enduring addi-tional clauses – waiver, war risks and frustration.

Further destruction of shipping contributing to the general air of ruin was caused by one man in a remarkable twenty-eight day cruise round the British Isles. Captain John Paul Jones was an unsavoury character, a renegade Scot who was disliked by his peers, but who possessed a savage fighting instinct. Born in 1747 in Kirkudbrightshire, he began his career in the British mercantile marine apprenticed to a Whitehaven ship-owner. On his first voyage Jones visited his elder brother who had emigrated to take up tailoring in Fredericksburg, Virginia, opening Jones's eyes to possibilities in the colonies. When Jones's employer went bankrupt his indentures were broken and Jones shipped in a slaver. By the age of nineteen he had risen to chief mate but he then gave the trade up in the West Indies. Taking passage home from Jamaica, Jones took command of the vessel when the master and mate both died. The ship's owners granted him and the crew 10 per cent of the freight and offered Jones the position of master of the *John* of Dumfries.

Jones made several voyages to the West Indies in the *John*, on one of which he flogged the ship's carpenter for neglect of duty. The man afterwards died and Jones was accused of murder by the carpenter's father and consequently arrested. Tried in Dumfries, he was acquitted, found employment as master of the *Betsy* of London and by 1773 was back in the Antilles. Jones's conduct towards his men provoked a mutiny when the *Betsy* lay off Tobago, evidence that Jones was typical of the harsher master of his day. His later apologists claim that in the confrontation the ring-leader of the mutineers ran upon Jones's sword but among the seamen of the islands his name stank, particularly as he avoided facing charges by escaping to lie-low in America. Here he was unemployed until the outbreak of the rebellion, when he went to Philadelphia where he helped fit-out the first Congressional man-of-war, the *Alfred*. Ingratiating himself with two congressmen involved with establishing what became the Continental Navy, Jones was offered a commission as lieutenant in December 1775 and served in the *Alfred* without distinction until, in 1776, he was given command of the *Providence*. It was now that he began to take prizes with the dash and élan that ultimately ensured his place in the pantheon of American naval heroes. As a consequence of his success he was given a small squadron, promoted to captain and repaid the confidence by taking sixteen prizes.

However, Jones was a man of touchy pride and a notion of his own superior abilities. His placing as eighteenth on the seniority list irked him and he began to make himself unpopular until Congress gave him command of the *Ranger* and sent him to France. Here he was to have assumed command of a larger, Dutch-built man-of-war, but found the ship had been given to the French by the American Commissioners in Paris so, leaving Brest in disgust, he headed for the Irish Sea, landing and raiding Whitehaven on 27-28 April

1778, burning the shipping in the harbour before crossing the Solway in an attempt to kidnap the Earl of Selkirk. The earl was disobligingly absent, so Jones and his crew helped themselves to what they wanted before heading for the Irish coast. Off Carrickfergus the *Ranger* fell in with HM Sloop-of-War *Drake*. In a furious action in which Jones lost eight killed and wounded to his opponent's forty, he took the *Drake* and returned triumphantly to Brest on 8 May with another seven prizes. The alarm his raid – particularly that upon Whitehaven – caused along the British coast was augmented by reports of sightings of other rebel vessels. Jones's presence with his prizes in Brest, demonstrating weaknesses in Britain's seaward defences as it did, occurred as the French ministry were meditating revenge upon Britain for her victories of 1759 by a declaration of war. Jones was summoned to Paris for consultations and on 4 February 1779 he was informed that he would be put in charge of a former French East Indiaman fitting out as a man-of-war which Jones renamed as the *Bonhomme Richard*.

In addition, Jones was given a small squadron of French officered, manned and financed vessels with which to repeat his raid upon the British coast. His French colleagues – officers of the *ancien régime* – disliked him for his lack of manners, regarding him as a *parvenu*, but his successes spoke for themselves. Leaving L'Orient on 14 August 1779, Jones's squadron returned to the Irish Sea, striking terror by the seizures of coasting vessels, rumours of which exaggerated the effects of his raid so that Jones's successful cruise against merchant shipping around the British Isles added to the unsettlement of the entire British countryside for the whole of that summer.

> [I]t was announced in the newspapers that the Duchess of Devonshire, and Lord and Lady Spencer, on their return from taking the waters at Spa, had arrived safe and sound at Harwich, although their ship had been attacked on the passage by two French cutters. The enemy had been beaten off by the *Fly* sloop, under the command of Captain Garner, after a long engagement in which an officer of the British vessel had been shot dead, and several of her crew killed and wounded; and it was allowed on all hands that the ladies had behaved admirably.[14]

Even the sight of the homeward Jamaica convoy caused confusion in Brighton, where 'the quality' took it for an invasion fleet. The actual and imminent descent of a combined fleet of French and Spanish men-of-war had been reported, Spain having opportunistically joined the war in anticipation of recovering Minorca and Gibraltar, and avenging herself for the loss of Florida and the coast of Honduras. This enemy fleet in the Channel was, in fact, a more significant threat than that of John Paul Jones and was aimed at Britain's naval heart: Portsmouth. However, the Combined Fleet dithered, so it was August before the twin forces

of the fleets of France and Spain were at large. The British Channel Fleet under
Sir Charles Hardy, operating in misty weather, caught sight only once of their
enemy as they slipped past and the allies might have affected the landing so anxiously desired by Choiseul and Vergennes, had not a lack of supplies exacerbated
by outbreaks of scurvy forced them to retire. Thus did inefficiency snatch defeat
from the jaws of possible victory.

Meanwhile John Paul Jones had better luck. His ships worked north,
through the Hebrides, where: 'Our Northern sea-board was everywhere
exposed to insult. The packet which plied from Tarbet to the Western parts of
Argyllshire was captured in the Sound of Isla[y]'. After his appearance before
Leith, which he unsuccessfully attempted to 'lay under contribution', towns-
folk all along the coast feared his coming. A public assembly was called in the
town hall of Kingston-upon-Hull to arrange defences for the River Humber
and the Marquis of Rockingham promised to 'treat the town with a battery of
eighteen-pounders'.

Jones's presence was an affront to the Royal Navy, particularly when on
23 September 1779, having passed north-about, he fell upon a Baltic convoy
off Flamborough Head. Jones's ships succeeded in defeating the escort, HM
Frigate *Serapis* and her consort, a sloop-of-war, in a fierce, celebrated and
bloody action which ended in the surrender of Captain Pearson and the
sinking of the *Serapis*. Within hours the shot-battered *Bonhomme Richard* also
foundered, drawing Jones's teeth, but he escaped with his prizes to reach the
Texel.[15] While Jones had established a legend, Pearson had at least largely succeeded in defending his convoy and, at terrible cost, ended Jones's cruise.

The day after Jones's victory the French corsair *Dunkerque*, Capitaine
J.B. Royer, took the merchantman *Three Friends* of Liverpool, Captain Samuel
Maine, who was caught off the Island of Jura. Not only the French and the
Americans, but the Irish were active, the *Black Princess* taking the *Lively*,
Captain Watts, in the English Channel in January 1780. However, a high sea
was running and the prize-crew was unable to board, so Watts was ordered
to follow his captor. He did this until darkness enabled him to run, but two
days later the *Lively* had the misfortune to be captured by a 44-gun French
frigate. Watts and most of his crew were removed and an officer and twelve
seamen were placed on board, joining three of the ship's boys who had been
left behind. The *Lively* now grew leaky and the prize-crew tired of incessant
pumping, fell asleep, whereupon the three boys seized some cutlasses, repossessed themselves of their ship and, shortly afterwards arriving off Kinsale,
made a signal of distress. This was seen by the local population who oppor-

tunistically boarded the *Lively* and began plundering her but, with the help of local pilots, the *Lively* was brought into port where Captain M'Arthur of the privateer *Hercules* took her over and beat off the looters.

The appearance of rebel Irish on their doorstep prompted the Liverpool merchants to petition the Admiralty for better protection and Their Lordships responded by increasing the number of cruisers in the Irish Sea by two frigates and a brace of cutters. There was much need for this. The scandal of enemy privateers operating in home waters with impunity was bad enough, but greater opprobrium attached to a navy that failed to protect tax-paying merchants from a home-grown menace. Although Edward Macartney had lived in France for some years and his ship, the *Black Princess*, flew the Bourbon ensign and carried a French Letter-of-Marque, her commander had been born in Ireland. Macartney's *Black Princess* seized the *John* of Newcastle off the Mull of Galloway in July 1780 despite a spirited defence by Captain Rawson and his crew. Badly hurt and with his second mate also wounded and one man dead, Rawson hauled down his colours. Taking possession of his prize, Macartney agreed to the *John*'s release upon a surety for a ransom of £1,000, a sum which Rawson considered rapacious, refusing to sign the requisite documents. At this opposition Macartney withheld the services of a surgeon from the wounded and, on Rawson's further protestations, gave the intimidating order to burn the *John* and her crew with her, whereupon Rawson capitulated. Some time later Macartney was captured and imprisoned at Plymouth.

A more notorious Irish privateer was Patrick Dowling who cruised in the Western Approaches and among whose prizes was the *Olive Branch* outward-bound from Liverpool to Charleston in 1781. She was ransomed for 7,700 guineas but Dowling, like Macartney, appears to have adopted extreme measures, perhaps because unlike his countryman who flew the French flag, Dowling could not avail himself of the prize-system and was more pirate than privateer. At the time of his taking the *Olive Branch* he had on board his own ship some seventeen 'ransomers' out of a tally of twenty-two prizes. The five who would not – or could not – oblige Dowling, were sunk. Clearly Dowling found ransom satisfactory, restoring his captures to their owners – at a price – and banking large sums himself, presumably thereby avoiding attracting too much unwelcome attention. The *William* of Bristol was released for 900 guineas, the *Elizabeth*, bound for Cork raised 800, the *Sally* for Guernsey 700, and a Maryport vessel put another 750 guineas in Dowling's pocket.

Dowling and Macartney were by no means the only Irish commerce-raiders attacking British shipping in those last years of war. Nor were the Irish the only practitioners of ransom: the French were equally good at it. When the corsair *Le Comte de Guichen* was taken by HM Frigate *Aurora*, Captain Collins recovered a sheaf of ransom documents: the *Peace* of Whitehaven, 2,000 guineas; the *Spooner* of Glasgow, 1,800; the *Six Sisters* from the Isle of Man and *Fortitude* of Greenock, 1,500 each; the *Sally* of Strangford, 500 guineas; the two Workington vessels *Lark* and *Glory*, 450 between them, with two other bottoms adding 1,610 guineas to the total.

It was a see-saw war on both sides, but despite the serious effect the enemy's war on trade had upon the British economy – the aspect most emphasised in conventional assessments – the British privateering war on American trade was itself of some counter-vailing significance. Our old friend William Boats, in partnership with William Gregson, commissioned several privateers and employed a number of energetic and able commanders. One of these was Captain Jolly who in early 1778 commanded the *Ellis*, in which he took the *Endeavour* and *Nancy*, both loaded with sugar and rum. Later, handing over the *Ellis* to Captain Washington, he transferred to the *Gregson* and then cruised in company with his old vessel. Both these privateers were substantial, the *Ellis* of 340 tons burthen, 28 guns and 130 men; the *Gregson* of 250 tons, 24 guns and 120 men. Between them they took *La Ville du Cap* from St Domingo to Nantes with sugar, coffee, cotton, rum and indigo, and the *L'Aigle* from port-au-Prince to Nantes with a similar cargo. Separating, Jolly next took a small privateer which he disarmed and released, followed by the snow *La Genevieve*, outward from Nantes for St Domingo with flour, wines and a general cargo. Captain Washington, meanwhile, was busy seizing the snow *Josephine*, full of oil, soap, brimstone and straw hats destined for Dunkerque.

Curiously a reduced form of trade between the belligerent powers some-times continued, so that a wine merchant in Manchester was able to learn from his shipper in Bordeaux that:

> Very many rich and respectable merchants here, have been already ruined by the great success of your privateers and cruisers. Many more must fall soon. May God, of his mercy to us, put an end speedily to this destructive and ridiculous war.

This contribution of privateers to the general war-effort is largely ignored by the eulogist extolling the exploits of naval 'cruizers', but the wine-merchant's *cri de coeur* is eloquent enough. On the British side investment, in prospect of attractive return, was not confined to the usual ship-owning classes. The Marquess of Granby had an interest in several privateers, including the *Lady Granby* and the *Marchioness of Granby*. Such was the impact of the enemy war on British trade on the one hand, and British retaliation in the same vein with prizes said to have been worth £100,000 coming into the Mersey alone, that in October 1778 it was patronisingly announced that:

Several ladies of the first rank are about following the patriotic plan of the *Marchioness of Granby*, by opening subscriptions for fitting out privateers, and it is expected, in a very little time, several will be manned and sent to sea against our perfidious enemies, merely by pin-money.

The *Marchioness of Granby*, jointly owned by the marquess and Mr Nicholas Ashton, was a 20-gun ship of 260 tons and 130 men commanded by a Captain Rogers. She sailed in the fall of 1778 and soon sent in her first prize, a Dutch ship with a French cargo, but the prize-master lost her on the Irish coast and all but two of her people perished. In January Rogers took *Le Labour* from St Malo to Massachusetts with a general cargo, and a Dutch snow bound for Cadiz with brandy, before encountering the French frigate *Le Sensible*. After a sharp engagement, Rogers was obliged to strike his colours.

Ashton did better on his own account in the *Jenny*, commanded by a relation. In company with the *Betsey* and *Buckingham*, Ashton's *Jenny* 'captured a very valuable prize called *Le Marquis de Brancas*…also a brig from Newfoundland for [Le] Havre, with fish, and sent both of them into Cork'. The value of some prizes was fabulous. After a run of luck, Captain Fairweather of the large 24-gun frigate-privateer *Bellona* completed his cruise in Jamaica taking a vessel said to be worth £4,000. This was handsome enough, but modest compared with the prize sent in by Captain Robert Bostock of the *Little Ben*, a small slaver of 14 guns and fifty men. Bearing a Letter-of-Marque, Bostock had had a bit of luck on his outward passage to West Africa and in October 1778 wrote to his Liverpool owners from Exeter declaring that he had just arrived there with the *Molly*, privateer, of that port. The two had captured *Le Mallie*, a snow well freighted for Bordeaux and valued at £20,000, together with an un-named Dutchman of some unspecified value. Bostock reported speaking with the *Gregson*, just then parted from the *Ellis*, whose commander, Jolly again, had reported seeing French men-of-war and feared they had taken a Liverpool ship. It would seem that a French squadron was at sea in anticipation of meeting and safely escorting homeward French East Indiamen into L'Orient. But there were jack-pots yet to be taken, the first by the least significant of Liverpool privateers.

Captain Ralph Fisher of the *Two Brothers*, an undistinguished vessel of 150 tons, 16 guns and only – significant when handing out prize money – thirty-nine men, had sailed from the Mersey in company with Captain Currie in the larger *Young Henry*. On 3 October 1778 Fisher wrote to his owners, Messrs Roberts & Co., from Spithead thus:

Gentlemen, I have the pleasure to acquaint you we arrived safe here this day with a French East Indiaman of 500 tons, deep laden, from Bengal which we took on Tuesday the 29th September, in lat. 47° 28' N. long. 10° 30' W. At six in the morning we discovered two sail in the N.W. quarter, wind at S.S.W. upon which the *Henry* and we gave chace (sic) to the northwardmost of them. At eight…I left the *Henry* chacing and hauled for the westernmost ship. At ten I just weathered her, at a long shot (she was standing to the Eastward) notwithstanding her formidable appearance, I wore round and gave her a broadside, which was well directed. She still stood on, thinking to outsail us and get clear, which I believe she would had not the second broadside of grape and round shot, which we poured into him, immediately cleared his decks, and he struck to the *Brothers*. The *Henry* had given over the other chace, and passed us a league to leeward; and when she struck he was a long way astern. As she is such a valuable prize, we thought it most prudent for both of us to convoy her into port. I put two mates (Mr Callow and Mr Pugmore) and twelve men on board; Currie the same number. She is called *Le Gaston* (her first voyage)… She has only 6 nine-pounders on board and 60 men including passengers, amongst which is a French General… By the General's account she is worth 2,000,000 livres; I think she is worth more. I beg you will write me by return of post…but I think one of you coming yourselves post would be requisite. As dull as the *Brothers* sails we have stumbled upon a noble acquisition…

Scarce able to believe his luck, Fisher goes on to say that he had later that day fallen in with the *Ellis* and *Gregson* who had reported running from a squadron of French men-of-war the previous day, adding that in addition to the French master's manifested cargo, he had gleaned from the passengers that there were also 'four trunks of valuable merchandise, and other packages of value' which were presumably the commander's private trade goods.

But the caprice of fate could dash expectations, and although the French naval squadron missed Fisher, they caught Captain Holland of the *St Peter*, who had engaged and captured another French East Indiaman *Aquilone* – valued at £100,000 and probably the ship in company with *Le Gaston* abandoned in her chase by the *Young Henry* – only to run into the French. The 74-gun line-of-battle-ship and a frigate captured the *St Peter* and took her into L'Orient, the incident being witnessed by Jolly in the offing. At 320 tons, mounting 22 guns and bearing 147 men, the *St Peter* was no mean prize herself and a great loss to Messrs Holme, Bowyer and Kennion.

The fates and fortunes of men became curiously entwined: a Captain M'Bride captured two Dutch vessels only to discover in the masters of both not only that the men were father and son, but that he had seized both of them twenty-one years earlier. It was indeed a see-saw war.

Capture by the enemy was one risk, getting one's prizes home another. Messrs Drinkwater & Co. sent their 16-gun, 130-ton privateer *Mary* on a cruise under Captain Bonsall in the autumn of 1778. On Sunday 2 October, the day before Fisher sat down to write to Roberts & Co., Bonsall had brought into the Mersey the *La Grand Athanase*, a richly tobacco-laden vessel which had been bound for Nantes. In December he repeated his success, bringing in *L'Equité*, a ship bound to Bordeaux from St Domingo with sugar, coffee, indigo, cocoa, cotton and tortoise-shell, in prospect of which Messrs Drinkwater & Co. must have been licking their lips. Alas, in entering the Mersey, *L'Equité* first went aground then:

> beat off her rudder, which was washed away; when very bad weather coming on, no boats could be got to tow her into dock. A temporary rudder was sent off to her, but after cutting three cables, being three times ashore, and losing three boats, she at length was run ashore near the New Ferry, with one anchor and cable at her bow, which were never let go. 'Tis to be feared the ship will not be got off, but the materials and greatest part of her cargo are saved

This report proved optimistic; although lighters had been brought alongside to effect the removal of the cargo, the next day:

> the people from the country, assembling in their hundreds, swooped down upon the vessel, threatening destruction to all who opposed them, forcibly seized and carried off great quantities of the cargo, in consequence of which lawlessness it was found necessary to call in the aid of the military. Application was accordingly made to the Mayor of Liverpool, and the commanding officer of the Leicestershire Militia stationed there, both of whom declined interfering, the transaction being in another county [Cheshire]. The owners of the privateer then sent over arms to their people, for the defence of the vessel. On the following night a numerous mob again assembled, and in spite of the entreaties of the four men who guarded the property, proceeded to renew their depredations. The guard then fired several times over the heads of the most desperate of the plunderers, and at last, for the preservation of their own lives, fired directly on them, killing one man. This resistance, however, only exasperated the mob, and in the end, to prevent further bloodshed, the men upon guard took to their boat, and left the prize to the robbers.

Bonsall must, of necessity, again go a-cruising and in the spring of 1779 he was at sea, taking a number of prizes which depleted his crew by fifty-five so that, when in April he encountered the American privateer *Vengeance*, Captain Wingaze Newman, the *Mary* was badly mauled in a fight lasting one and a half hours. Three of Bonsall's remaining crew were killed and twelve wounded, the *Mary* had her main-topmast shot away, her mainmast wounded and she received over thirty shot in her hull, five of which were near the waterline. Three of her sixteen guns were dismounted, circumstances that obliged Bonsall to strike his colours to Newman. The *Mary* was soon afterwards recaptured and carried in to Antigua.

Similarly mixed fortunes afflicted Captain Wilson of the 18-gun privateer *Knight* belonging to Hindley, Leigh & Co. In that same October of 1778 Wilson captured *La Plaine du Cap*, which was loaded with West Indies produce and valued at £25,000. In December the *Knight* took a French East Indiaman, *Le Deux Amis*, but in trying to get her into the Mersey in a northerly gale the prize grounded on the Flintshire coast under the Point of Ayr while the *Knight* was driven into Conway Bay, stranded and sent her masts over the side. The prize-crew climbed into the rigging of *Le Deux Amis* to avoid drowning as seas swept over the stricken ship but 'the night being intensely cold, only nine Englishmen and one Frenchman survived it'; as the ship broke up beneath them, the remaining thirty-two all perished. Refloated and refitted, the *Knight* set off again, only to be engaged and sunk off Portugal by a French frigate, her crew escaping in the boats and landing at Oporto.

Roistering ashore, flush with prize-money, the privateersmen of Liverpool were often as lawless as the daring and insolent inhabitants of Cheshire. The mayor, William Pole, was driven to issue a caution in which, among the enumerated crimes of annoyance and disturbances of the King's peace, the chief offence was 'forcibly breaking open, and rescuing several impressed seamen out of the houses for the reception of them.' The disorders and outrages committed towards the end of 1778 marked a particularly fruitful period in the annals of Merseyside's privateering fraternity, for it was a private Liverpool ship which actually scooped one of the great prizes of the war.

The homeward passage of the French East Indiamen, like their British counterparts, was an annual event. Inevitably some of the ships became separated and although it is probable that she had left Pondicherry at the same time as *Le Gaston* and *Les Deux Amis*, the French East Indiaman *Carnatic* was some way behind them. The seasonal approach of these vessels was as well known to the English as were the movements of the British East Indiamen to the French, and ambitious privateer commanders went in search of them. One such was John Dawson, whom we have met previously and who had been exchanged after his captivity. At this time he was master and commander of the large, ship-rigged 400-ton *Mentor*, owned by Baker & Co., mounting 28 guns and manned by 102 men. She appears to have both traded and acted as a privateer and Dawson was intimately connected with his owners, having married Baker's daughter and entered into partnership with his father-in-law. Messrs Baker & Dawson & Co. had invested in a ship-building business on the Mersey's riverside, becoming part of the Liverpudlian establishment.

In the autumn of 1778, Dawson took the *Mentor* to sea and headed south, his instinct being rewarded on 28 October when a large Indiaman hove in sight. This proved to be the *Carnatic*, as deficient in fighting qualities as other homeward Indiamen of both belligerent powers and she fell a lawful prize to Dawson and the crew of the *Mentor*. On being condemned, she was valued at £135,000. On board was discovered 'A box of diamonds of an immense value,' the newpapers reported to a gawping public. All-in-all the capture of the *Carnatic* was 'to no small satisfaction of the captors'.

No doubt as a result of this sudden wealth, Dawson handed over command of the *Mentor* to a Captain John Whiteside who was engaged in the Jamaica trade and in August 1779 took two prizes when outward-bound. Then, in October, when in the Western Approaches, Whiteside had a nasty encounter with French men-of-war. His letter to Baker and Dawson gives a vivid picture of the vicissitudes of an armed merchantman in time of war.

On Wednesday, the 27th…saw four sail bearing S.E.; bore away for them. As we came near, found two of them to be ships, one having Dutch colours hoisted, the other English; the other two sail being a sloop and a schooner. At nine A.M. came so near one…as to perceive she was a frigate, on which we hauled upon a wind to the southward. She immediately hoisted French colours, fired several shot, and gave chace (sic) to us. We, finding she came up very fast, kept away with the wind abeam [the fastest point of sailing] and set every studding sail and small sail in the ship to the best advantage. At noon the frigate was about two miles astern in chace. The 28th October [the ship's day then changing at noon, or 'the meridian'] moderate winds and clear weather; the frigate in chace all these twenty-four hours, sometimes coming near us, other times dropping, according as the breeze freshened and died away. We…could not get distance enough from him to alter our course in the night. At ten A.M. saw three sail astern, steering after us. At meridian, the frigate about a mile and a half astern, coming up fast with us. The 29th October, at half past meridian, the wind dying away, the frigate came up with us fast, in consequence of which, we in studding sails, up courses, and got all clear for engaging. At one P.M. came to action, which continued very warm till ten minutes past two, when she made all the sail she could, and stood away from us to the southward.

She was a frigate of 36 guns, carrying 28 twelve-pounders on one deck. We weighed one of their shot, and found it 15lb. weight. We had our main-top-mast shot away, a great deal of our rigging and sails, and one shot through our main-mast head… Our officers and men behaved exceeding well.

Quite why the French frigate abandoned her chase is unclear but the *Mentor*'s final fate was shared with that of the *Sarah Goulburn* – now under a Captain Orr – when, homeward-bound from Jamaica in 1782, both foundered in a severe gale on the Grand Banks off Newfoundland. Whiteside and one of the ship's boys were picked up, the remaining thirty-one of the *Mentor*'s crew drowned.

Another jackpot was secured by Captain Charles Lowe Whytell, commander of the 14-gun *Amazon* who, after a reasonably successful cruise in the summer of 1779, set off again and on Tuesday 24 August, 'saw a ship, which proved to be a Spaniard'. Shortly after noon Whytell came up with her and engaged.

She looked exceeding large, and shewed fifteen guns on a side, but we could not tell whether they were metal or not until we tried; so run up and received her fire, and found she had only fourteen metal guns, but they were heavy ones. [It was not unusual for ships to mount dummy, wooden guns to deter an enemy from attacking. Because of their martial uselessness, they were nick-named 'Quakers'.] We gave her two broadsides for one, and continued the engagement for three [half-hour] glasses very briskly, and then lost sight of her for ten minutes in a cloud of smoke, and feared she had sunk. When it cleared up we perceived her endeavouring to make her escape, and gave chase to her again; came up with her, received her broadside, and returned only a few guns before she struck her colours. A Bristol privateer (which we afterwards found to be the *Ranger*) came up during the engagement, but kept aloof and never fired one gun. We having received much damage in our rigging and sails, and our yard teacles (sic) [tackles for hoisting out the boats] shot away, the Bristol privateer took the advantage and boarded her first, and received the Captain's sword and papers, which they did not deserve.

She proved to be the *St [Iñez]*. a Spanish frigate, commanded by Fernando de Reynosa, from Manila bound to Cadiz; larger than any of our thirty-six gun frigates, and pierced for forty guns. She had two eighteen and twelve nine-pounders mounted, and upwards of 150 men, of whom forty-seven were killed and wounded in the action, and in the explosion of gun-powder; thirty-three of the forty-seven are dead.

We only lost one brave fellow (the master's mate) who had his arm shot off by an eighteen-pounder, close to his shoulder, and he died in about an hour. My officers and ship's company all behaved like men of true courage during the whole engagement. I believe the prize is very rich; but known not yet what she is loaden with, therefore cannot ascertain her value.

Whytell and his unwelcome colleague, with whom he would be obliged to share the spoils if judged a lawful acquisition, sent their prize into Cork where,

accompanying her, he discovered the details which were transmitted to his
owners and soon afterwards appeared in the newspapers. The prize was an
800-ton Spanish man-of-war armed *en flute* – that is to say with much of her
armament struck down into the hold – running as a heavily armed cargo-car-
rier with a reduced crew. The explosion Whytell refers to might have lost him
the entire ship had it occurred in her magazine, but it was a single powder-
cask which blew up and killed forty of the *St Iñez*'s men. According to a
second letter from Cork she was:

> deeply laden with gold, silver, coffee, china, cochineal, and indigo... She is
> deemed the most valuable prize since the rich Acapulco ship by the late Lord
> Anson. In her after hold the King of Spain's cargo is stowed, which is supposed
> to be gold and silver, but not yet opened. The captain and crew were not per-
> mitted to see it when shipped, as she was laden by porters, which is the usual
> custom at Manila; nor is it supposed it will be examined until the owners of the
> privateers from England arrive here.

A little later the Liverpool newspapers announced the arrival of the *Amazon*
at 'Hoyle-Lake [Hoylake in the Dee estuary]. Letters from Ireland say the
above prize is worth one million'. Among the cargo was a zebra, loaded at
the Cape of Good Hope, which instead of joining the royal menagerie in the
Escorial Palace at Madrid, was exhibited for the amusement of the populace
of Liverpool. Whytell was a redoubtable commerce-raider, enjoying further
successes the following year when in command of the cutter *Tartar* in which
he took three Frenchmen and one Dutch ship before being captured himself
by two French frigates.

Another Spanish frigate, the *Soledad* which was homeward-bound from
service in the Pacific, was taken by two large privateer-frigates from Liverpool,
the *Telemachus*, Captain Ash, and the *Ulysses*, Captain Briggs. The *Soledad* was
sent into Crookhaven, her prize-master narrowly avoiding recapture by an
American privateer cruising off Mizen Head. A further action with a Spanish
warship occurred between the *Ellen*, Captain Borrowdale, and the sloop-of-
war *Santa Anna Gracia*, Don Juan Morallas commanding. The Spanish sloop,
mounting 16 guns and loaded with stands of small arms was taken in mid-
Atlantic by Borrowdale on 26 April 1780. Although the 16-gun *Ellen* had on
board a detachment of the 79th Foot under a Captain Blundell, Borrowdale
had no intention of attacking a man-of-war, intending only to defend his
own vessel. For this he prepared himself thoroughly, confusing the enemy
by hoisting American colours and in the delay double-shotting his guns and
exhorting his men. This done the *Ellen*'s crew and the infantrymen of the
79th calmly awaited the outcome. As the *Santa Anna Gracia* ranged up close,

Morallas hailed the *Ellen*, whereupon Borrowdale hauled down the American ensign and ran up the British, firing a broadside supplemented by a volley of musketry from Blundell's infantry. Edging away, Morallas tried to escape but Borrowdale tacked and gave the *Santa Anna Gracia* his other broadside after which a running fight ensued. This ended in the surrender of the Spaniard and her triumphal carriage into Jamaica. Later in the war, in the mid-summer of 1782, Borrowdale sent in another prize, the *Isabella* homeward from the Mascarene Islands with cotton, cloves, pepper and coffee. That October the *Ellen* arrived off Liverpool from Jamaica:

> having on board forty-two of the ship's company of the *Ramillies*, flagship of Rear-Admiral Graves, which had foundered. The Mayor received a letter from the Admiral requesting him to convey to the captains of the merchant ships belonging to Liverpool, who were the preservers of the lives of the Admiral, officers, and company of the *Ramillies*, the approbation of the Lords Commissioners of the Admiralty, of their humane conduct.[16]

Perhaps the most worthy engagement of the period between a British merchantman and a naval vessel was that between the *Watt* and the Continental Naval ship *Trumbull*. The *Watt*, commanded by Captain Coulthard, was on her way to New York with a general cargo including military stores. Coulthard carried a Letter-of-Marque under which he had previously taken the American vessel *Nancy* and a French brig, *La Pégase*. On 1 June 1780, in mid-Atlantic, the *Watt* fell in with the *Trumbull*, Captain James Nicholson, a 36-gun, 12-pounder frigate. The *Trumbull* was well manned, superior to the *Watt*'s 164 men and their thirty-two 12- and 6-pounders. The New York papers happily related the event:

> The action was obstinate and bloody, and the carnage on board the rebel frigate amazing, as the vessels were a considerable time yardarm to yardarm, and the *Watt*, by the superior skill of her officers and the alertness of her crew, had the opportunity of twice raking her antagonist fore and aft, which made her a perfect slaughter house. Her stern was drove in almost down to the water, many of her guns dismounted, hundreds of shot through her sides, her foreyard and topmast shot away, and all her sails and rigging greatly damaged. She at last put before the wind, and run from the *Watt*, which chased her eight hours; but having a cargo on board, and her [own] masts so damaged that she could not venture to carry a great press of sail, she lost sight of the chace on the 2nd inst. The *Watt* has a great number of shot holes through her sides and sails, four of them through her powder magazine. She has certainly fought a more glorious battle than any private ship of war since the commencement of hos-

tilities. The most exalted encomiums are inadequate to the merit of the brave Captain Coulthard. The determined courage he exhibited during the action, and the cool, deliberate manner in which he issued his orders, does him the highest honour; nor ought the approved behaviour of his gallant officers and crew remain unnoticed…

A later edition of the same New York newspaper told something of the other side:

> By a flag of truce arrived last night from the eastward, we are informed the Lieutenant of the *Trumbull*, Rebel frigate, had with much difficulty got the ship into New London, after being torn down to a mere wreck in an engagement…with the Letter-of-Marque ship *Watt*… We have as yet only been able to learn that Captain James Nicholson, the *Trumbull's* commander, was killed at the first broadside…and that there were fifty-seven men killed on board the *Trumbull*; the number of wounded has not yet been declared.

Damage to the *Watt* was severe and her casualties were not insignificant either, though far fewer than the *Trumbull's*. At first they were reported as eleven killed and several wounded, but a petition for charitable relief by the widow of 'Nicholas Rigby, late a mariner aboard the *Watt*' states the butcher's bill as 'thirteen men killed and seventy-five wounded. Described as 'truly invincible', Coulthard had taken a massive risk.

Another action fought between British privateers and the embryonic American navy was that between two Liverpool ships named *Jenny* and an unspecified Continental 28-gun frigate on the Grand Banks during 1781. Both the British vessels were well appointed and copper-bottomed. Captain Thomas Walker's ship-rigged *Jenny* mounted fourteen 6-pounder carriage guns, besides swivels and small arms, while Captain William Gill's *Jenny* bore two additional 6-pounders and 'sails like the wind'. Both afterwards enjoyed successful cruises.

A classic privateering cruise was accomplished by Captain Taylor in the *Snapper* that same year. In the Bay of Biscay off the Gironde on 24 July Taylor met with a convoy of seven coasting vessels under convoy of a 20-gun corvette which gave chase to *Snapper*. Taylor ran all day, drawing off the escort until, after dark, he changed course and then turned back towards his quarry. His appearance caused three of the convoy to run themselves ashore to avoid capture while the *Snapper* took the remaining four, a munitions-laden snow, a small sloop with a cargo of iron and two brigs carrying naval stores.

Whether responsible for a commissioned privateer or a freighted merchantman operating with a Letter-of-Marque, a ship-master had to have due regard for his owners' property. Avoiding a superior enemy was part and parcel of his duty and the circumstantial failure to do this is nicely expressed by Captain

Beynon to Messrs Hindley, Leigh & Co. of Liverpool whose 220-ton *Nanny* mounted 14 guns and was manned by fifty men. She was in the wine trade with Oporto and had taken a brace of prizes under Beynon, one the recapture of a British vessel. The *Nanny* had fought a three hours' engagement with an enemy privateer before meeting another on a homeward voyage. Writing from Cadiz on 2 June 1779, Beynon had to exonerate himself.

> On 20th of May, of Cape Finisterre, saw a ship in chace of us. Being resolved to know the weight of his metal before I gave up your property, I prepared to make the best defence I could. Between eight and nine o'clock, he came alongside, with American colours, hailed, and told me to haul my colours down. I desired to begin and blaze away, for I was determined to know his force before I gave up to him. The engagement began, and lasted about two hours, our ships being close together, having only room to keep clear of each other. Our guns told well... We were soon left destitute of rigging and sails... [and] were sadly shattered below and aloft. I got the *Nanny* before the wind, and fought an hour that way, one pump going till we had upwards of seven feet water in the hold. I thought it then almost time to give up the battle, as our ship began to be water-logged. We were so close that I told him that I had struck and hauled my colours down. The [enemy] privateer was in a sad shattered condition. By the time we were all overboard [had abandoned] the *Nanny*, the water was up to the lower deck.

The American privateer was the *General Arnold* and Beynon had cheated Captain Brown of his prize, for so fierce had the fight been that the *Nanny* sank, taking one of her crew with her. Sensible of the unrequited cost to Brown, Beynon boarded the *General Arnold* under some anxiety.

> When Captain Brown heard the number of men I had, he asked what I meant by engaging him so long? I told him, as I was then his prisoner, I hoped he would not call me to any account for what I had done. He said he approved of all I had done, and treated my officers and myself like gentlemen.[17]

Although the *General Arnold* was herself taken some time afterwards by HMS *Experiment*, it was not before she had captured Davenport & Co.'s *Swift*, Captain Brighouse, who had become separated from the Jamaica convoy. The *General Arnold* was under a new commander, the Bostonian James M'Gee, a man of different stamp to Captain Brown. 'Most of the captain's [Brighouse's] letters, papers and clothes were taken from him, and he was nearly stripped naked of everything he had'. Nevertheless, Beynon himself was exchanged, for he was later in command of the *Hypocrite* in which, in company with the *Vengeance* and *Surprise* off Belle Isle in the Bay of Biscay on 5 June 1780, he took *La Dauphine*, a richly laden snow carrying wine, cognac and naval stores 'on the French king's account'. A month later he returned to Liverpool escorting a Genoese vessel full of wheat, a trick he repeated in August. The following year Beynon shifted his cruising ground to the West Indies, seizing a schooner bound from St Eustatia to Marie Galante, but shortly afterwards the *Hypocrite* fell foul of a French corsair and, in a fierce action, she was captured and Beynon killed.

French and American seizures continued. In February 1780, after an action of 'nearly an hour, in which Captain Jackson, the first and second lieutenants, and seven men were wounded, the Continental sloop-of-war *Thorn*, took the *Sparling* on her way to New York and carried her into Boston. In the summer the *Albion* heading for Archangel, the *Speedwell* on her way from Peterhead to Bergen with oatmeal, the *Ashton* and three other brigs were all taken by the American Letters-of-Marque *General Washington*, *Alexander* and *Maryland* who interrupted their commercial voyages to Amsterdam to raid British shipping.

Such was the fluidity of the struggle at sea that the most bizarre fortunes attended many voyages, the most extreme of which was the fate of the slaver *Hero*, Captain Wilcox. Bound for the Guinea coast in the spring of 1780 the *Hero* was captured by the French, then retaken by HMS *Champion* 'within a league of Cherbourg'. Continuing on her voyage, on 1 May she was again taken by a French privateer and again recaptured before reaching port. Wilcox tried to reach Africa once more, but then fell in with the combined fleets of France and Spain, from which there was no escape.

Although the balance-sheets in the counting-houses on Merseyside and elsewhere showed some profit from privateering ventures during 1779, in contrast to the fears of invasion on the coast of the English Channel – which was, according to Sir George Otto Trevelyan, at this time English in name only – British shipping losses mounted steadily. The merchantman *Tyger*, the privateers *Adventure* (taken in company with an unnamed Glasgow ship) and the *Spitfire* – but not until her side had been beaten in by shot so that it was 'like a rabbit warren' – are but a few, and must stand proxy for the rest. In 1779 alone these amounted to 656 vessels.

Many British merchant seamen imprisoned in France were ill-treated, as in the previous war. A letter of that fateful August of 1779 tells in 'what manner we have been used'.

> In the first place we have a pound and a half of bread, such as is the cause of all the sickness, beef is just good enough for dogs, sometimes it amounts to half a pound a day, but more often to six ounces, sometimes we have peas, and those so bad that one half of them are as hard when they come out of the furnace as when they went in... We have nothing to lie on but straw full of vermin, which

deprives us of rest. The beds we had at first are taken away, and we are now treated as if we were horses. We dread the thought of another winter, and expect nothing but to fall victims to death.

Many men who, in prospect of prizes, willingly took risks at sea, found themselves ill-equipped to cope with the corroding effects of imprisonment: cold, damp and a wretched diet. An exception is a spirited Scottish seaman writing from Dunkerque who recorded the loss of all his possessions, including gifts he had purchased for members of his family. His final indignity was that 'the French dogs unrigged me in an instant, and left me nought but a greasy jacket of their ain'. He also assured his sweetheart that he would make all well for:

> I have sixpence (sic) a day from the King of England, God bless him; and I have bread and water from the French King, God curse him… [K]eep a good heart, for I'll get out of this yet, and win meikle Siller, and get a bottom [ship] of my ain too; and then have at the French dogs…

So much for 'the auld alliance'.

But liberation and a light-hearted and unwary spirit carried its own ever-present danger: that of the press. On 4 March 1780 the appropriately named *Happy Return* entered the Mersey. She had been sent to L'Orient as a cartel under Captain Webb in order to exchange prisoners and was homeward-bound to Plymouth with 300 liberated British seafarers. On the passage the seamen rose and took over the ship, altering course for Liverpool, fearful of impressment were they to arrive in the Hamoaze under the guns of the Royal Navy. The authorities were not to be cheated. On the night of Friday 17th, the officers and seamen of His Majesty's Impress Service stationed on Merseyside gathered outside a house in which a number of those who had seized the *Happy Return* had barred themselves, determined to avoid forced abduction into the Royal Navy. The house-owner, one James Richards, refused to open his doors to the naval-party and a fire-fight ensued, continuing for about thirty minutes until Richards was twice dangerously wounded and a man inside the house was killed.

Heavy losses of shipping continued through 1780 and 1781, but the latter year saw a second remunerative period for British privateer owners as prizes came in under their prize-masters and crews. Even the whaler *Betty*, Captain Wilson, on her way to the whaling grounds of the Davis Strait, operating under her Letter-of-Marque, sent a Dutch ship into Lough Swilly, as did the *Seacombe*, Captain Pagan, hunting Sperm Whales off the Azores. The *Betty*'s prize was the *Johannes*, bound north-about from St Eustatia to Amsterdam loaded 'with 292 hogsheads of sugar, 100 hogsheads of tobacco, 158 bags of coffee, 103 bags of cocoa, and 9 casks of indigo'. Indeed, the Dutch were particularly unfortunate at this time, but others also suffered, including the Swedes, who had joined the Armed Neutrality of the North against Great Britain. In May Captain Fayrer was cruising off the Azores in the *Harlequin*, privateer. He chased and took a Swedish brig which, 'by stratagem' – which ruse is regrettably expunged from the record – he discovered that 'she was sent out to give advice to the [home-coming Swedish] East Indiamen'. And in September the privateer *Lightning*, Captain Walker, took 'a large Swedish ship of about 500 tons, from Bordeaux to St Domingo, laden with bale goods, wine, flour, etc, value as per invoice, 330,118 livres'. The *Lightning* also took 'a Spanish packet, from the Havannah to Cadiz', with 12,000 dollars on board and, in the following May, the *Maria* from L'Orient with wine and salt; the *St George*, La Rochelle to Martinique; an unnamed French vessel and 'a French East India packet from the Cape of Good Hope, for St Malo, with passengers and despatches for France. The mails were thrown overboard...' This vessel had previously been the British privateer *Resolution* but at the time bore the name *Le Mars*.

The *Harlequin* performed one final service in the war when on her way out to Jamaica in the fall of 1782. Falling in with the *Bella* of Liverpool which he found to be waterlogged, Captain Fayrer sent a boat to assist her in her distress and discovered the ship in the hands of her crew. It transpired that the ship's company had risen upon Captain Burgess and his mate, marooning them on a rocky island known as the Jordans. Fayrer took possession and placed the muti-neers in irons, eventually returning them to Liverpool and, presumably, rescuing Burgess and his colleague. Fayrer derived little but trouble from this encounter, for the *Bella*'s hold was flooded and, beyond redemption, she was sunk.

Like many privateers, the *Harlequin* was involved in a dispute over prizes. These usually arose when one or more privateers were in sight of one another when a capture was made. Since privateers tended to concentrate on the foci of trade-routes, many commanders cruising in company came to an agreement to share the proceeds, without which disputes ensued. If ships-of-war were in sight of one another when one took a prize, the other was deemed entitled to a share because her mere presence had an intimidat-ing factor and may have decided the issue in favour of the captors. Despite the naval practice of automatic right-of-share, in the privateers' case this could not be assumed. Cruising in company with the *Patsey*, the *Harlequin* and her consort had taken a valuable Dutch West Indiaman, the *Eendracht*, within sight of the Bristol privateer *Caesar* whose commander lodged a claim for a share in the prize. The case was hotly disputed and passed from the local Vice-Admiralty court – established worldwide to settle matters of lawful prize quickly – to the High Court of Admiralty in London. The case was eventually settled by a judgement in favour of the two Liverpool ships, gratifying their owners, Henry Rawlinson and Messrs Earle & Co. By this time, however, the crisis of the war in North America was over and hostilities were grinding their weary way to an end.

As Cornwallis approached his nemesis at Yorktown, the Royal Navy, which would fail him in his hour of dire need, had greatly improved its arrangements for convoying the West India trade. On 17 March 1781 this left Jamaica, under the protection of six line-of-battle-ships and amounted to over 120 merchantmen. This large convoy avoided a powerful Franco-Spanish squadron mustered to intercept it by passing through the Windward Passage where, in their turn, the British ships fell in with the French 64-gun *Marquis de la Fayette*. The French man-of-war had in her hold eighty pieces of artillery, uniforms for ten regiments, sufficient stores for two men-of-war 'and about 2,000,000 livres in specie'. The homeward convoy also encountered and recaptured the British merchantman *James and Rebecca*, Liverpool to New York, which had been taken by an American privateer.

The depletion of seamen available to serve in British merchantmen during this arduous and now largely forgotten war at sea had begun to tell by 1780. The nature of the conflict inhibited a ready exchange system, while the enforced migration of man-power from the merchants' service to the King's was ceaseless. In order to address this problem and to avoid the necessity of obliging the Royal Navy to be careful of the legality of its recruiting policy, Parliament passed an Act in May whereby:

> Merchant ships are allowed to have three-fourths of their crew foreigners; and all the foreigners who shall have formerly served, or shall hereafter serve, two years on board any of His Majesty's ships, or any privateer, or merchant ship, being British property, shall be deemed a natural born subject of Great Britain, and enjoy all privileges and immunities thereto belonging.

One such 'privilege', accompanied by no immunity whatsoever was, of course, the vulnerability to being pressed. As ever, this seemingly ineluctable process was accompanied by violence, although the press-gang was not always the winner. On the evening of Sunday 3 March 1782 as two seamen of the Impress Service in Liverpool were taking a sailor into custody for shipment to the press-tender, the man writhed free, drew a pistol and shot one of his captors dead before escaping into the twilight. The coroner's jury returned a verdict of manslaughter.

Two and a half months later, in May 1782, news came in that cheered the nation in the miserable wake of Cornwallis's surrender at Yorktown in the previous October. Admiral Rodney had destroyed De Grasse's hitherto victorious fleet off Les Saintes in the West Indies, rescuing the Royal Navy's reputation. Arriving with the news of this victory was that of the safe arrival of 'the Jamaica fleet' of 1782, a relief to the ship-owners, shippers and West India merchants in Liverpool, London and Glasgow, but the war against trade continued on both sides for a little longer with its complex vacillations. Despite the disaster to their battle-fleet at Les Saintes, French frigates remained active, capturing – among others – Captain Burrows's *Spy* on her way to the West Indies with 250 slaves and six tons of ivory. Nor were the American privateers idle. On the other hand Captain Butler, outward to the Guinea coast in the *Stag*, took a Spanish vessel bound from Barcelona to Buenos Aires. Valued at £8,000, this added to the profits of carrying 700 slaves to Jamaica which 'no doubt satisfied the owners'.

But whatever Rodney's victory of Les Saintes had achieved by way of adding lustre to Old England's glory in these dog-days of an unpopular war, her very doorstep remained mired by the activities of Irish piracy. There was an unequivocal quality about the depredations of Captain Kelly, whose 22-gun privateer *Terror of England*, armed with a privateering commission signed by 'Le Roy de France', roamed British home waters unchecked. Efforts by the navy to seize him had failed and he had fought and overcome HM Cutter *Hope*, Lieutenant Vickers, after a barbarous action at the conclusion of which Kelly continued to fire into the smaller *Hope*, refusing quarter 'even when they had pulled down their colours… Some of his infernal crew', the Dublin newspapers reported, 'after they boarded the cutter, cut and abused, in a shocking manner, several of the men'. The paper – partial and devout – hoped 'Kelly will add one more to the numerous throng that occasionally make their exit from that tree which so often has promoted the good of humanity by ridding the world of villains disgraceful to human nature'. Kelly's last victim was Captain Jordan of the *Molly*. Kelly discovered and fell upon the *Molly* off the Tuskar rock as she headed for Liverpool from Jamaica. Captain Jordan fought off Kelly for three hours until Jordan was killed and his ship captured. In a gale which followed the action Kelly's prize-crew were overwhelmed by the *Molly*'s people as the ship was running through the North Channel and she was taken in to Glasgow.

Kelly's luck was now out; his reputation had run so high with the taking of the *Hope* that the Royal Navy was moved to finish the task Vickers had been inadequately prepared for. Within days of the taking of the *Molly*, Captain Robert Cooper of HM Frigate *Stag* retook the *Hope* and engaged the *Terror of England*, carrying Kelly and his ship prisoners into Dublin.

During a long war which involved large bodies of British and Hessian troops, many vessels were chartered as military transports. The former East Indiaman *Clive*, sold and renamed *Kent* by M. Adams of London, was put in the North

American timber and mast trade in 1772. When war broke out Adams, one of many owners to do so, chartered her to the Government as a transport to earn a steady income from her, but even this could be a risky business. After the British evacuation of Boston in 1776 a number of British ships unwittingly sailed into the port to be seized by the Americans. Among these was the *Lord Howe*, originally the first of several East Indiamen named *Glatton*, which, having been taken up as a military transport, left with reinforcements for the garrison of Boston in convoy under HM Frigate *Flora*. Unfortunately the *Lord Howe* became separated in heavy weather and fell into the hands of the enemy, her troops becoming prisoners-of-war without firing a shot.

As the war escalated, so did the demand for transports and redundant East Indiamen were purchased for this purpose. One of the last, the *Duke of Richmond*, was actually bought from the ship-breakers by the Navy Board for the purpose, while many other vessels similarly chartered were worn out. The *Grenville*, renamed *Tortoise*, acquired by the Navy Board in 1777, foundered off Newfoundland two years later but the market, as markets will be, was ruthlessly exploited. Close to the heart of military planning and the Admiralty itself, the London ship-owners had the advantage in this. John Durand, a member of the East India Company's inner circle, also had other interests and was involved in the transatlantic timber trade. He bought several second-hand East Indiamen including the *Fox* in 1770 and the *Duke of Grafton*, acquired in 1782, both of which became transports. Messrs W. Wilkinson of London bought the ex-*Europa* and the ex-*Lord Mansfield*.[18] Other East Indiamen were chartered as military transports directly from the Company, such as the *Harcourt* in 1774 and the *Speaker*, which served from 1776 to the end of the war in 1783.[19]

Another source of transports was sought among the owners of whalers, many of whom were content to swap the risks of whaling, increased by enemy privateers, for the steady income derived from Government trooping contracts. Since all whalers were subject to the rudimentary inspections necessary to obtain the Government bounty, they were known to the state and their taking up was a simpler matter than with some other vessels. These demands, accompanied with shifts in man-power had a profound effect upon the whaling fleets, which increasingly divided their time between the Davis Strait and the old grounds west of Spitsbergen, affecting the personal fortunes of individuals. A few whalers remaining in the fishery operated under Letters-of-Marque and, as we have observed, acquired prizes. Some, like Captain John Gee's *Caroline* of Hull, sailed on a deliberate privateering cruise before heading for the whaling grounds.

On the outbreak of the war HMS *Lion* had been ordered to escort the whalers heading for the Davis Strait, after which she was to attempt the North

West Passage and link up with Cook, coming from the Pacific. This failed and the following year the *Lion* repeated the task, escorting the seven whalers bound for the strait and again unsuccessfully trying to find the desired passage to the Pacific. By 1777 the bounty to whaler-owners had been reduced, driving more vessels out of the fishery, exacerbating the inroads of the press-gangs and increasing the numbers of press-exempt apprentices carried.[20]

As in the previous conflict whalers heading for the fishing grounds sailed from their home ports as an armed squadron. Early in the war, following news of the *General Mifflin's* cruise and before the Hull fleet was almost entirely chartered for trooping, they formed themselves under an 'admiral', Captain Thomas Franks, whose *Marlborough* was covered by a Letter-of-Marque. The other ships, most of whose commanders were brethren of the Trinity House of Hull, were fully armed and manned, with carriage guns and small arms in addition to the formidable tools of their trade.[21]

But such precautions were unavailing against the machinations of the state. Just as their ships were known to Government as suitable troop-ships, so were their seamen earmarked for the Royal Navy with its insatiable appetite for man-power. 'What think you of taking the Greenlanders?' the Attorney-General Lord Thurlow enquired of Lord Sandwich, the First Lord of the Admiralty, on 21 June 1779, adding 'under a promise to return them before the season for fishing'. Was Thurlow disingenuous? Did he really think all the men, dispersed throughout the fleet as they surely would have been, could be returned in this way? Promise or not, Sandwich thought it a splendid idea and the result was an order to ignore all press-protections so that, as the *Newcastle Chronicle* of 3 July reported, shipping movements ceased on the Rivers Tyne and Wear. '[E]very ship that enters our harbour is immediately boarded and stripped of men and boys...since the impress broke out here it is supposed that upwards of 600 men have been taken'. Even this number was scarcely sufficient to man a single 74-gun ship-of-the-line. As on the Mersey, the Geordie and Yorkshire sailors were no less anxious to avoid serving His Majesty. Once word had got out, it seems that if the weather was suitable the master of a whaler approaching her home port agreed to let part of his crew go ashore by boat, trusting in the press-exemptions of himself, his mates and the apprentices, along with those seamen who remained on board, to enable him to work the ship safely into port. Presumably the escapees, who had probably drawn lots, would re-muster later to receive their proceeds from the voyage, or appoint delegates to do so on their behalf. When off the Tyne on 4 July, a number of seamen released from the whaler *Adamant* by boat, were pursued by boats from HM Sloop *Fury*, caught and impressed. The *Fury* herself then followed the *Adamant* down the coast and upon her arrival off Whitby, where the Impress Tender *Advice* was lurking, boarded her and took all the remaining hands out of her.

On the 30th the whalers *Kitty* and *Noble Ann*, both of Newcastle, were homeward-bound when word of the hot press reached them, probably from fishing cobles encountered off the Farne Islands. By arrangement most of the *Kitty's* men got ashore before their ship arrived off Tynemouth, but the same means of escape was not taken advantage of by the men of the *Noble Ann*, which sailed into an ambush. Off the Black Midden Rocks she was surrounded by boats from the brand-new frigate *Syren*, then commissioning at Shields, along with boats from the several Impress Tenders also lying in the Tyne and from the Impress Rendezvous. The attack on the *Noble Ann* was led by Captain Edmund Dod of the *Syren* who was desperately in want of seamen. There was a bloody clash which left two Greenlanders dead and a third seriously wounded, his life feared for. As for the rest, they were forcibly entered into His Britannic Majesty's Royal Navy.

In reaction to the wave of resentment that rippled along the crowded river-bank, Captain John Bover, the Regulating Captain for the area, wrote to Dod on 1 August, advising him 'that you are in the utmost Danger of your Life if you stay at Shields a single Day'. Bover was quite explicit about the consequential illegal-ity of Dod's over-zealous action, adding that 'it is clear that you will immediately be taken up, tried and condemned for wilful murder'.[22] Dod took Bover's advice, disappearing south under cover of darkness in the small hours of the following day while HM Frigate *Syren* was conducted to Sheerness by her first lieutenant. Here Dod rejoined her on 5 September and – needless to say – escaped justice.[23]

Despite this tacit admission of guilt, the navy were unrepentant over this incident and by the middle of August Bover had stationed an armed ship, the *Content*, to intercept the homeward whalers and prevent the landing of seamen to evade impressment. On the 15th the *Content* detained the whaler *Freelove* off Alnmouth, only to be interrupted in pressing thirty seamen out of her by two large French corsairs. The *Content* 'Engaged both the French ships till about twelve minutes after two when they being sick of it, run away...' Soon afterwards the *Content*, sighting five more homeward-bound Whitby whalers, pleaded the presence of French privateers on the coast and escorted them south, only to board and take out of them a number of seamen as they closed the River Esk. As a post-script to this affair, it was afterwards circulated that Captain John Brown and the remainder of the *Freelove's* people, had failed to join the *Content* in her action with the corsairs and thereby secure two prizes having 'being afraid'. The *Newcastle Chronicle* was pleased to publish this imputation on 21 August: it was not enough that Brown should be faced with the risks of working his inadequately manned ship into port, but that he must be publicly stigmatised with cowardice!

Although a number of seamen taken in these circumstances were released in time for the next whaling season as Thurlow had suggested, the great shortage of man-power and the consequent hazards resulting from it, was a persuasive reason encouraging many owners of all classes of merchant ships to charter their vessels to the Government as troop-transports. In these dismal circumstances it is unsurprising that many British seamen opted for signing-on American privateers when the opportunity offered, as Captain Symerson of the *Dick* deposed after his release by Daniel McNeil of the *General Mifflin*, and although rich bounties were offered to American harpooners captured by British ships to induce them to make up for the deficiencies in British whalers, this seems to have been of a far lesser order. It was, of course, this migration that a few years later – during the run-up to the war of 1812 – induced the Royal Navy to adopt its hard-line attitude to British-born seamen discovered in American ships. One way or another, the Royal Navy was determined to have them.

It was, in a sense, a similar tale for many whalers. In the short-term, like many of her sister-ships, the *Noble Ann* did not return to whaling. Instead she sailed for Gibraltar where the besieged garrison was much in need of the coal and military stores with which she was now laden and where she was wrecked in April 1781. Exceptionally, the *Kitty* fared differently. In 1782 and 1783 the whaling fleet was reduced to a fraction of its pre-war level and almost entirely composed of ships from Whitby and Newcastle. But prices were high and profits considerable. Of the forty-seven whales taken by a handful of Newcastle ships in these two years, twenty-nine were taken by Captain John Lattimer and the crew of the *Kitty*, hunting on the traditional grounds off east Greenland.[24]

The preliminaries of a peace treaty with the United States were agreed in November 1782, those with France, Spain and The Netherlands by February 1783. Among the political settlements, freedom of navigation through the Dutch spice-islands was conferred on British shipping and, despite a disgraceful abandonment of the claims of many thousands of loyalists – many of whom were involved in commerce – trade with the newly emergent nation recovered almost immediately. *Williamson's Advertiser* summed it up thus:

> The Mercantile World is in a hurry and bustle unknown at any former time. The merchants are endeavouring to outstrip each other in the race of traffic. European goods, and particularly the produce of England, being greatly wanted in the ports of America, the destination of many of the vessels now in the river [Mersey] is altered from the West India Islands to the American ports, where it is expected the cargoes will sell at an immense profit.

This galvanising of the British commercial instinct was timely; despite the pro-active exploits of British privateers, on balance British shipping had had a very rough time of it. So too had the institutions behind shipping, not least the under-writers for whom the practice of ransoming was particularly abhorrent because it invited on-the-spot collusion between captor and captured. Even small enemy privateers plundering the coastal trade had affected the insurance market as a report in *Lloyd's List* in May 1780 makes clear:

> [A] French privateer, of 26 twelve and Nine-pounders, and 300 men, appeared off Sunderland, and took the following loaded Colliers, viz. the *Minor*, *Howe*, and *Albion*, *Whitehead*, of Sunderland, and two Brigs belonging to [King's] Lynn, and ransomed as follows. 800 guineas, 750 ditto, 850 ditto, 600 ditto.

While another in July rubs the point in:

> Extract from a letter from Swansea, 3 July. Last Night arrived a Vessel from Cornwall, with Copper Ore, after being taken and ransomed for 130 Guineas, by the *Mayflower* Privateer, of Dunkirk, a lugger of 2 Guns and 20 Swivels; she also took the *Diligence*, from hence to Cornwall, with Coals, and ransomed her for 150 Guineas; she has taken many more. Names not known.

The *Mayflower* had continued her cruise, capturing the *Susannah*, Captain Lamport, from Cork to Bristol, which she ransomed for 1,100 guineas. In the closing years of the war the North Sea, had become even more dangerous with the addition of the Dutch as enemies. The complex rules of engagement in eighteenth-century European war often provided immunity from attack for mail packets which continued running between belligerent countries, but on 28 October 1782, Kapitein L.W. Sextroth of the Zierikzee privateer *De Goede Verwachting* suspected the packet running between Hellevoetsluis and Harwich was carrying 'war intelligence' as well as the legitimate mails. Consequently the *Dolphin*, Captain Flynn, was detained and examined, but nothing was found and, at the peace conference later the Dutch delegation were compelled to apologise for Sextroth's action.

Further complications had arisen from the practice of London under-writers insuring foreign vessels. 'It was,' a later commentator points out, 'by no means unusual for Lloyd's underwriters to pay out on enemy merchant-men captured by the Royal Navy'. The same historian notes that: 'Not only did they have to pay out…but drunken fools of British seamen could not even keep a prize when they had taken one', referring to an incident which occurred in May 1780 when a prize-crew from a British privateer was put aboard the Dutch vessel *Hethuys Ostenburgh*, Kaptein Pieters, from Sète to Dunkerque. '[T]he six Men put on board her getting drunk, were over-powered by the Dutchmen who carried her into Helvoetsluis'.[25] Such incidents were common enough, exemplifying the lawlessness that without strict discipline was endemic among British seamen who, it must be admitted in partial exoneration, inhabited an extremely precarious world.

News of the official peace treaty travelled slowly and one of the last casualties of the enemy's action was the slaver *Fancy*, Captain Greaves, of Liverpool, which sailed from Cape Mount on 22 March 1783 with a cargo of 390 slaves, two tons of ivory and 'a quantity of rice'. She was taken later that day by a French 50-gun man-of-war that carried her prize all the way to Cape François. Notwithstanding these last gasps of warfare, the energy invested in a resumption of trade was formidable. Liverpool alone, exposed to the enemy as it had been by geography and the Royal Navy's deficiencies, had seen a vast reduction in her trade and had been compelled to rely upon her marauding privateers to try to make up deficiencies in her revenues, both commercial and official.[26]

Recovery was mercifully rapid. The deeply unpopular nature of the war, particularly among the educated merchant classes who saw it as an abused prerogative of the oligarchical establishment, meant a swift return to pragmatism, particularly with their transatlantic colleagues for whom the war had been but a temporary estrangement. Not only was there an eager and ready market for British manufactures in the new United States, but the new Government of George Washington was near bankrupt, so economic revival was essential to both the former protagonists. Along with revival in general trade went a resuscitation of whaling. In retrospect the 1780s became boom years, culminating in 1788 when 216 English and thirty-one Scottish whalers left for the Arctic.[27] This was also the year that the British turned greater attention to the hunting of the Sperm Whale and whalers from London began to venture further south.

Thus, almost in Cook's wake, whalers entered the Pacific in an enterprise conducted with vigour and involving considerable investment. One of Cook's protégés, James Colnett, late of HMS *Resolution* but afterwards master of the *Rattler*, was despatched to the South Pacific in 1793 on a commercial exploring voyage on behalf of the whaler-owners Enderby & Co. of London. His brief was to seek out safe anchorages and a possible base in that vast ocean, for Enderby's ships were by then carrying out long cruises in hunting the Sperm Whale that were soon lasting for several years.[28]

Despite the peace of 1783 bringing a restitution of trade and a return to normality, the seaman's traditional enemy, the weather, remained. Accounts of two post-war losses may suffice to exemplify the inherent risks in seafaring and the uncertain navigation of the day. On 4 March 1783 the *Count Belgioso* of Liverpool, a new ship, recently fitted-out and commanded by Captain Pierce, left the Mersey bound for the east having on board a cargo of lead, bale-goods, a consignment of ginseng and a huge quantity of silver dollars, all valued at £130,000. The weather was fine and the wind fair but before she had cleared St George's Channel, the *Count Belgioso* encountered 'a violent storm of wind, and a great fall of snow' which drove her down upon the Irish coast. Here, only three days out of Liverpool, she struck the Kish Bank and shivered asunder. Captain Pierce and 146 souls perished in the wreck.

Two years later the *Whale Fisher* of London, proceeded north and on 30 April she was struck by a heavy sea which so damaged her bows that Captain Allen had to seek shelter amid the pack-ice to effect repairs. By the time this was accomplished, the *Whale Fisher* was beset, remaining ice-bound for three weeks. Breaking free Allen succeeded in killing a whale on 4 June and on the 8th he conducted his ship into a bay on the Spitsbergen coast. Here his boats struck another whale which they lost in an accident in which the lines parted and the mate was mortally injured, his body being cremated ashore. On 29 July a second whale was taken, upon which Allen headed for home with a poor tally. Sailing on her next voyage in late March 1786, the *Whale Fisher* seemed accident-prone after a yard broke, a circumstance which seems to have disturbed the ship's company and persuaded them the voyage was doomed. However, in June and July two whales were caught and by August the *Whale Fisher* was in company with several other whalers, some of them Dutch. Then she, the *Sally* of London and the Dutch vessels were again caught in the ice and on 1 September the *Sally*'s hull was pierced and she foundered. Her crew was dispersed among the other ships but the *Whale Fisher* remained in the ice until, on the 10th, she was herself crushed and rapidly sank. With little more than what they wore at the time, Allen and his men spent six days on the floes before being picked up by the three Dutch vessels. However, these had little rations to spare and Allen determined to make for the distant land. In this he was frustrated and returned to the Dutch ships, but their crews now refused to allow them on board, despite promises of bills drawn on London in exchange for blubber on which to subsist. Eventually the Dutch relented, and on 27 September a south-easterly gale began to break up the ice and the ships reached open water. However, the paucity of provisions reduced them all to a state of near starvation until, on 31 December, they reached the Norwegian coast, from where Allen and his crew were able to take passage to Peterhead. Such incidents became all too frequent in the succeeding years, not helped by the Government regulation that 'clean' whalers had to remain on the grounds until 1 August to qualify for the bounty. In many cases the delay was fatal.

Despite these vicissitudes, the swift revival of trade ought to have brought stability to the life of the seaman. Throughout the wars of the eighteenth

century the merchants' service had had to contend with the demands of the
Royal Navy with whom, it is no exaggeration to state, its men were in a state
of private hostility. As we have observed many times, forcible entry into the
navy was a commonplace in wartime but in time of peace it was – at least in
theory – illegal. This did not deter the captain of the frigate *Boreas* from sending a press-gang ashore at Bridgetown, Barbados, on the evening of Friday
14 April 1786 when his men were led by the ship's boatswain, John Scotland.
In the course of a struggle with some unwilling recruits Scotland shot and
mortally wounded a merchant seaman named James Elliott, and was shortly
afterwards found by the captain of the *Boreas* who was ashore with one of his
officers, with the dying man. Hurrying back to the *Boreas*, Scotland was concealed and when a warrant was served for his arrest, the captain of the *Boreas*
prevaricated, denying any knowledge of Scotland's whereabouts, continuing
this evasion even when Admiral Hughes, the flag-officer of the station, was
requested by Governor Parry to locate the suspect. In due course the matter
was referred to the Admiralty and Hughes was ordered to determine 'how it
happened that the Boatswain of the *Boreas* was suffered to make his escape'.

The *Boreas*'s captain continued to maintain Scotland was not aboard his
frigate and to deny his men were ashore as a press-gang. On the contrary, he
claimed, his complement was complete to within 'a man or two' and 'dozens
were daily refused [entry to the *Boreas*] from merchant ships': an improbable
fiction at best. Far from pressing seamen, the party had been ashore hunting deserters and certainly one man, Able Seaman Hugh Robinson, had run
that very day. But five men had been entered on the *Boreas*'s books the same
day: one deserted five days later and another was found to be an alcoholic
and discharged, strong evidence that they were pressed from the stews of
Bridgetown. Of the others, one was James Elliott, entered as captain's servant
on 14 April and, incredibly, discharged dead on the 15th. Scotland was, according to the ship's books, present aboard *Boreas* for musters on 16 and 23 April,
his discharge being recorded on the 30th, despite evidence that he seems to
have slipped aboard the store-ship *Cyrus* on the 15th. The *Cyrus* was shortly
afterwards wrecked, but Scotland survived and appears to have escaped the
noose to return home to England.[29]

The *Boreas*'s captain was Horatio Nelson, whose conduct was typical of
his contemporaries, but his high-handedness was often as risky as it was
unjust, perhaps motivated by that 'zeal for the service' that was his trade-
mark, and a protective loyalty towards his own men that was, in the face of
murder, misplaced. At the beginning of the *Boreas*'s commission, Nelson had
pressed eleven men out of Dutch East Indiamen, claiming in a letter that 'the
Admiralty have approved my conduct in the business' but when his frigate
reached Portsmouth, whither she was bound, Admiral Montagu ordered the

men to be discharged and Nelson 'received a far from supportive letter from the Admiralty'.[30] On the other hand the Admiralty itself had no compunction in the forcible seizure of *British* merchant seamen. When the *Boreas* returned home from the West Indies at the end of her commission in 1787 she was stationed in the Thames Estuary to intercept in-bound merchantmen and press seamen out of them as we have noted in the previous volume.

Not all naval officers shared an enthusiasm for the press. Though driven to it as an expedient, Graham Moore frequently animadverted upon its disadvantages in his journal.

> While that violent practice (i.e. pressing) is resorted to that class of men, the seamen, have much to complain of. The Country loves them and is fully sensible of their merit and of their importance, then is it not worthy the attention of Government to conciliate the affection by rendering more comfortable the lot of this meritorious but hard used body of men.[31]

On merchant seamen in general Moore remarked:

> Let it always be remembered that we have Seamen ready made and that it is not in a Man-of-War that the best of them are formed. In this the navy and Army differ materially, you may make a good private soldier in six months but a sailor must have served five or six years in a merchant ship before he can be deemed as Able Seaman, and even then he has much to learn. There is something in the nature of a Seaman's profession which many men of superior endowments never acquire and which many comparatively dull men frequently excel in.[32]

Quite apart from the fates of individual merchant seamen and the ruin that the American War had brought upon many merchant houses, the fortunes of others were laid during these difficult times. In 1779 William MacAndrew moved from his native Elgin in Scotland to Liverpool to set up business as an importer of citrus fruits from Spain, Portugal and the Azores. For this purpose MacAndrew chartered small but fast schooners and brigantines, of which Liverpool with its history of slaving and privateering had plenty, and his activity established what would become one of Britain's longest-lived shipping enterprises. However, the palm for the oldest shipping company – marked until recent years by the flying of their house-flag at the fore-masthead rather than the main – was that of Brocklebank & Co. whose flag first flew on ships registered at Whitehaven.

The company was founded by Daniel Brocklebank who was born in Westmorland in 1741 the son of a clergyman whose sons were attracted to the sea. John, Daniel's elder brother, had started in the coastal trade and risen to command a Greenland whaler, Daniel seemed more eager to build ships than sail in them, for he married at Whitehaven and a year later, in 1770, having emigrated to New England, set up a ship-building yard near Sheepscut on the Gulf of Maine. By 1775, when the stirrings of rebellion were compelling men to take sides, Brocklebank had built his fifth vessel, the brig *Castor*. Aware of the state of affairs round Boston, Brocklebank had also heard that 'the Provincials were fitting our two schooners at Kennabeck (sic) to endeavour to take one of the men-of-war that lay at Casco [in Nova Scotia] and had enlisted four hundred men for the purpose'. Having made up his mind where his loyalties lay, on 8 May 1775 Brocklebank abandoned his yard and the vessel on the slipway that the rebels would afterwards commandeer and complete as a privateer, to slip away in the *Castor*. The brig only had on board one barrel of bread and some beef, so Brocklebank invited his crew to choose whether to run for Nova Scotia or fish on the Grand Banks of Newfoundland for cod before heading for England. They settled for the latter and the *Castor* arrived at Whitehaven in early June after a passage of thirty-three days. Here Brocklebank communicated the state of affairs in New England to the authorities and soon learned of the opportunities that Government chartering offered ship-owners. Within a week Brocklebank sailed for Nova Scotia where the *Castor*, based on Halifax and sailing regularly from there to London, was caught up in momentous events.

In sight of the Irish coast in February 1779 Brocklebank fell in with the American privateer *General Sullivan* and her prize. Coming up with another British merchantman, the *Lively* of Bristol, Brocklebank attacked the *General Sullivan* and drove her off her capture, which the *Castor* and *Lively* retook and escorted into Cork, eventually receiving the customary reward of salvage and prize-money. As a result of this Brocklebank applied for and was granted a Letter-of-Marque for the *Castor* and by the end of the war he was employing her in the West India trade. In 1780 he began acquiring more tonnage, handing over the *Castor* to her former mate, James Williamson, and himself taking command of the ship-rigged *Pollux*, soon afterwards renamed *Precedent*. While commanding her he learned of the loss of the *Castor* which, having been chartered as a trooper, had been approaching St Kitts when her foremast carried away and the brig was wrecked on the adjacent rocks. The loss embroiled Brocklebank in a legal argument of long-standing but his faith in Williamson saw him put in charge of the *Precedent* while Brocklebank bought a share in the brig *Love* and shortly afterwards acquired an interest in the *Castor II*.

Daniel Brocklebank retired from the sea in 1788 to found a shipyard at Whitehaven but continued his business in ship-owning. In the boom years that followed he became a principal- rather than a part-owner, and by the outbreak of war with France in 1793 he owned eleven vessels which were by then trading to Russia as well as the West Indies and North America. Predeceased by his son, also named Daniel, Brocklebank was to die in 1801, aged only fifty-nine, but after his death the company he had founded prospered, migrating to Liverpool in 1822 by which time it had become Thos. & Jno. Brocklebank.

The establishment of dynastic ship-owning houses such as MacAndrew and Brocklebank typified was slow, but it was matched by greater cohesion in other institutions associated with shipping, particularly the Society of Lloyd's. Such confederacies were small at first but they gained momentum, power and influence as time passed and began to militate against the old monopolies enjoyed by the Hudson's Bay Company and, more aggressively, the Honourable East India Company. Their success and profile encouraged greater investment and provided the vehicle for it. Sole-ownership of vessels and an accrual of tonnage both enabled and took advantage of imperial expansion, industrial development and such other straws-in-the-wind that fell in the way of vigilant ship-owners.

Meanwhile the burgeoning technology of civil engineering was providing increasing numbers of enclosed wet-docks for cargo work, graving docks for ships' maintenance and such aids to navigation as the world's first isolated lighthouse on the Eddystone Rocks. These improvements went hand-in-hand with slow advances in the navigational methods outlined in Chapter Three of *Neptune's Trident*.[33] Alongside all this, an ultimately largely beneficial regulatory authority was emerging, helped – after a century of argument – by an Act of 1786 which required the registration of all vessels over 15 tons burthen. War also contributed; if Lord Sandwich had been an indifferent First Lord of the Admiralty, at least he had overseen the copper-bottoming of the British fleet in imitation of many merchant ship-owners, making men-of-war faster and more efficient; while the humiliations of the American War had not only been the nursery of a new generation of sea-warriors who were to excel their forebears in the business of naval warfare, but the experience had considerably increased the operational capabilities of the Royal Navy.

Upon the back of such enterprise, the merchant seamen of the day were also poised expectantly. Unlike their masters they rarely thought in the long-term, for nothing in their fragile existences persuaded them of the least necessity to do so. Theirs was the old path of duty, even if it was the bleak one that gained them only their daily bread and was to be cast off the minute their feet set foot ashore. For the benighted mercantile seafarer, though he was yet to undergo almost a quarter of a century of being exposed to the evils of impressments and, after the Great War with France, a further fifteen years of slump, he would feel something of the benefits of a much-improved convoy system.

In the decade between the whimpering end of the American War in 1783 and the outbreak of the struggle with a transformed France, there was a brief, gilded age, the first of the booms – before the busts – that were to characterise the history of British merchant shipping in the next two centuries.

NOTES

1. Described as 'Close to the Antarctic seas, and most southerly of all British colonies, the Falkland Islands are bleak and inhospitable, even in the short southern summer. The rest of the year rain and hailstorms sweep the hills and moors. Only hardy sheep and hardy settlers of Scots origin survive... The wild life of the sea is their chief interest...'

   Territorial claims to the islands were intermittent: the British landed first, in 1690, when a Captain Strong of the *Welfare* set foot ashore and named the claimed territory after the Treasurer of the Navy, Lord Falkland; next Malouine corsairs made a loose claim on the archipelago and in 1764 Bougainville landed to formally claim East Falkland for France, naming Port Louis. The following year Commodore Byron, in HMS *Dolphin*, claimed West Falkland for Britain and founded Port Egmont, named after the then First Lord of the Admiralty. Receiving Byron's survey of the anchorage by way of the *Florida* in June 1765, Egmont despatched Captain McBride in HMS *Jason* to establish a settlement 'which Byron claimed to have made on the strength of an act of possession and of a vegetable garden laid out by his surgeon'.

   After the Seven Years War all French claims were ceded to Spain in 1767, and in 1770 a Spanish expedition, at the instigation of the French Minster of the Marine, the Duc de Choiseul (who had been planning a maritime war of revenge against Great Britain for some time) was sent from Buenos Aires. This drove the tiny British garrison out but it was re-established the following year, Madrid and London having reached a curious accommodation, 'without prejudice to the question of sovereignty'. In 1774 the British garrison was withdrawn from West Falkland, leaving it to sealers, but a small Spanish enclave remained at Soledad, as Port Louis had been renamed, until in 1811 it too was withdrawn.

   The years following the Napoleonic War in Europe were marked by the wars of independence of the South American colonies of the Iberian powers. Having declared themselves an autonomous state, the Argentinians of the La Plata Vice-Regal territory of Buenos Aires landed and hoisted their own flag, reoccupying Soledad. Unfortunately, in 1831 the Governor of Soledad seized three American sealers engaged in what had become a regular trade for the Americans as well as the British. The United States Government despatched a sloop-of-war to enforce the restitution of American property and to disperse the colonists and dismantle the Spanish fort. Following this, however, a small Argentinian garrison returned.

The Argentine claims had been contested by Great Britain which, in the following December, sent two men-of-war to reoccupy West Falkland and remove the Argentine presence from Soledad. This latter was accomplished in January 1833. British trading interests in Buenos Aires, led by the Lafone brothers, encouraged settlers, and in 1841 a civil administration was established. Samuel Lafone and his brother had by this time opened up a steam-ship service, acquired extensive land, rights and interests in the islands. In 1851 they sold out to the newly formed Falkland Islands Company which took over the running of the steamers. These ran not to Buenos Aires, but to Montevideo in Uruguay. In 1828 the Oriental province of Uruguay seceded from Argentina, contesting sovereignty of the wide estuary of the Rio de la Plata. Largely pro-British, the new independent Government acted in defiance of Argentine claims against the British occupation of the islands, consequences of which have erupted in more recent years.

For the British mercantile marine, the islands' inlets were much valued refuges for South Seas whalers and other troubled sailing ships, many of whose bones lay, and still lie, upon their lonely shores.

2. The 321-ton *Baffin* was built by Mottershead and Hayes.

3. See Barrow, T., *The Whaling Trade of North-East England, 1750–1850*, p12 *et seq.*

4. *An Authentick Narration of all the Occurrences, in a Voyage to Greenland in the Year 1772*, written and published at Durham by William Kidd and quoted by Tony Barrow to whom I am indebted for much detail in this section.

5. *Newcastle Journal*, 16 April 1757, quoted Barrow, p16.

6. As with so many of the East India Company's ships, names were repeated. Angerstein's ship was the first of the name and should not be confused with the second *Lord Camden*, owned by Nathaniel Dance senior and commanded by his son, nor the *Earl Camden* of which Nathaniel Junior was also commander. The first *Lord Camden* had been sold in 1778 to James Mather who renamed her *Juliana*, chartered her to the Admiralty as an armed escort ship and military transport before selling her to Angerstein in 1786.

7. But also the Danes who led the Scandinavian countries in an Armed Neutrality of the North which objected to the Royal Navy's insistence upon stopping neutral merchant ships – even when under the convoy of national men-of-war – to search for contraband cargo which might aid the rebels.

8. Even before the entry of France into the war the Americans had adopted a practice described by D.E.W. Gibb in his *Lloyd's of London, A Study in Individualism*. 'In the early days of the American war…the Americans sent to France bundles of Letters of Marque signed in blank by a competent American authority. On reaching Paris they were filled in with the name of a French ship, and taken as good justification for the Frenchmen to ply the profitable trade of interfering with British commerce. It was co-belligerency carried to an extreme, and it served its purpose until France openly joined the Americans be declaring war on England in 1779.'

9. Later in the war, in command of another privateer, Allanson captured a number of prizes chief among which was a French slaver coming from Angola bearing 692 slaves. These sold in Jamaica for £25,560 'a stroke of business which must have caused great satisfaction in the office of the owners, Messrs J. Backhouse & Co.' writes Gomer Williams, p237.

10. Captain Reid of the *Greenwood* fought off his assailant, killing the *Vengeance*'s captain with his first broadside but was compelled to submit to *force majeure*. The *Tom* was purchased from her captors as a cartel to bring the ransomed ships' companies home.

11. The *Minerva* was recaptured by the Royal Navy in 1781.

12. The *Sturdy Beggar* also took a rich Spanish ship, *La Salta Nostra Señora del Rosario* but on 29 October 1779, when anchored in a gale in Fayal Road, parted both cables, drove ashore and was dashed to pieces with the loss of four men in ten minutes. Several other anchored ships suffered the same fate.

13. The quotation is from Donald L. Canney, *Sailing Warships of the US Navy*, Naval Institute Press, Annapolis, 2001, p12. Canney quotes the figures published by George F. Emmons in his *Statistical History of the Navy of the United States* (1853).

14. *The Morning Post and Daily Advertiser* of 30 September 1779.

15. Although Jones is today held to be the 'father' of the US Navy and is interred at Annapolis, he was neglected in his lifetime by Congress and died in poverty in Paris in 1792. Ironically, given subsequent events, after the war he found employment in the Imperial Russian navy of Catherine the Great and served in the Russo-Swedish War.

16. Other sources state that the *Ramillies* was burnt and scuttled after receiving severe storm damage on the Grand Banks.

17. Quoted by Williams, p245.

18. To both of which Roland Hackman ascribes a renaming to the *Grand Duke of Russia*.

19. Other former East Indiamen included the second *Salisbury*, sold to James Mather of London; the second *Ranger*, sold to Camden & Co. in 1788 for the West Indies trade but which was also used as both a convict and – after the American War – a troop transport. About a score of chartered merchantmen were lost with Cornwallis when he surrendered at Yorktown in 1781.

20. There were no less than eight out of a crew of thirty-six in the *Caroline*, Captain John Gee, and aboard Captain Samuel Lazenby's *Humber* there were four apprentices and eleven first voyage greenhorns. Many other ships' muster lists show the same proportion of inexperienced men and boys.

21. The other ships were *Addison, Adamant, Delight, Freelove, Friendship, Hercules, Henriette, Jenny, Nancy, Perseverance, Providence, Speedwell* and *Volunteer*.

22. Bover to Dod, National Archives, ADM 51/209

23. Dod, who had been born in 1734, soon afterwards turned the *Syren* over to another captain who wrecked her on the coast of Sussex in 1781. Dod himself took over HMS *Lizard* and by the outbreak of war with France in

1793 he was in command of HMS *Charon*, 44 guns, then lying as guardship off the coast of West Africa. In 1797 he was promoted to flag-rank and had risen to full Admiral of the White at the time of his death in December 1815, though he appears not to have been much employed during the long conflict with France. He was never accused of having been an accessory to the murder of the whalers.

24. Barrow, p30. The *Kitty's* catch in 1782 was 12 whales, rendering 144 tun-barrels of oil with a value of £3,744; five tons avoirdupois of baleen valued at £1,725. The *Kitty's* owners received a bounty of £702 at £2 per ton burthen, all of which gave an overall profit of around £4,400 for her voyage.

25. Cameron, A., and Farndon, R., in *Scenes From Sea and City, Lloyd's List, 1734–1984*, p36 where they quote *Lloyd's List*, May 1780.

26. Customs revenues were £274,655 at the beginning of the war and had fallen to £188,830 by 1780. Tonnage owned in the port fell from 84,792 to 79,450, much of which was privateering. The population declined and the numbers of the poor requiring parish relief rose sharply, while: 'The manners of the common people at this period made a retrogression towards barbarism…' One effect of the war was to reduce its popularity as 'a bathing place' largely through fear of the press-gangs. The *Liverpool Advertiser* states that: 'During the war, very few…durst come down, on account of the warmth of the impress…'

27. In 1784 the long-lived *Truelove* made the first of her many voyages north and in 1785 William Scoresby, Senior, sailed as an ordinary seaman aboard the *Henrietta* of Whitby.

28. See Chapter Two, note 9 in reference to Colnett's exploring voyage, but where he will be found to have played another, more extraordinary role in the Pacific Ocean.

29. See Knight, *The Pursuit of Victory*, p102, and for detail Sugden, *Nelson; A Dream of Glory*, pp320–329.

30. See footnote Knight, p137.

31. Quoted Wareham, *Frigate Captain*, p233.

32. Quoted Wareham, p214.

33. John Smeaton's Eddystone lighthouse of 1756 was the fourth structure on the reef, but the first masonry tower which was the prototype for other isolated seamarks, such as Stevenson's Bell Rock lighthouse of 1812. Other technical advances in this period presaging things to come include Jonathan Hornblower's patent for the principal of compounding steam, canal barges built of iron by John Wilkinson of Ilkley in 1787, experiments in North America in 1788 where the Scotsman Patrick Miller rigged a central paddle wheel between two hulls and made 5 knots and, specifically for the benefit of seamen, Henry Greathead's *Original*, the first purpose-built lifeboat of 1789.

TWO

'A LYING AND
TROUBLESOME PEOPLE'

British Shipping in the Far East, 1763–1793

In the years of peace between 1763 and the outbreak of the American Revolution, the Honourable East India Company steadily consolidated its political power and increased its trade with India. By 1777, as the crisis in North America approached among the wooded hills of Saratoga, the Company was also engaged in a growing trade importing woollens, cotton goods and lead into China to defray the costs of homeward cargoes, otherwise paid for in quantities of silver, a factor directly impacting upon the Company's viability. As a consequence of this increasing trade the numbers of Indiamen sailing seasonally from the Thames had risen slowly, from about fifteen to twenty over the first eight decades of the century, to some forty ships around 1780, peaking at seventy-five in 1795, before stabilising at between forty and fifty until 1810. Thereafter a slow and inevitable decline began. Sailings to India remained fairly constant throughout, though outward-bound the ships were loaded and operating increasingly in support of the Company's political and military objectives in India, rather than as pure traders. Among the homeward commodities loaded, saltpetre was a basic lading, filling the ground tiers of their lower holds. East Indiamen were also involved with military operations elsewhere in the greater war against the French and Dutch, particularly during the final decade of the Napoleonic War, after Trafalgar when Indiamen took part in operations in the West Indies, the taking of Java and the assaults on the Mascarene Islands.

In support of the Company's ambitions, the India-bound ships carried members of both sexes as the Company's ex-patriate community of civil servants and military officers grew. Regular troops were also sent out to consolidate the Crown's stake in the *Raj*, though the Company had to pay for the privilege, while hopeful young women – those prospective brides whose annual arrival became unkindly known as the 'fishing fleet' – tore down the rigid bastions of a social fabric dominated by male *sahibs* and their clubs and messes.

The Company's operations in China were of an altogether different complexion, necessarily adapted to local sensibilities and the prerogatives of the distant Emperor. While the inevitable clash of cultures produced impasses – protracted, ludicrous and serious in nature – interaction was actually the more remarkable for its successes than its failures. In July 1777 an Imperial edict from Peking forbade trade in cotton goods because the people of Pegu were financing a rebellion against the Rule of the Son of Heaven by the sale of cotton goods to Europeans. The crisis was short-lived, the Peguese submitting to Chinese suzerainty, but it demonstrated the arbitrary nature of the conditions by which trade was constrained.

During the trading season the Company continued to maintain a 'Select Committee' at Canton in the British factory situated on the waterfront with the other foreign concessions. The Indiamen arrived around July and negotiations began for their homeward cargoes on the basis of what they had brought outward. Loaded up, they left at the end of the year, often as late as the following spring. Once they had sailed the Selectmen were obliged to withdraw to Macao. Direct trade between the Select Committee and shop-keepers and merchants was illegal. A little went on clandestinely for cash, but general trading was conducted through the accredited Chinese merchants of the Hong which had been established by the Emperor K'ang-Hsi a century earlier, and this was overseen by the imperial Hoppo whose especial responsibility was to oversee the farming of the Emperor's Customs dues and to act as the commercial arm of the imperial bureaucracy. For this purpose every incoming Indiaman was formally 'measured' and appropriate dues were paid to the Hoppo.

To take 1780 as an example, trading began with the Company having a credit balance of 975,239 taels, one tael being worth six shillings and eight pence, or one third of a pound sterling. Trade was carried on in Spanish dollars at about four to the pound, with slight variations. For instance all salaries and fixed charges at Canton were paid at the rate of £100 equalling 416.67 dollars whereas bills of exchange on the Company in London varied between four shillings and ten-pence and six shillings the dollar, for bills payable 365 days after sight. Spanish and Mexican silver was reckoned by 'touch' that is by the percentage of pure silver in the metal coin. That year twelve ships arrived to load: the HCSs *Earl of Oxford*, *Earl of Sandwich*, *Halsewell*, *Britannia*, *Stormont*, *Lascelles*, *Bessborough*, *Atlas*, *Granby*, *London*, *York* and *Bridgewater*. The imports they brought amounted

to 403,462 taels-worth of woollens, 30,195 taels-worth of lead, and 'Indian produce to the value of 45,522 taels'. All, except the *Britannia* which was wholly
owned by the HEIC, were the usual chartered tonnage. During this season bills
on London to the value of some 1.4 million taels were given, of which about
183,000 taels were at 730 days after sight at five shillings and four pence per
dollar and the balance at 365 days payable at five shillings and one penny. The
year's advances, drawn by certificates on the Company's Court, amounted to
182,415 taels, half at 90 days after sight, half at 365 days.

But the twelve Company ships were not alone; they arrived accompanied
by a similar number of British-flagged Country-vessels that traded between
the sub-continent and China, many of which were owned by Indians, usually Parsees. Neither groups of ships imported any silver at this time, though
thirty-five chests were brought in by the four Dutch, three Swedish, three
Danish and the single 'Imperial', or Austrian, Indiamen, the last registered at
Ostend and probably a beneficially British-owned interloper under a flag-
of-convenience. On the occasions when silver specie was shipped from Fort
William at Calcutta to fund the year's trade it was usually carried in a man-of-
war, the captain receiving 1 per cent of the amount as a perquisite. Following
this initial fleet of two dozen vessels, five more Indiamen which had loaded
for the 1780 season arrived in February of the following year, and in total the
seventeen Indiamen bore home 99,396 piculs of various teas – Hyson, Bohea,
Congou – amounting to about 5,916 tons. Tea, apart from being easily tainted,
was a high-volume commodity and the ships required additional bottom-
weight and this was normally provided by porcelain and the commoner
blue-and-white 'china' crockery that has ever since enjoyed a long vogue in
Britain. The other high-value cargo carried was, of course, silk.

The Country-ships bore similar cargoes, importing Patna and Malwa opium,
some having called at Benkulen to pick up pepper. When the Select Committee,
having seen the last of the loaded ships depart from the anchorage at Whampoa,
headed for Macao, they left a few hardy hands behind. These included a
Mr Fergusson (sic) who 'came to Canton from Bengal last year [1779] in the
[Indiaman] *Calcutta*. ...he bought a small Vessel at Macao and brought her to
Whampoa to manage an Opium concern, where he still remains'.

At this time the Hoppo – properly the Sea Customs Commissioner for the
Province that was then known as Kwantung – was Yüeh-hai-kwan-pu, styled
informally as Kwanpu and liaison with him and the Chinese merchants of
the Hong – usually conducted through Chinese interpreters known as 'the
Linguists' – was enhanced by the arrival of a Mr Bevan. Thomas Bevan was
one of two young men who had been sent out by the Court of Directors
in London in 1753 and was allowed to travel by the Chinese authorities to
Nanking where they had, unusually, learned Mandarin Chinese.

Matters were complicated by the outbreak of war between Great Britain and Spain as a consequence of Spain's ally France espousing the cause of the rebellious American colonists. In 1779 the East India Company's forces had captured Mahé, Pondicherry and Chandanagar, precipitating war with Hyder Ali (the First Mysore War) on the sub-continent and thereby drawing France and Spain into the American War of Independence. The French despatched a number of corsairs – privateers with Letters-of-Marque-and-Reprisal – to prey on the Indian trade and most therefore operated in the Indian Ocean.

In 1780 one French corsair, mounting twelve 6-pounder guns, in addition to seizing several small ships from Bengal, took the Country-ships *Concord*, Captain Jamison, and the *Prince*, Captain Scott, in the Straits of Malacca. However, in August 1780 Captain John Tasker, then commanding the Country-ship *Hornby*, engaged and captured a vessel wearing Spanish colours off Macao but, as the *Hornby* had no Letter-of-Marque and was therefore not able to legitimise her capture, Tasker's prize was taken by the resident British naval officer who had been sent by the British Commander-in-Chief of the East Indies station to convoy the Indiamen westwards. Captain John Panton of HM Frigate *Seahorse* claimed the Spaniard 'for the king, and Captain Tasker delivered up to him the value found on board amounting to in money and Bird's Nests [a much-prized Chinese gastronomic delicacy] 8,299 Dollars'. The ship herself was ransomed for a further 2,000 dollars. Despite this set-back Tasker appears to have gone on to prosper as a Country-ship-owner.

War with Spain choked off the supply of silver dollars and a financing crisis developed. Although produce brought from India in the Country-ships helped, it was also necessary to bring in silver and gold, the latter of which slumped in price owing to a flooding of the extremely local market. Such variations in the means to trade were absorbed very often by the versatility and accommodation of the Hong merchants themselves, led at this period by the redoubtable Puankhequa, senior. Later, Chinese disinterest in sophisticated British manufactures would combine with a shortage of silver to create another such crisis. This – and periodic refusals from the Governor-General at Madras to advance any from the Indian treasury – would lead to an increasing use of opium to fund the export trade from China to Britain. However, in the last quarter of the eighteenth century the trade, though subject to hiccups, ran according to organised procedures:

Advances for tea, silk and nankeens [the yellow cotton cloth from Kiangsu province and brought from the provincial capital Nanking] were now an established custom, as the only means of ensuring the delivery of full quantities on the due dates (nine months or more ahead), and so of avoiding delay to the Company's ships, now more numerous and of greater carrying capacity. In making their

contract in February for delivery in 300 days, the Select Committee decided
that they could make advances to only three of the Hong Merchants, and that
it would not be safe to trust the four others…at that date doing business. Under
those contracts advances of Tls. 601,500 were made to Puankhequa, of which
the sum of Tls. 562,500 was for 2,250 piculs (3,000 bales) of raw silk…[1]

The intrigues of trade in this exotic milieu were complex, frequently attended
by cultural and attitudinal impasses, and bedevilled by the British insistence
of respect to their nation – usually forcibly expressed by a naval post-captain
from distant Bengal – all compounded by the subtler counter-vailing Chinese
nicety of 'face'. Generally the Select Committee who, as resident supercargoes,
managed the Company's affairs 'knew no Chinese, cared little for Chinese
politics, and considered primarily their trade'. On the whole, however, the
fact that vast sums of 'cash' were regularly exchanged for cargoes predomi-
nantly consisting of tea and silk is evidence that matters worked reasonably
harmoniously. Nevertheless there were spectacular ruptures invariably caused
by the floating population who annually arrived in the Pearl River and demonstrated the truth asserted by Admiral Charles Napier a generation later that
seamen were 'the Devil in harbour'. At the Whampoa anchorage where the
Indiamen lay awaiting their cargoes, the crews were 'constrained to a life little
less monotonous than they had while at sea'. War only exacerbated matters,
embroiling the French and Danes, and 'aroused the boisterous patriotism of
the sailors of all nationalities, a class always difficult of restraint…' Boredom
and the juxtaposition of the merchant ships of belligerent nations in a neutral's waters for many months only needed the catalyst of spirituous liquors
to cause mayhem. This was further complicated by the varying nationalities
employed on board different – but particularly the British – East Indiamen
and Country-ships.

In December 1780 a French seaman from the crew of the Country-ship
Success fell into an argument with a Portuguese sailor from the HCS *Stormont*.
The men had met in one of the Hong merchant's premises and the Portuguese
had been killed. The Frenchman then sought asylum with the French consul
claiming self-defence until, some days later, he was given up and by order of
the Fooyuen, or city governor, publicly strangled. This worried the European
community who disliked one of their nationals being punished by the rigour
of Chinese law without any chance to state his case. The Fooyuen hit back,
issuing 'a Chop' or edict over his distinguishing signature (his 'chop'), justify-
ing his action on the grounds that it was his duty to maintain order, that he
had no assurance that the prisoner would be properly punished if withdrawn
to stand trial in his own country, that such a device would remove him from
the public eye in Canton and that the seamen 'who are addicted to drunken-

ness riot and quarrels' could only be kept in order by such Draconian and intimidating punishments.

Such instances of summary justice became commonplace on both sides. In the case of a Dutch seaman murdering one of his own countrymen, the request by the mandarins to give up the accused was refused, but the malefactor was hanged at the foreyard arm in full view of the Chinese passing in the Pearl River. To be fair to the Mandarin Government when, in 1785, an English seaman from the *Earl of Chesterfield* was killed in an affray on Dane's Island – the only location recreational shore-leave could be given to foreign sailors aboard the ships anchored at Whampoa – the murderer was in due course given up to the mandarin who had him executed. The eye-for-an-eye principal inherent in Chinese justice was upheld again in 1796 when a lascar from the Country-ship *Hornby*, who was shopping for vegetables, was killed by a stall-holder.[2] The homicidal vendor was swiftly arraigned and, after due if summary process, publicly strangled.

While the conduct of the East India Company's own vessels was subject to some control by their own commanders and the authority of the Select Committee, the same could not be said of the Country-ships belonging to the private free-traders. These were sometimes commanded by fiercely independent mavericks, often – though not invariably – despotic to their lascar crews and verging on the piratical in their general behaviour. Such was Captain John McClary of the *Dadaloy*. Having obtained a Letter-of-Marque-and-Reprisal from the Governor-General at Fort William, Calcutta, the *Dadaloy* left Macao on 20 May 1781 in pursuit of a Spanish vessel bound for Manila. The consequence of the chase was that the Spanish vessel ran upon a lee shore and was lost. The Portuguese authorities at Macao imprisoned McClary, threatening to deliver him to the Chinese 'on purpose to be executed as a pyrate'. McClary escaped this by paying 70,000 dollars compensation, but on 17 August breached the neutrality of Chinese waters when the *Dadaloy* was anchored at Whampoa. Hearing of the war with the Dutch, McClary ordered his men to seize the Dutch vessel *Felix* from Surat, after which he prepared to carry his prize out of the Pearl River through the narrow entrance of the Bocca Tigris. The Select Committee were understandably furious while the mandarins, concerned at this flagrant contempt of their neutrality and fearful of the consequences from Peking (Beijing), mustered 2,000 troops to contest the passage of the Narrows.

Confronted by this McClary abandoned his prize but the Chinese attempt to get the Select Committee to discipline him and force him to make restitution failed. The Selectmen stated that they wielded power only over the Company's ships and men, not private traders, whereupon the governor of Kwantung complained that: 'You English are a lying and troublesome People, for other nations that come to Canton are peaceful and do not hurt any one, but you English are always in trouble...' In response the Selectmen complained that:

> We have many times seen the whole Trade of the Company under an Embargo on the most trifling pretence; and we think it may hereafter suffer the most material detriment; from the Wickedness or Folly of Country Commanders. Long Experience has shewn the Chinese that we must suffer almost any thing to avoid an impediment to our Trade: but Country ships are every day committing some irregularity...[3]

This was not the end of McClary, for the following year, in company with a privateer named the *Death and Glory*, the *Dadaloy* captured two ships outward-bound from Macao on the pretext that they carried cargoes consigned by Dutch principals. McClary's justification was said to be 'to reimburse the loss sustained by him last year'. He then went on to plunder a junk belonging to one of the Hong merchants, Chowqua, again on the pretext that the goods on board were Dutch. Chowqua promptly demanded compensation from the Selectmen and once again the supercargoes wrung their hands over their inability to regulate the private merchants and mariners.

Another example of arrogance in a so-called Country-*wallah* was that of Captain Richardson who caused the Select Committee grief when he arrived from Calcutta at the end of 1785 in the *Bellona*. Freighted entirely with illegal opium, no Hong merchant would stand security for such a lading until opportunity got the better of their consciences and they agreed to do so in a body. Having received this mutually convenient accommodation, Richardson refused to reimburse the Hong the cost of the *Bellona*'s measurement, the principal revenue-raising duty applied by the Hoppo which would turn away imperial wrath, should it be directed against what was a contraband cargo. Upbraided by the Select Committee for his contemptuous treatment of the Chinese, Richardson was impervious to appeals to his sense of fair-play and compounded this with intemperate language to the British representatives. He also threatened to order his first officer to take the ship down river without himself if necessary. However, the Select Committee instructed the East India Commanders of ships anchored at the Second Bar to throw a cordon across the river and prevent the passage of the *Bellona*. This determined stance persuaded Richardson to pay his dues in full, whereupon he received the Grand Chop – or outwards clearance granted by the Hoppo – and departed.

Although theoretically only able to trade on their own account under the Company's licence 'for urgent private affairs', which generously extended for two or three years, the private traders refused to leave at the expiry of their terms, facilitating this flouting of the Company's authority by means of the system of *cumshaw*, or bribery, without which little happened in China and was but the mirror image of the perquisites prevalent in contemporary British public life. One such was George Smith who had been granted a two-year licence in 1764. He did not leave until 1781 and only then after regular and seemingly interminable remonstrance from the Select Committee.

Threats to the smooth running of 'the trade' could quickly develop and get out of hand, as in the case of the *Lady Hughes* affair of 1784 in which George Smith reappeared as supercargo. In firing salutes, the gunner of the Country-ship *Lady Hughes*, Captain Williams, carelessly discharged his gun across the deck of a licensed lighter and severely wounded three men, two of whose injuries proved mortal. Apprehensive of the exemplary severity of the Chinese system of justice, though innocent of any criminal intent, the gunner deserted his ship. The Chinese had recourse to the Selectmen who pleaded their inability to intervene and referred the matter to the supercargo of the *Lady Hughes*, George Smith. Failing to locate the gunner, the Chinese authorities decoyed Smith out of his factory and seized him on the basis that the supercargo was responsible for the actions of his subordinates and could stand as proxy.

This action stopped all trade and the factories of all nationalities, being surrounded by Chinese troops, were deserted by their Chinese employees; the Hong acted likewise and all commerce was suspended by the Hoppo. The representatives of the Danish, French, American and Dutch factories joined the British and armed all the boats of the combined ships at Whampoa. On their way upstream shots were fired from the shore, slightly wounding two men, but no fire was returned and the boats pushed past the Mandarins' war-junks and sampans to stand guard on the factories and their national representatives. Negotiations proceeded, the Chinese still holding Smith in lieu of the gunner. In the meantime the elderly gunner had turned up, and on 30 November he was brought to Canton; trade consequently resumed on 6 December and the *Lady Hughes* sailed for Bombay next day.

The abandoned gunner was arraigned and the Provincial judge delivered a lecture to the Company representatives 'observing how gracious the Emperor was to allow us to trade here & that we ought always to bear in mind his bounties.' He also expressed his displeasure that it had taken five days to deliver up the culprit who would be held until the distant Emperor's pleasure was known; in fact, however, the poor man had already been strangled. Whenever an affray occurred between a seaman and a Chinese subject, if the victim was the latter, the Selectmen ordered the guilty sailor secured pending the outcome. When a seaman was killed by a Chinese, the Hong merchant standing security for the Indiaman or Country-*wallah* was requested to apply to the magistracy and the malefactor was apprehended and usually executed. However, as will be seen in a subsequent volume, *Masters Under God*, the affair known as that of 'the gunner of the *Lady Hughes*' was to have long-term and far-reaching effects half a century later.

However, it was not only the Chinese Mandarins who judged the conduct of the *fan-kwai* as two junior officers from the HCS *Ponsbourne*, Captain Frederick Le Mesurier, discovered. For the ships' officers, shore-leave to Canton was limited largely because the only way to reach the city was by river sampan. When, in November 1781, Surgeon's Mate Evans and Midshipman Burton of the *Ponsbourne* were travelling thus, Burton was thrown overboard by the sampan's crew and Evans disappeared. The midshipman saved himself and a complaint was lodged. Six days later the boat-men:

> on being put to the Torture confessed they threw the Surgeon's Mate overboard soon after the Midshipman. The reasons alleged for this uncommon Act of Cruelty were, that these People insisted on having more Girls brought [to] them, which the Boatmen refused to comply with... [4]

Against the personal vicissitudes that such a yarn represents, there were larger issues at stake. In 1782 the Select Committee found themselves financially embarrassed when of the thirteen or fourteen expected ships for which cargoes had been contracted, only four arrived. The money at Canton was quite inadequate to fund the year's trade, despite cancelling some of the Bohea tea on order, and no help was forthcoming from Bombay or Madras. Calcutta was in no better position until the Governor-General in Fort William, Warren Hastings, invited subscriptions in large sums of rupees for which he gave certificates for dollars exchangeable at Canton for bills of exchange to be drawn on London. The risk was covered by shipping 1,466 chests of Patna opium in the *Betsy* and a further 1,601 chests in the private armed-yacht *Nonsuch*, owned by Lieutenant Colonel Henry Watson, but commanded by the adventurer William Richardson. Both voyages were eventful.

The *Betsy* was ordered to sell as much opium as possible on the Malay coast and convey the rest to Canton; her master, Robert Geddes, disposed of 60,000 dollars' worth of the drug before the *Betsy* fell in with a French privateer off the Rhio Islands. Geddes and the *Betsy* escaped with the money and made their way to Canton where his dollars augmented the Company treasury. The *Nonsuch* was well appointed and appears to have borne a Letter-of-Marque-and-Reprisal, for Richardson's orders suggest a 'cruise against the enemy' as the *Nonsuch* was to pass east of Java and through the Macassar Strait, the Celebes and Sulu Seas and coast the Philippines under the French ensign. After leaving the Luzon coast Richardson was to head for Macao

wearing Spanish colours and in due course enter Macao Road, which he did
on 21 July, though without any prizes.

Informing the Selectmen of his action, Hastings thought 'it necessary to
observe that the *Nonsuch* will enter the River at Canton as an armed Ship, and
will not be reported as bearing a Cargo of opium, that being a contraband
Trade.' The gentlemen at Canton thought otherwise, paying the usual duty on
measureage and treating the *Nonsuch*, whatever her pretensions, as a normal
Country-ship, many of which had for long been importing opium into the
Middle Kingdom. The consignment was handled by Sinqua who 'had large
dealings' in the illegal drug, and he disposed of some of it in Macao. More was
distributed along the coast south of Tongking in what was, of course, but the
prelude to a deluge of the drug in the years to come.

The escalation of the American rebellion into a major war among the
European powers stretched across the globe. In the east it consisted largely of
a series of five major encounters fought off the Coromandel coast between a
British squadron under Vice Admiral Sir Edward Hughes and a French fleet
commanded by Admiral Pierre André de Suffren.[5] Throughout the hostilities
the Honourable East India Company's fortunes had been mixed. Although its
war losses were not excessive overall, they were dreadful when a large outward-
bound convoy, consisting of East and West Indiamen, military transports and
victuallers, was attacked to the north of Madeira on 9 August 1780. This disaster was touched upon in the previous chapter, but merits further comment
here for, as Sir George Otto Trevelyan points out: 'All through that autumn
and winter the prosperity of the country was profoundly affected by the far
reaching consequences…' The convoy was deemed of sufficient importance
as to have been escorted by the might of the Channel Fleet as far south as
Cape Finisterre where 'at the exact point where any serious danger began, the
admiral in command, obeying the specific orders of Lord Sandwich,' the First
Lord of the Admiralty, 'turned homewards and handed over his charge to a
single vessel of the line' which was accompanied by two frigates.

Unfortunately, this mass of shipping with its wholly inadequate escort then
fell foul of the combined squadrons of France and Spain under Admiral Don
Luis de Cordoba, resulting in one of the worst convoy disasters ever to befall
British shipping. No less than fifty-two vessels were taken by the enemy, sev-
eral of which have been mentioned in the last chapter in connection with the
trade and military supply of the West Indies. Five of these captured ships were
East Indiamen, namely the Honourable Company's Ships *Gatton*, Captain
James Rattray; *Royal George*, Captain Thomas Foxall; *Hillsborough*, Captain Pitt
Collett; *Mount Stuart*, Captain John Stewart, and the *Godfrey*, Captain Francis
Read. Along with these prizes was the *Houghton*, a quondam East Indiaman

by now owned by Sir William James, the victor of 'Severndroog'. As befitted this old warrior, he had fitted her out as an armed transport and auxiliary escort, but his ship was overcome by *force majeure*.

This was not a glorious moment for the Royal Navy either, for the convoy's escorts, His Majesty's line-of-battleship HMS *Ramillies* and the frigates *Southampton* and *Thetis*, abandoned their charges and ran for safety, escaping capture along with a mere five West Indiamen. Cordoba took his prizes into Cadiz where the Company refused an offer to negotiate any ransom and lost the lot, all being converted either to 5th Rates, or to Register ships for the carriage of bullion from Central and South America. Besides the cargoes of seventeen victuallers and store-ships 'of inestimable value, and vast consignments of military stores for the defence of our remote colonies and dependencies' the enemy also captured 'crews of prime sailors, with many hundreds of officers and soldiers in the service of the Crown and the East India Company, and with a multitude of passengers of every rank and calling'.

A lieutenant from HM Frigate *Thetis* carried the bad news to London where it was received at Lloyd's Coffee House, then in Pope's Head Alley, with dismay. Losses were between £1.5 and £2 million, an enormous sum which the under-writers managed to meet. As for the senior officer of the escort, Captain John Moutray of the *Ramilles*, he was arraigned before a court-martial at Jamaica and sentenced to be dismissed. Importantly – though it was no comfort at the time – the disaster laid the foundations for a closer co-operation between Lloyd's – as the only centralised point of contact between ship-owners – and the Admiralty, which was to secure a better convoy system in the wars of 1793–1815.

Other merchantmen engaged in the eastern trades, both Country-ships and East Indiamen encountered the enemy with varying fortunes of which a couple of examples may be given. The 775-ton *Fortitude*, built in 1780 and commanded by Captain Charles Gregorie, was captured by a French frigate on 23 June 1782 but was soon afterwards retaken by a British man-of-war and as a prize-of-war was sold back to the Company at Madras for 35,000 rupees. She subsequently carried General Stuart and his suite home before being sold, whereupon her name was changed and she was re-chartered to the Company as the second HCS *Pitt*. The enemy had less luck with the Country-ship *Shah Byramgore* which beat off the 44-gun French frigate *Pourvoyeuse* in an action in the Malacca Strait. After the Peace, the East India Company honoured the British admiral who had defended the eastern seas and named a new ship, the *Sir Edward Hughes* in his honour. Teak-built of 958-tons burthen in 1786, she was constructed to the Company's own account in Bombay and put under the command of Captain Joseph Smith.

Meanwhile a warlike state of affairs existed between the Chinese and the bored and fractious seamen confined to the limitations of Dane's Island in the Pearl River. Here, adjacent to the wooden warehouses, or bank-shalls, stood wooden shacks from which Chinese vendors sold adulterated liquor which transformed recreation into riot. One wretched Chinaman, stuck on the island with a board about his neck announcing his crime of theft from the *Belvedere*, was further humiliated by a beating from Captain William Story's seamen from the *Lansdown*, while men from Captain Henry Churchill's *Walpole* 'cruelly beat some Lascars and insulted the Captain of a Country-Ship'. The culprit of this assault at least had the decency to desert, though he was later found hiding aboard a sampan. These events were overtaken by the more serious misbehaviour of the men of Edward Fiott's *Belvedere* who mutinied on 2 December 1787.

Captain William Greer commanding the *Belvedere* sent for assistance to the senior commander, or Commodore as he was commonly styled, aboard the *Earl Fitzwilliam*. James Dundas ordered a muster of armed boats from each of the eighteen Indiaman then at Whampoa and sent them to retake the *Belvedere*.[6] After a fierce fight the deck of the *Belvedere* was cleared and the ten leading mutineers were first brought aboard the *Earl Fitzwilliam* before being confined separately on different ships. None of the Selectmen or commanders wished the matter to fester and, as this was not thought to be an occasion when the prisoners should be sent home, notwithstanding the fact that mutiny was a capital offence and a Company-court did not have powers of life-and-death, it was dealt with immediately. A court of sixteen commanders assembled aboard the *Earl Fitzwilliam*, sifted evidence and questioned the accused. They concluded that the men had not been ill-used but that because 'they were on board of a Merchantmen…they would not meet with due punishment' and had pushed their luck.

Refusal of their crews to knuckle down and to submit to discipline was to bedevil British merchant ships at various periods, most frequently in port and only occasionally at sea when danger threatened. The relatively relaxed regime generally prevailing aboard merchantmen, including the rather stuffy and pretentious East Indiamen, was easily accepted by both the governors and the governed, until the men misbehaved to the extent of drawing attention to themselves and provoking a necessary reaction from their officers. Once mutiny has been fomented, it tends to generate a life of its own and invites suppression by its very insolence. This was the case in the Pearl River in December 1787 when the assembled court of commanders, convened to consider events aboard the *Belvedere*. These men worried in case:

this Spirit spreading to the Fleet in general, where there are above Three Thousand of His Majesty's Subjects, the greater number of which might have by joining the Mutineers committed Depredations against the Inhabitants and put a Stop to the Company's Trade, and the Loss of many lives.

The court sent its findings to the Select Committee and the Selectmen upheld the court's judgement and, as a consequence 'severe and immediate Corporal Punishment' was meted out to the mutineers. The ring-leaders, Berry and Lilly, were to receive at different ships of the fleet a total of 170 lashes, respectively. The remainder were to be flogged aboard the *Belvedere* with a lesser number. This, though short of a death sentence, was harsh and probably condign in the circumstances.

A more pernicious and more durable crime that bedevilled British cargo-vessels up until the age of the container was that of theft or pilferage of the cargo. Captain John Pascall Larkins, having brought the HCS *Warren Hastings* out to Bombay and discharged her cargo there, freighted the ship with cotton goods for discharge at Canton. During the lighterage of this cargo upstream from Whampoa to the Company factory at Canton, a large quantity of the cargo was stolen and Larkins found himself unable to deposit the promised two lakhs of silver rupees, a valuation of the missing 731 piculs of cotton amounting to 12,183 Spanish dollars. Most bales were of the requisite 400 pounds avoirdupois weight, but others:

> had been shortened by about a Foot and then sewn so completely at the Ends as scarcely to be perceivable from the Bombay Package…the greatest Part of the Bales [were found] to have been thus plundered.

Larkins, contending this had been done by Chinese coolies working the cargo, complained to the Hoppo and after a month's deliberation the Hong merchants generously bore the loss to the value of 8,000 dollars. The ship's own security agent, Geowqua, provided 3,000, the two merchants buying the cotton, Skey Kinqua and Eequa, each put up 1,500, and the balance was raised from 500 dollar contributions from Puankequa, Chowqua, Munqua, Pinqua and Howqua. In the face of this co-operation, the Selectmen complained that Geowqua should bear the loss entire, because:

> the Boats were his and…his Boatmen were notorious for robberies of this kind, which was doubtless owing to his supineness and inattention to the Conduct of the Person (sic) he employed.

An increasing number of vessels lay in the Pearl River in 1787. Among the British, in addition to twenty-seven Indiamen, were two ships, the *Queen Charlotte* and the *Prince of Wales*, laden with furs brought from the Pacific north-west, the first shipment of its kind. Furs were in great demand at Canton, and this initial cargo sold for a princely 64,235 dollars, whetting the appetite for more and from which would arise a problem of international significance, as will be seen. Against this opportunistic triumph the vexed question of opium continued to simmer, its importation becoming a growing but under-hand and illicit trade. In 1785 the Emperor had banned the export of silver *sycee* to pay for opium, thus admitting the ineffectiveness of his policy to exclude it, while its import in Country-*wallahs* by way of Macao embarrassed the Portuguese governor. In this trade it appears that Lord Cornwallis, now Governor-General of Bengal, played a part, largely to fund the greater annual trade in the most general sense, but also to protect the East India Company from loss. Cornwallis was equally concerned that good prices were obtained for all Indian exports to China which were providing some 53 per cent of the investment in the annual uptake of Chinese exports. His lordship was in fact attacking the Selectmen at Canton, whom he suspected of price-rigging, and seeking to moderate all losses made in the trade, so the significance of his interest in exporting Indian opium should be taken at its face value.

Others were involved besides the Selectmen. In October 1788 allegations were made against Mr Lane by a Portuguese merchant at Macao who deposed that Lane:

> did for his Private advantage embark personally on the Sloop *Flayte* in order to sell 50 chests of Opium…as is publickly known… Mr Lane has built a Sailing Vessel in which he carries on a contraband Trade…

Lane denied the charges, admitting the import but attributing the lading to 'the Association of 1786', a cosy coterie to which the Selectmen Lance and Fitzhugh were themselves a party. A large quantity of opium had also been imported in the HCS *Lansdown* and the Country-ships *Tyronne* and *Resource* under special licence to a Portuguese *Monador* with the approval of the governor of Macao and Lord Cornwallis.

In 1791 another opium-laden ship arrived, but the Selectmen advised Captain Stevenson, the supercargo, that he would not be welcome at Macao, where he would compromise the Company's relationship with the Portuguese. They recommended Stevenson take the *Phoenix* to another anchorage but, 'as there has been of late many Chinese pirates on the coast that you be constantly prepared against a Surprise'. Stevenson disregarded them, sailed the *Phoenix* up to Whampoa and had her measured for dues by the Hoppo. Reporting her as a Company's ship he claimed to have a cargo of lead and iron, but the Hoppo was undeceived, doubting 'so small a Vessel with such a Cargo would subject herself to pay the Port Charges'. The Hoppo demanded to know which Hong merchant was standing security but the Selectmen disavowed her, leaving Stevenson to get himself out of his own mess. He did so by proceeding to the open anchorage of Lark's Bay, 'to the Westward of Macao' where, despite 'a stagnation' in the sale of opium owing to the quantity on the market, he disposed of the *Phoenix*'s cargo at a profit. Despite their disinterest in Stevenson's plight and disavowal of any interest in his 'concerns' the Company's treasury accepted a substantial deposit of 90,000 dollars and issued a certificate for the Bengal treasury. On 17 November Stevenson left for Bombay in the HCS *General Elliot*, Captain Robert Drummond, presumably clutching his certificate.

Stevenson's was not the only ship to off-load opium in Lark's Bay, for Captain Canning of the *Nonsuch*, a fast-sailing and copper-bottomed Country-ship (not the armed yacht mentioned earlier), followed Stevenson into the anchorage. Canning had 250 chests and it 'realized…exceeding slow; owing to the… Merchants at Macao…they being able to undersell me Head Dollars fifty per chest'. Canning did sell his cargo, but it took him four months and he departed indebted to the Company, taking until June 1794 to pay off his debt when the Country-ship *Surprize* discharged 70 chests of Patna opium at Lark's Bay. Long before this the conduct of ships in this unapproved anchorage had drawn a complaint from the Hoppo. The illegal and dangerous practice of discharging cargoes of opium anywhere but at Whampoa was to be increasingly used and sanctioned on a quasi-official basis with the permanent anchoring of 'receiving hulks' for the secure reception and holding of the drug, until local junks could trans-ship it ashore. But at the time of Stevenson's and Canning's actions the risks from piracy and official Chinese interdiction were considerable. The anchorage at Lark's Bay was also used by entrepreneurial masters arriving with furs and the Selectmen fulminated that 'however convenient or advantageous it may be for Private Traders to resort to this place, as it is undoubtedly repugnant to the Laws of the [Chinese] Empire'. In fact the Hoppo's complaint affected only one additional British vessel, the fur-trading *Halcyon*, Captain Barkley, the other three being Americans; all had cargoes of fur and they saw no reason to reduce their profits by submitting to the heavy port-duties imposed by the Hoppo at Whampoa or submitting to those of the Portuguese at Macao.

Such uncontrollable elements and their own constant obligation to the unwilling and compromised Portuguese authorities were becoming increasingly irksome to the Select Committee and equally difficult for the Portuguese to manage. The aggression of their powerful trading ally, even when only manifested by the influential Selectmen – and the inner workings of their Secret Committee – made their own relationship with the Chinese impracticable. For both the Company and eager British and Indo-British traders, it was ever more irksome not to have their own, sovereign base on the Chinese coast just as the Portuguese had. Consequently an agitation began among the interlopers and Country-traders in which both opium and the affair of 'the gunner of the *Lady Hughes*' would play their part in due course. Such a grand design began to find advocates at home where a growing awareness of the weakness of the Indian economy and its fragile dependence upon the China trade combined with the difficulties of trading at Whampoa to provoke a diplomatic initiative to arrange more favourable trading conditions.

Occasional such attempts had been made to improve matters between the two trading nations before, and in 1787 another of these had set out headed by Lieutenant Colonel Charles Cathcart. Cathcart was an emissary of George III's Government, not the East India Company, though the Company paid his salary, his expenses and provided a stock of suitable presents for the Emperor! The British Government was contemplating relaxing the Company's monopoly and, finding reliance on Macao and the unsatisfactory state of affairs at Whampoa unacceptable, in reaction to representations from East India House, it now sought a port where a British depot might be established. One solution was the ceding of Macao to the British but a better solution would be a depot near Amoy and the seat of tea and silk producing areas further north-east. Cathcart's proposal was that within such a Pale the Chinese would abide by Chinese law and British subjects to the Law of England. Cathcart left Spithead in HM Frigate *Vestal*, Captain Sir Richard Strachan, on Friday 21 December on a doomed mission, for he died when the *Vestal* was in the Banka Strait and Strachan was obliged to put back to Java and bury the ambassador in a Dutch cemetery at Anjer Point before returning to Britain.

However, matters of international moment now affected the business world of the Pearl River from an entirely different direction. The increasing influx of furs from the north-west coast of America to Canton suddenly provoked a serious rupture with Spain. The quarrel arose from imperial Spain's grandiose claims to uphold the Treaty of Tordesillas of 1494 which, in the perception of Madrid, gave the Spanish crown rights stretching indefinitely northwards from the ill-defined area of California, to embrace what was later called after its first surveyor Vancouver Island. Here, on Nootka Sound, lay an outpost of the Spanish state, established by Capitán Estéban Jose Martínez of the Spanish Royal Navy in 1789. Martinez had earlier advised the Viceroy of Mexico, Manuel Antonio Flores, that Russian encroachment from Alaska was threatening Spanish territorial rights along the Pacific coast. He had also heard reports of others having been in the area. The first of these was an American vessel under John Hanna, followed by two British ships. Martínez's task was to prevent these intrusions but he was, in fact, too late.

A scheming and unscrupulous Briton named John Meares had arrived to build a small fort from which he intended to hunt the sea-otter for its pelt.

Meares's first venture into these waters in the *Nootka* had ended disastrously but now he had come from Macao in two ships, the *Iphigenia* and *Felice*, under Portuguese colours and with a work-force of Chinese labourers to build his settlement. With a few sheets of copper, Meares purchased land from the local Indian chieftain, one Maquinna, and began building in Friendly Cove. The year following, while Martínez was raising his own fort nearby, Meares and his men built a small vessel, the *North West America*. As winter approached Meares's associate, Captain William Douglas, took the *Iphigenia* and the *North West America* to Hawaii for supplies and Meares returned to China with a cargo of furs in the *Felice*.

At Macao, Meares ran into James Colnett who was backed by a London merchant trading with the orient named Richard Etches. Intending to profit from the pelts of the sea-otter to be found in great numbers in the Sound, Etches had employed three masters, all of whom had seen naval service in the Pacific and had been midshipmen with James Cook. The first two, Portlock and Dixon, had arrived in the Pearl River in 1787 in the *Queen Charlotte* and *Prince of Wales*, as has already been mentioned. The third of Etches' vessels, the *Argonaut*, refitted in Macao in April 1789 before leaving for Nootka Sound with the *Princess Royal*.[7] The *Argonaut* was under the command of Colnett who, after serving in the *Resolution* under Cook, had been commissioned a naval lieutenant in 1779 but lacked further employment.[8] Like so many in his predicament and with Pacific experience, Colnett had taken up trade as a ship-master, carrying out commercial surveys on the Pacific littoral of north America partly on behalf of the Hudson's Bay Company and partly in Etches' interest. Now, however, he was in partnership with Captain Thomas Hudson of the *Princess Royal* and, backed by Meares who remained behind, Colnett and Hudson intended to expand the British settlement and embarked more Chinese artisans and supplies for the purpose.

Meanwhile Martínez and two Spanish men-of-war arrived under orders from the Viceroy to expel the British 'invaders'. Martínez found Douglas back in Nootka Sound and the *Iphigenia* lying at anchor wearing Portuguese colours. Presumably recognising the dubious validity of her papers, Martínez initially seized the *Iphigenia* but, perhaps considering the complications arising from a dispute with Lisbon, he released her on condition Douglas sailed away. Martínez next arrested the *North West America* on her arrival with a load of otter pelts from a hunting cruise, but inexplicably ignored the next to arrive, the *Princess Royal*, from which on 24 June Hudson observed Martínez formally take possession of the British post – under the Papal Bull, *Expeditu Motu Proprio*, of Alexander VI – in the name of His Most Catholic Majesty Don Carlos III. A few days later Martínez suffered Hudson to sail on a hunting cruise unopposed and it was now that Colnett arrived in the *Argonaut*.

Within hours Colnett and Martínez were involved in a violent quarrel. Colnett expostulated in terms conceived of as insulting by Martinez, who drew his sword and seized Colnett and his ship. Later, on his return to the anchorage, Hudson and the *Princess Royal* were likewise arrested and all were carried south to St Blas on the Gulf of California. From here Colnett was sent for interview by the Viceroy, Flores. He was detained for thirteen months during which time, on 11 February 1790, the Spanish ambassador in London demanded recognition of Spanish sovereignty along the whole coast of north-west America and the punishment of British subjects trading there illegally. This was refused by London and, as both governments rejected compromise, orders were passed to mobilise the Spanish Navy. Meanwhile Meares, hearing of this development, set off for London to present a memorial to Parliament:

> In presenting his case, Meares, knowing that he was on to a good thing both politically and financially, did not allow truth to stand in the way of his claims against the Spanish Government. His exaggerated and imprecise account of the land he had 'bought' at Nootka, and of the large house he had built there, were to be the source of confusion and embarrassment for years to come. He estimated his probably total losses would amount to half a million Spanish dollars.[9]

When, on 6 May, William Pitt, the thirty-year-old Prime Minister, demanded 'ample restitution to the individuals injured and full satisfaction to the nation for its insulted honour', matters took on a grimmer aspect. The two countries now stood upon the brink of war; the Royal Navy was ordered to fit out a powerful battle-squadron intended to force the issue under Lord Howe. Known as the 'Spanish Armament' the immediate effect was to compel the Spanish Government to back down over 'the Nootka Incident'. On 24 October a convention was signed in Madrid which effectively opened the Pacific coast of north-west America to free commerce. Not only the British, but the Americans and the Russians, were soon trading upon the long-disputed littoral.[10]

News of the convention liberated the *Argonaut* and Colnett, who had 'lost four of my five vessels, with most of my officers and half the crew, who had become victims of disease'. However, Colnett and his remaining men received with their liberty compensation from the Viceroy of £40,000. 'After suffering incredible hardships from a want of provisions, and the ship getting several times on shore... [Colnett] procured another valuable cargo of furs and proceeded to China,' arriving on 30 May 1791. Here he found his luck no better, for the Hoppo had issued a decree closing the fur trade which, although lucrative to the British and prized by the Chinese, was thought by the Emperor 'from an Idea that they are purchased of the Russians' with whom the Son of

Heaven had 'been at variance with for some years past'. Undaunted, Colnett refitted the *Argonaut* in the Typa at Macao and afterwards sailed north, disposing of his cargo on 'the West side of Japan, and east side of Corea (sic); a coast which had never before been visited by a European vessel. Here an encouraging prospect of a new and valuable commerce for my country unfolded itself,' he wrote, but he was caught in a typhoon off the Korean coast and obliged to anchor off Chusan in north east China to put right the *Argonaut's* rudder which 'was repaired, as well as could be contrived, without the professional aid of a carpenter'. Colnett's presence was not welcome and he was attacked by a fleet 'of thirty six armed junks' and, obliged to cut his cable, made his way back to Canton.

Not all of Colnett's skins were disposed of in Japan and Korea, a consignment was shipped home in the HCS *Governor Coote*,[11] the furs being part of Captain James Baldwin's 'Indulgence of Private Trade' and probably the result of a private deal with Colnett.

The other ships seized by the Spaniards in Nootka Sound appear to have been restored too, for on 11 August a sloop under Spanish colours arrived at Macao from Manila and anchored in the Typa. Towards the end of the month the Select Committee received a letter from their Spanish counterparts at Macao stating they had received:

> an Order from His Excellency the Governor & Captain-General of the Philippine Islands to deliver to Messrs James Colnet (sic) & Thomas Hudson the vessel *Princess Royal* in the same state as she was when she was detained by an Officer of our Royal Navy in the Port of St Laurence in Nootka situated in the Septentronial Coast of California.

In the interim and in consequence of 'a very severe Gale of Wind' the *Princess Royal* had lost her mast and been driven ashore from her anchors where she lay wrecked. Her cargo of:

> Three Thousand Sea-Otter Skins, which the Chinese have with much difficulty permitted to be landed at the Custom House of the City, where they are to remain under the Seal of the Mandareens (sic) until the Emperor's pleasure is known.

In the absence of either Colnett or Hudson, the Selectmen rejected receiving the sloop on the grounds that it did not belong to the East India Company and her owners were absent, submitting 'an account of the Losses they had sustained to be adjusted in Europe'.

Ignorant of the Emperor's embargo, other vessels continued to traffic in furs and one, the *Nootka*, which the Selectmen informed the Hoppo they disowned in case she should proceed up the Pearl River, brought 8,000 otter pelts. Although on her arrival from America on 22 July the *Nootka* flew the British red ensign, she was afterwards listed as 'Prussian'. This was Meares's old ship but by this time she had passed to a John Henry Cox whose business partner at Macao (who in common with the other merchants moved up to Canton during the trading season) was a Daniel Beale. Beale held the honorary office of consul for Brandenburg-Prussia and was thus empowered to register ships under the flag of the Hohenzollerns. This sort of commercial legerdemain was commonplace and facilitated the circumvention of many of the constraints laid upon free trade in part by the Chinese but more so by the Company's monopoly. In fact the *Nootka* had been originally been built at Bombay as a Country-*wallah* by John Meares and sent after otter skins in his first disastrously mismanaged expedition largely rescued by George Dixon in the *Queen Charlotte*. Afterwards the *Nootka* was sold to a Portuguese owner at Macao until she was acquired by Cox.

The extent to which Country-shipping had by now penetrated the China trade is clear from the foregoing. Whereas these free-traders operating in the Indian Seas comprised the widest spectrum of owners, most ships employed in the China Seas were commanded by Britons and it came to be a repository for unquiet spirits, as David Scott, Secretary to the Company wrote in February 1802: 'I am aware what gentlemen in the seafaring way must expect in India but his merits, with the countenance of friends, will carry him on.' The vast majority were owned by partnerships wholly or partly involving Parsee houses. As with all Country-ships they were manned by lascars and a few were commanded by Indian *nacodas*. They traded widely: from the Persian Gulf in the west, along the Malabar and Coromandel coasts; up the Hughli to Calcutta, across the Bay of Bengal to Chittagong and the Arakan coast of Burma; south to the Mergui archipelago, Penang and the Straits of Malacca. From there a few went to Botany Bay, but most headed north for Canton and the riches to be had in the Pearl River. Such ships never ventured south towards the Cape and the route to Britain, a trade that in theory at least was barred by the monopoly of John Company.

Of course other nations possessed Indiamen and loaded and discharged cargoes at Whampoa: the French, Danes, Spanish, Swedes, Dutch, Americans and Portuguese all visited the Pearl River, but British owners were not supposed to break the Company's monopoly. They did so, however, by means of 'interlopers', vessels that traded illegally by virtue of being beneficially British owned – and usually British officered – but legally by sailing under a foreign ensign as a proto-flag-of-convenience, as Beale's use of the Prussian ensign exemplified. These men 'never sought publicity,' their vessels 'were the mystery ships of the illicit trade and may often have changed their colours to

suit the occasion'. They operated out of Ostend, a European port convenient to London and they flew 'Tuscan, Savoyard, Genoese or even Russian
colours'.[12] The Austrian ensign of Ostend was most usually favoured, the
Ostend Company having been formed for this very purpose was owned
by Britons. Many engaged in this lucrative trade were otherwise entirely
respectable persons and one at least was yet another maverick British naval
officer.

Home Riggs Popham, an inventive, original and unconventional officer
whose contemporaries considered 'a damned cunning fellow', had an obses-
sive interest in trade and, setting aside for a while his naval career, indulged in
wild private enterprise. His prominence gives us an insight into this obscure
business. Indeed, when unemployed after the American War, Popham gave
up his half-pay in order to 'follow his private affairs in the Danish settlement
of Fredricknagore'. This appears to be somewhat disingenuous, for Popham
sailed in the *Madonna* and 'by his own testimony' was in India in 1787:

> where he followed his own pursuits without…restraint, and without being
> aware that he was violating any law of his country by so doing: That he
> was well-known to Lord Cornwallis…and kindly received by him; and at
> his lordship's request, whilst lying with his foreign flag [i.e. his own foreign-
> flagged merchantman] at Calcutta, he undertook to make a survey of Laccam's
> Channel and Harbour, of which he made a report that obtained his Lordship's
> approbation.

Whether or not Popham lay in the Hughli in the *Madonna* is uncertain, for
he seems to have sold her and bought another vessel. More certain is the
untruth of Popham's assertion that he knew nothing of the unlawful nature of
'interloping'. He can hardly not have known, given that his ship was freighted
and registered at Ostend, while his ingratiating offer to carry out a survey
and to solicit Cornwallis's good opinion is equally illuminating, sure evidence
of his cunning, if not his lordship's. Going into partnership with a certain
John MacArthur, Popham purchased the 500-ton *Stadt van Weenen*, clearly an
Ostend-flagged vessel, changing her name from the Flemish to the French,
Ville de Vienne. For some time Popham employed a Captain Williams to command her and she plied a profitable local trade until in late 1788 when she
sailed for Ostend laden with cotton piece-goods with Popham in command
and in possession of a bride.

Back in Ostend by March 1790 Popham had remortgaged his ship for
£5,000 at 1.25 per cent to the Leghorn (Livorno) firm of Valle and Borghini,
renaming her *L'Etrusco*. He was obliged to ship a Genoese master, Francisco
Coppi, of whom he was to:

'make use' in order to acquire a passport for a voyage to the East Indies and permission to sail under the Tuscan flag from Prince Leopold…and among his other titles, Grand Duke of Tuscany. To such labyrinthine legal dodges were merchants and ship-owners driven in their determination to evade the monopoly of the East India Company.

Loading 'a cargo of masts, spars, iron, lead, copper, marble and bale goods,' Popham sailed from Ostend in July.[13] Before his departure he had received a warning from his brother William, an officer in John Company's Bengal Army, who had written to state:

> I hope you will attend to the necessary ceremonies respecting the flag you sail under, even to the number of Englishmen you carry with you as part of the ship's company; orders are positively sent to India to be very strict with regard to foreign ships, and yours, I have reason to believe, will be particularly marked. Do not give way [to] ideas contrary to this opinion of mine, lest you and your friends [and backers] should materially suffer…

William's warning arose from the provisions of Pitt's India Act of 1784 – the same which caused old William James a fatal apoplectic fit – which had to some extent curbed the Company's political powers by making it subject to a Board of Control. Under an Act of 1718 the Company had been empowered to seize the person, goods and chattels of any British subject trading independently, and significantly, 'under the auspices of the Ostend Company'. Despite this 'there were not wanting enterprising spirits who sought to make a profit by taking service with its (i.e. the East India Company's) foreign rivals'.[14] Matters were no less explicit under the India Act: 'his Majesty's subjects…are strictly prohibited from trading to, or being in, India, unless licensed by the Company.' Moreover, 'the ships and cargoes of such illicit traders, and also their persons, shall be seized by any of the Company's Governors or Agents, and the illicit traders shall be sent to England to answer for their offences…' As for interlopers, 'British subjects trading to India under the authority of any foreign Prince or State, shall forfeit £500 for every such offence', so the very act of trading under pretended colours was an offence and explains Popham's protestations of ignorance. So, by mortgaging his ship to a Tuscan trading-house at Ostend, and adding a change of name, Popham's *L'Etrusco* was definitively not a British ship, indeed she was nominally commanded by Senhor Coppi, and Popham probably assumed the character or a supercargo. He himself was, however, liable to a fine of £500, a process that would have been seen not so much a fine but either a licence-fee or a tax.

Whatever the pretence, the fact was that such interloping was widespread and connived at in Bengal by the Company's own servants, the British Government's representatives and all the merchants, many of whom used the interloping ships to carry home their own private trade-goods. Indeed, when in later years Popham – by then, unsurprisingly, a Member of Parliament – was charged with illicitly trading to India, he defended himself by a bold and candid admission that at Bombay he 'witnessed vessels taking in goods and trading contrary to the law, which was evidently relaxed in their favour. How then was he wrong...?' Furthermore at Calcutta:

> Lord Cornwallis knew he was a British subject, and that he was in command
> of a foreign ship. It was in his Lordship's power, as Governor-General, to
> have put him under arrest and to have sent him back to England; but on the
> contrary, that Noble Lord...had abstained from noticing the trade in which
> he had been engaged.

During the voyage Popham, as was customary, loaded wine at Funchal, Madeira, for the London market, it being believed that the wine improved by a voyage to India and the rocking of the ship. Once off the coast Popham, with the luck of the devil, found further official approval: *L'Etrusco* was chartered by the Company to assist in its military campaign against Tippo Sahib by conveying foodstuffs for the troops on the Malabar coast. However, a strong south-westerly monsoon drove the ship to the eastwards, across the Bay of Bengal to 'the Company's new Settlement on the Prince of Wales Island (Penang)'. Ever ready to make a virtue of necessity Popham, with his customary energy, promptly sold his cargo to the commander of a Bombay-bound Indiaman and set about surveying the waters round Penang. He discovered that the Kra Channel, leading south into the Strait of Malacca, was suitable for ships of up to 24ft draught, thereby giving direct access to the southward and saving the doubling of Muka Head on the island's north coast.

L'Etrusco now began loading a new cargo, taking in betel nuts and rattans before sailing down the Malay coast in search of more, including pepper, which she eventually unloaded at Calcutta. Here, it appears, Popham sold his ship, discharged Coppi, with whom he had fallen out over the sale of the military cargo, and abandoned his contract with Valle and Borghini. This required the ultimate delivery of *L'Etrusco* to Leghorn but instead Popham purchased for the large sum of £20,000 an American vessel of 980 tons, armed with French 6-pounders. He then gave her *L'Etrusco*'s name, a transparent subterfuge to confuse the issue, and without Coppi as passport-holder and titular 'Etruscan master' he set sail for Bombay. In so doing Popham disregarded his brother's advice, for his insurance became invalid, and he put his whole enterprise and person in jeopardy.[15] John Burgh, the Calcutta merchant whom Popham used as agent, warned him that a disaffected Coppi was dangerous and that he had himself acted too precipitately. '[L]ike a mole in the dark' Coppi went about his work of discrediting Popham but in November 1791 the wretched man died – probably of malaria – while so doing.

Popham's trading at this time is obscure, though he is known to have made enemies other than Coppi. Having survived a run on the Bengal banks, he had not only sold the old *L'Etrusco* to his new ship's former owners, but on 2 January 1792, before heading for Canton, he had secured the services of a new Tuscan master, Giacomo Pons, to whom the ownership of the new vessel was assigned on paper. Thus it was that in 1792 Popham was back at Penang, while in Calcutta the authorities had been informed by his enemies that the 'new' *L'Etrusco* was engaged in illicit trade. An investigation was set in train but by this time Popham (whose leave of absence from naval service had also expired and resulted in him being removed from the list of lieutenants) had loaded a Company cargo of rice and saltpetre for Madras. From there *L'Etrusco* returned to Penang with a cargo of cotton. This was discharged and stored ashore while the vessel was careened and cleaned. The cotton was then reloaded along with lead, betel nut, rattans and pepper, and *L'Etrusco* departed for China. It was now that Popham himself acted as pilot, actively demonstrating the practicability of the Kra Channel by leading out the convoy of five Indiamen and several Country-ships on passage towards Whampoa.

According to his biographer and descendant, Hugh Popham, Popham appears to have been in correspondence with a merchant named Prendergast in Dacca who was negotiating an eventual homeward cargo. 'Let me know,' wrote Prendergast:

> your terms for freight…and whether you can effect the landing of a few bales of very fine goods in England at the usual terms… Do not be offended by my proposing illicit commerce to you…there are many [trading] houses in London whose principal attention is given to this line of business…[to avoid] the exhorbitant charges at India House and infringing their monopoly rights.

In fact the Canton voyage furnished Popham with a valuable homeward cargo and he was not to return to India.

Arriving at Whampoa in September, Popham concluded negotiations on 23 October 1792 with the Swiss merchant Charles Samuel Constant de Rebeque and a French merchant named Jean-Baptiste Piron for a cargo destined for Ostend and valued at about £50,000. De Rebeque, a former employee of the French East India Company which had been dissolved at the Revolution in 1789, also acted for John Company. Their Hong Security agent was Skey Kinqua and he found them a lading which included eighty chests of chinaware, 'powdered sugar candy', Souchong tea, nankeen cloth, 'benjamin' or gum benzoin (which was a balsam extract used in paints, varnishes, ointments and perfume), sago and rhubarb root. This last was used as a purgative and without which the Chinese Emperor – with a touching prejudice combined with a belief in its medicinal qualities – believed the *fan kwei* could not exist. In addition to this there was a quantity of private cargo. While at Whampoa Captain Pons fell ill and was advised to resign for his health. The wily Popham promoted the ship's surgeon whom he had engaged at Calcutta. Balthazar Georgi was a Venetian but – of benefit to Popham – possessed Tuscan citizenship.[16]

L'Etrusco sailed on 2 January 1793 with a few passengers including De Rebeque and Popham's brother-in-law. They called at Penang and then St Helena, arriving on 30 March and staying ten days. Two weeks later they exchanged news with a Portuguese frigate and learned that war had broken out in Europe and that Ostend had been over-run by the French revolutionary army. Popham and De Rebeque promptly drew up papers assigning the entire cargo to De Rebeque, in which Popham clearly enjoyed a consideration, but from which the absent Piron was expunged.

Uncertain of the state of affairs in Europe and short of water, *L'Etrusco* put into Crookhaven in south west Ireland where, joining the East Indiamen *Pitt* and *Swift*, she was escorted to Cork by a British revenue cutter. Here the ships were convoyed to Spithead by HM Frigate *Diadem*, Popham blustering his way through any awkward questioning and – being wise to naval practice – hiding his English seamen below to avoid their being pressed. Off the Isle of Wight *L'Etrusco* left the convoy and headed up Channel, lying-to off Hastings on the evening of 14 July where, according to the testimony of a Danish sailor, Popham went ashore briefly. A number of boats approached, whereupon 'several chests of tea and one chest of Rhubarb were taken out of the ship'. A Mr Wenham, one of the partners of Robert Charnock, Popham's British business-associate in Ostend, lived near Hastings, though Popham afterwards denied any such incident occurred and, since a pilot was taken aboard at the same time, hinted that this quantity of cargo was a *douceur* to the pilot and his boat's crew.

On the following day the ship was stopped by a British naval cutter whose commanding lieutenant came aboard and had a lengthy conversation with Popham. Whether or not Popham and De Rebeque convinced the naval officer that *L'Etrusco*'s flag and cargo were *bona fide*, the inquisitor cannot have been insensible to the fact that the ship was from India and that Popham was British. It is more likely that Popham invoked his naval links and appealed to the fraternal sensibilities of a fellow lieutenant – an officer in a cutter probably not enjoying great prospects of patronage or promotion and so perhaps susceptible to an advantageous arrangement. Given what happened next, some collusion seems probable. At all events Popham learned that Ostend was back in Allied hands and L'Etrusco continued on her voyage, anchoring off Ostend next day. Popham landed immediately with all his effects. Towards midnight Lieutenant Mark Robinson of HM Frigate Brilliant boarded L'Etrusco and seized her as a prize. This was a blatant act and was to initiate legal proceedings that would rumble on for fifteen years. Lying within the Austrian Netherlands, Ostend was an allied port and a vessel flying her flag was, at least superficially – and setting aside the true nature of the Ostend interlopers – entitled to the protection of the Royal Navy. Robinson, in possession of his prize, remained at anchor off Ostend for three weeks before receiving orders to bring L'Etrusco up the Thames to Deptford. During this period, it was maliciously rumoured that Popham offered Robinson a huge bribe to leave L'Etrusco, a preposterous idea but one which indicates the sentiment surrounding the case and which may have been true if De Rebeque made the actual offer.

Depositions were taken from L'Etrusco's crew and submitted to the High Court of Admiralty where, despite a defence mounted on the grounds of 'Jurisdiction and Territory', the ship and her cargo were judged a prize-of-war and forfeit to the Crown. Popham and De Rebeque appealed and the case dragged on-and-on. Popham moved heaven and earth to recover something, humbly petitioning the King, but the matter was not finally settled until 1809. By 1803 L'Etrusco herself had been sold for £7,050, a more accurate reflection of her true value. De Rebeque eventually settled for £12,000, said then to be a third of the entire cargo's value; Skey Kinqua received £16,000 and the 'captain of convenience', Georgi, had a mere £1,036. Popham himself had lost not merely his investment, but the freight charges of £27,000. Robinson, by then a post-captain, received 'general expenses' of £2,450 and the remainder eventually fell to Popham, in all about £25,000 out of which he had to pay huge legal fees.

He was not quite out of the wood for, as touched upon earlier, he was attacked later in Parliament, especially by Richard Sheridan. In the end the Advocate-General justified the settlement, saying that 'it was perfectly well known to the Indian Government that he was there, and it was the policy at that time to encourage exportation from India in foreign vessels'. Moreover, although Popham had unequivocally broken the law by bringing goods out of China:

> was the *captain's property* a fit forfeiture for the Crown to take advantage of?
> The Advocate-General, by a channel of legal sophistry too subtle for the lay
> mind to follow, thought that it was not, and that therefore his share should be

returned to him. It was a conclusion at last, but Home Popham would never be allowed to forget it.[17]

Perhaps not, but in the short-term Popham's persistent usefulness *to* – though unemployed *by* – the East India Company, ensured that he finally brought home not only a dubious cargo, but testimonials to the Court of the East India Company and the Admiralty, along with a handsome piece of plate for his house. For all his faults, Popham was an energetic seaman and a competent surveyor, so 'his zeal and the gratuitous direction of his professional talents to the advancement of the public good…claimed more than common notice'. It was not long before his name reappeared on the list of lieutenants and he was to enjoy a naval career as contentious as his mercantile ship-owning. Popham's experiences as an interloper allow us to peek into a shadowy world; he represents the culpable tip of a vast amount of illicit trafficking, the most expert practitioners of which remain hidden behind the cunning of their acumen. At the end of his mercantile venture, the flamboyant Home Popham was not quite cunning enough.

Curiously Popham was to reappear in eastern seas in 1800 when, in command of the 44-gun *Romney,* he was sent to escort troop transports bound for Egypt by way of the Red Sea and to conduct a secret mission. The troops were to join reinforcements sent to Egypt from India and, having disembarked them at Kosseir, Popham proceeded to Mocha. He had been charged with reviving the trade between Mecca and the Yemen, which had fallen off in recent years. Most eagerly sought was the *Arabica* coffee bean, grown in the Yemen, that Felix Arabia of the Romans. The erratic Popham compiled a detailed report of all the commodities traded in the area but his embassy to the Imaum at Sanaa was a humiliating failure, not least because conditions under Popham's command resulted in a number of defections following the 'enticing of his Majesty's subjects to desert from their ships, and embrace the Mahometan religion'. Eventually, and probably to restore his fortunes, Popham was the driving force in the launching of an ill-advised and disastrous military adventure from the Cape of Good Hope to the shores of the Rio de la Plata in 1806-1807. Ostensibly in support of the established British traders accepted as a necessary evil by the Spanish, but who were portrayed as under duress by the authorities, Popham's grand design was really intended to break into the Spanish monopoly. His collusion with General Baird at Cape Colony drew in a reinforcement of troops from home and resulted in the defeat and abject surrender of the British expeditionary force before Buenos Aires, the cashiering of General Whitelocke, but the miraculous exculpation of Home Riggs Popham.

Popham is the most extreme example of what mischief an interloper could cause, but his actions go some way to explain the jealously with which the East

1 Richard Thornton, the richest ship-owner of his age and one of the richest men in the world, was nicknamed the 'Duke of Dantzig', owing to his fortune deriving largely from trade with the Baltic. (© Courtesy of the Worshipful Company of Leather Sellers)

Clockwise from bottom left

2 With her fore topsail blown out, something of the difficulties experienced by the small crew of a merchantman may be seen here as the 267-ton brig *Peter Proctor* reduces sail and prepares to anchor off Capetown. Teak-built in India in 1808 for Smith & Co. of London, the *Peter Proctor* was originally put into the West Indies trade and was armed with eight guns during the war. She ventured further afield after 1815. Detail of a painting by George Chambers. (© Private Collection/Photo Courtesy of the N.R. Omell Gallery)

3 The *John Bull*, shown here outward bound and having just dropped her pilot off the East Mouse near Amlwch, Anglesey, with the Liverpool pilot smack No.7, the *Liver*, off her port quarter. The *John Bull* was frigate-built in 1799 for Taylor & Co., of 480 tons burthen and mounted 34 guns. Put into the Africa trade, she was probably used as a slaver. Sold on, she was acquired by the Benson family in 1803 and remained in their ownership trading to the West Indies until 1820, when she was sold to Hibberson and placed in the Liverpool to New South Wales trade until her breaking up in 1832. From a painting by Joseph Parry. (© Private Collection/Photo Courtesy of the N.R. Omell Gallery)

4 The ship *David* of Bristol was built in that port for Messrs Vaughan & Co. in 1813. She was commanded on her maiden voyage to Jamaica by Captain T. Payne and is shown here off Flatholm in the Bristol Channel. She was sold in 1832 and lost the following year. From a painting by Miles Walters. (© Private Collection/Photo Courtesy of the N.R. Omell Gallery)

5 This painting by Robert Salmon showing a ship-rigged and armed merchantman in the Mersey with the Wirral coast beyond is signed and dated 1808. The vessel otherwise shows the characteristics of a vessel under the colours of Jardine, Matheson, pre-dating the establishment of the company by over twenty years. However, the vessel is typical of a medium-sized merchant ship at the end of the Napoleonic War. (© Private Collection/Photo Courtesy of Richard Green)

6 Loading sugar in the West Indies. Having been brought down to the beach in carts, the hogsheads are being rolled into small rowing boats and taken out to small sailing craft which take several out to the ships anchored offshore. On the headland in the distance is a windmill powering the mill where the cane is crushed and the sugar boiled. Note the back-breaking work of the labourers and the supervisor checking the consignees' marks on a hogshead awaiting shipment. Aquatint by an unknown artist. (Private Collection)

7 The brig-rigged Post Office packet *Lady Hobart* being abandoned after striking an iceberg in the North Atlantic, 1803. Note the ensign hoisted upside down as a signal of distress and the hurried abandonment of the vessel as she founders by the head. From an aquatint by R. Pollard after a painting by Nicholas Pocock. (Private Collection)

8 Three small armed merchant ships of the John Gladstone & Co. fleet in the Clyde off Dumbarton Rock. This spirited painting by Robert Salmon shows the relatively small size of even ship-rigged vessels around 1800. All three fly the Gladstone house-flag at the mainmast-head. The nearest has a scroll-head and the vessel on the right bears no decoration on her bow. John Gladstone's ships ran out to the West Indies and were also engaged in the slave-trade. He was the father of William Ewart Gladstone, later Liberal Prime Minister. (© Private Collection/Photo Courtesy of Richard Green)

9 A privateer in two positions leaving Whitehaven Harbour. The bellicose intentions of this Letter-of-Marque-and-Reprisal are shown by the adoption of the blue ensign and the firing of a salute by the left-hand image. In the late eighteenth century regulations regarding the wearing of specific ensigns were not always observed to the letter, though they remained open to challenge. The flag at the fore and the pendant at the main mark her as a private ship-of-war. From a painting by Robert Salmon. (© Private Collection/Photo Courtesy of Richard Green)

10 Robert Surcouf in *La Confiance* boards and captures the East Indiaman *Kent*, Captain Robert Rivington, off the Sand Heads, River Hughli, on 7 October 1800. The painting is by Louis Garneray who served with Surcouf. (© Photo Courtesy of the Musée de Saint Malo)

11 Scourge of the Indian Seas and doyen of the corsairs, Robert Surcouf's memorial statue at St Malo. Surcouf turned down the command of a frigate squadron offered him by Napoleon to pursue a purely commercial career. (Author)

Clockwise from bottom left

12 While the pilot comes aboard, the forecastle party on the HCS *William Pitt* lower the crown of the starboard bower anchor by its shank-painter so that it hangs vertically under the cat-head ready for letting-go in the anchorage off Deal known as The Downs. The heavy rope cable has been 'bent' onto the anchor ring in readiness. The full plate is shown in *Neptune's Trident*. (© Private Collection/Photo Courtesy of Richard Green)

13 A pilot boarding the homeward East Indiaman *William Pitt* from his lug-rigged Deal 'punt' or 'galley'. The men who manned these, the Deal 'hovellers', were quick to take advantage of any mishap as well as serving as tenders and pilot boats as the previous plate shows. (© Private Collection/Photo Courtesy of Richard Green)

14 One of the few East Indiamen actually owned by the Company. Built in 1806 by John and William Wells at Blackwall on the Thames, the *Britannia* was of 1,273 tons and made two voyages to China under Captain Jonathan Birch. She was anchored in The Downs in company with the 816-ton *Lord Gardner* on 25 January 1809 when she dragged her anchor and drove ashore on the Goodwin Sands in a severe gale. She flies an inverted ensign as a sign of distress and the small lugger in the foreground is a Deal 'galley' whose crews assisted – and profited – from such disasters. From a painting by Thomas Buttersworth, Senior. (© Photo Courtesy of the N.R. Omell Gallery)

15 A British admiral in full dress and wearing the Order of the Bath. British sea-power rested on the flag-officers responsible for blockading the enemy's ports and providing escorts for convoys from the Indian Ocean, the West Indies, from Whampoa in China or the White Sea in Russia. Admirals such as Collingwood, Pellew and Saumarez were as important in the winning of the war as Nelson. (Author's Collection)

Above: 16 A regiment of light dragoons is embarking for foreign service. The holds and 'tween decks of the transports had to be specially fitted out for the carriage of both men and horses, and loaded with stores, including hay and extra water. (© Courtesy of the National Maritime Museum)

Left: 17 Captain Mitchinson of the whaler *Blenheim* was brought before York Assizes charged with the murder of two members of a press-gang in March 1801. The jury found him 'Not Guilty'. (© Courtesy of the Trinity House of Kingston-upon-Hull)

18 The Post Office packet *Antelope* beating off an attack by the French corsair *Le Atalante* in the West Indies, 2 December 1794. This is one of the large, ship-rigged packets whose commanders were ordered to run rather than fight and risk losing the mails, but if forced to fight make certain that the mails were not captured. The mails, which besides private and government letters included commercial correspondence, contracts, bills of exchange, etc., were of fundamental importance to trade itself. (© Courtesy of the National Maritime Museum)

19 This painting by Robert Salmon depicts a revenue brig, one of the larger vessels used to pursue smugglers. She is identified by the gold crown in the fly of her ensign and on the pendant as her masthead. Similar such vessels were built for the Post Office packet service and would have borne a post-horn in place of the crown. They were manned from the merchant service. (© Private Collection/ Photo Courtesy of Richard Green)

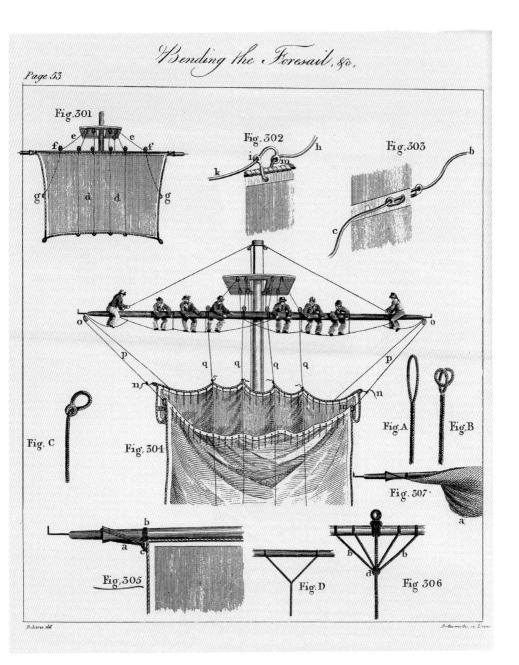

20 Bending a foresail. The skills of practical seamen are shown here in this illustration from D'Arcy Lever's *The Young Sea-Officer's Sheet Anchor*. (Author's Collection)

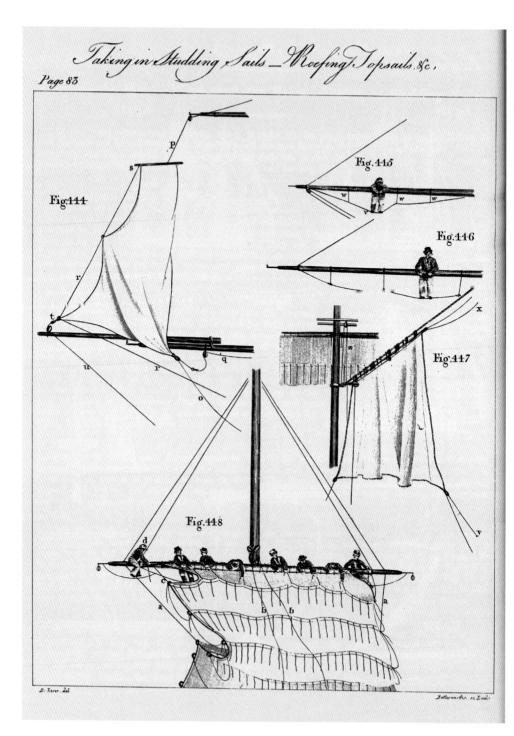

Fig. 444

Fig. 445

Fig. 446

Fig. 447

Fig. 448

21 Another plate from D'Arcy Lever's seamanship handbook for the young officer from the 1818 edition. The plate shows the method of hoisting studding sails and of reefing topsails. By the end of the Napoleonic War seamanship had acquired almost scientific status. (Author's Collection)

22 Thwarted in his attempt to escape to the United States, Napoleon Bonaparte
surrenders to Captain Frederick Maitland aboard HMS *Bellerophon* blockading Rochefort
after his ruinous defeat at Waterloo in June 1815. He was to be held on the island of St
Helena in the South Atlantic Ocean, leased for the purpose by the British Government
from the Honourable East India Company. (Author's Collection)

23 The *Princess Charlotte* was built by the Brocklebanks after the end of the Napoleonic War in 1815 to inaugurate a service to India after the East India Company was compelled to relinquish its monopoly. She was oak-built and, at 540 tons burthen, the largest vessel thus far owned by the Company. She was abandoned at sea in 1854. The Company was to adopt the white ribband on a black hull as its livery. From a painting by H. Collins. (© Photo Courtesy of Liverpool Museums)

24 George Cruikshank's wry view of 'An interesting scene on board an East Indiaman, showing the effects of a heavy lurch after dinner' depicts the land-lubberly passengers including a civilian gentleman, army officers, children and a lady in some distress, who have yet to find their sea-legs. The commander reviews the scene with detached amusement but note the cannon, and the balls that have come loose, causing the steward to lose his footing, and the powder-horns and gun-sponge that have fallen from their stowage on the deck-beams. (Private Collection

India Company guarded its monopoly. While interlopers were, by design, outside the British mercantile marine, their beneficiaries were chiefly British, or British-linked and their business-interests united the wider commercial community that, as it always has done, stretched the fragile bonds of patriotic and political nationality. In addition these ships provided employment for British seafarers, particularly masters and mates, who travelled to Ostend to seek employment when none was forthcoming at home. One such was William Richardson, late of the slaver *Fly* (see *Neptune's Trident*) who joined the *Prince of Kaunitz* in 1791. Hoping for a berth as second mate, Richardson settled for that of a quartermaster in which capacity he sailed for Bengal. He wrote of his new ship:

> The *Prince of Kaunitz* was a fine ship of about 800 tons, built at Bombay of teakwood, her masts and yards of the same, and belonged to Mr Gregory, a Scotchman, and a Monsieur Blanche, a member of the French National Convention: as she was to sail under Genoa colours, a captain of that nation was on board *pro tempore*; the rest were Captain Tennant, a Scotchman and commander; Mr Palmer, chief mate, and Englishman and half-pay lieutenant in the British navy; all the other mates were Scotchmen – the second too a half-pay lieutenant; but such a crew as I never would wish to sail with again, they being a mixture of English, Scotch, Genoese, Italians, French, Flemings and Prussians.

The polyglot nature of the crew was typical of many British merchant ships, and would become more so in the coming century, but also of interest are the astonishing alliance of Revolutionary French and British commerce, united under the flag of the Genoese Republic, and the presence of otherwise unemployed British naval officers willing to serve in the merchants' service. Richardson goes on to give us an insight into his personal circumstances:

> When ready for sailing, we received each two months' advance of pay, thus with my fourteen dollars, river pay and night watching [for which he had received one shilling a night] I had a pretty good sum; so after paying what I owed…and getting myself a good rig-out, and remitting two-guineas to my landlord at London (which I had the pleasure of hearing he received), I was perfectly content and clear of debt.

And thus happier with his circumstances than when in the slave-trade, Richardson left for Calcutta, the *Prince of Kaunitz* bearing a few passengers, including ladies, who kept Captain Tennant's wife company.

In an age when movement was dictated by the wind, time was not regarded in monetary terms. East Indiamen, especially when carrying passengers, were not hard-driven, as, for example, the later emigrant ships were. Not only were the social conventions of Georgian society held to be a mark of civilisation, and therefore to be preserved as far as possible even in the sometimes turbulent environment of a ship, but it behove a commander not to take risks in pressing on at night, or when the visibility was poor, for fear of losing the ship on some uncharted – and unseen – danger, as had happened too often. To these pragmatic considerations one has to bear in mind the prevalent psychology on board. All knew they were in for a long voyage and must make the best of it; no one needed to embrace unnecessary anxiety and, in doing things with a measure of care, accidents were best avoided. The commander and his officers also had to consider the well-being of their cargo, avoiding damage by motion or the ingress of water, not least because a substantial amount of it was their own property. Thus passenger-comfort and prudence dictated a cautious approach to passage-making and it became an habitual procedure to 'shorten-down' at nightfall.

East Indiamen are conventionally regarded as lumbering and cumbersome, but the evidence, though conflicting, tends to suggest otherwise. They were built for cargo-carrying capacity rather than speed and their so-called 'kettle-bottomed' hulls do not, on the face of it, suggest they were anything other than capable of making slow passages.[18] However, many were inferior to their peers and such exceptions perhaps prove the rule. Admiral Pellew anathematized the *Sir Edward Hughes*: 'She sails uncommonly bad in all points', which is telling, and a few were over-sparred or over-canvassed. Nor were they as generously manned as naval men-of-war of comparative tonnages, so that manoeuvres had to be taken one-step-at-a-time, and not in that flurry of multiple activity – such as tacking and reefing topsails simultaneously – by which means flamboyant post-captains demonstrated they commanded crack frigates. This, especially in the company of men-of-war, would tend to infer that they were indeed sluggish, which is not synonymous with inefficient. That said there were notable exceptions.

On the occasions they were chased or went into action, many gave a good account of themselves, often deceiving a more powerful enemy by the boldness of their handling, as we shall see in a later chapter. Occasionally they were the chasing vessel and some did carry unconventional sail-plans. The most extreme example of this was the 1,257-ton HCS *Essex*, built at Perry, Wells and Green's Blackwall yard for Henry Bonham in 1803. Apart from her maiden voyage under Captain George Bonham, when she ventured no further than Ceylon (Sri Lanka) and Bombay, the *Essex* traded to India and China over six further voyages, most of which were under Captain Richard Nisbet. Her spread of additional sails when running before the light breezes of the tropics was immense, crossing eight yards on her mainmast and with a span of studding sails, both inner and outer, equalling the height of her fore-mast. Even in moderate conditions she carried skysails on all three masts and Nisbet added a personal idiosyncracy by painting each side of his ship differently as a form of deception to confuse an enemy.

Flying-kites – as light weather sails were called – were adopted by other commanders in the post-1816 period when competition began to have an impact and speed was a growing consideration. Most notably among these were Captains Walter Campbell, Peter Cameron, John Barrett Sotheby and Timothy Smith, successively commanding the *London*, and the two Cruikshanks of the *Farquharson*. These ships turned in creditable speeds of 11 knots. Passage-times varied, but it was perfectly possible in the large Indiamen of the first quarter of the nineteenth century to make England a little over 100 days after leaving China, a by no means contemptible accomplishment.

There were also good commercial and competitive reasons for 'cracking-on' as are revealed in this extract from the journal of the well-connected Reverend William Money who took passage in the HCS *Walthamstow* under the command of his cousin and near-namesake Captain William Taylor Money. The ship was outbound from London, in the southern Indian Ocean and Captain Money was a 'runner', parting company with his convoy for obvious reasons as the *Walthamstow* spread her wings to the prevailing strong westerlies in 37° South and 062° East:

June 14, 1800. Having effectually parted from our dilatory commodore...we were of course making the best of our way for Madras, which place, should we reach before the rest of the fleet [convoy], our exertions would be amply repaid by the considerable advantage of having the first of the market for European investments. In this attempt the wind was determined to lend us every assistance blowing still a fair and very stiff gale. Last night there was an amazing degree of motion, and this morning the heaviest sea we had yet witnessed. The swell at a distance exactly resembled a chain of immense mountains, which following with superior speed overtook and raised us to an immense height, when suddenly shifting from under [us]...down we rushed into a valley proportionately low. During the voyage we had been particularly unfortunate in springing masts, which proceeded from two causes, having badly seasoned timber and encountering bad gales. About 10 am in continuation of the old story, we sprang our foretopmast, but replaced the damage without loss of time. At noon 202 miles [run since the preceding noon].

Hull construction in an Indiaman differed from that of a man-of-war principally in having less sheer and less tumblehome, the latter reducing the need for locating the increasingly scarce compass timber needed for sweet curves.

After the long-serving and innovative Company surveyor Gabriel Snodgrass introduced iron knees and pillars in new tonnage, they were also fitted retro-spectively to 'all old ships and to those which had made three voyages'.[19]

Mention has been made of vessels bound for China coming thither by way of Botany Bay, taking out supplies to the struggling colony. The experiment of transporting felons from Great Britain to the Antipodes which began in 1787 with the despatch of the so-called First Fleet, apart from using a hand-ful of chartered bottoms, was to have momentous consequences, not least for British shipping.

   The First Fleet, which sailed from Portsmouth on 13 May 1797 and arrived in Botany Bay on 26 January 1788, consisted of eleven vessels, eight of which were chartered merchantmen, the other two HM Ships *Sirius* and *Supply*. The convicts comprised 543 men, 189 women and twenty-two con victs' children, besides the ships' companies, colonial officials and a large detachment of marines with their families who had volunteered to settle as guards. During the voyage sixty-one men and eight women either died or deserted, while twenty-two babies were born. Each ship carried a surgeon and some bore an assistant.

   The nine merchant vessels consisted of three store-ships and six convict transports. These latter were the *Alexander*, Duncan Sinclair master, which returned home in June 1789; the *Charlotte*, Thomas Gilbert, which then ran up to China under charter to the HEIC, returning with a cargo of tea in November 1789; the *Lady Penrhyn*, which carried over 100 female convicts and was also chartered for a homeward cargo of China tea. Her master, William Sever, was co-owner, along with William Curtis, a manufacturer of ship's bis-cuits and sometime Lord Mayor of London. Having loaded tea at Whampoa, the *Lady Penrhyn* arrived back in the Thames in August 1789. Laden with over 200 male convicts, the *Scarborough* was commanded by Dennis Considen. On her homeward voyage by way of China for tea, she called at Lord Howe Island for birds and vegetables. She was also part of the Second Fleet carrying 253 male convicts, seventy-three of whom died before arrival. Out-bound at the Cape she took aboard eight convicts which had been landed there when HMS *Guardian*, Lieutenant Edward Riou, arrived in Table Bay in a sinking condition after striking an iceberg on her way to Australia. Under the command of John Mason the *Prince of Wales* carried one male and forty-nine female convicts, but Mason died of scurvy before his ship arrived home by way of Rio de Janeiro at the end of April 1789. Last of the transports was the smaller brig *Friendship*, Francis Walton, which transferred female convicts at the Cape of Good Hope to load livestock. She left Botany Bay in com-pany with the *Alexander* but both ships had scurvy on board and, with their number reduced, her crew transferred into the much larger *Alexander*, and the *Friendship* was scuttled. The three convict-transports were the *Borrowdale*, Hobson Reed master, which returned to Britain via Cape Horn with her crew ravaged by scurvy; the *Fishburn*, Robert Brown, which came home similarly afflicted in May 1789, and the *Golden Grove*. The latter took thirty-two mixed-sex convicts on to Norfolk Island before heading homeward in company with the *Fishburn*. They lost contact but the *Golden Grove* reached England in June 1789.

Subsequently many vessels bore convicts to Australia, either shipped aboard from Millbank prison to the transports waiting in the Thames, or embarked at Spithead. The vessels included a number of former East Indiamen, including the *Baring*, which had been sold to Messrs Buckle & Co. of London, and the *Barkworth* which, in 1824 was spoken to by Captain Cairns of the West Indiaman *Cumberland* after which she disappeared. In 1792 the third *Neptune* was chartered directly by the Company to convey convicts to Botany Bay before proceeding to Canton. On the outward voyage the commander died, being succeeded by the chief officer, Donald Trail. There was subsequently an affray on board, in which a convict was killed and Trail and his new chief officer, William Ellerington, were eventually charged with murder and brought to trial at the Old Bailey. Both were acquitted, the attorney bringing the charge being afterwards struck off the Rolls.

Chartered initially to support the infant settlement with basic commodities, within a lifetime British ships were carrying every conceivable artefact out to a vast new country which, besides its furniture and furbelows, wanted a population other than that composed of miserable criminals. This diaspora also rapidly produced an export trade and, as we shall see in a subsequent volume, the entire trade of Australia and New Zealand, not to mention every rivet of Sydney's harbour bridge, was carried largely by British shipping companies. No hint of such a momentous traffic was perceptible at the time, for New South Wales strove to survive and it was at the other end, diagonally speaking, of the Pacific Ocean where events produced more immediate results.

The Nootka Incident of 1792 which had led to the 'Spanish Armament' also had other consequences. Having commissioned many men-of-war in expectation of a war with Spain, a similar diplomatic breakdown a few months later with Russia over Turkey maintained the war-footing of the Royal Navy and meant that when a hot war between Great Britain and France broke out in January 1793 the navy was all but fully mobilised.

As is usual with hostilities, they merely made more difficult the trade of Britain's merchant ships and the already fragile lives of her seamen. In the two wars that were to occupy the period 1793-1815, the War of the French

Revolution and the Napoleonic War, known collectively – until a greater
catastrophe overtook western civilisation in 1914 – as the 'Great War', the
wealth-generating capability of shipping was vital to the survival of Great
Britain, funding not only her own war-chest, but enabling her to subsidise
the efforts of her Continental allies. This was necessary to field allied armies
of enormous man-power which Britain could not muster from her own
resources, but which were essential if Napoleon's legions were to be overcome.

NOTES

1. H.B.Morse, *The Chronicles of the East India Company Trading to China, 1635–1834,*
   Vol.II, p53.
2. The *Hornby*, at 600 tons and built in Bombay had been a new ship in 1780. By
   this time she was owned by Sorabjee Muckcherjee and was commanded by
   William Watson – see A. Bulley, *The Bombay Country Ships, 1790-1833,* note on
   p267.
3. Morse, Vol.II, p65.
4. Morse, Vol.II, p72.
5. All were fought towards the end of the American War of Independence, the
   first four in 1782. The first, at Sadras, near Madras, was an indecisive action on
   17 February; it was followed by the French occupation of Cuddalore. In April
   Hughes attempted to recapture Trincomalee but was intercepted north-west of
   that bay at Providien on 12th and a furious battle ensued. Both fleets fought to
   a standstill and, after remaining in sight of one another, the French withdrew,
   allowing Hughes to retake Trincomalee. Suffren then embarked troops at
   Cuddalore to the south of Pondicherry and moved further south against the
   British at Negapatam. The two squadrons were evenly matched and another
   fiercely contended action on 6 July was followed by stalemate. Hughes stayed
   protecting Negapatam and a frustrated Suffren withdrew to Cuddalore. Two
   months later with Hughes off Madras, Suffren fell upon Trincomalee and took it.
   Hearing the news Hughes hurried south with twelve ships-of-the-line and met
   Suffren with fourteen off Trincomalee on the afternoon of 3 September.
   On this occasion Hughes was defeated, though not overwhelmed, for Suffren
   was not well supported and lost *L'Orient* on a reef as he returned to Trincomalee.
   Hughes, however, was compelled to withdraw to Madras, leaving Suffren with
   the advantage until, in the spring of 1783, he learned that Cuddalore was under
   siege by land and blockade by Hughes from seaward. Leaving Trincomalee with
   fifteen ships-of-the-line, Suffren sailed north. Hearing of his approach Hughes
   weighed to intercept, but Suffren outwitted him and took up the anchorage
   off Cuddalore where he took aboard additional men to work his guns. Hughes
   was now in the offing and three days of manoeuvring followed until action was

joined off Cuddalore on 20 June. This too was a drawn battle: after three hours inconclusive fighting Hughes withdrew north to Madras while soon afterwards Suffren raised the blockade of Cuddalore. The Peace of Paris of autumn that year terminated hostilities in the Indian Ocean.

6. Not to be confused with the contemporary and larger 800-ton Indiamen of the same name and mentioned earlier. Stevenson's accounts for this voyage are indicative of the value of the trade. He landed 258 chests with one damaged and only realising part of its full value. The cargo yielded 98,320 dollars. He paid commission at 5 per cent amounting to 4,916 dollars and Measurage of the *Phoenix* at 2,275 Taels which equated to a charge of 3,223 dollars. Sundry additional expenses such as boatmen and possible off-loading or lightering charges amounted to 298 dollars, leaving a deposit for transfer to Bengal of 89,883 'Head Dollars'. Morse, Vol.II, p189.

7. Not to be confused with the Indiaman of the same name. Some accounts of the Nootka incident claim four ships were taken, Colnett states, somewhat proprietorially, five.

8. Colnett's pioneering was soon afterwards followed up by the formal naval surveying of the eponymous George Vancouver. Failing to obtain employment in the navy, the indefatigable Colnett himself was back in the Pacific the following year in command of the *Rattler*, an ex-naval sloop which he and the whaling firm of Enderby & Co., sent thither on a voyage of exploration to locate harbours suitable for the support of the British Sperm Whale fishery in the 'Great South Sea'. After the start of hostilities with France in 1793 Colnett re-entered the navy, was promoted Master and Commander in 1794 and post-captain two years later. He commanded the frigate *Hussar* and during the invasion scare of 1803–1805 carried out a detailed survey of the defences of the coast of south-east England upon which the building of a chain of Martello towers, forts and redoubts was based. He died in 1806.

9. Naish, G., *The Interwoven Lives of George Vancouver, Archibald Menzies, Joseph Whidbey and Peter Puget, Exploring the Pacific Northwest Coast*, p10 et seq.

10. In the sixteenth century Francis Drake had landed on the coast of present day California and claimed it as 'New Albion'. The Russians penetrated as far south as Bodega Bay and the Russian posts were not sold to the United States until the middle of the nineteenth century. Of immediate consequence Captain George Vancouver, another of Cook's protégés, was dispatched on a surveying expedition.

11. I have here followed Morse, Vol.II, p186; Hackman, p113, states the ship's name was *General Coote*.

12. Holden Furber, *The John Company at Work*, Harvard, 1948. Quoted Hugh Popham, *A Damned Cunning Fellow*, p42, Tywardreath, 1991. Popham later developed a code of flag signals for the Royal Navy designed to expand the vocabulary available to naval officers who were then curtailed by the formal Naval Code of Signals. It was by using the expressive and popular 'Popham's

Code' that Nelson signalled his fleet on the morning of Trafalgar that he expected every man to do his duty.

13. Popham, p32.

14. *The Cambridge History of India*, Vol. V, p313, quoted Popham, p33.

15. The price and nature of the deal accompanying Popham's acquisition of the second *L'Etrusco* suggests a deal through the vendor to launder a substantial sum of money.

16. Details of such cargoes are rare but Georgi's private cargo is known and its contents are illuminating: silk, lambskins, elegant rosewood fans, clocks, forty pounds of madreperle (a species of decorative coral), a large collection of rare Chinese watercolour paintings, sea-otter skins, two richly gold-worked pieces of Malay silk, ten bundles of dragon-blood canes, 1,400 'Malacca' canes, 300 tooth-pick cases, preserved ginger, wooden carved work including two large figures with articulated parts, porcelain and jade and mother-of-pearl curios.

17. Popham, p183.

18. A number were considered capacious enough to be converted to whalers. Whaling was a trade which demanded capacity and sea-kindliness rather than speed.

19. MacGregor, *Merchant Sailing Ships, 1775–1815*, p183 *et seq.*

THREE

'HIGH NOTIONS OF HONOUR AND CONSEQUENCE'

Acts of God and Other Disasters in the Eastern Trade, 1793–1816

The war-scares of the Spanish and Russian Armaments, in provoking the mobilisation of naval squadrons, called for a 'hot-press' in which merchant seamen on leave in Britain's ports were effectively kidnapped by the Royal Navy for service in men-of-war. The subject has been touched upon earlier and such conduct by the authorities instilled hostility in the psyche of merchant seamen which is, once the method and extent of the state's interference is understood, scarcely surprising.

Fear of impressments became so ingrained that it almost led to the capture of the Indiaman *Lord Eldon* which, in June 1802, had hove-to off the Needles at the western extremity of the Isle of Wight to await a boatload of late-joining passengers. The watch on deck had seen a ship-rigged vessel that they assumed was a British frigate nearby and, when a sudden sea-fog closed in and the neighbouring ship suddenly loomed alongside, they instantly assumed her to be intent upon pressing them. Running below, they left the officer of the watch defenceless against a boarding party of French privateersmen. Alarmed at the ruckus on deck, Captain Jasper Swete ran from his cabin and, seeing a stranger at the wheel of his ship, drew his sword and cut the man's head from his neck. Calling for his crew to rally, Swete and his men drove the enemy off their decks, whereupon the French privateer sheered off.

The fear of the *Lord Eldon*'s seamen was far from groundless and their reaction commonplace. On one Indiaman boarded by a press-gang in home waters 'every sailor writhed his limbs and features into the most ludicrous distortions: some limped, some stooped, and all did their utmost to appear decrepit and unfit for service,' but it did little good as six men were carried off.[1] In April 1803, although the war with France was in temporary abeyance during the brief Peace of Amiens, the homeward East India convoy was obliged to lie-to off Plymouth under the lee of Bolt Head owing to strong easterly winds in the Channel. The convoy included five Indiamen and was under the 'protection' of the 50-gun *Romney* and the frigate *Daedalus*, which now proved their mettle by boarding the Indiaman and taking 'from them nearly 300 seamen'. The merchant ships were now incapacitated and had to bear away for Plymouth Sound where drafts of naval seamen from the ships laid-up 'in ordinary' in the port were put aboard as 'run-crews' to see the Indiamen safely into the Thames. It was not unusual for Indiamen to be completely immobilised by lack of men after a visit from His Majesty's sea-officers, indeed it became a curiosity for the quality to observe this by way of a diversion. On 4 August 1804 Joseph Farrington, whilst staying at Broadstairs, took a boat trip to The Downs where 'the homeward bound Indiamen were laying at anchor, having had their men pressed'.

Sickness as well as impressments reduced the crew of Indiamen and it became common practice in the Far East to make the numbers up by employing, besides Chinese and Indian seamen, any waterfront riff-raff that answered the description of sailor. Travelling home to retirement in the HCS *Castle Eden* in 1808, William Hickey wrote of the 'strange motley crowd' that manned her.[2] Besides a polyglot crew from every country in Europe, the *Castle Eden* was manned by nine Americans and eighteen Chinese, there not being above ten native Britons among them. This did not prevent twenty-two seamen being pressed out of the Indiaman on her arrival in The Downs by a party led by a lieutenant from a sloop-of-war who replied to a remonstrating Captain Alexander Cumine that he had 'Orders, Captain, orders! I am bound to be obedient to my superiors!'

The following year there was a worse encounter when the HCS *Asia* was boarded in the east. Such was the dearth of officers as well as ratings in the men-of-war in the Royal Navy's East Indies squadron that midshipmen were promoted acting lieutenants when still in their teens. Thus the 'lieutenant' seeking out men aboard the *Asia* was 'aged about fourteen' and on coming aboard he:

> Began the interview by ignoring the chief mate's bow, and calling out rudely 'Call your hands out. I am come to press your men.' As he held no commission and showed no press warrant, some dispute then followed… [The adolescent] lieutenant…on 'being touched gently on the shoulder and desired to keep calm' – this was after the exchange of shots – shouted 'Don't touch me. You're poison-

ous. You are no gentleman...' until the chief mate threatened to kick him over the side. The details of such an incident are childish enough, but the upshot is not. The Indiaman had given up her proper quota of men and received a 'protection' for the remainder from Admiral Drury. Despite this she was boarded in an irregular manner, and eventually forced to give up thirty-three more. On her officers showing their resentment – more at the incivility than the injustice – a scuffle ensued: and the result was that the first, second and fourth mates of the *Asia* were suspended from office for armed resistance to His Majesty's flag.[3]

As a result of this incident the *Asia's* commander, Captain Henry Tremenhere, was moved to comment:

> The young men in the Navy are too often impressed with such high notions of the honor (sic) and consequence which attach to them from being in His Majesty's Service that they are apt to forget what is due to the Officers in the Company's Service, of equal respectability with and possessing as nice a sense of honor as themselves, and imagine they may just speak and act towards them as they think proper.

As a consequence of this great nuisance, the Court of Directors was constantly complaining to the Admiralty, to little effect however, even when Their Lordships were graciously pleased to issue press protections. These were customarily ignored, as was the case when the sloop-of-war *Tyrian*, Commander Henry Davies, took men out of the HCS *Juliana*, Captain Jeremiah Toussaint, in 1810. Even when a former Admiralty Commissioner was present, the malpractice went on. On 5 February 1807 Captain James Tweedale of the *Perseverance* reported from Whampoa that his 'ship's company had been weakened to a very great degree by having no less than forty-one of the best seamen pressed by HMS *Blenheim*'. Tweedale had lost six men to sickness since leaving Penang on 7 December and at the time of writing had 'no less than thirty-four men in (sic) the sick report from dysentery and scurvy'. With a long passage home, this left Tweedale in a difficult position. HMS *Blenheim* was the flagship of Rear Admiral Sir Thomas Troubridge, a renowned hot-head with definite ideas on discipline, though it gives little pleasure to record that she, Troubridge and all his men were lost in a cyclone off Mauritius shortly thereafter.

During enquiries into the foundering of a number of Indiamen held in 1808 and 1809, it was considered that the case of Tremenhere's previous command (also called the *Asia* and which had been wrecked on a sandbank in the Hughli in June 1809), along with his experience in her successor when he lost so many men to the press, may well have revealed a contributing factor of some importance. A disturbing number of Indiamen had been posted missing in the preceding years. Most had been in convoy and all had succumbed to extreme weather, either off Cape Agulhas, ever a graveyard of ships with exceptionally large waves being generated in the locality, or from cyclones in the Indian Ocean. On 8 June 1804, when outbound for Bombay and Madras on her first voyage the *Prince of Wales*, Captain John Price, had been seen in distress off the Cape before disappearing. The Extra-ship *Exeter*, Captain Andrew Dunlop, foundered in the South China Sea in October 1806; the *Ganges*, Captain Talbot Harrington, also foundered off Cape Agulhas when homeward from China in May 1807. In October 1808 the *Experiment*, Captain John Logan; the *Glory*, Captain Horatio Beevor, and the *Lord Nelson*, Captain Charles Hutton, were likewise overwhelmed. Then, in a cyclone off Mauritius in March 1809, a further four went missing: the *Bengal*, Captain Richard Sharpe; *Calcutta*, Captain William Maxwell; *Lady Jane Dundas*, Captain John Eckford, and the *Jane Duchess of Gordon*, Captain John Cameron. They vanished without trace, though an unidentified and capsized hull was spotted that October.[4]

The depletion of man-power following impressment told upon the handling and pumping of a ship *in extremis*. This obvious weakness was laid at Their Lordships' door and the Admiralty was sufficiently moved to issue a code of practice which in theory increased the protections 'offered' to petty officers, midshipmen and mates of Indiamen. One consequence of these losses which, by impinging upon the war effort, directly implicated the Admiralty, was the loss of large quantities of Indian saltpetre. This commodity, stowed deep in the holds of the Indiamen, was a vital ingredient in gun-powder which was not only required by the Royal Navy, but also by the British army in the Iberian peninsula after 1808, when the contract was for the Company to supply 6,000 tons. By 1810, this had doubled to 12,000 tons but by this time, as the East Indies squadron diminished in size after the taking of Mauritius, these inter-related problems tended to solve themselves.[5]

The Admiralty, of course, always had the upper hand, not only because they invoked the superiority of the state's case backed by the force of law, but the Company depended upon the Royal Navy for convoy escorts which, in time of war were provided to-and-from St Helena. Later, when the French deployed squadrons in the eastern seas, the navy was obliged to increase its East Indies squadron, though this was always short of ships, officers and men as was noted in connection with the outrage upon the *Asia*'s quarterdeck.

Just as the men-of-war operating in the Indian Seas might require assistance from the master ship-wrights at the Company's dockyard at Bombay, Indiamen sometimes sought help from the naval dockyards of Plymouth and Portsmouth. The anchorage at St Helen's, just seaward of Spithead, was a convoy rendezvous, and Indiamen came and went, submitting to raids by press-gangs and repairing damage after a hard passage.

Typical of the losses through poor navigation on passage – of which there are numerous examples – was that of the *Doddington*, Captain James Samson. This ship was wrecked on a rocky islet east of the Cape of Good Hope in Algoa Bay at about 01.00 on 17 July 1755. Samson and 248 others lost their lives, though Evan Jones and John Collett, first and second officers, were among the survivors. So too was Richard Topping, the ship's carpenter, who built a boat in which the survivors escaped at the end of October from what became known as 'Bird Island'. After many privations they made the St Lucia River on 6 April 1756, moving on later to Delagoa Bay where on 20 May they found the *Rose*, Captain Chandler, and 'begged a passage to Bombay'.

Another ship to be lost near the Cape of Good Hope was the *Colebrooke*, Captain Arthur Morris. Morris had lost his last command, the *Earl of Chatham* (see below), and had been placed in command of the *Colebrooke* in 1771. Outward-bound for Bombay on his third voyage in the ship, Morris had the misfortune to strike an uncharted rock at the entrance to False Bay. Signalling the danger to the accompanying Indiaman *Glatton*, the *Colebrooke* became a total loss. The South African coast was also the graveyard of the HCS *William Pitt* in December 1814 when she was on her way home from Batavia, which had recently been captured from the Dutch. A number of articles and identifiable wreckage were picked up by the transport *Morley* and it was at first feared that she was one more Indiaman to have foundered off this notorious coast. However, evidence came in of a ship firing guns during a westerly gale and it was concluded that the *William Pitt* had driven ashore near Algoa Bay and had rapidly broken up with the loss of Captain Charles Butler and all hands.

Poor navigation accounted for the grounding of the *Grosvenor* on the Pondoland coast of South Africa on 4 August 1782. She was homeward-bound from the Hughli on her fourth voyage when Captain Coxon discovered – as his ship struck – that he was over 100 miles out in his reckoning, although evidence suggests he was misled by a faulty chart on which the land was incorrectly laid down. Only fifteen people lost their lives in the actual disaster, but a mere fourteen survived the ordeal of the march to safety, the rest being lost to exhaustion, hunger, thirst and attacks by native warriors.

That same month, the *Brilliant* was clearing the Madagascar channel when she ran aground on a rock off the island of Joanna (Anjouan), one of the Comoro group. Originally a man-of-war she had been purchased and fitted-out as an Indiaman by Sir William James, now the Deputy Master of Trinity House and the *Brilliant*'s ship's husband. On her first voyage as a Company's ship under the command of Captain Charles Mears, she was outward-bound for the Hughli when she was wrecked with heavy loss of life as she carried a large detachment of Hanoverian infantry on their way to serve in India. Three officers and over 100 soldiers lost their lives and although some reached the shore they died from hunger and exposure. Some of the survivors made a boat voyage to Bombay and in due course three officers and forty-four other ranks arrived for duty at Tellicherry at the end of the following year.

Another serious wrecking was that of the *Winterton* which sailed in early May 1792 for the coast of Coromandel and Bengal. Her commander George Dundas was a member of an influential family and he had risen rapidly. It was his second voyage in the *Winterton* but although Dundas had previously sailed in the Company's service at no higher rank than second mate, he was both the possessor of a chronometer and an avid practitioner of determining longitude by its means. In addition to the conventional cargo of woollen broadcloth, the ship carried some spare anchors for the Company's stock and seventy-five cases containing 300,000 silver dollars worth £60,000. With crew, passengers and a draft of 123 newly recruited soldiers for the 75th Regiment of Foot the *Winterton* had passed the Cape of Good Hope and Dundas headed her north, up the Mozambique Channel to the west of Madagascar. As with the *Grosvenor*, the probable cause of the *Winterton's* loss was the wrong 'laying-down' of the vast island, an error that was compounded by the shoals extending seawards from its south-west corner.

On the pleasant evening of 19 August 1792 Dundas had ordered the ship shortened down for the night and she stood north-east under easy sail making about 6 knots. He was anxious about the ship's progress, though confident of his position, and in particular his longitude. He finally turned in half way through the middle watch on the 20th, leaving Third Mate Dale on deck. Unwisely, Dundas took no soundings, nor did he order Dale to do so during the night. A little later the ship touched, barely perceptibly at first, then she lifted on a ground swell and crashed down, driving the rudder upwards and toppling her masts. Suddenly a peaceful night at sea was transformed into chaos: within hours the ship was breaking up and attempts to escape by cutting off the poop were only partially successful, the extemporised raft going aground. Loss of life was heavy, Dundas and his first mate, Charles Chambers, were among those drowned in the wreck. In the weeks and then the months that followed, others would succumb, even after getting ashore and finding the local Malagasy king sympathetic to their plight. The belated rescue was engineered by John Dale, who undertook a journey across to the mainland in the remaining ship's boat and was finally able to charter a small vessel to rescue the survivors. Less than half of those aboard the *Winterton* finally reached Bombay and only after being captured by a privateer following the outbreak of war.[6]

Country-ships must also be included in this tally of disasters. In June 1795 the *Juno*, an old ship employed running teak from Rangoon to Madras, left her loading berth and dropped down the Irrawaddy on the ebb only to strike on a sand-bar. Captain Alexander Bremner was obliged to await the next high-water before the *Juno* refloated and he could resume his voyage. The ship had on board Bremner, his wife and her maid, a few European passengers, forty-five lascar sailors and eight Malays. A fortnight later the *Juno* encountered a cyclone in the Bay of Bengal and began to leak so badly that her pumps were incapable of coping and the vessel began to fill. However, loaded with timber as she was, she did not founder, but wallowed with her upper deck awash. Having cut away the main topmast to reduce the motion, the entire ship's company took to the mizzen rigging. A few tried to swim to the main and fore masts, but were swept away and others, Bremner among them, died of hypothermia. Eventually, after drifting over 500 miles to the north-east, the *Juno* grounded off Cox's Bazaar south of Chittagong. Another Country-ship to get into trouble, though with less serious consequences, was the *Shah Munchah* of Bombay which, in 1796, was entering the Singapore Strait on her way home from Canton, when she struck a reef. Launching the boats, all hands reached Malacca safely. Despite the work done by Dalrymple, Horsburgh and others, uncharted, or inaccurately laid-down reefs were a danger to any vessel, particularly east of the Cape of Good Hope, where they proliferated in the Madagascar Channel, the Malay, Indonesian and Filipino archipelagos, and the South China Sea. They were impossible to detect at night in fair weather, even when sounding, for they rose rapidly from the deeps to pierce a ship.

In the small hours of 1 February 1797, the HCS *Ocean* of 1,190 tons, Captain Andrew Patton, struck such a reef off the island of Kalatoa in the Flores Sea. The ship seemed immobile and, judging the tide to be low, Patton sent the cutter ashore with two officers to make contact with the local people. While they were away other boats were launched and as the tide made the ship lifted, then rose on a swell and fell back in the trough so that her rudder was beaten off. Getting a spare topmast over the side to prevent the vessel from falling on her side, the crew now tried to land, but a heavy surf began to upset the boats and three men were drowned in the attempt. In the succeeding hours, however, the remaining crew and passengers got ashore with some provisions, stores and sufficient sails for tents. While they watched helplessly as the ship broke up over the following days, Patton opened negotiations with the natives for the purchase of boats, but relations between the two groups grew strained and on the 15th an affray led to the deaths of seven of the *Ocean*'s crew and the wounding of four more. However, Patton had managed to secure three *praus* which, with the surviving longboat, provided accommodation for the 100 survivors. They left Kalatoa on 18 February and made the 500-mile voyage to Amboina without further incident.

The Pratas Reef, Paracels and Macclesfield Bank in the South China Sea are among a number of hazards that lie in the grain of any ship making for, or leaving, the Pearl River. On an unknown date around October 1800 the large, 1,400-ton Indiaman *Earl Talbot*, Captain John Dempster, struck one of these and went to pieces with the loss of all hands. All that was seen was some identifiable wreckage, picked up by the homeward-bound *Houghton* off the Pratas Reef and which was reported on her arrival at Bombay. As a consequence the Company cruisers *Intrepid* and *Comet* were despatched to search for survivors, as is narrated later. The *Houghton*, though built as an East Indiaman in 1782 and the fifth of her name, had been sold out of the service in 1799 to Captain James Rees, who ran her in the tea trade from Whampoa to Bombay. She too was to be lost in these waters on an outward passage in August 1803 when she was caught in a typhoon and foundered with all hands.

It was always the death of passengers which drew the most attention and forced shipwreck upon the public's collective consciousness. Given the risks inherent in a voyage to India in the eighteenth century and the number of passenger-carrying Indiamen involved, human losses through shipwreck were relatively small. However, it is always the exception that proves the rule and is longest remembered. On New Year's Day 1786 the *Halsewell* – the same into which the firebrand Nelson had fired a few years earlier – was outbound on her third voyage towards India. Having made a good passage down Channel and come abeam of Plymouth, Captain Richard Pierce was sufficiently disturbed by a serious leak to put back towards Portsmouth. Pierce, who was on his last voyage prior to retirement, had his two eldest daughters, two of their cousins and several other young women on board, most of whom were returning to their families in India. There were also about 300 military personnel embarked, so the anxiety felt by Pierce over the leak is understandable. However, on the return passage the weather deteriorated, frustrating the commander's intention of making directly for Portsmouth and he was forced by a fierce gale and heavy snow to anchor in Swanage Bay. Here, on 6 January the *Halsewell* parted her cables and drove ashore on a rock off Peverill Point that now bears her name.[7] In the ensuing disaster 386 people were killed. Pierce and all his officers except two, all the young women and most of the soldiers were drowned, circumstances that made the wreck a public sensation. The two surviving officers were her first mate, Henry Meriton, of whom more will be heard, for he was an outstanding officer in the Company's service, and Third Mate John Rogers.[8]

Nor was a ship safe when she reached either of the great estuaries at each end of her voyage to India. Total losses occurred in the Ganges Delta where the hydrodynamics of the multiple estuarial channels, of which the Hughli was the principal navigable one, caused a constant shifting of sand bars and shoals. The river passages were a nightmare of unpredictable navigation and, despite the establishment of a pilotage service, employing Company officers who made themselves masters of the river's secrets, a number of Indiamen continued to be lost in the delta. It was here that Captain Tremenhere lost the *Asia* in 1809, while among other Indiamen whose groundings proved fatal were the loss in September 1769 of the *Lord Holland*, Captain Fasham Nairn, whose orders the pilot is said to have countered; and the *Duke of Albany*, Captain Alexander Stuart in 1772. On 10 April 1783 the HCS *Hinchinbrooke*, Captain Arthur Maxwell, ran ashore on the Long Sand in the Hughli estuary when on her way up-river to refit before making her homeward voyage to London. Sadly, these are but a representative handful.

The open roadsteads in which Indiamen frequently anchored often exposed them to danger, even when generally recognised as safe havens, such as The Downs, in the lee of Kent. In January 1809, the *Britannia*, commanded by Captain Jonathan Birch, and the *Admiral Gardner*, Captain William Eastfield, both parted their cables and were driven onto the Goodwin Sands. Plymouth was hated by seamen on account of the exposure of the Sound, a danger until the construction of the breakwater begun in 1816 but not completed for some time. Admiral Earl Howe grumbled that it would be 'the graveyard of the British fleet' and in January 1796 it proved so for the HCS *Dutton*. In the autumn of the previous year she had sailed with a large military force intended for the West Indies as a troop transport under the command of Captain Peter Sampson. The force ran into extremely bad weather and separated. With his troops prostrated by sea-sickness and a revolting shambles between decks, Sampson put back into Plymouth where, despite having two anchors out, the *Dutton* drove ashore beneath the citadel and broke her back. Hearing of the wreck, the indefatigable Captain Edward Pellew of the Royal Navy organised an heroic rescue.

Indian anchorages could prove little better in the cyclone season, that at Madras being particularly dangerous. Cyclones struck in 1734 and 1737 when the *Grafton* and *Pelham* were lost off Fort St George, and the *Devonshire* was wrecked in the Ganges. Another occurred in 1761, sinking the *Protector* off Pondicherry. As a consequence of Indiamen being driven from their anchors and wrecked in cyclones off Madras in particular, a general order was issued forbidding ships to lie at anchor off Fort St George between 11 October and 11 December. On 20 October 1768 the HCS *Earl of Chatham*, on her maiden voyage, arrived at Madras with cargo and passengers. As the weather was favourable and the surf low, Captain Arthur Morris intended landing his passengers and discharging his cargo before proceeding onwards to Bombay. Unfortunately, having accomplished this, he was ordered to remain at anchor by the governor at Fort St George, Charles

Bouchier. For several days the ship lay in the road when, with a lowering glass and obvious signs of approaching bad weather, Morris and his purser went ashore to remonstrate. Waiting on Bouchier to protest at further delay, Morris found himself too late; in his absence the threatened cyclone struck, the *Earl of Chatham* was driven from her moorings and although the first mate, Mr Robert Sedgeley, had a full crew on board, the ship foundered, drowning all hands. There were other losses off Madras, such as that of the *Earl of Hertford*, Captain David Clarke, in 1782, which sank in similar circumstances, all of which gave the anchorage a bad name.

As the general trade of Bengal increased it was Fort William and the adjacent city of Calcutta that became the centre of the Company's business. The Ganges estuary, although dangerous, nevertheless provided several good anchorages for an increasing mass of shipping. Indiamen large and small, plus a vast number of Country-wallahs and indigenous coastal craft all made use of the anchorages off Fort William, Diamond Harbour or Saugor Island. This accumulation of commerce began to erode the importance of Madras as a major port.

And it was not only in the Bay of Bengal that a mariner might encounter a tropical revolving storm. This seasonal danger is an added complication to the predictable monsoon and it occurs elsewhere. Known off the east coast of India and in the Southern Indian Ocean in the vicinity of Mauritius as a cyclone, the tropical revolving storm is encountered around the world between latitudes 10° and 30° North and South of the Equator. What is a cyclone in the Indian Ocean is a hurricane in the West Indies and typhoon in the China Seas. Such a disturbance remains a very real danger to any ship, but a sailing ship was particularly vulnerable. An account written by the unknown but surviving second mate of the Country-ship *Nautilus* is of interest. On the morning of 17 November 1802 the *Nautilus* was making for the Pearl River, approaching the Chinese coast in pleasant weather. During the forenoon soundings were taken and a little later the outlying islands of the Lema group were sighted. At noon, as the *Nautilus* neared the end of her passage, the ship was struck by a hard squall but this soon cleared. The land came in sight again and with it:

a great number of fishing boats going in different directions, and seemingly in great confusion…[later, it was] still squally with heavy rain. At eight o'clock at night, the squall increasing, and dismal looking weather, handed our topsails and courses, and lay-to under the mizzen staysail, heaving the lead through the night; at midnight, blowing hard with rain, the wind about NE. At three o'clock next morning wore ship to the southward and eastward, blowing furiously, and a tremendous sea. At four o'clock wore ship again. At daylight saw an island

An able seaman is lashed outside the ship's side in the fore-chains to heave the lead and so determine the depth of water. When the bottom could be found in under 100 fathoms, a ship was said to 'be in soundings'. The end of the lead itself was hollowed and 'armed' with some tallow to pick up a sample of the bottom to assist location, while the lead-line was marked at intervals with distinctive materials such as bunting, serge, leather and knotted yarns so that by feel a leadsman could feel the wet mark at night. Heaving the lead was a wet but highly responsible and skilled task and was also carried out as a ship approached a shore or open anchorage. After a drawing by George Cruikshank. (Author's Collection)

under our lee: let go both the bower anchors; but at this time the wind being so
very violent the anchors had no effect on the ship, and she drove bodily on the
island and went to pieces shortly after she struck.[9]

The survivors were helped by local Chinese and eventually reached Macao,
though some trouble was encountered when the local mandarin refused to
allow the seventeen surviving lascars permission to travel. The intervention of
the Portuguese governor secured their release and they rejoined the second
mate and the gunner. That same night a Spanish frigate had been lost a few
miles away, not far from modern Hong Kong, driving ashore in Brandon's
Bay. She had been on passage from Manila bound for Whampoa with 800,000
silver dollars, all of which was lost, though her crew scrambled ashore.

Another Country-ship to succumb to a typhoon was the *Fanny* of Bombay.
She was bound from her home port to China in August of 1803 under Captain
Robertson loaded with cotton piece goods. The captain had just engaged a
new second mate, Thomas Page, who had come out from England in the HCS
Elphinstone. On passage through the Malacca Strait the *Fanny* ran aground and
'knocked off their rudder, but soon shipped it again, and went on...till the
middle of September, when the moon plainly indicated blowing weather'.
By now the *Fanny* was in the South China Sea, not far from the dangerous
Paracel Shoals and by the 19th the typhoon was upon them with:

a fresh gale, with increasing sea, until the 20th, on which day the sky presented a
vivid appearance; the clouds, which were greatly agitated, were flying about in all
directions, and the sea tossing about with equal irregularity. Convinced that these
were omens of something unusual, they prepared their vessel for the worst...
On the 21st, by noon, the gale came on, and by eight o'clock, P.M. it blew so
exceedingly hard that they could not carry a stitch of canvas; it increased in violence through the night, attended with a very high sea, until eight next morning,
when suddenly this heavy gale of wind became a downright calm. They were
now assured of the approach of a typhoon, which accordingly came to pass in half
an hour. The sea was amazingly high, and the rising waves, counteracted by the
violence of the hurricane, turned back, and made an irregular froth all over the
ocean, resembling a boiling chaldron(sic). About nine o'clock the foremast went
by the board; and the wreck going astern, tore away the rudder. There were now
three feet of water in the hold, and the ship was driving to and fro at the mercy
of the wind and sea. All hands were employed at the pumps; the captain was very
much dejected, and the first mate was out of his senses. The second mate, Mr
Page, used all his endeavours in cheering the men at the pumps.

At midnight the gale abated, and...next morning they had reduced the water
in the hold by incessant pumping to nine inches; still...the vessel, from the loss

of her rudder, was drifting... They were now in the most perilous situation; the wind was dying away, and they were not able to carry sail to steady the vessel, on which account she rolled about most dreadfully. At ten at night her main top-mast went overboard, killing one man and wounding five. On the 24th they got up a jury fore-mast...steering by the sails...they at length gained the coast of Hainan, October 13, where they came to an anchor...

By extraordinary exertions the following day they rigged a jury rudder. However, the wretched mate now decided to abandon the ship by deserting from a boat sent ashore for fresh water on the 15th. He took his servant with him 'to take his chance among even wild beasts'. However, while the boat and her four-man crew were away, a wind came offshore in such strength that the *Fanny* dragged her anchor, then parted her cable and was driven out to sea. The gale continued the next day but thereafter moderated, so that they were able to stand inshore and anchor in Tongsoi Bay where they lay for three weeks, repairing damage and finally replenishing their water. However, such was the fear of strangers and the injunctions against intercourse with them laid upon the Hainanese by the imperial mandarins, that the *Fanny*'s crew were unable to obtain provisions and had saved only a few bags of *dahl*, or chick-peas, all the rice being spoiled. Robertson was obliged to cut rations which: 'The poor men bore...with great patience, but soon began to droop.' They did, however, buy a small sampan, probably to facilitate their repair work.

Robertson now received a letter from his mate informing the master that he repented his desertion which had only resulted in his incarceration by the authorities at Tongsoi. The letter had been smuggled aboard at some risk to the Chinese bearer, but it did not prevent four men deserting, taking the longboat and wrecking her in the surf. Robertson had intended to secure the mate's release and, hoisting in the little sampan, prepared to stand into the bay with his four 6-pounders manned, but again an offshore gale got up, split their mainsail, broke off the extemporised rudder and drove the *Fanny* out to sea again. The ship was now drifting helplessly and miraculously avoided running aground. In the meanwhile they again made up a jury rudder and, on 21 November 'got it shipped', which could have been no mean feat. 'Having the vessel once more under their command, they felt themselves more at ease, and stood to the SE that night.'

After their run of luck, this was a near-fatal decision, for: 'Early next morning they perceived rocks and sands round them in every direction, and tried in vain to get out; therefore they came to anchor'. It is impossible to determine their location but having crossed 'the southern tail of the Paracels', they appear to have got among the Spratly Islands where they were in the gravest danger. The next three days were spent in rendering the sampan fit for the

task of discovering a way out of the encircling reefs, over which 'the sea broke
with tremendous violence' and upon which they threatened to drag at every
gust of wind. Unable to make the sampan seaworthy and with the nearest
rocks only 100 yards distant, on 26 November Robertson decided to take
his chance, weighed one anchor and cut the second cable, paying the *Fanny*
off and heading for a gap in the reef surveyed from the uncertain vantage-
point of the masthead. At the critical moment, just as they stood clear of the
rocks, the wind shifted and 'at one o'clock…the *Fanny* struck! The first blow
knocked off their second rudder, which cost them so much trouble to make.
The vessel struck very hard, driving in further among the rocks'. It was high
water and they cut away the mizzen mast, only to find at low water that they
lay in a pool of water surrounded by rocks and sand bars which stretched for
several miles. Anxious now that the ship would fall over, the last yards came
down as props, and while 'at present the *Fanny* was perfectly tight…it was
impossible that she could continue so long . It did not; next morning the
Fanny was bilged, her bottom open to the sea.

Robertson and Page, who with the gunner 'were the only Englishmen on
board', now decided to cut off the poop and fabricate two flat-bottomed
boats. Fortunately, in breaking open the hatches for timber they found some
dry rice from which: 'The poor Lascars had now a hearty meal, after which
they laboured with greater cheer'. A fortnight later, while they laboured at
the rafts, the sodden cargo of cotton decomposed and emitted an unpleasant
'effluvia'. This affected them all, many falling ill and ailing with a mysterious
facial swelling. Robertson was among the sick and kept his bed while the lascars quietly began to die. On 22 December an American brig, the *Pennsylvania*
of Philadelphia, came in sight and hove-to when she perceived the red ensign
hoisted union-down as a signal of distress. Page went off in the sampan to
guide the brig's boat in through the reefs and a curious negotiation ensued.
The brig's opportunist master wanted some stores out of the *Fanny*, to which
Page readily agreed, but Robertson would not leave his ship on anything
other than the rafts. This was a curious decision, the first hint that Robertson's
mental state was precarious. Page loyally declined to abandon his commander
while both men urged the lascars to leave. However, the American master
would only take four Christians, so four Portuguese seamen transferred to the
Pennsylvania, which obligingly left some provisions in exchange for cordage
and sails before resuming her passage to Whampoa.

In the wake of this bizarre encounter, Christmas was depressing, though the
food obtained from the *Pennsylvania* helped revive Robertson. By the end of
the year two boxy, swim-headed boats were ready and on 4 January 1804, armed
with some muskets, Robertson, Page and 'twenty-three Europeans' embarked
in one raft with the sampan in tow, while two dozen lascar sailors cast off in the

second. The simple craft could only run down-wind but it took a day and a night – with several near-disastrous groundings – before they cleared the reefs. By this time Robertson's boat leaked badly and lascars remained entrapped within the reefs, so the sampan was sent back with Page to extricate the lascars' boat and having got her off into deep water Page returned to report to Robertson that one of the lascars had poisoned himself in the night, tortured by his fellows' reproaches for refusing to help on the wreck.

For days they struggled south-west before the prevailing north-east monsoon accompanied by two sharks until the 8th when at dawn they had lost sight of the lascars' boat. The sampan which had been towing astern as a rudder manned by two sea-cunnies now overset and while one of the men was pulled in on the painter, the other was lost to the sharks, calling upon Allah in his death agony. A fortnight later:

> their situation was truly deplorable: the captain had lost the use of his limbs, and a dreadful scurvy had broken out among the crew; ten of them were incapable of doing any duty, their gums and throats having become so putrid that they could scarce swallow; even wounds which had healed many years, now broke out with all their former inveteracy, and one man lay dead before them…

Only Page remained tolerably fit when, on 23 January he sighted the Anambas Islands. They landed on Pulo Tingley where they obtained water but little relief for their scurvy. On the 30th a brig came into the bay and handed them some provisions but, since she was bound for the Rhio Islands to trade for pepper and the intransigent Robertson was equally determined to reach Malacca, he declined to be rescued. The brig's master warned them of pirates – the *orang laut*, or sea-people, from the Borneo coast – with whom he had recently had an engagement, lost his mate and had himself been wounded. Robertson took no notice and pressed on. Quite incredibly they made their way through the Singapore Strait and succeeded in reaching Malacca on 4 February. Now, however, the indomitable Page, devoid of any money, clothes or basic necessities, stood guard over the only asset attached to the *Fanny*, the crazy box-boat. This was sold on Robertson's orders and Page, having passed the cash to the master and written a full affidavit of the affair, found himself cast out and abandoned by the perverse Robertson who 'took no more notice of me than if I had been a foremast man'.

It was at Malacca that a ship came in with the sole survivor of the lascars' raft. This had run ashore on an island off the Singapore Strait where the seamen had been attacked and from which only the one man had escaped by stealing a canoe. After a three-week stay at Malacca the convoy from China to Bombay arrived. 'Captain Robertson procured a passage…for himself, but refused to take Mr Page with him, alleging that the ship were too much crowded already...' Page secured a place in the *Minerva*, thanks to the kindness of Captain Pope. Of the seventy-five aboard the *Fanny* when she had left Bombay, twenty-five survived. The long ordeal of the *Fanny's* people shows the extraordinary courage and tenacity of the human spirit, as much as its meanness in Robertson's 'scandalous' treatment of his young mate which, one might charitably assume, was due to a complete nervous breakdown.

Moreover, the *Fanny's* tremendous strength attests to the durable nature of teak ships built in the Wadia dockyard at Bombay. The 770-ton *Britannia* – the fourth Indiaman of the name and built in 1777 by Wadia – would have lasted for more than twelve voyages if she too had not run hard-aground. Outward-bound in charge of a convoy in the small hours of 1 November 1805, the lookout aboard HM Frigate *Leda* spotted breakers ahead. The officer of the watch promptly fired a warning gun and wore round, so close to the Rocao Rocks off Brazil that her quarter boat was said to have over-hung them. At daylight, however, the artillery transport *King George* was seen to have run ashore, as had the *Britannia*. In the act of promptly tacking clear of the danger, the *Britannia* had been run into by the HCS *Streatham* which had yet to react to the *Leda's* signal-gun. In the collision the *Britannia* lost her bowsprit and fore-topmast and, unable to manoeuvre, had consequently drifted onto the rocks, lost her rudder and been bilged. The Company ships *Europe*, *Comet* and *Veruna* stood by, their boats rescuing Captain Jonathan Birch and about 400 people including, besides the *Britannia's* passengers and crew, the Company's military and administrative recruits. Birch also managed to bring off the ship about twelve of the 160 chests of silver dollars she was freighted with before the *Britannia* broke clear of the rocks to sink in deeper water. The Indiamen's boats also joined those of the *Leda* in taking off the people in the *King George*, where only the elderly General York lost his life through refusing to co-operate with the seamen arranging the rescue by means of a rope.

An almost identical fate overtook the *Lady Burges* in April 1806. She was one of a convoy under the escort of HMS *Leopard*, 50 guns, which had left St Helen's on 31 March and by 13 April was off the Selvage Islands. In addition to the *Lady Burgess*, the HCSs *Walthamstow*, *Nelson*, *Sovereign*, *Asia* and *Melville* were in company. At 02.00 on 20 April a warning gun was fired from the *Lady Burges*, her watch having seen white-water ahead. Immediately the convoy hove-to, but daylight revealed the *Lady Burges* dismasted upon Leyton's Rock, a reef off Boa Vista in the Cape Verde Islands. A heavy surf soon began its work, frustrating the boats working their way in to the rescue. By 09.00 the Indiaman had broken up with the loss of thirty-four of the 184 on board and including Chief Mate Thomas Cock, the purser William Dick, eighteen seamen, three Company cadets and Midshipman Swinton, son of her commander, Captain Archibald Swinton.

Just as a sinking arising from action with an enemy was a comparative rarity in the days of wooden ships, so was it from a simple collision, but it was not unknown. On 26 December 1778 the sixth Indiaman to be named *London* left for St Helena, Benkulen and China under Captain Daniel Webb. Two days later, off Berry Head at the southern extremity of Tor Bay, she was in collision with HMS *Russell*, of 74 guns. Both ships were badly damaged, so badly that the *London* filled and sank, though the *Russell* and her boats rescued the passengers and crew from her. Sometimes a squall could strike out of a blue sky, consigning men and women to oblivion in a matter of minutes. On 2 July 1814 the HCS *Devonshire* was lying at anchor in the Ganges at Saugor Roads completing her cargo for China when a squall laid her over on her beams-ends and she filled through the lower ports kept open to air the lower decks.[10]

Throughout its long history the Company lost ships from many causes: heavy weather, being caught off and driven upon a lee-shore, and through lack of visibility due to fog. Fog was a particular hazard on the home coast. It was common for Indiamen to pick up a naval escort off Portsmouth, and a convoy would assemble at St Helen's Road, in the lee of the Isle of Wight a short distance from the naval anchorage of Spithead. However, while the approaches to St Helen's are not difficult in clear weather they are transformed when fog closes down, as occurred on 9 December 1798. Several Indiamen working their way to the rendezvous were caught out. The *Henry Addington*, outbound to Bombay and China under Captain Thomas Wakefield, struck the Bembridge Ledge off the eastern end of the island. The ship was loaded with military and naval stores, guns, shot, powder and spare anchors and when the tide left her she was soon bilged, to become a total loss, despite the efforts of her crew to cut away the masts and lighten her. During these exertions a boy was killed when a block fell from aloft and struck him. After Wakefield had given the order to abandon ship five more seamen were drowned attempting to get ashore on a raft, although the remainder were saved by the ship's and local boats – which were soon on the scene in anticipation of trouble in the fog – leaving the *Henry Addington* to break up. At the same time the West Indiaman *Thames* had struck the Owers, some miles away to the south of Selsea Bill, and she too broke up, but not until most of her cargo had been salved. A second West Indiaman, the *Taunton Castle*, Captain Henry Bond, ran aground in Sandown Bay but fortunately floated off with the rising tide.

If it is possible to conceive of a worse fate than shipwreck, it must be that of fire. Unlike other acts of God, fire was a constant danger and many Indiamen were lost from an overset lantern, or carelessly handled candle. In this matter passengers were an outright liability. Whether incapacitated by sea-sickness or drink, a foolish passenger of either sex could, from a moment's thoughtlessness, cause catastrophe. Equally dangerous was the exposure a merchant ship had from the necessity of having on board gangs of labourers to work and handle her cargo. This was thought to be the cause of the loss of the *Ockham*, Captain Jobson, who had distinguished himself against a Maratha attack in 1732. She lay at Calcutta loading in November 1734 when she was consumed by fire. Another terrible example was that of the *Duke of Atholl*, commanded by the Captain James Rattray whose first mate, Mr Denton, was to so delight the ladies of Calcutta with his stock of haberdashery brought out in the *Phoenix*. The *Duke of Atholl* was lying at anchor in Madras Roads in April 1783 when, on the morning of the 18th, Rattray and his first mate were breaking their fast in Fort St George with the governor, Lord Macartney. Suddenly, to Rattray's mortification, 'a prodigious column of smoke' rose above his anchored ship, indicating an explosion. A steward was supposed to have ignited a cask of spirits by dropping a candle in the lazarette. The fire spread rapidly and boats were sent from HM Frigates *Juno* and *Bristol*, then lying in the road, but the flames quickly took hold and, after some time later the *Duke of Atholl*'s magazine ignited and blew up. There was considerable loss of life including three passengers, twenty-two of the ship's company, officers and men from the two men-of-war and thirty-two soldiers, six women and two children belonging to the 52nd Regiment. The *Duke of Kingston*, Captain Justinian Nutt, was – besides his passengers – also carrying a detachment of the 52nd Foot when, off the north coast of Ceylon a few months later that August, the ship caught fire. Three passengers, twenty-two crew and thirty-two soldiers along with six wives and two children belonging to the regiment were killed.

The Country-ship *Malabar* was also 'set on fire by a cask of rum and a candle' in 1798. Captain Kent, Eastwick's wife's brother-in-law, had to bear the loss, as his ship was not insured despite the establishment of the Bombay Insurance Co. six years earlier. The disaster brought upon Kent a 'settled melancholy' and an early death. Other losses by fire included the *Fairford*, Captain John Haldane, on 15 June 1783 while loading a homeward cargo in Bombay, and forty souls were lost from the HCS *Princess Amelia*, Captain John Ramsden, which caught fire off Pigeon Island, near Goa on 5 April 1798. Worse occurred the following August. Two Indiamen, the *Royal Charlotte* and the ill-fated *Britannia*, lay at Culpee on the Ganges about 50 miles below Calcutta. The former was an Extra-ship, specially chartered by the Directors to provide additional tonnage and not to be confused with a contemporary vessel in the Company's service of the same name. Commanded by Captain William Logie Smith, she was of 680 tons burthen and had been built in Bombay for Greenway & Co. Like the *Britannia* nearby, the *Royal Charlotte* was loading for London and both vessels had embarked a large number of passengers, including women and children. They had also each loaded some 500 casks of gun-powder manufactured at Calcutta and destined for the Cape.[11]

On 7 August, with preparations for departure almost complete, a heavy thunderstorm broke over the anchorage. Neither ship was fitted with a lightning conductor, so Captain Thomas Barrow of the *Britannia* had ordered his men to place wet swabs round the masts at deck level. This was in hand when the *Britannia* was shaken by a terrific concussion as the *Royal Charlotte*'s foremast was struck by lightning. The magazine was constructed about its heel deep in the ship and the charge ignited her powder. In the explosion all on board perished, some 140 souls, including fifty women and children and seventy-five lascar sailors.

The carriage of gunpowder was a constant hazard, even when properly secured. The Company's armed schooner *Ganges* was lying at anchor in the Hughli on the evening of 11 January 1799 when her officers, who were then walking the deck, smelled burning. A small flask of tung oil had ignited, it was believed, spontaneously. All the efforts of Captain Wade and his men to douse the fire before it got a hold were in vain. Having swung the boat over the side as a precaution, some of the terrified men made off in it and in extreme haste Wade and those that remained were obliged to construct a make-shift raft. With a strong ebb-tide and the prospect of drifting out to sea, Wade attempted to attract the attention of those aboard the HCS *Laurel*, anchored about twelve miles away. After some six hours as the fire burned to the water-line and the *Ganges* sank, Wade's party drifted on the stream, fortunately being seen and picked up by the *Laurel*'s boats.

Another terrible loss by fire occurred to the *Queen*, Captain Milliken Craig, which had left the Thames bound for the Coromandel coast and China in May 1800. On 9 July she was anchored off São Salvatore, Bahia Bay, Brazil, in company with other vessels. The ships were taking in water and, as a consequence, Craig, several of his officers and most of the passengers had gone ashore for the night. In the small hours, at about 02.30, the officer of the watch aboard the HCS *Kent*, anchored nearby, noticed thick smoke pouring from the gunroom ports of the *Queen*, aboard which, with many of her crew ashore, the fire spread before anyone was alarmed. The vigilant *Kent*'s boats were put down and loaded with:

the fire-engines, buckets, &c…but within a few minutes of our discovering the smoke she was completely in flames from stem to stern, and in a few minutes more the three masts were overboard. Unfortunately it blew very fresh and a current of three or four knots rendered it very difficult for the boats to go alongside to save the people; and so rapid were the flames that about thirty soldiers perished below decks, being unable to get up the hatchways… The scene was dreadful, from the cries of between 200 and 300 men, and many perishing in the flames or the sea. Those that are saved are almost entirely naked from being hurried out of their beds. The remaining troops and all the passengers, about 300, proceed in the *Kent* to India.

The *Queen*, which had burnt through her cable, drifted out of the bay some distance and, at 07.00, blew up. Since no one had been in the gun-room 'with a candle' the fire was attributed to the crew of a Portuguese coast-guard boat that had lain alongside the previous afternoon. The guard-boat had been seen to have a fire on board and it was rumoured that out of malice some smouldering wood had been tossed in through the gun-room scuttles. Among those passengers rescued by the *Kent* were General St John, his family and suite, and five ladies who all now crowded into Captain Rivington's cabin. The numbers indicate the often crowded state of these ships, now doubly uncomfortable aboard the over-burdened *Kent* whose voyage to India was now resumed, with consequences we shall presently observe.

Soldiers were involved in the loss of the Country-ship *Caledonia* which left Balasore Roads on the Hughli for Bombay on 18 May 1803. She had on board a draft of men for the 78th Foot along with four women and several children belonging to the 78th and the Bengal artillery. On 29 July, when making their landfall in strong winds and soundings with Captain Thomas attempting to resolve his longitude by means of a double-altitude, smoke suddenly poured from the forward hatchway. Within seconds the ship was ablaze and the watch on deck ran to cast loose the boats. Thomas and his wife escaped in the longboat, as did fifty-six others including two wives and a child. A further ten sea-cunnies and lascars escaped in the pinnace, with the ship's gunner and fourteen lascars getting clear in the jolly-boat. Just after the boats had pulled away the mainmast fell, a little after which the raging fire reached the magazine, whereupon the *Caledonia* disintegrated in a massive explosion. As the boats attempted to land near Malabar Point the heavy surf upset the jolly-boat, drowning four lascars, while the pinnace drove onto rocks nearby, killing a further seven. Of the 157 souls on board the ship, eighty six were lost.

During the rather futile operations in support of Balambangan in October 1803 mentioned in *Neptune's Trident*, the Country-ship *General Baird*, which had been chartered to carry troops to the island, caught fire while at anchor and was burnt to the waterline. Only five weeks earlier another Calcutta-registered ship, the *Anstruther*, had been lost nearby. She had been fitted up at Malacca with 12 and 9-pounder carriage-guns as an armed-ship by the adventurer Captain William Richardson for the carriage of reinforcements to the garrison of Balambangan and had on board a detachment of European infantry and artillery, with sepoys embarked as marines. However, a strong south-westerly gale blew the *Anstruther* past the island and drove her amongst the shoals off Banguey Island (Pulo Banggi) where she was wrecked with heavy loss of life.

It is clear that unprotected lights and inflammable spirits were the most common cause of fires aboard these ships. Shortly after reaching the homeward convoy rendezvous off Pointe de Galle on the south-east point of Sri Lanka in January 1815, Captain George Nicholls had the mortification of finding his ship, the *Bengal*, on fire. The gunner, in securing a bung in a cask of rum, found that upon striking it, it drove into the barrel and rum spewed out, the fumes catching from a candle-lantern close-by. 'All,' Nicholls reported:

> was instantly in flames: and though every possible exertion was promptly made to arrest the progress of the flames, in less than an hour the ship was so far destroyed, that she sunk a blazing ruin. The ship's company behaved admirably, they were to a man orderly and obedient; not a man quitted the ship or relaxed from duty to the last moment. The number of sufferers was unhappily great, I fear upwards of twenty, principally occasioned by the sinking of boats alongside, although some perished in consequence of the dreadful rapidity with which the fire swept through the ship. Captain Newall of the [Extra Ship] *Alexander*; Mr Barker, second mate of the *Surrey*; Mr Miller, midshipman of the *Bengal*; together with the master and a lieutenant of the [convoy escort, the frigate] *Malacca*, were all drowned. It is, after this melancholy detail, some consolation to reflect that all the females and helpless children were saved.

Though loss to piracy, such as that of the *Cassandra* mentioned in *Neptune's Trident*, was rare by this period, the Indian coast was not entirely free of it. Attacks on Indiamen were unknown, but Country-ships were not immune and their seizure usually arose over the old question of *dastaks* – the licences to trade issued by local rulers and disdained by both the Company's and Country-ships wearing British ensigns. These were now objected to by any coastal vessels conceiving themselves to 'belong' to Indian ports under British rule. There had been some incidents in 1799 and in 1801 the *Sallamatty*, a *pattamar* on passage from Goa laden with paper, sandalwood, wine, beeswax and betelnut for Bombay, was seized off the Gurria River. A ransom was demanded from the master, *Tindal* Rama, and a tedious negotiation followed before Rama, his crew and vessel were suffered to proceed. Nor was the old Angrian lair quiescent, for as late as April 1803 the *Bhowany*, a *pattamar* armed with four carriage-guns, arrived at Calcutta to report an attack off Suvarnadrug. Her *nacoda* complained of six heavily armed and manned *gallivats* which he had only escaped by standing offshore under full sail in a stiff breeze.[12]

If piracy now had little impact upon the Indiamen there were a few cases arising from a similar turbulent lawlessness: mutiny.[13] One such insurrection occurred aboard the *Hartwell*, on her maiden voyage under Captain Edward Fiott, a relative of her owner, John Fiott of Jersey. In view of the consequences, Fiott's career is of interest. He was by no means an inexperienced master having first gone to sea before the mast on a voyage to Venice in the snow *Hunter*. He then joined the Royal Navy as a midshipman but remained only twenty months before securing several posts over the next three and a half years as second and first mate in vessels trading to Newfoundland, Lisbon and the western Mediterranean. Edward Fiott continued in these trades but as supercargo and agent until, on the outbreak of the American War of Independence, he commanded the Jersey privateer *Willing Mind* in which in 1778 it appears that he captured a French ship, the *Tartar*. This vessel was briefly commissioned as a privateer under Edward Fiott until later that year she was taken up by the East India Company on charter. Although John Fiott is listed as her master at this time, he appears not to have sailed in command of the *Tartar* when she left for the Coromandel coast on 26 June 1781.[14] Instead the thirty-one-year-old Edward Fiott was her captain, and the voyage, which concluded on 7 August 1783 appears to have gone sufficiently well for him to be appointed to the HCS *Hartwell*.

The Fiotts must by now have been on the fringes of the Marine Interest, for the *Hartwell* was built at Itchenor, near Chichester, for John Fiott for service with the Company and sailed with Edward in command for China-direct on 13 April 1787. Forty-one days later the *Hartwell* piled up on a reef off Boa Vista, the most easterly of the Cape Verde Islands. The news was reported at Calcutta in August as being due to 'the bad discipline of the crew, who four days before had behaved in a most extraordinary mutinous manner'. A different view was taken in London where Fiott was dismissed from the Company's service in June, the loss of the ship being in large measure attributed to his indecisive manner in handling his men. What lay behind the mutiny is unclear, but 'the loss to the Company will amount to £80,000'. Not that this seems to have greatly checked Edward Fiott for, five days after the *Hartwell* sailed, her builders at Itchenor, Crookenden and Taylor, launched a 988-ton Indiaman named *Belvedere* to his personal order. The *Belvedere* sailed under the command of one Captain William Greer only two months later on 9 June 1787, not long before her principal managing owner, Edward Fiott, was dismissed from the Company's Maritime Service. It has to be presumed that John Fiott saw matters to a conclusion in Edward's absence, but the *Belvedere*, which was to make six voyages to the east until sold into the West India trade in 1803, remained under Edward Fiott's titular ownership until 1789 when she was bought by Samuel Bonham, a member of the Company's inner circle. She too was to be the scene of a mutiny.

Towards the end of the Company's history in the early part of the nineteenth century, there were to be a number of mutinies, most of which were minor and soon suppressed. In the present more robust period there was only a handful. In contrast to Fiott's apparently abject conduct, that of Captain Edmund Elliston of the HCS *Ranger* stands in marked contrast. This vessel had been built in France for the French *Compagnie des Indes* but in 1777 she was captured – possibly by a privateer – and purchased into naval service as a 30-gun armed ship with the name *Ranger*. Redundant at the end of the War of Independence, she was sold in 1785 to Anthony Calvert & Co. of London. Calvert, who we have previously encountered, was an influential owner who had been born in Whitby and, having gone to sea, rose to command of merchantmen. He soon acquired shares in several vessels and later became an outright ship-owner. Elected and sworn-in as an Elder Brother of Trinity House, he lived in the City and owned farm-land in the Isle of Thanet. Among his other ships was the *Tartar* – formerly owned by the Fiotts – which he hired out as a government transport, but the *Ranger* was chartered to the East India Company and sailed for China-direct under Elliston on 11 April 1786 with a cargo of silver. The presence of this 'Company Treasure' was too great an enticement for some members of her crew, who plotted to seize the ship. Fortunately the conspiracy was betrayed by a seaman loyal to Elliston and he and his officers collared the four mutineers and clapped them in irons.

Prompt and decisive action, without recourse to remonstrance, often detached the mass of a crew from its ring-leaders – it was probably in this that Fiott failed so dismally – precipitating the collapse of an incipient rebellion, and so it proved aboard the *Ranger*. The mutineers remained shackled until the *Ranger* arrived in the Pearl River, when Elliston laid the matter before the Select Committee. The Selectmen instructed each of the four mutineers to be transferred to a separate homeward-bound Indiaman, an order not immediately obeyed until each commander had been furnished with a bond of indemnity against the consequences of any civil action brought against them by the individual for illegal detention. The commanders of Indiamen were acutely susceptible to such a risk of private prosecution and nervous of the outcome, chiefly because any such action could threaten them personally and the widespread perception of their personal wealth by private trade, although often true, exposed them to such proceedings. Any civil action fuelled by the jealousy of either the aggrieved person or the cupidity of his lawyer thus had wider implications, not just to the commander trying to make good previous losses, but to his own private backers. In this case, however, the four were brought home in the bilboes, sent for trial and on 21 January 1788 the two ring leaders, Henry Parsons and George Steward were hanged at Wapping.[15]

Not all such prosecutions ended as the law intended. In October 1737 Michael Smith, fourth officer of the HCS *Royal Guardian* was murdered by the ship's sail-maker, James Buchanan. The culprit was arrested and, on the ship's return from China in the autumn of 1738, Buchanan was tried and condemned to death. On 20 December, Buchanan was taken to Execution Dock and hanged, but less than five minutes later a well-organised gang of seamen appeared, drove off the curious crowd, the hangman and the court's officers, and spirited the half-asphyxiated Buchanan away in a boat. Nothing further was heard of him, despite a widespread hue-and-cry.

The risk of more serious and bloody mutiny was more likely in a Country-ship where racial and cultural differences, exacerbated by a master's cruelty, might combine with the lure of a valuable cargo to tempt the usually loyal lascars to revolt. In late February 1801 as the *Marianne* approached the Sand Heads at the mouths of the Hughli on a passage from Penang, her four sea-cunnies, or quartermasters, killed Captain George, the first and second mates and 'a native woman' – presumably George's mistress. Having robbed the cabin of all portable valuables, they brow-beat the lascar crew and put the *Marianne* about for Chittagong. When in sight of the shore the conspirators hoisted out the boat, 'laid a train of gun powder between decks and were in the act of pushing off from the vessel' and setting fire to her when the *serang*, or boatswain, jumped into the boat and plunged a knife into one of the sea-cunnies.[16] The *serang* was stabbed in retaliation and both men fell into the sea to be drowned, whereupon the lascars realised the extent to which they had been betrayed and turned on the three remaining mutineers before the boat could be cast off. Two were quickly laid hold of, but the third took to the rigging, scrambling up to the maintop armed with a brace of pistols and a large knife. Here he remained for two days until his shipmates enticed him down with promises of compromise. Once on deck they broached some arrack and soused the man until, fast asleep, they placed him in irons and returned to Penang.

If the total loss of his ship or a successful mutiny did not deprive a ship-master of his life, it could still have a devastating effect. To a Country-ship-master, his vessel represented his fortune and its loss spelt personal ruin. In the case of mutiny aboard an Indiaman, a commander risked dismissal and the probable destruction of his standing in the eyes of the Court of Directors. Of only slightly less hurt to a commander's reputation were the occasional strandings which – though they might avoid the loss of the ship – could occasion damage. Such a plight occurred to the *Nassau* in January 1737, when she struck the Galloper Sand to the east of Harwich. The ship appears to have been on an intermediate European voyage, between Indian trips, and Captain William Hutchinson 'forc'd her off again with her head sails, but had the misfortune at the same time of losing our Rudder, Main and Mizen Topmast[s] which obliged us soon after to come to an anchor'. With a veering of the wind consequent on the passing of the cold front, Hutchinson worked the *Nassau* into Margate Roads and eventual repair.

Indeed, as with the distant destination of the River Hughli, the estuary of the River Thames was almost equally dangerous to a deep draughted and laden Indiaman. Although partially buoyed, at this date the provision of seamarks in the Thames was inadequate to meet the demands of this large class of ship and the shifting nature of several of the shoals meant that what had been a safe passage on an outward voyage, may not be so on the Indiaman's return perhaps two years later. As at the Sand Heads off the Hughli the Company provided a pilotage service for the Thames, maintaining its own cruising pilot vessel in The Downs. This did not guarantee the safe passage of a ship, however, and an outbound Indiaman was at as much hazard as an inward one. The *Lyell*, Captain John Acton, was outward-bound for Bengal and Benkulen just before Christmas 1736, running downstream before a strong north-westerly breeze. It was close to high water when the *Lyell*, 'by the Unskillfullness of the Pilote has been [put] Onshore on the Spaniard Sand, in going down for the Downs'. The Spaniard Sand lay south of the deep-water channel and Acton had no doubt that it was the pilot's error for he had missed 'the buoy of the Spill' (Spile). With a strong wind blowing the *Lyell* onto the sand, the vessel was soon pounding heavily and water was flooding into her hold. Seen from the shore, it was not long before local fishermen approached from Whitstable, eager to help and perhaps to profit from whatever washed out of the laden argosy. Acton was lucky; the northerly wind caused a tidal surge and the following high water made sufficiently for him to: 'Thank God the ship floated and we got her off.' Worked into the East Swale near Faversham, the *Lyell*'s intended voyage had to be abandoned and Richard Mead, her owner, informed before she returned into the Thames for repairs. These took some weeks, for it was not until 28 February the following year before she again sailed for India. She was not a lucky ship, for although this was only her second voyage, it was to be her last in the Company's service. On her return she was sold to the Portuguese but never reached her new owners, being wrecked after running aground on the Goodwins in the spring of 1740.

An earlier incidence of such a stranding occurred in March 1734 when the *Derby* sailed for Bengal on her fourth voyage. Again in the hands of a Company pilot, Captain Abraham Anselme had the mortification to find himself run upon the Mouse Sand, not far from the Nore lightvessel. Here the *Derby* pounded so heavily that she could only limp across the estuary to the sanctuary of the naval dockyard at Sheerness, where repairs were put in hand. She was not ready to resume her voyage until the following year when, as we have already noted in *Neptune's Trident*, she was captured by Kanhojii Angrey and carried a prize into Gheriah. While the evidence in these cases almost always blames the pilot, it is easy to assume this exonerates the commander. Pilots always tender 'advice' to a ship's master and the occasional conflict of personality has to be added to the more obvious one of professional opinion. Generally the master had more to lose, so laying the blame on the pilot was a convenient method of self-exculpation and it has to be remembered that, as Captain Frederick Marryat wrote, 'no man is fit to command a ship that cannot contrive a log-book to his own advantage'.

That said, wrecks in the Thames Estuary were a scandalous disgrace and, with so many of the Marine Interest also serving the Trinity House, the institution responsible for marking dangers to navigation, it begs the question: why? The answer is largely attributable to inadequate funding. Although the numbers of buoys was slowly increasing they remained insufficient to warn mariners of all possible obstructions to their safe passage. However, in December 1800 the *Walpole*, homeward from Coromandel and Bengal, went ashore and was also stranded on the Mouse. Although much of her cargo was taken out before she broke up, she was just one of a number of Indiamen lost almost within sight of their destination.

NOTES

1. So recorded Acting-Quartermaster John Shipp of the 24th Dragoons, a passenger aboard the third *Warren Hastings* in January 1809. (This ship had been built after the loss of the second *Warren Hastings* in 1806 and was commanded by the same man, Captain Thomas Larkins, who had been wounded and exchanged after a gallant defence – see Chapter Five. The second *Warren Hastings* was recaptured when Mauritius was taken in 1810.)

2. Hickey was returning home after serving the HEIC in Bengal since 1783.

3. C. Northcote Parkinson, *War in the Eastern Seas, 1793-1815*, p341 *et seq*. Youthful promotions went beyond lieutenants, the most blatant being that of the post-captaincy of Fleetwood Pellew, the son of Sir Edward, one time C-in-C of the East Indies station. Fleetwood was sixteen, his advancement a combination of nepotism and opportunism. Parkinson emphasises the outrage felt by HEIC officers, but also the desperation of the Royal Navy to maintain the East Indies squadron in distant waters. It is of passing interest that the Navy's longest commission, that of the frigate *Fox* of fifteen years, was in these waters. Such was the mortality among her original company that not one farthing of their wages was paid by the state.

4. It is a curiosity that the last two were both named after the same lady, before and after marriage. They were the only two Indiamen to be named after the same person, to both be in service simultaneously and lost together.

5. The abuse of impressments never extended into ships of the Country-trade since they were invariably manned by lascars. While a few Indians – and a number of black Africans and Afro-Caribbeans – found their way into the Royal Navy, a definite prejudice existed at this time against 'men of colour' being entirely suitable for His Britannic Majesty's service. One reason, not applicable to black Africans, was that lascars were held to be enfeebled in extreme latitudes and unsuited to colder climes, a prejudice that lasted until the Second World War. For the saltpetre shortage, see Taylor, *Storm and Conquest*.

6. For the full story see Hood, J., *Marked for Misfortune*, Conway, 2003. A similar fate overtook the HCS *Degrave* earlier in the century, see Pearson and Godden, *In Search of the Red Slave*, Sutton, 2002.

7. There is extant a charming engraving of a party of passengers in the great cabin of the *Halsewell* on a previous voyage enjoying a concert while the ship is at anchor.

8. Meriton, a child of Rotherhithe was born in 1762. He finished his career as a competent but unpopular and unbending Superintendent of the Bombay Marine (1813-1825). He was nevertheless a highly competent seaman who distinguished himself in the Company's Maritime Service if not in its Marine counter-part. Prior to the loss of the *Halsewell* he had served a seven-year apprenticeship in West Indiamen and was successively gunner, second and first mates, then master of the brig *John and Richard*, plying to the Antilles, a period totalling eight years. Between 1785 and 1814 he made a record thirteen eastern voyages in the HEIC's employ, first as third mate in the *Pigot*, then as first mate in the *Bridgewater* and *Albion*, before joining the *Halsewell*. After her loss he made three voyages as first mate of the *Exeter*, being sworn-in as her commander on 9 October 1799. It is in the *Exeter* that we shall next meet him.

9. The *Annual Register*, 1803, quoted Grocott, *Shipwrecks of the Revolutionary and Napoleonic Eras*, p133.

10. Another account suggests she either ran, or was driven, ashore. The name *Devonshire* was not auspicious. Of the four in the HEIC's service only one, the third, survived to be broken up.

11. By 1798 the Cape had been taken from the Dutch.

12. A *pattamar* was and remains a lateen-rigged Indian cargo-vessel used in the Arabian Sea. It has a high sheer and long stem and sometimes an upwardly curved keel. Larger, sea-going *pattamars* were two-masted with a square stern.

13. The more heinous crime, that of barratry, when a master stole the ship from his principals and owners, was unknown in the Company's Maritime Service though a former Indiaman, the *Barwell*, when sold in 1804 to the London owners Fletcher & Co., was run away with in 1811 by her master, Captain John Poole, when trading regularly to Lisbon.

14. This seems the most likely way the Fiotts acquired the *Tartar*. The subsequent career of this ship is not without interest, showing the vagaries of a vessel's fate as much as that of her erstwhile commander. Having returned from India the *Tartar* was sold to the firm of Wilkinson & Co. of London as a South Seas Whaler but

in October 1792 she was again chartered by the HEIC and made a second Indian voyage, though under whose command is unclear; it was not Edward Fiott. She returned from Bengal at the end of 1793 and is next heard of as sold to Anthony Calvert & Co. who hired her to the Transport Board for trooping.

15. The *Ranger* made no other voyages east but was sold by Calvert to Camden & Co. to be put into the West India trade, only to be hired as an Admiralty transport and a convict ship for Botany Bay. Calvert died in November 1808. During the Nore mutiny in 1797 he was captured from the Trinity House yacht and threatened with hanging by Richard Parker and the mutineers aboard HMS *Sandwich*. He escaped by informing the mutineers that their cause was doomed, by which 'manly bearing' he impressed them and they allowed him and the yacht to proceed. Calvert, a wealthy man, died without direct issue and left £5,000 to his friend, Captain Morton, who succeeded him as an Elder Brother.

16. 'Sea-cunny' is an Anglicisation of the Persian word *Sukkānī* or the Hindustanti form *Sükunni*. These words derived from the Arabic *Sükān* meaning helm or rudder and refer to the sea-cunny's duty as a quarter-master. In a British merchantman the quartermasters acted as helmsmen at sea and attended the gangway of a ship in port. Among the other ranks used by Lascar crews in British ships the senior was the *Serang*, from the Persian *Sarhang*, meaning Boatswain, or Bosun. The rank of *Tindal* is occasionally substituted for Boatswain, it being a originally a Malay word of rough equivalence to *Serang* in status and often qualified by the adjective *Burra*, meaning senior, or 'big'. When used in conjunction with *Serang*, particularly in after years when the etymology had become confused and the terms being indiscriminately assimilated into a maritime *patois*, the *Tindal* was usually the Boatswain's Mate, immediately subordinate to the *Serang*. Thereafter, in descending order of rank, the Malay word *Casab* was used to denominate the Lamp-trimmer and the ordinary seamen, often simply referred to as 'lascars', were also known as 'Kalassies', from *khalâcis*.

Indian craft manned by Indians were commanded by *Nacodas*, a word deriving from the Persian *Nā-khudā*; while an Arab dhow's skipper was a *Raïs*. An entire and complex vocabulary, much corrupted and altered over time, prevailed on the various coasts and on board ship throughout this entire era. Among the most common forms were the Malay noun *Crani*, meaning a tally-clerk and the curious adoption of 'Tiger' reserved for a ship-master's personal steward where he was allowed one. Sadly this rich etymology, closely muddied by the Indian caste-system and imperial British racism, has cast it irredeemably into the realms of the politically incorrect, however Hobson-Jobson's Anglo-Indian Dictionary and C.T. Wilson's *The Mālim Sahib's Hindustani for Ship's Officers*, are recommended. Wilson was in the Bombay Pilot Service and I am much indebted to Captain Aris Finiefs for his expertise and elucidation.

PART TWO

'Long and Dangerous'

*The Merchants' Service in the
Great War
1793–1816*

'I consider the protection of our Trade the most essential Service that can be performed.'
Vice Admiral Horatio, Viscount Nelson

'If a person' wishes to know what trouble and anxiety mean he may find an index to it during the war in the countenance of a careful conscientious shipmaster.'
Captain Samuel Kelly

FOUR

'HAUTEUR AND CONTEMPT'

War in the Western Ocean, 1793–1816

On the eve of the great conflict that was to overwhelm the nations of Europe for a quarter of a century the British merchant marine occupied a commanding position as the world's largest carrier of trade. The generality of deep-water bottoms were by now exceeding 200 tons burthen, some 150 such vessels – aside from East Indiamen – being built in Britain in 1791 alone. Most were ship-rigged and were employed in a variety of foreign trades, chief of which were the transatlantic runs to Canada and the United States, the West India and slave-trades, the Baltic and North Russia routes and the long-established 'Levant' traffic into the Mediterranean. As in eastern seas, there were also some cross-trades, such as those between North America and the West Indies, and between North America and the Mediterranean. Smaller vessels were employed on shorter routes such as the east coast of Scotland and England – from Leith to London, chiefly with coal and passengers, and that known by its customs receipts as 'Coasting and Foreign-Coasting' which covered traffic between mainland Great Britain and Ireland, the Channel Islands and Isle of Man. There was also the short sea trade across the southern North Sea to Holland and Flanders. This – which sustained the important political and diplomatic links between the Court of St James and its Continental allies – included the all-important packet-routes, particularly that between Harwich and Hevoetsluis. It was highly significant during the period, for the occupation of Antwerp by Revolutionary French troops was the key *casus belli* of the first phase of the long war. Antwerp in enemy hands was, it was said, 'a pistol pointed at London,' a direct threat to the security of the kingdom. In the event this trade was – if we except the later problem with the United States between 1812 and 1814 – the only significant casualty of the greater war with France.

To service these worldwide trades the newly established register of shipping contained in September 1792 the details of 16,079 vessels, 12,776 of which were owned in Great Britain. A further 1,558 were owned in Ireland, the Channel Islands and the Isle of Man and a 1,745 in the twenty-six colonies now numbered as British possessions overseas. Most of these were small coasting vessels, but the chief interest in these comprehensive figures lies in the fact that despite what amounted to twenty-one years of global war with a heavy attrition rate, the combined privately owned merchant marine had by 1814 grown to a total of 24,418 vessels, 19,585 of which were owned in Great Britain. Taking vessels of 1,000 tons burthen or more, the number rose from 1,107 in 1792, to double at 2,329 in 1814. These were almost all owned in Britain.[1]

These figures included fishing craft, which continued their important business in the North Sea and on the Grand Banks off Newfoundland, and also the whaling fleet which was now clearly divided between the Arctic – the so-called 'Greenland fishery' – and the Pacific, known as the 'South Sea fishery'. As in previous conflicts, many whaler-proprietors joined those other ship-owners minded to fit their vessels out as privateers. The figures do not, however, indicate the losses of ships due to heavy weather, enemy action or faulty navigation. As may be inferred from the previous chapter, these were prodigious and it is impossible to accurately calculate them. Some authorities claim a universal rate as high as 2,000 per annum between 1793 and 1815, though this includes 'vessels of many nations, naval and mercantile'.[2] Nonetheless, the wrecking of shipping, particularly on the home coast, was beginning to impinge upon the public consciousness, particularly insofar as loss-of-life was concerned, prompting the life-saving efforts of men like Henry Greathead, chief among the designers of early lifeboats, and Captain George Manby, inventor of the line-throwing rocket apparatus.[3] Since they ventured world-wide, the bones of British merchant ships lie in even the remotest places, from Archangel bar where the *Westbury*, Captain Fisher, homeward for Bristol was lost in 1793, to Cape Agulhas, scene of the wrecking of the military transport *Arniston* in May 1815 when homeward-bound under convoy from Ceylon with troops on board. Over 330 bodies were discovered along the shore from this wreck alone.

Occasionally the very means by which merchantmen could be protected from the enemy, sailing in convoy, contributed to their mass destruction. Homeward-bound from Jamaica, Captain Thompson of the *Diana*, arriving in The Downs after a passage of thirty-six days, wrote to his owners on 17 March 1794. He had left Jamaica:

> on 6th February under convoy of the *Convert* frigate, with about fifty sail. I am sorry to say that my time under protection was of short duration, as the frigate with nine sail of the convoy was unfortunately wrecked between twelve and one o'clock on the morning of the 8th. At daylight I was a spectator of their total destruction on a reef that lies to the east of the Grand Cayman. The fleet stood on and off until three o'clock in the afternoon, endeavouring to get people off, but I having no boats could give no assistance and immediately set sail. I cannot give you the names of any except the *Sally* of Kingston.

Specifically, prior to the outbreak of war, there were some 5,500 vessels engaged in foreign trade. In 1792 vessels clearing outwards from British customs houses for trans-oceanic voyages amounted to 1,495; 878 cleared for Iberia and the Mediterranean and no less than 3,101, for the Baltic, Scandinavia and Russia. Such clearances were made by the individual ship-master who sought permission to depart by means of a 'Jerque Note'. Such men were, as we have previously noted, bound by duty to both the state and to their owners and consequently required not only to engage in business, but to risk suffering because of commercial failure.[4] In the year the war broke out:

> the Bank of England stopped discounting bills, being aware of the great extent of false credit in the kingdom, the consequences of which are well-known by the multitude of bankruptcies that took place in the year 1793. Liverpool was especially affected by the storm, so that business for a while lay dormant and a vast many houses were shut up.
>
> Whilst lying at Bristol…a merchant had stopped payment, and when this was known to his creditors, without resorting to law, the tradesmen boarded one of his vessels ready to sail for the West Indies and seized on the property that originally belonged to them, and what was more surprising the captain assisted in the delivery, for I saw him standing at the hatchway to bear off the goods hoisted up by the tradesmen…[5]

The war which began in 1793 was to last – with a fifteen-month break after the Peace of Amiens in 1802 – until 1815, and it was to affect British trade worldwide. It would fulfil Edmund Burke's early prediction that it would be 'long and dangerous' and, up to that time, 'the most dangerous we were ever engaged in'. During the first phase, the struggle with Revolutionary

France between 1793 and 1802, the French National Navy was relatively effective at prosecuting its *guerre de course*. Despite the ultimately successful British policy of blockade, the enemy was occasionally able to mount an offensive against British trade at squadron strength. Indeed a strong argument can be mounted that after almost ten years of war Britain had, in fact, suffered a defeat at sea. Despite a series of British naval victories, the French Revolutionary Government and its successors had survived and, under First Consul Bonaparte, was about to be transformed during the period following the Peace of Amiens of March 1802 into an imperium.[6] The most serious effect of the Peace of Amiens upon the British mercantile marine was the return of the Cape of Good Hope to the Dutch Batavian Republic. It was not to be retaken until 1806.

But after war was renewed in May 1803 the British blockade began to bite deep and, after Trafalgar, the incision proved fatal. However, Trafalgar neither ended the war at sea, nor conferred naval superiority to the British, but in its advantageous wake the Royal Navy, whose subsequent ten years of worldwide exertion ensured that it never lost the upper-hand and, by that very exertion and the consequent experience gained, it constantly improved its technical ability to keep the sea and wage war. With this went the concomitant expertise of increasingly efficient trade protection, though French tenacity in holding the Île de France and the Mascarene Islands brought this late into the Indian Ocean. Although in 1812, by which time it had expanded to its greatest extent with just under one thousand men-of-war in commission, the Royal Navy's global dispersion and consequent variable quality exposed it to some humiliating single-ship defeats by the new United States Navy, this was of little real consequence. Nothing after Trafalgar seriously challenged the Royal Navy's overall ability to project British sea-power, though this puissance did not prevent large scale losses of British merchant ships. In fact, despite the humiliations it inflicted upon its proud foe, it was the Americans who failed in their objectives during the War of 1812–1814. For the British the hostilities with 'Cousin Jonathan' were a furious aside, distracting them from their principal struggle with France.

Nevertheless, Nelson's victory was in fact very far from the end of the French navy. In addition to the battle squadrons of France which still lay at Brest and Toulon, and the ships scattered in the West Indies and the Indian Ocean, the French strove to acquire more warships. This they did partly by building in such arsenals as Venice and Antwerp, and partly by acquisition as a consequence of the shifting alliances that followed the turbulent military campaigns of Austerlitz, Jena, Friedland and Eylau. For several significant years (1807–1812) the Russian navy changed from a British to a French ally, while Napoleon attempted to seize the Danish and the Portuguese navies in 1807,

A sturdy South Seas Whaler outward-bound around 1810, from a study by Baugean. Note the double-ended whale-boats hoisted in davits on the quarters. The smaller vessels on the right are a mercantile sloop and, in the distance, a lugger. (Private Collection)

both moves frustrated by the British. The first was pre-emptively seized or destroyed at Copenhagen, the second was spirited away that same year, along with the Portuguese Royal Family, to their vast colony of Brazil. The effect this had upon Portuguese *vis-à-vis* British influence in Macao and Canton is not hard to imagine.

In spite of these frustrations and the constant obstacle of the naval blockade, the French managed to take occasional advantage of offshore winds and despatch flying-squadrons to sea, mostly from Brest. These usually consisted of four heavy frigates of 40 or 44 guns with an attendant corvette and they had a dual purpose, to reinforce and re-supply beleaguered colonial garrisons overseas and afterwards to raid British trade routes. Fortunately such were the numbers of British cruisers at sea – ships of all sizes, mostly sloops and frigates but including some fast and seaworthy 74-gun line-of-battle ships – these overloaded and encumbered French squadrons were usually intercepted, chased and captured. Nevertheless, their very presence at sea was a constant anxiety to the British Admiralty and they were not without their successes against British merchantmen, particularly in eastern waters where, using as a base the Mascarene archipelago, their effectiveness against the ships of the Honourable East India Company was almost crippling. It was not until 1810, after a series of bloody actions in which the British did not always have their own way, that the Mascarene Islands were taken, the Île de France recovering its former name of Mauritius. In the Far East the final defeat of the Dutch in the East Indies followed the capture of Mauritius, all of which we shall remark in due course.

Until its capture in 1810, Mauritius was used by both French naval cruisers and French corsairs. It was ultimately the latter which proved the greater problem to the British, and not only in the Indian Ocean. If the French were less than successful in formal naval warfare, they remained adept at this private war on trade, prosecuting it with all the vigour they had so readily demonstrated during the American War of Independence. And, as before, this promoted uncertainty among merchants and shippers, drew criticism upon the Admiralty for its failure to adequately protect British merchantmen, and raised insurance rates. The climax of the French *guerre de course* in 1811 was to coincide with economic crises affecting both sides which arose from poor harvests and affected currencies. Napoleon's solution at this critical moment was to fall out with his new ally, Tsar Alexander I, and attack Russia, with dire and fatal consequences. The British weathered bad harvests and economic vicissitudes by their wealth and their superior ability to enforce their policy of a commercial blockade of Europe, drawing resources from the four corners of the world by means of their commercial merchant marine operating on exterior lines of communication.

In the post-Trafalgar period it was this sea-power – mercantile and naval – which combined formidably and allowed the British, with their vacillating allies, to balance the books – just. The economics of the day were, despite the war, undergoing a change: the old mercantilist theories were on the wane, undermined by the notions of free-trade expounded by Adam Smith in *The Wealth of Nations*, published in 1776. Unsurprisingly, such ideas found fertile ground in the United States, growing in the thirty years following independence to form one platform from which the war against Britain was launched in 1812. British resistance to such ideas was entrenched until, as will be seen, the life-and-death struggle with Napoleonic France compelled an abandonment of the Navigation Acts.

Little of this was obvious at the beginning of the war. The British economy was thought to be fundamentally unsound because, unlike France, Britain lacked a strong agricultural base and was saddled with a vast National Debt, £230 million in 1793 rising to a staggering £507 at the conclusion of the Peace of Amiens in 1802. Adam Smith himself pointed out that British manufactures paid for victory in the Seven Years War and therefore a vigorous interdiction of British overseas trade would be disastrous for the country. Once again the West India lobby howled its dire-warnings, but nothing changes things like change itself: whereas revolution was to fracture French society so that in 1794 the survival of the revolutionary Government was to rely upon a single convoy of American grain, across the Channel English agriculture was benefiting from improved methods and mechanisation. And while war in the West Indies might affect the lifestyle of absentee landowners and slave-masters in England, the islands' trade actually contributed only *one tenth* of the whole of British commerce, with income derived from West India investment varying between 7 and 10 per cent.

On the other hand, the exported ideology of *liberté, égailté et fraternité* when translated to France's West Indian colonies with their dependence on slave-labour could only provoke a slave-rebellion – and a consequent disruption of *one fifth* of the French economy. Indeed, the conflict of interest provoked by the new ideology and its exporters in the National Assembly, the desire for liberty among the mulatto population of Saint-Domingue and the competing interests of the French plantation-owners – who asked for help – enabled the British to take over the island. The fierce war among the colonial Antilles, in which the Peace of Amiens operated to the French advantage, can only be touched upon here, but it should be noted that, in terms of economic wealth the acquisition of the revenues of Saint-Domingue compensated the British exchequer for the loss of the Thirteen Colonies of North America *in their entirety*. Moreover, *inter alia*, possession of the island closed the port of St Nicholas Mole to French privateers.

France was to cling to some of her West Indian possessions almost until the end of the war but by then French mercantile shipping was almost at a stand-still, re-supply from France coming – when not stopped by the Royal Navy – by way of the French flying squadrons mentioned above. However, the French West Indian trade had employed a quarter of her merchantmen manned with about 20 per cent of the man-power enrolled on the *Inscription Maritime*, and this provided a massive pool of man-power, not merely for France's navy, but for her corsairs.

Despite these apparent advantages to the British, the predictions of doom seemed, in the early years of conflict, to be accurate. Possession of Saint-Domingue was lost, owing largely to bad weather and yellow fever, Government stocks fell and peace overtures were rejected by the French Directory.[7] The fortune of war in the West Indies swung hither and thither, though Jamaica was held fast, despite the revolt of the Maroons in its heartland. Meanwhile at home the poor rioted over lost work on the land and rising food prices, and the game seemed to be up entirely when in 1797 the seamen in the Channel Fleet mutinied at Spithead; and then – just as a resolution was reached at Spithead – the unrest spread to the North Sea fleet at the Nore and Great Yarmouth. England's very wooden bulwarks looked about to crumble, swept away by the perfervid heat of imported sedition and revolution. All seemed in turmoil: the Bank Restricting Act released the Bank of England from its duty to redeem paper money and rampant inflation seemed in prospect; Ireland erupted in rebellion the following year and, while Britain's naval defences were down, French expeditionary forces appeared off the Irish coast, the west of England and Wales, actually landing troops. Nothing like this had occurred since the Dutch wars.

Astonishingly, rebellion, invasion and revolution all failed: the naval mutineers were met and largely conciliated, the French adventure foundered under the onslaught of the weather and, unsupported, Irish rebellion was bloodily suppressed. As for the financial situation, this was stabilised by Mr Pitt's 'temporary' introduction of income tax and the abandonment of excess spending on military failure in the West Indies.[8] Most importantly British shipping continued to conduct its business, under-pinning the economy so that, by the peace in 1802, re-export of colonial produce had increased by 80 per cent of its pre-war value. During 1798-1802, following the stabilisation of the political and economic situation, domestic imports – largely those of West Indian sugar and coffee – rose overall by 58.5 per cent.[9] In this period domestic exports rose 57.7 per cent and re-exports by no less than 187 per cent of their pre-war level. All this was made possible by an expanding merchant fleet which, by the Peace of Amiens, was manned by 144,558 seamen.[10]

During this period of economic augmentation more subtle weapons were brought into play by the opposing protagonists. On the British side, under-writers at Lloyd's and the other exchanges such as Liverpool and Glasgow were forbidden under the Traitorous Correspondence Act from insuring enemy shipping. Hitherto this had been a common practice in wartime, compelling an enemy to stump-up high premiums to purchase war-risk cover. But these events were hard-won, set against social turbulence and poor harvests in 1795 and 1800, the latter of which pushed up the price of wheat three-fold and caused disturbances among the poor. A select committee of the House of Commons recommended increased importation of wheat from the United States and influenced the decision to send an expedition to the Baltic in 1801. Thanks to Nelson's victory at Copenhagen, this eliminated the potential strangle-hold of Denmark on the free-passage of shipping through the Øresund and neutral vessels brought grain to British ports under naval convoy. In the second phase of the struggle – the Napoleonic War of 1803 to 1815 – there was to be a reprise on this with a second attack on Copenhagen in 1807 which annihilated the Danish fleet and prevented it falling into French hands.

On the French side, the rapid conquests of the revolutionary armies and, particularly the Napoleonic armies under the later Empire from 1804 onwards, levied compensating reparations from the conquered countries of Europe. The relentless militarism of the Napoleonic French Empire, operating on interior lines and finite resources, never really attempted to balance its economy. Happily for Great Britain this invoked the law of diminishing returns, for the unpopularity of such impositions naturally played into London's hands. Crucially for Britain, her prudent Government and steadily increasing economic muscle enabled the accrual of sufficient resources for the subsidising of a succession of European Coalitions which – though several of these foundered and much gold was lavished in vain upon unsteady allies – would finally end the French Empire of Napoleon. Thus it was that British merchantmen were the catalyst that transmuted the value of trade-goods into gold that conjured the vast armies of Russia, Austria and Prussia into the field against the French. So, in the war between sea-power and land-power – of what has been described as that of 'the whale and the elephant' – the former finally won through.

The plight of the individual ship-master during these years of turmoil may be gauged from the memoirs of Captain Samuel Kelly whom we have met previously. He had left school at the age of fourteen and went to sea first in the Post Office mail packets from Falmouth where he remained for four years. He then spent three years in military transports, taking part in the American War of Independence and its aftermath, when his ship took displaced Loyalists to the Bahamas and New Brunswick. '[D]uring these several years I suffered innumerable hardships and ill-treatment,' he wrote. From the age of fifteen he afterwards claimed that 'I earned my livelihood, and from this period never received five shillings as a gift from any relative, nor ever sailed from a port to the best of my knowledge one shilling in debt.'

Appointed master of the *Thetis* in 1794, he had great difficulty in manning her and, having done so, keeping his crew, not from desertion but from sequestration by the Royal Navy. Alongside his mate, who was young and inexperienced, he was obliged to make up his crew by shipping four boys as apprentices, not from any desire to train young officers but because 'it was war-time'. His problem was complicated by the *Thetis* arming as a 'runner' to sail officially without convoy and, as soon as he recruited a few men, he 'sent the ship into the river' to prevent desertion or absconding. Eventually, having resorted to 'a Jew[ish] crimp', he found his ship's company and sailed for the West Indies. Upon arrival at St Nicholas Mole, boats from HMSs *Belliqueux* and *Intrepid* came alongside, and although Kelly managed to dissuade the *Intrepid*'s lieutenant from pressing any of his seamen, the *Belliqueux*'s insisted on doing so: 'Finding I could not divert him from his object I gave him one who had given me much trouble'. A day or two later he lost another to the same ship, an officer taking a sailor from a party landed to fill water-casks. Kelly then sailed to Jamaica where, off Port Royal, HM Sloop *Siren* impressed three seamen, leaving him 'only the mate, the second mate, carpenter, and a lame, sick man, besides the boys…' A day or so later the second mate, the lame man and carpenter had deserted, leaving him with the mate and 'four small boys' whom he now tried to insure against yellow fever by paying an apothecary ten pounds to attend them if any fell sick. In a week or two all four boys were laid low and Kelly employed 'a Negro named King' to attend them and was greatly impressed by the man's compassion, though this did not prevent the death of one of the apprentices.

Having discharged his outward cargo and his private venture 'of cheese, potatoes, onions and bottled porter', Kelly next had to find a homeward lading. It took him some time before he picked up consignments of sugar and rum. On the homeward run across the North Atlantic one morning:

> a heavy squall laid us nearly on our beam ends, its approach not being observed owing to the fog. As I was at my post watching the sails I called loudly to let fly the main sheet, but no one being quick enough and seeing the carpenter panic-struck, I was tempted to seize hold of his jacket and fling him to leeward to execute my orders. The sheet was accordingly cast off and the sail immediately rent in pieces.
>
> By urging my carpenter to his duty I now laid myself open to the discipline of the gentlemen residing in Doctors Commons, who give no allowances for any situation a master of a ship may be placed in to save the ship and cargo as well as the lives of the crew. But they keep close to the letter of the law, embracing every advantage of the harassed and perplexed situation of the poor shipmaster.[11]

The *Thetis* crossed the Atlantic in convoy but as she approached the Isle of Wight where the convoy dispersed, the character of naval protection reversed and Kelly resumed his private war with the Royal Navy, the galling of which he felt personally. Off the Needles the *Thetis* was intercepted by:

> a sloop-of-war lying in wait for homeward-bound ships [which] fired several shots at us, wantonly, to bring us to, when one gun would have answered every good purpose, but young men in arms are fond of hectoring over those from whom there is no danger of retaliation.
>
> Three of my English seamen had previously hid themselves among the cargo before the [sloop's] boat boarded us, and as no British could be found a Swede

was taken, but after examination on board the man-of-war he was sent back to me, and I was allowed to proceed up the English Channel.

[Having entered the London River] we anchored near the convict ship off Woolwich, having two Custom House officers and two excise men on board from Gravesend to keep each other honest. This night my three British seamen landed on the Essex side and proceeded to London... Soon after passing Blackwall the pilot ran the ship on shore on the Isle of Dogs, but as the flood tide was running we got her off by the help of a kedge anchor during a great fall of rain. Before sunset we entered the Pool. We had been twelve weeks from Jamaica, and as I had been sadly harassed during the whole time with a slow-sailing, leaky ship, and an unprincipled crew, I was much rejoiced at finding myself safe in the Thames.

Having been obliged to ship a crew at Kingston on 'runs', that is sums demanded by the seamen for the single passage, Kelly paid out 45 guineas per man for twelve weeks work, whilst his own wage amounted to £15 – the only voyage, he claimed pointedly, for which he was paid a decent wage. Having discharged his crew and needing to secure the ship and unbend his sails, he had to engage and pay 'lumpers', a shore-gang who at fairly exorbitant rates would help him out of his predicament. Having reported the poor condition of the ship, his owners agreed to advertise her for sale. 'Accordingly on exhibiting a broom at the mast-head many people came to inspect her'. However, the ship was in such a state that no buyer could be found. Kelly himself was in equally poor shape after:

seventeen years regularly at sea... During this time I was never in a vessel that was stranded, wrecked, or that lost a mast by the board, larger than a topmast, and I believe that the Underwriters never lost a sixpence by me during the whole of my seafaring life...

Kelly was justifiably proud of his record, but it came at a cost: 'If a person wishes to know what trouble and anxiety mean he may find an index to it during the war in the countenance of a careful conscientious shipmaster.'

One source of this anxiety was the omnipresent threat of enemy privateers. The Dutch and Danes commissioned private commerce-raiders but it was always the French who proved the perennial foe, exerting themselves in this traditional form of warfare against their old enemy. From its beginning until the very end of the war, French corsairs were active and effective. As we have previously observed, the key to the success of a corsair was the energy, resource, cunning and resolution of her commander, and the French produced some exceptionally daring and able privateer-captains. The doyen of these exponents of the *guerre de course* was the Malouin, Robert Surcouf, who carried out several raiding cruises, the most spectacular of which, as we shall shortly see, he directed at the artery of British trade with India and China in the Indian Ocean. The French employed many types of vessels as corsairs: relatively small, fast open boats hoisting a lugsail when the wind served, but equally capable of escaping pursuit in calms or directly to windward by plying their oars; heavier luggers known as *chasse marées*, which could, and often did, double as smugglers, being well-acquainted with their counter-parts in the remoter coastal communities of southern England; and larger vessels varying in size from small brig-corvettes to large private frigates. All such corsairs were well armed by their *armateurs* and all were exceptionally well-manned. With the Royal Navy officially pressing merchant seamen at an unprecedented rate, a corsair inevitably had the advantage in both fighting men and weight-of-metal if it came to an engagement with a British merchantman.

The answer was convoy, which was introduced soon after the outbreak of war and enforced first by the Convoy Act of 1798 and later by a second act in 1803 on the breakdown of the Peace of Amiens. On receipt of the news of the outbreak of war a deputation of the heads of a number of trading-houses had – at the invitation of William Pitt, the Prime Minister – met with members of the Government to discuss measures to be taken to protect shipping. Convoy was discussed, along with the issuing of Letters-of-Marque, for which there was less enthusiasm than in the previous war. More was expected from a Royal Navy better acquainted with the matter of trade-protection than it had been in 1776 and both merchants and ship-owners were unwilling to either disrupt profitable trade or reach in their pockets to fit out private ships-of-war, particularly once they were paying income tax. However, all would depend upon the degree to which the enemy affected trade and whether, as in 1779, privateering would offer a better return on investment in shipping that was unable to function normally owing to the disruption of hostilities.

Convoy on a global scale took some time to establish and could not extend to vessels homeward-bound in the early months of the war. In May 1793, only weeks after the outbreak on 1 February, Anthony Calvert's *Albemarle*, of which mention was made earlier, was homeward-bound from the West Indies and had fallen in with another of Calvert's ships, the smaller *Active*. The *Active* was returning from a voyage to Botany Bay and Canton as an Extra-ship under Captain George Bowen. The two vessels had the misfortune to encounter the largest French privateer then at sea, the 450-ton *Duguay Trouin*, a fast, ship-rigged frigate fitted out at considerable expense by the *armateurs* Guillemaut and Bodinier of St Malo.[12] Well-manned and handled by an experienced commander, Dufresne Le Gué, the *Duguay Trouin* rapidly overwhelmed Calvert's two vessels and sent them both into Morlaix.[13]

Post-war analysis by Lloyd's determined no more than 3 per cent of British shipping fell into the hands of the enemy and that actual losses of merchantmen taken out of convoy was tiny, so-much-so that from this arises the assumption that the impact of the enemy's war on trade, whether by national cruiser or privateer, was minimal. This overlooks several important circumstances, the first two of which relate directly to convoy management. The maintenance of convoy under sail was difficult and many ships straggled behind, to be caught by corsairs. Moreover, ships proceeding alone or in small numbers to or from the appointed convoy rendezvous were again vulnerable to attack. As the *guerre de course* reached its climax around 1811–1812, it became common practice for small, handy corsairs to lie under English headlands, perhaps masquerading as fishing boats, only to spring into life as an unwary merchantman, having left the protection of a naval escort, made her way to her destination. Partly for this reason the Admiralty established a line of signal stations on such promontories to deter the practice by the enemy, to warn merchant master of the presence of an enemy, and to summon any British cruiser in the offing to the rescue.

Loss of property and profit – even of life itself – were matters of grave importance to British seamen and their dependants. Ultimately, in their cumulative effect, enemy corsairs were of equal importance to the nation, its economy and its means to wage war. Thus, the threat and impact of attack by French corsairs were, from the perspectives of both a ship's master and owner – and, by extension the underwriters and insurers of her hull and cargo – of a very different order. The low overall loss expressed in a small percentage has misled naval historians to largely dismiss the *guerre de course* as of little significance, not least because the Royal Navy tended to eliminate French national cruisers with ruthless efficiency. Private corsairs were a different matter. Just as an enemy 'fleet-in-being' poses a strategic threat and, without any actual need for it to proceed to sea, soaks up blockading forces in its confinement, so did the *threat* of privateering – unquantifiable at the time – operate upon the smooth running of trading voyages. It would have been a very different story had Britain not possessed a mercantile marine capable of accepting a level of attrition – howsoever hard that might be upon the individuals affected.

Unfortunately for many merchantmen, convoy escort was not a popular duty with ambitious young frigate captains for whom war was a business opportunity as much as a means of covering themselves with glory. Trade-protection was tedious and troublesome, the different rates of sailing of a disparate body of merchantmen made station-keeping a nightmare and the cohesion of a convoy difficult, especially in bad weather. The social differences that existed between the two sea-services did not encourage co-operation or mutual understanding, and efficient convoy-escort required an active sea-officer possessed of a high sense of duty and little hope of reward. In short it could become a task disdained by some naval commanders. To counter this mind-set, on the renewal of the war in 1803 the underwriters of London established Lloyd's Patriotic Fund to remind naval officers of their prime – and patriotic – *obligation* to protect trade. Gifts of plate or suitably inscribed swords of fifty or 100 guineas value were presented to officers judged to have earned them by meritorious service of this kind, acting as *douceurs* to others.[14]

Indeed, despite the plundering of their crews, merchants set this aside, going to some trouble to encourage individual officers vested with the escort of a convoy of their ships. In March 1798 Mr Gladstone – the ship-owning father of a future Prime Minister – presided over 'a very elegant entertainment' laid on at Bates's Hotel in Liverpool given by the merchants and ship-owners trading to Hamburg and Bremen to Commander Richard Raggett and the officers of HM Sloop *Dart* which had been detached from the North Sea squadron and was under orders 'to convoy a number of valuable ships from Liverpool to the Elbe and Weser'.[15]

Nothing was fool-proof, however, and losses of merchantmen occurred despite these blandishments such that, in due course, the mood of the merchants would sour. To those more closely involved the consequences could be serious, even fatal. War in any age immediately embroils merchant shipping, turning it into a military objective, increasing the already high risks of sea-going and interrupting the normal ebb-and-flow of trade. Such interruptions were not always taken quietly, particularly when convoy constrained a number of ships engaged in a competitive trade, compelling them to arrive simultaneously, causing a glut on the market and a consequent depression in prices. Such a state of affairs was inimical to the instincts of commerce and this was the most common cause of disobedience among ship-masters. Occasionally a master would therefore buck the system and risk bringing down ruin upon himself and his ship, by running ahead of a convoy to gain a market rate favourable to a cargo. This was an illegal practice unless the master concerned had, like Kelly, first obtained a licence to 'run'.

At the very beginning of the war in May 1793, an assiduous naval officer, Graham Moore, when Master and Commander of the sloop *Bonetta*, noted that:

> Many of the Convoy are exceedingly troublesome, by their total disregard they pay to their Instructions; they are continually striving to slip ahead of the *Bonetta* whilst she is obliged to stay by the dull sailors (sic). I frequently awaken their attention with a shot athwart their bows...

One vessel, the *Peggy*, Moore contended, ran ahead deliberately and he took 'the first opportunity to write to Lloyd's Coffee House about him.'[16]

It was still going on twenty years later. On 12 February 1813 the *Coquette* of Glasgow sailed from St Thomas's in the West Indies in convoy under the escort of HMS *Kangaroo*. The *Coquette* must have been a fast sailer for she became a 'runner', Captain Newlands abandoning the *Kangaroo*'s protection. In 1814, following a prosecution brought against him by The Lords Commissioners of the Admiralty under the Convoy Acts, Newlands was banged-up in the Marshalsea for a month.

The system was riddled with problems of which runners were but one manifestation. While discipline was important throughout the conduct of convoys, delays could be counter-productive. Some cargoes possessed dangerous properties, particularly those containing oils, as was demonstrated in November 1799, when the *Malvena* of Shields caught fire in Riga. She had a cargo of hemp – a vital 'naval' commodity – the loading of which had begun five months earlier, and she had been kept waiting for a convoy for half that time. Captain Bell was obliged to fall in with the port-authorities who ordered the burning vessel to be carried up the harbour into shallow water, scuttled and filled to save both ship and cargo. Other cargoes spoiled through delays, while crews held idle at anchorages grew fractious, stores were run down, costs rose and ships grew weedy, only contributing to the problems of maintaining station at sea.

Notwithstanding these drawbacks, the convoy-system was remarkably well-organised and drew public praise. Even early in the war its efficacy was clear, *Lloyd's List* reporting in the summer of 1797 the arrival of 192 ships from the West Indies, an encomium repeated in a Liverpool broadsheet which pointed out this was:

> exclusive of those at Liverpool, Lancaster, and Whitehaven. There is not a missing ship…a circumstance unparalleled in any former war. What a delightful view of the vigour of our navy, and of the prosperity of this country, to see our…merchantmen arrived safe in the midst of war.

As the war progressed a close liaison developed between Lloyd's as the centre of British maritime mercantilism and the Admiralty, so that although basic, the convoy-system grew remarkably symbiotic. Intelligence was drawn from other sources, not least the gossip that accompanied the dealings of merchants and the consequent conversations they may have with ship-masters, but also by way of the ship-masters themselves and through such agencies as the General Post Office whose packet commanders – themselves conveyors of mercantile contracts, letters of credit, bank-draughts and so on – were encouraged to report on commercial, political and military developments abroad. Indeed the clerks-in-waiting in the General Post Office in London issued a *General*

Shipping and Commercial List which publicised some of this information where it was conducive to the public good.

The convoy system began on the home coast with a series of fortnightly coastwise sailings enabling vessels to safely reach the appropriate long-distance assembly points. These were located at in the protected anchorages at St Helen's Road, off the Isle of Wight; in The Downs off Deal; at the Nore at the confluence of the Thames and Medway; in the Humber; off Leith and in Scapa Flow in the Orkneys. Overseas there were similar meeting points such as Barbados and Jamaica in the West Indies; Malmo and Vinga Bay in the Baltic; St Helena in the South Atlantic for the East India trade and so on. The most significant convoy routes were those to and from the Baltic where they were supervised by the naval Commander-in-Chief, Admiral Sir James Saumarez from his flagship *Victory*, which will be touched upon later. Special naval escort was provided to the annual Hudson's Bay Company ships out to 30° Westerly longitude; south to St Helena accompanying the East India Company's highly valuable fleets; and to the north from Scapa Flow towards the North Cape escorting merchantmen to ports as remote as Archangel. Frigates cruised to protect – often rather feebly – in support of the Arctic Right-Whale hunt and the Grand Banks fishery. The fate of the South Sea Sperm-whaling of the Pacific is dealt with in the following chapter.

Ocean convoy routeing was compelled to follow the global wind system but, within this constraint, it avoided as far as was possible the traditional choke-points where privateers lurked, favouring safety over speed and utilising rendezvous points where a straggling ship might catch-up, or join a later convoy. For this, the Atlantic is generously provided with islands, chief among which were Madeira in the north and St Helena in the south.

Along with tables of signals, these details were included in the printed sailing instructions issued to masters upon joining a convoy and without which the appropriate clause in insurance policies – 'to sail with convoy and return' – would not be honoured. Unlike the system devised for warfare in the twentieth century where a senior officer was appointed commodore to govern the convoy, leaving the senior officer of the escort to defend it, the contemporary system required the senior naval officer to command both convoy and escort – a taxing task, adding to its unpopularity and probably reducing its efficiency.

Several convoys were badly mauled by the enemy, resulting in heavy loss of ships, cargoes, men and money. In 1795 the Italian victories of General Bonaparte had an effect on British shipping when Leghorn – that centre of British trade with its ex-patriate mercantile community – fell to the French on 30 June. Then Admirals Ganteaume and Richery were sent to sea to raid British commerce across the Atlantic. Richery slipped out of Toulon on 14 September with a squadron consisting of six ships-of-the-line and three frigates, headed for the Strait of Gibraltar evading the British blockading squadron commanded by Admiral Hotham. Having withdrawn to Corsican waters, Hotham had meanwhile sent home two of his own battle-ships, the *Fortitude* and *Bedford*. These, under the command of Captain Thomas Taylor in the 74-gun *Fortitude*, were escorting a French prize, the *Censeur* which was only partially armed and jury-rigged. Calling at Gibraltar, Taylor left the Rock on 25 September having been joined by the 44-gun *Argo*, the frigate *Juno* and the fireship *Tisphone*, which had in turn been entrusted with a huge convoy from the Levant, the old 'Smyrna fleet' consisting of sixty-three sail of merchant bottoms. That night the convoy became divided, thirty-two of the ships finding themselves under the escort of *Argo*, Captain Richard Burgess, and the *Juno*, Captain Lord Amelius Beauclerk, while the remainder proceeded with the main force.

Off Cape St Vincent on 7 October Taylor's ships encountered Richery's squadron which comprised the 80-gun *Victoire*, the *Barras*, *Jupiter*, *Berwick*, *Résolution*, *Duquesne*, all of 74 guns, plus the frigates *Embuscade*, *Félicité* and *Friponne*. Taylor at once threw out the signal for the convoy to disperse and *Fortitude*, *Bedford* and *Censeur* formed line-of-battle to present as bold a face to the enemy as was possible, whereupon the damaged *Censeur* rolled her foremast overboard and fell astern. Considering his chief duty to assist the hapless captain, John Gore, Taylor bore up with the *Bedford*, commanded by Captain Augustus Montgomery, to the support of the *Censeur*, abandoning the convoy to the French frigates which made off in hot and eager pursuit. Fifty minutes later Richery's leading ships reached the *Censeur* before Taylor, engaging her at about 13.50. The *Censeur*, armed *en flûte*, was no match for his opponents though Gore fought his ship until his remaining masts had gone by the board and most of his powder was expended, but at 14.30 he struck his colours. In the meanwhile the *Embuscade*, *Félicité* and *Friponne* had picked up all but one of the fleeing merchantmen, some thirty ships, all of which Richery triumphantly carried into Cadiz.

Demanding and receiving the protection of a Spanish squadron to accompany him clear of the British blockade the following year, Richery subsequently crossed the Atlantic and raided the coasts of Newfoundland as instructed. 'The expedition destroyed about 100 fishing and merchant vessels and took a great many prisoners, most of whom were, however, sent in a cartel to Halifax.'[17]

Ironically the Levant convoy had been the specific target of the second squadron sent to sea from Toulon that autumn under Commodore Honoré Ganteaume. This was formed from the 74-gun *Mont Blanc*, the heavy 40-gun frigates *Junon* and *Justice*, the 36-gun *Artémise* and *Sérieuse*, the 28-gun *Badine* and the 16-gun corvette *Hasard*. French intelligence was flawed, for the convoy was still thought to be east of Malta and Ganteaume missed it as his squadron swept eastwards, but he 'not only made many prizes but raised the blockade of Smyrna, in which port two French frigates and a corvette had been shut up...' With a British squadron under Troubridge in *Culloden* in pursuit, Ganteaume escaped, to return to Toulon. However, the cumulative effects of French military victories and diplomatic coups, was to make the sustaining of a British fleet in the Mediterranean impossible, with a knock-on effect on trade. The British struck back and in due course, with a string of naval victories culminating in Nelson's destruction of Bruey's fleet in Aboukir Bay on 1/2 August 1798, repossessed themselves of the Mediterranean.

As in previous wars, some ship-owners – particularly those owning slavers – decided to fit their ships out as privateers with Letters-of-Marque once the Admiralty had announced their intention of 'issuing Reprisals'. However, the early limited enthusiasm for privateering on Merseyside took a knock on 10 March 1793 when the brand new 20-gun privateer *Pelican*, fully equipped and with – besides her crew of 100 men – a large number of shareholders and their friends and families on board, was:

> cruising to-and-fro in the river with a moderate breeze, according to custom in such cases... While they were making merry...to the strains of music, the ship, on being put about...suddenly capsized, filled with water through the lee ports, and sunk in ten minutes with all on board. Seventy or eighty persons were drowned... The ship was never raised, and the top of her masts stood above water for years after the fatal event.

Such an event seems clearly a consequence of incompetence and the tragedy was somewhat offset on 5 April when Thomas Barton's privateer *Harriet*, commanded by Captain Caitheon, brought in *L'Agréable*, a French brig taken on her way to Bordeaux from Martinique with sugar, coffee, indigo and cotton and valued at £7,000.[18] This was Liverpool's first prize of the war, though it was to be followed by many others. Before the end of May the *Ann*, Captain Worthington, sent in the 10-gun corsair *La Porquin*; Captain Huston's *Thomas* followed with *La Expeditif*; the *Princess Elizabeth*, under Captain Beasley, sent in *Les Bonnes Freres*; the *Earl of Derby*, Captain Perrin, took the brig *Victoire* and the *Prince of Wales*, Captain Thompson, *Le Federatif*, whose cargo was valued at £32,000.

Perrin took more prizes and the Liverpool privateers made several recaptures, numbering sixty-seven by the end of July, but they suffered losses too, and the old, familiar see-saw war began all over again. That April, for example, the privateer cutter *Dudgeon*, Captain Gullin, captured the French brig *St Roman* from South Carolina to St Valery-en-Caux laden with rice, tobacco and cow-hides worth some £5,000. Four days later she took another Frenchman from Cayenne to Le Havre with sugar, indigo and cotton valued at £15,000 and on 4 May she recaptured the brig *Argyle* of Greenock and sent her into Milford Haven. On 9 June, Gullin brought the *Dudgeon* into the Mersey with a Spanish brig he had taken within sight of her home coast after a voyage from Caracas; she carried cocoa, indigo and hides. Refitting, the *Dudgeon* sailed a week later in company with the *Jenny* and they jointly seized *L'Esperance*, which arrived off Liverpool on 19 June. Gullin left the *Dudgeon*, handing over to Captain Egerton who in February 1794 was compelled to throw all his guns overboard to lighten her as she rode out a gale of wind while lying at anchor in Liverpool Bay. Then, rearmed in March, Egerton retook a Danish *galiot* which had been carrying sugar, oranges, figs and sugar from Lisbon to St Petersburg when taken by a French corsair. Soon afterwards, however, the *Dudgeon* and another Liverpool ship, the 500-ton *Ann and Jane*, were themselves captured and taken into Brest. The *Dudgeon* was commissioned into the French navy and Egerton and his men imprisoned, but the cutter herself was retaken in September and brought into Falmouth.

This early period of the war yielded several rich prizes, chief among which was the French East Indiaman *La Liberté*. She had been sighted in the vicinity of the Azores by the *Pilgrim* on 4 May and Captain Hutchinson had cracked on sail to intercept her. A long and stubborn running fight ensued; on the evening of the 5th a shot killed *La Liberté*'s commander, but matters were undecided until the following morning when *La Liberté*'s colours came down in submission. She was a Danish-built 800-ton ship that had been out from France over two years, trading on the west coast of the sub-continent and she consequently bore an extremely valuable and varied cargo the contents of which are of interest. It consisted of some bewildering commodities:

138,557 pieces yellow and white nankeens, about 150 hogsheads of sugar, 71 chests of chinaware, 18 chests mother-of-pearl, 139 chest of cinnamon, 183 bales of Surat goods, 2 chests Nankeen silks, 1 chest cotton woollen stuff, 4 bales nicanees, 17 bales casileys, 1 bale tapsel, 1 bale muslin, 500 cardels of pepper, 500 chests tea, 20 cases images, 2 bales coral, 2 chests silk manufactory, 1 case Nankeen calico, 1 chest painters' paper, 108 sacks Malabar pepper, 3 bales white linen, 90 bales cotton, 13 bales Bejuta pants of Surat, 1 bale Bengal goods, 1 bale embroidered waistcoats, 1 parcel medical roots, 6 parcels sugar-candy, 1 parcel Fontanagu lacca.

Hutchinson saw his prize into Barbados where, duly condemned, she realised the prodigious sum of £190,000. Such was the war waged 'in reprisal' against the old enemy by British privateers.

Most British ships were obliged to run a gauntlet when trading between the islands of the Antilles and until they joined convoys at the prescribed rendezvous. In addition to the sending to sea of scores of corsairs, French national frigates were at large, big powerful cruisers capable of taking on anything smaller than a ship-of-the-line. Among them were the *Semillante*, *La Proserpine* and *La Felicité*, news of which was accompanied by familiar horror stories of brutality as captured masters, mates and seamen were dragged off to durance vile. When north of the Azores the Liverpool ship *Olive* was chased and attacked by *La Felicité* on 24 September 1794. The captain of this 40-gun ship:

> behaved in a most villainous manner, sheering up alongside and pouring nine of his heavy guns right into us before he hailed, which killed one man and wounded another... They boarded and stripped us of every article but the clothes on our backs, and in that state we were landed at Brest...

From such custody some were released by exchange and cartel, and a few escaped. James Scallon, the carpenter of the *Ellen*, Captain Raphael, which had been taken by *La Proserpine* in March 1794, broke out of prison in Quimper on 1 July. With six others, Scallon marched for seventeen nights, holing up during day, until they reached the coast where they took a small boat. It had neither mast nor sails but they found a pole suitable for a mast and cobbled their shirts together for a sail. With a favourably light breeze and little sea they reached Sidmouth in three days, Scallon reporting that about 2,700 British prisoners were in the hands of the French at Quimper. These included both naval and mercantile mariners whose treatment had worsened after Lord Howe's victory of The Glorious First of June.

To these French annoyances – and in due course those of their European allies – must be added a number of privateers fitted out in America against the old colonial power, all scrupulously flying French republican ensigns, but many including American nationals in their crews.[19] Given the trade between Britain and the United States, these had an easy time preying on British shipping, joining French frigates like *L'Ambuscade* which cruised off Sandy Hook and picked off the trade. Such men-of-war entered American waters to take on stores and water and the American authorities did not always comply with the laws of neutrality in preventing belligerent men-of-war from sailing within twenty-four hours of an enemy merchantman. When Captain James of the Halifax Packet applied to the American authorities for this ruling to detain *L'Ambuscade* in port after he had sailed, his application was rejected with indifference. Applying to the French consul, James received a four days start. He was right to be anxious, as a merchant in Philadelphia points out, expressing incredulity to his business colleague in Liverpool in a letter of 13 May 1793:

What can all your frigates, of which we are told you have such an immense number in commission, be about, to permit… *L'Ambuscade*, Citizen Bompard, commander, to insult your flag, take your merchantmen, and 'ride triumphant o'er the western waves'? She is now abreast our city, and has taken five or six prizes since her departure from France, two of which are at present alongside of her, the *Little Sarah* of Kingston, Capt. Laury, built in Liverpool, taken ten leagues at sea, and the *Grange*, Hutchinson, of your port also. This vessel it is expected will be delivered up [released] as she was taken at anchor with the pilot on board, ten or twelve miles up the Capes [therefore well inside Delaware Bay]… The ship *William*, of Glasgow, Capt. Nageto, is just sent up as a prize to a little privateer of six guns.

The *Grange* was released by the Americans as an illegal acquisition by Bompard, but the unknown American merchant's enquiry has to be seen as more than just that: he is a man questioning the safety of shipping his goods in British bottoms. Such anxieties preoccupied others; the case of the *Grange* was an embarrassment to the American Government who did not wish for their economy, in the full spate of its recovery after their war for independence, disrupted by a failure of commercial intercourse between Britain and the United States, whatever opportunities that might throw in the way of American shipping. For the time being at least, it was in the mutual interest of Britain and America at this high level, to maintain the *status quo ante bellum*. The United States was neutral and they clamped down upon the fitting out of privateers for French – or vengeful American – *armateurs*. Intelligence of this debate in Congress was brought across the Atlantic by a Captain Heavysides of Liverpool where it echoed in the counting-houses along the Mersey.

The courage with which some merchantmen defended themselves often threw off an attacker. Such actions were occasionally deemed sufficiently meritorious to receive mention in the *Naval Chronicle*, an example of which is that of Captain Alexander Speers's defence of the *Amelia and Eleanor*, a Liverpool slaver which had sailed from London, loaded slaves on the coast of Angola and had begun the Middle Passage. On 1 October 1798 the *Amelia and Eleanor* was running in the heel of the south east trade winds when, during the forenoon she sighted a French privateer of 18 guns which gave chase and brought the *Amelia and Eleanor* to action. Writing to his owners, Brettagh & Co., from Barbados on the 26th, Speers had this to report:

At eleven the action commenced and continued until half-past two… Early in the action I lost my bowsprit and foremast… when he found I was disabled, he renewed the action with double vigour and hoisted the bloody flag at his main top-gallant masthead, sheered alongside within pistol shot and hailed me, 'Strike you --, Strike!' which I answered with a broadside, which laid him on a creen;[20] he then stood away to the northward to plug up his shot holes, as I could see several men over the side. In about twenty minutes he came alongside again and gave me a broadside as he passed; he then stood to the southward and got about a mile to windward, gave me a lee gun and hauled down his bloody flag, which I answered with three to windward. I have received a deal of damage in my hull; on my starboard bow two [gun] ports [beaten] in one; several shot between wind and water; I lost all my headsails and my after sails ruined. I lost one slave and four wounded; for of the people [his crew] wounded, two are since dead of their wounds. I shall not be able to proceed from hence till January as my hull is like a riddle.

Not least in this account is the understated minor epic of bringing the shattered *Amelia and Eleanor* from a position 210 miles south of the Equator and half way across the Atlantic safely in to Bridgetown, Barbados, while the salutation of guns by both antagonists fired *away* from the opposition, signalled a formal end to the action.[21]

Within weeks of this, another letter from Barbados was sent by a passenger on board the *Barton*, Captain Cutler, which had run into a corsair sixty miles east of the island. The strange sail gave chase 'in the wake of the *Barton* most part of the night, receiving a constant fire of stern chasers, without returning a shot'. At sunrise the enemy 'which proved to be a French privateer schooner, of 18 guns...

bore down with a press of sail upon the *Barton*, who again opened her fire as soon as she came within shot, and soon after a close action commenced, which lasted two hours and a half, the schooner repeatedly attempting to board; but by the heavy and well directed fire from the ship, was prevented from getting near enough to effect their purpose, and was at last so dismantled in her rigging, that she sheered off; but having refitted, commenced a second attack at noon, with a most sanguinary design of boarding, and notwithstanding the incessant cannonading from the ship, ran plump on board, and endeavoured to throw her men into her. But well prepared to receive the enemy, the whole of the *Barton*'s crew being assembled on the quarter-deck, and headed by their gallant commander, who was spiritedly seconded by his passengers, an attack, sword in hand, commenced and the enemy were driven back with considerable loss, many of them being spiked from the [boarding] netting and shrouds of the ship, while by a well directed fire from the cabin guns, numbers were swept from their own deck; and great part of her rigging being cut away, she dropped astern and gave over the contest, amidst the victorious huzzas of the British tars, whose bold commander, calling from his quarter-deck, defied the vanquished republicans to return to the attack. Captain Cutler's conduct on this occasion cannot be too highly spoken of, and such was the enthusiasm of all on board the ship, that his passengers bear a proportionate share of honour, while his mates have a just claim to the approbation and applause of their merchants... The second mate and three seamen were wounded on the *Barton*.

Some of these engagements were of considerable duration and must have tested stamina on both sides. In March 1798 Captain Williams sighted a large schooner from the deck of the *Abigail*. Realising she was faster than his own ship, Williams shortened sail, bore up and sent his men to clear away and man the guns. The enemy, a corsair mounting 14 guns and manned by about 180 men ranged up alongside and opened fire.

We fought him within pistol shot, for seven hours, and kept a steady and well-directed fire with grape, double-headed and langridge shot. He attempted boarding us three different times but we repulsed him with small arms... During the action we carried away the privateer's main-topmast, shot her fore-sail to rags, and killed and wounded a great number of her people. My officers and men behaved as Englishmen, steady and collected...

Williams's long action must have been interspersed with breaks, for his men mustered aft at one point to declare 'they would stick to their guns and be true to me,' he wrote later, or else the enemy were deplorable shots, for the *Abigail* was little damaged and only her carpenter was wounded, and that not seriously. Other masters endured similar testing encounters, often exacerbated by insufficient men for which the press was not always responsible. On the morning of 11 October, the slaver *King William*, on her way to Barbados with slaves below, fell in with a 16-gun French privateer manned by a large crew, some 150 men. Against these Captain Theophilus Bent had 'only 15 effective hands able to stand to their quarters', nevertheless he fought his ship for two and a half hours 'when the privateer, having sustained considerable damage, and an immense loss of men, sheered off'. Counting the cost, Bent found the *King William* 'almost a wreck, having received 602 shots, and her rigging cut to pieces.' One of her crew had been killed and four wounded, while eight male slaves were hit while under hatches and two subsequently died of their wounds.

French commerce raiders were cruising in the West Indies throughout the winter and the spring of 1799. The ship *Benson* was among several British ships to encounter one off St Kitts, in her case at daylight on Thursday 6 December. Captain Croasdale's ship possessed a Letter-of-Marque and had, on a previous voyage, taken a Spanish prize valued at £7,000; she was now bound for

Jamaica when a ship and brig under a press of sail were seen standing towards the *Benson*. The *Benson* was also under studding sails and running fast but could not outpace her pursuers and at 10.30 the brig crossed her stern under American colours. The more powerful ship now ranged up upon the *Benson's* weather quarter under a British ensign. It seems probable that, as occurred during the Franco-American Quasi-War, the *Benson's* pursuer had most likely been in chase of the American brig and abandoned her for a British prize, because fifteen minutes later she broke out the tricolour and opened fire.

Croasdale immediately doused his studding sails and lay-to, ready to offer a warm response. The enemy also clewed-up and for an hour and a half the two fought it out 'within pistol shot of each other' until 'the firing ceased, and both vessels, which had been ungovernable, lay-to for the purpose of refitting'.

> At twenty minutes past one, the action again commenced and continued till about a quarter past two, when our opponent hauled his wind to the southward, and left us in such a crippled state in our rigging, masts, sails, as to be unable to follow, Fortunately no lives were lost in the contest, from…the enemy chiefly aiming to disable us aloft.

Later that evening Croasdale learned from a neutral vessel that they had fought and beaten off a 20-gun French National corvette – that is to say a man-of-war, not a privateer – with a crew of 170; information afterwards 'corroborated by a gentleman, a prisoner at that time on board, who got down to Jamaica shortly afterwards, and says that they have twelve killed, and ten wounded'. On the following day, by which time she was off the west extremity of Puerto Rico, the *Benson* ran into a 'large schooner privateer, of 12 guns, and full of men, which she drove amongst Cape Roxen shoals'. Then:

> On the 11th December, she chased a French cutter of 17 guns, which had an American ship, her prize, in company. The privateer liberated the prize, on seeing the *Benson* gaining upon her, but the wind dying away in the evening, the cutter out sweeps and escaped.

Another action with a National corvette was fought by the 20-gun *Dick*, Captain Isaac Duck. Duck had fought a long action with eight Spanish gun-boats when approaching Gibraltar early in the year and on his way to Barbados he picked up three prizes. By October, Duck turned for home and on the 13th the *Dick's* lookout sighted a ship and both, with hostile intent rapidly closed and came to close action. The corvette mounted 22 guns of a heavier weight-of-metal than her opponent and the gunfire was intense. The French also kept up a smart small-arms fire from their tops until Duck cleared these, but the corvette's broadside guns were uncharacteristically trained to hull the *Dick* and her captain was soon informed that there was 4ft of water in the hold. Undaunted, Duck came within half-pistol shot of the corvette and kept up a sustained fire for another hour when the corvette made sail and ran ahead. The *Dick*'s people set-to to repair the damage, plug the shot-holes beneath the waterline and pump their ship out while the corvette, having hove-to a short distance away, awaited events. Having made all ready, Duck re-engaged, but the corvette fled, leaving the British to lick their wounds, which were extensive. For this engagement in which Duck commended his chief mate, Mr Hugh Morris, Duck was presented with a purse of 200 guineas.

A year later the *Dick* was in action again off the coast of West Africa, where she was going for slaves under a different master, Captain W.Grahme. On this occasion her opponent was a 22-gun corsair, *La Grande Decide*, and the two fought for over seven hours during which Grahme and ten of his men were severely wounded while the first lieutenant and thirty-nine of the corvette's crew were killed or mortally wounded. The top of Grahme's skull had been shot away by a canister shot and, with the ship reduced to a wreck, the colours were struck. Grahme was taken aboard *La Grande Decide*, placed in the commander's cabin and attended assiduously by the French surgeon but he died on 21 October. Soon afterwards, however, the corsair and her prize fell in with two British cruisers, HMS *Clyde* recovering the *Dick* while the *Fisgard* went in chase of *La Grande Decide*.

Such courageous defences as Grahme put up often proved in vain and personally costly. In the early weeks of the war the *William* of Liverpool was in company with the *Joseph* of Appledore and the *Fanny* of Greenock. The ships were homeward-bound from Virginia when they were chased and engaged by a fast schooner-privateer, one of the vessels referred to earlier as being fitted out in America. After 'a desperate engagement' of three hours, the *Joseph* was taken, but the others escaped, the *William* arriving with the news of the *Joseph*'s capture on 23 July 1793. During the action Captain Prance twice drove off his assailant, sighting one of the guns himself, but as the enemy made a third attempt to close the *Joseph* and board her, Prance's gun exploded. The master lost both hands, a shard of the gun deeply gashed his thigh and he had one eye badly damaged. The *Joseph*'s mate was also wounded and Prance was obliged to strike. Prance was unlikely to have survived, for at the time 'his recovery was despaired of'.

Such risks did not deter an opportunist master from seizing the day. Captain John Ainsworth of the slaving schooner *Polly* fought a running engagement with a Spanish privateer-brig that lasted four and a half hours and ended with Ainsworth capturing the Spaniard. The *Polly*'s people 'expended 160 cannon cartridges, and upwards of 400 musquetoon cartridges' before the *Santa*

Antonia, on passage between Tenerife to Buenos Aires, surrendered. The *Polly* was on the Middle Passage; her rigging and sails were 'much cut up' and a number of her slaves were hurt from a 'shot that went through our side under the main chains' into the 'women's room'. Ainsworth landed his prisoners and left his prize at Barbados before proceeding onwards to Jamaica, but the following day a French schooner gave chase. After running for some hours during which the French corsair gained on him, Ainsworth decided to fight and settle the issue before nightfall, heaving-to. The enemy:

> came up under our quarter and I gave him what guns I could get to bear. We had a number of our men slaves with small arms, which they fought very well, and killed and wounded several of the privateer's people. She then attempted to board us on the quarter and carried away our main sheet... In their attempt to get up the side, I took a boarding pike, and threw it at them, which went through the side of one man, into the thigh of another and they both fell. He then sheered off. I can safely say he had 20 men, or upwards killed and wounded his decks being full of blood. We gave him three cheers and chaced him in out turn, but could not come up with her. She was full of men, but cannot say what force, I have one man wounded, and our hull full of musket shot, and our sails and rigging very much cut and shattered.

An example of gallantry in the face of superior odds was that of the schooner privateer *Earl St Vincent* of Falmouth which was 18 miles north of Cape Spartel in June 1799 when she was attacked by two French corsairs. The enemy was supported by four Spanish gunboats and Captain Smith decided to engage the corsairs before the gunboats could come up in the hope of disabling them. In this he was disappointed; after an action of an hour Smith found himself beset by a 'heavy fire of great guns and musketry'.

> Finding it useless to contend with such superior force he ordered his stern and quarters cut [away] and made a battery out of his stern chase [guns], from which he kept up a constant fire upon the enemy making at the same time all the sail he could to reach Tangier Bay, which he did after an action of five hours and a quarter... During the action she had three men wounded but no-one killed.

Examples of meritorious service may be found in the conduct of many seamen, particularly the masters and mates. When the *Townley* of Liverpool, on a voyage to Russia, was taken by a French privateer off the Shetlands, the corsair commander took out of her all her crew except the mate, a Mr Atkinson, and one other man named Overton. The prize crew consisted of six men, including the prize-master. Three days later Atkinson, 'assisted by Overton took an opportunity to fasten three of the Frenchmen below and attacked the rest; the prize-master fired his pistols without effect and fell in the conflict when his men submitted'. The two men then worked their ship into the safety of Vaila Sound in the Shetlands.

In late November 1799 Captain Stephen Urwin was making a passage in the vicinity of the Kentish Knock in the outer reaches of the Thames estuary when his ship, the *Marquis of Granby* of Sunderland, was brought-to by a French *chasse marée* to which he was compelled to surrender. Having lowered a boat to put a prize-crew on board and withdraw Urwin and two of his mates, the corsair commander made sail after another potential prize. The *chasse marée* was soon five miles distant and Urwin suddenly grabbed the boat-officer's sword from his hand and put it to its owner's throat, ordering the boat's crew to put about and return to the *Marquis of Granby*. Thinking the boat's return was due to the disappearance of the *chasse marée*, the prize-master let them approach, whereupon Urwin 'gallantly boarded her, sword in hand, and soon cleared the deck of the Frenchmen, who precipitately plunged into the sea and were picked up by their countrymen in the boat.' The *Marquis of Granby* resumed her voyage and, in due course, Urwin received a handsomely inscribed piece of plate from his insurers.

Such cool conduct was equalled by Captain Samuel Whitney of the ship *Hiram* whose ordeal is extraordinary and may best be told in his own words of explanation to his owners, written from Martinique on 22 October 1800.

> I have a very unpleasant account to give you of the *Hiram*, which, after being twice taken and retaken, arrived here the 13th inst. After being one hundred and two days at sea; the circumstances are these: On the 13th September, being in long. 55. and lat. 30. I was overtaken by a French sloop of war brig, called the *Curieuse*, Captain Ratlett, for Cayenne, on a cruise of two months, and then to France, who after an examination of my papers, pronounced the greater part of my property to be English. Then they took out all my people, (except my brother, one green hand, and a boy of 12 years of age), and out on board two officers and eight men, and ordered us for Cayenne, and after keeping us company for two days, and robbing us of a lower yard, a cask of water, a ship glass, and sundry small matters they left us. I, on first discovering her to be French, went below, loaded my pistols, and hid them away in a crate of ware, which if I had not done I should have lost them… The [prize] officers would not allow the[ir] men to off deck at any time, and they eat (sic), drank and slept on deck themselves…therefore I found I had no other chance but to engage them openly by daylight. I directed my brother to have a couple of handspikes in readiness, and when he saw me begin, to come to my assistance. Therefore, at four o'clock on the afternoon of the fourth day after being taken, I secured

my pistols in my waistbands, went on deck, and found the Prize-master asleep on the weather hen-coop, his mate at the wheel, and their people on different parts of the main deck, my brother and [the green sea]man on the lee side of the windlass. Under the circumstances I made the attempt, by first knocking down the mate at the wheel. The Prize-master jumped up so quick that I could get but a very slight stroke at him. He then drew his dirk upon me, but I closed in with him, sallied him out to the quarter rail and hove him overboard, but he caught by the main sheet, which prevented him from going into the water. By this time I had the remaining eight upon me, two of whom I knocked backwards off the quarter deck; by this time my people got aft with handspikes, and played their parts so well that I was soon at liberty again. I then drew a pistol and shot a black fellow in the head, who was coming to me with a broad axe uplifted, the ball cut him into the skull bone and then glanced, but it stunned him and amazed all the rest, who had no suspicion of my having pistols. By this time the mate whom I first knocked down, had recovered and got a loaded pistol…and…fired it…in my man's face, but the ball missed him. The Prize-master got on board again and stabbed my brother in the side, but not so bad as to oblige him to give out until we had got the day. In this situation we had it pell-mell for about a quarter of an hour, when at last we got them a running, and followed them so close, knocking down the hindermost, as we came up with them, until part made their escape below. The rest then began to cry for mercy, which we granted on their delivering up their arms… We then marched them all aft into the cabin and brought them up one at a time, and after examining for knives, etc.' we confined them down forward. By this time it was quite dark, and my brother was obliged to give out, and lay in extreme pain for forty-eight hours, expecting every moment to be his last, but he afterwards recovered astonishingly, and was soon able to keep his watch. My man got so drunk that I could not keep him awake at night, so that there was only my little boy and I to work the ship, watch the French and attend my brother. I kept a French lad upon deck, the only one that was not wounded, and kept him at the wheel all night. The weather was extremely fine and the Frenchmen quite peaceable, so that I met with little difficulty. Thus we kept possession of her for ten days, when we had reached within two or three days sail of Savannah… On 27th September, was again overtaken by a French privateer, from Guadaloupe, who, without any ceremony of examining papers…came immediately on board… As her cruise was nearly at an end, having sent off their men [in prizes], they hove overboard all their empty water casks…and filled themselves as full as an egg out of us… They then took out my brother, man and boy (leaving me on board) and all the former French crew, except four men, and put on board eleven of their own men, and after plundering me of part of my cloaths, brass hanging compass, carpenter's tools, spare cordage, deep-sea line, and many other like stores, they left us, ordering us for Guadaloupe; and after being forty-six days longer in their hands, we were taken by his Majesty's ship *Unité*, and sent into Martinique [then in British hands].

Pursuing in detail the *guerre de course* against shipping in the Atlantic risks repetition and consequent boredom on the part of the reader, so this first year of its prosecution – from which, even so, much has been omitted – must stand exemplar in part at least for what followed.

The most successful British privateers were those operating from the Channel Islands. Close to France and with their own trade disrupted, it was an obvious recourse to keep the islands' economies afloat. During the war of the French Revolution the High Court of Admiralty issued 4,748 Letters-of-Marque of which 454 went to masters of vessels registered in St Peter Port or St Helier. Of the 266 prizes taken by privateers, 181 were seized by Jersey or Guernsey vessels.

Like slaving, privateering aroused strong feelings and it may be supposed that the opinion of Samuel Kelly was shared by others: 'I considered it in no other light but a kind of licensed robbery, or as a plunderage of peaceable and innocent individuals', he thought, going on to relate the consequences following the seizure of a Danish ship with a French cargo for the West Indies by *The Brothers*. The privateer's two mates behaved in a highly improper manner, as an outraged Kelly reported:

> The officers of *The Brothers* had wantonly tortured the Dane's captain by means of a thumbscrew in hopes he would confess what nation owned his cargo, but they failed of obtaining the desired information, leaving the owners of the ship open to the penalties of the law incurred by their bad conduct.

Such brutal behaviour gave privateersmen a bad name in some quarters, but it was by no means universal. As with naval actions, a rough formality still governed war at sea and among certain private ships of war, honour could be a touchy subject. Of universal application, however, was the seaman's oldest and most implacable foe: the weather which, irrespective of wars between states, dominated the seafarer's life and for near-constant heavy weather in the winter, the Western Ocean had a bad reputation. Militarily, its worst effect at sea in the Revolutionary War was the dispersal and partial destruction of a large convoy with troops and stores bound for the West Indies in late 1795 under Admiral Christian. Men-of-war and merchantmen, including chartered East Indiamen like the *Valentine* and the *Dutton*, suffered dreadfully. The failure of the expedition had a profound impact on British strategy in the theatre, causing among other things the abandonment of Saint-Domingue – and with it a serious loss of revenue – but behind this major disaster the annual attrition of ships by the forces of nature went on relentlessly.

The regular traffic in salted and smoked cod from Newfoundland was an important business. Vessels crossed the Atlantic to fish on the Grand Banks, an area notorious for fogs, icebergs and gales. In the winter of 1797 a gale drove a number of fishing vessels ashore at Harbour Grace and Carbonear Bay, including the *Eagle*, Captain Graves, which was lost with 4,000 quintals of cod, and the *Chance*, Green, 1,600 quintals.

An Atlantic weather-system brought hurricane-force winds into the waters of northern Europe on 2 November 1801 when shipping was in trouble in the Skagerrak and Kattegat. Losses were frightful. The *Elizabeth* of Hull rode out the gale in the lee of Anholt, in the Kattegat, from where Captain Lowe observed no less than fourteen vessels of different nationalities stranded and wrecked on the weather side of the island. Another Hull ship, the *Flaxton*, capsized, all her crew scrambling onto her upturned bottom until the storm abated and they could be taken off by a Prussian vessel and sent home in various ships bound for England. Two British ships seen from the Norwegian coast sank while at anchor and the *Dash*, Captain Hill and also from Hull, foundered at sea with all hands. Further south in the English Channel where the south westerly wind later veered to the north west with the passing of cold front, conditions were described as 'the most dreadful seen for many years; the sea ran mountains high' and many vessels were in distress while ships suffered damage as far south as the Bay of Biscay where HM Frigate *Galatea* rolled her mizzen mast overboard, taking with it the main- and fore-topmasts. It was reminiscent of the great storms of 1703 when literally hundreds of merchantmen and an entire naval squadron under Admiral Beaumont had been lost, or of 1707 when poor navigation and heavy weather drove part of Admiral Sir Clowdisley Shovell's fleet onto the Scillies.[22] The weather improved on the 3rd when the cost was counted but it was little better on the 30 November when the Newfoundland convoy approached Start Point. Although hostilities had actually ended six weeks earlier, the convoy of fourteen sail had left St John's in ignorance of the peace negotiations, escorted by the frigate *Aurora*, now commanded by Captain Caulfield. The south westerly gale drove the ships north of the Eddystone lighthouse and prevented them weathering the Start, so they ran for Plymouth Sound where they anchored in Cawsand Bay. Even here they were not safe, four parting their cables and driving across the Sound to fetch up aground under Mount Batten.

The New Year ushered in more bad weather; on 4 and 5 January 1802 nine colliers from the Tyne, tucking themselves into shelter in Tees Bay, off Hartlepool, dragged their anchors and were driven onto Seal Sands, off Seaton

Carew, with other ships in distress in the North Sea and Channel. On the 21st an even worse storm scoured British home waters. The *Peggy* of Greenock from Cork for Liverpool foundered off the Mersey Bar, drowning all but one of her people; the collier-brig *Newcastle*, Captain Thomas Dixon, went ashore in Hollesley Bay under Orfordness, then worked off to sink on deeper water; further north at Southwold the *True Friend* of Lynn ran ashore and caught fire and the *Industry*, from Shields to Liverpool full of glass bottles, was abandoned by Captain Hopkins and his crew believing she was foundering. However, she was afterwards salvaged and towed into Great Yarmouth where, offshore on the Cockle Sand, the *Rio Douro*, a wine-laden Portuguese vessel from Oporto for Newcastle, ran aground. Away to the south west, the *Swallow*, making for Dartmouth from Newfoundland, collided with the *Lord Duncan* and sank, her crew being saved by the latter vessel.

Even in 1800 poor charts, the expense of chronometers and the relative poverty of many ship-masters continued to complicate navigation. Even the simple task of determining latitude and running along a parallel was frustrated under the overcast skies of the North Atlantic and quite impracticable among the tides and shoals of the North Sea. Ships were frequently and disastrously 'out in their reckoning' and the numerous shipwrecks attested to the fact. Wrecks along the western coasts of Ireland, the Scillies, Cornwall and the Channel Islands were welcomed by the indigent populace when winter gales prevented fishing. The Cornish prayer 'Almighty God, send us, we pray, a mild winter or a good-wreck,' was occasionally attended by the burning of false lights in simulation of the steady coal-fired chauffers of the primitive lighthouses of the day, and such largesse as a rich wreck deposited along a shoreline was – since it was legally an 'Act of God' – perceived as a 'God-send'. The tale of the Scillonian woman cutting the fingers of the half-dead admiral, Sir Clowdisley Shovell, as he lay washed-up after HMS *Association* had shivered her timbers upon the Gilstone in 1707 is well-known, but such disasters could impact not merely upon the wretched seafarers involved, but upon the very conduct of commerce.

On 4 January 1801 the *Dictator* of Liverpool, on her way from Berbice, Guyana, for London was driven into Dingle Bay on the west coast of Ireland 'by one of the worst storms of the winter'. The Inch Peninsula lies athwart the run of the bay and the *Dictator* drove ashore there, only three of Captain Lovelace's crew surviving. As the *Dictator* broke up her cargo of cotton, coffee and rum spread along the coast, so did the news of the God-send, attracting scavengers intent upon 'scranny-picking'. It was four days before the authorities arrived to recover what was left, most important of which was not the cargo of the *Dictator* herself, but the remittances, bills of exchange and correspondence relating to a far wider traffic. Letters and London bank-notes with a face-value of £20,000 were found in the possession of one illiterate man, with a further £12,000 in bills belonging to a certain James Frazer, a merchant from Berbice who had taken passage with Lovelace and drowned in the disaster.[23]

Navigation in high latitudes added another danger to the environment: ice. In the vigorous timber and tar trades carried on with northern Russia during the summer months when the White Sea ports were open, ice was usually avoided, but the limit of the pack could vary. Seeking a cargo of timber, Captain Nazby had left Liverpool for Onega on 15 May 1797 when, some 250 miles east of Jan Mayen island, the *Three Sisters* ran into loose pack-ice. This rapidly closed about her until she was held fast. Fearing the worst, Nazby and his men cleared away the ship's boat and hurriedly built a foredeck upon her, covered this with canvas and fashioned two masts and a suit of sails. This done they provisioned the boat and had barely completed the task when the ice began to open. Unfortunately it had pierced the *Three Sisters* and the ship immediately filled and sank. Taking to the boat, Nazby, his sixteen men and boys, safely reached Lerwick from where they were able to take ship, arriving back in Liverpool on 1 July.

Being beset in the ice was a risk commonly run by the Arctic whalers. At the turn of the century in a single season several were thus held up, including the *Ariel, Oakhall, Molly, Mary Anne, Fountain* and the *Symmetry*. The last two spent respectively forty-eight and seventy-one days stuck fast, though the *Fountain* of Lynn, Captain Baxter, succeeded in taking five whales whereas the *Symmetry's* voyage was ruined. In 1804 the *Dwina* of Hull and the *East Lothian* of Dunbar were lost in the frozen wilderness.

Nor was the hazard confined to the polar seas, the Labrador current sending icebergs south to the waters off Newfoundland. Shortly after the renewal of the war, in June 1803, the Government packet *Lady Hobart* left Halifax bound for Falmouth. Commander William Fellowes set a course to avoid both Sable Island and the French cruisers he already suspected would have left Brest in quest of prizes. Shortly after midnight on the 28th the *Lady Hobart* was running before a westerly gale in thick fog when:

> going at seven knots [she] struck an iceberg with such violence that several of the crew were thrown out of their hammocks. The vessel then struck a second time…then swung round upon her keel…the stern post being stove in and the rudder carried away before anything could be done; the iceberg meanwhile was overhanging the ship about twice the height of the masthead and was estimated to have been about a third of a mile long.

Fellowes threw his guns and anchors overboard to lighten his vessel, manning the pumps and forming a bucket chain as the water rose in the *Lady Hobart's* hold but 'within minutes the ship had settled to her forechains'. Cutter and jolly-boat were hoisted out and eighteen people put in them, including a number of women. As the boats were being launched Fellowes saw one of the seamen, John Tipper, emptying a demi-john of rum on the deck. Tipper informed his commander that his intention was to refill it with water from the scuttle-butt on deck, an initiative that provided 'the only fresh water that could be got at'. The two boats were seven days at sea before they sighted the coast of Newfoundland about forty-two miles from St John's and received assistance from some fishing boats. Two days later they left for St John's in a hired schooner. Remarkably there had been no fatalities, although several of the survivors 'required surgical attendance, being so much frostbitten'. Tipper was to die in his native Falmouth, exactly one year after the *Lady Hobart*'s boats reached land; he had been married just sixteen days.

Occasionally a cargo caused trouble, though less so than in later centuries. Some were, however, highly dangerous and a mishap in the voyage could have profound effects. Gun-powder was carried in specially sealed casks and stock-piled before shipment in isolated hulks moored in the remoter reaches of a river or harbour, but other commodities could create trouble in unexpected situations. When the West Indiaman *Wildman*, Captain Cundall, went aground off Ramsgate in late November 1794, she might have survived had not her cargo caught fire. She was described as 'one of the finest vessels engaged in the trade, being a new ship of three decks and capable of carrying 800 hogsheads of sugar', but her lading of lime 'which the generality of [outward-bound] West Indies merchantmen always carried and which heated by the sea strik-ing the vessel and the water entering the hold' caused her to catch fire and burn 'to the water's edge'.

While Cundall's culpability in the loss of his ship must remain conjectural, such losses as the foundering of the Dublin packet *Viceroy* seem entirely the fault of her commander as much as her cargo. In late December of 1797 the *Viceroy* left the Mersey with fifty people on board, the most of them passengers. Among these was 'Mr Handy and his troop of equestrian performers' amount-ing to twenty-five men, women and children and, perhaps fatally, their twenty horses. Whether or not Mr Handy was a convivial companion and strong drink was taken, the *Viceroy* was observed to be heavily laden and she vanished after her departure. 'It was thought at the time,' *The Times* remarked, 'that the horses may have contributed to the loss…by their rolling to one side when the vessel heeled'. Whether or not the cargo contributed to the sudden, unexpected foundering of 50-ton *Prince of Wales*, Simcock master, as she lay anchored off the Mumbles Head in January 1795 is uncertain, but seems likely. The little coaster, registered in St Ives, was one of many such vessels employed hauling copper-ore from Cornwall to the smelting works at Neath and her entire crew perished with her.

Another potential threat to the success of a voyage was mutiny. The political turmoil in France was reflected to some degree in Britain where republicanism never took a real hold, but was not without its advocates. Of more effect was the social imbalance in Georgian society which was producing increasingly articulate disaffection that was not confined to the less fortunate. It was not republicanism that gained ground in these tumultuous years, but radicalism, and the seafarer – being a beast of burden serving both the state and private capital – was easily mobilised. The naval seamen's committee that had organised and run the mutiny of the Channel Fleet at Spithead in 1797 had been a remarkable model of collective discipline, though this could not be said of the outbreak at the Nore where it was savagely repressed. The mood of disaffection that swept Britain in 1797 and infected the Royal Navy did not transfer into merchant ships, where the men were better paid and enjoyed an easier discipline and liberty ashore, but it could be a different matter among the convict-ships making regular sailings towards Botany Bay. The outward-bound *Lady Shore* was taken over by an uprising of the convicts connived at by a mutiny among the soldiers embarked for long garrison duty in the Antipodes. The ship had been built in Calcutta for her commander, Captain James Willocks, who chartered her to the Government as a convict transport and must have rued the day he did so in his last moments of life, for he and his chief officer were murdered and thrown overboard, the *Lady Shore* afterwards being carried into the Rio de la Plata.

Where mutiny was a comparative rarity, the weather capricious and the malice of the enemy a misfortune, there was one horrible aspect of seafaring during the war which was as predictable as day following night. As the incident involving the impressment of 300 seamen driven into Plymouth Sound in April 1803 mentioned earlier makes clear, the curse of removing seamen from merchantmen was to reach an outrageous climax in this long war with France. Even before hostilities had broken out in February 1793 the great demand for seamen to man the rapidly expanding Royal Navy then mobilising against Spain and Russia, again required the seizure of men from merchant ships. The competence of merchant seamen both at seamanship and fighting made them invaluable recruits requiring little training, for naval commanders were allowed neither time nor a budget to undertake such a luxury and might find themselves in danger or the presence of an enemy within hours of leaving port. Both Robert Park of Ipswich, whose *The Art of Sea-fighting* was published in 1702, and Hutchinson's *Practical Seamanship* of 1777, touch upon the arming and defence of merchant ships, while the practice of taking out a Letter-of-Marque was pointless without a ship's company possessing, at the very least, a rudimentary competence in handling small-arms, swivel and carriage-guns. As for the liberties of Englishmen, much vaunted at the time in the face of the *sans-culottes* of the *faubourgs* of Paris, these were of course suspended, an infamous ruling in law establishing the principle that it was perfectly proper that merchant seamen should have no liberties if by oppressing that minority the far greater majority of Britons might be guaranteed freedom secured by a properly manned Royal Navy.

Such was the incontrovertible argument that consigned thousands of hapless men into what many must have found a form of purgatory. That they submitted and did their duty is no less remarkable, even though the captains of men-of-war possessed far greater coercive and draconian powers over their existences than their former mercantile ship-masters. The numbers of these legalised kidnappings and their often illegal prosecution was legion, yet so widespread was the problem that it cannot be passed over lightly.

Returning from the Davis Strait fishery, the Hull whaler *Sarah and Elizabeth* was approaching St Abb's Head on 19 July 1794 when she was fired into by Captain William Essington of HM Frigate *Aurora*. Upon the second shot the whaler's master, Captain Rose, being to windward, hoisted his colours and ran down towards the frigate in compliance with Essington's peremptory action. The *Sarah and Elizabeth*'s crew, however, were determined not to be impressed and Essington afterwards alleged that Rose had aggravated the situation, having 'desired them to arm and defend themselves, and [saying] he would do all in his power to assist them', an allegation Ellington is said to have had learned afterwards from one of the whaler's wounded sailors. As the two ships closed, Essington sent two boat's crews under his sailing-master to board the *Sarah and Elizabeth*. On boarding, the naval party discovered that the whaler's men were defiant and shortly afterwards ran below and refused to come on deck. Hailing Rose, Essington raised the question of Rose's ability to command his men, an insulting tactic designed to establish that the *Sarah and Elizabeth*'s people were in a state of mutiny, whereby Essington could justify armed intervention. With an affray brewing below and Rose surly upon his own deck, Essington's sailing-master took over the whaler's helm while the *Aurora* was run alongside her. Then, as *The Times* reports, apparently following Rose's account:

> the boatswain of the *Aurora*, holding a grenade in one hand and a lighted match in the other, asked Captain Essington if he should fire the grenade amongst the people, which his captain then ordered him to do; but on being told by the master of the *Sarah and Elizabeth* that the ship was full of oil and would blow up, he desisted. They then commenced to break up the hatches with crows, but the men still refusing to come on deck, the *Aurora*'s captain ordered the eighteen marines to fire down the hatchway, by which fire one man was killed and three

badly wounded. The crew of the ship asked for quarter long before the marines ceased firing, yet ordered by their officers to do so. The greater part of the crew of the *Sarah and Elizabeth*, together with the wounded men, were taken on board the *Aurora* and put in irons, and were still in irons on 1 August.

The whaler arrived at Hull on 23 July and the coroner's jury 'were unanimous in bringing a verdict of wilful murder against the captain and part of the crew of the *Aurora*; whereupon the owners of the *Sarah and Elizabeth* instituted a prosecution against them'. This charge was refuted by Essington who wrote a letter to the mayor of Hull claiming 'that the crew of the merchantman were in a state of mutiny and fired upon one of the [naval] officers first'.[24] Essington's effrontery was not uncommon; armed force was often even more deliberately employed and sometimes with more serious consequences for the perpetrators.

Arriving in Studland Bay from Newfoundland with a cargo and passengers in November that same year, Captain Randle's *Maria* was boarded from the Impress Tender based at Poole. The officers in charge, anticipating resistance, took with them 'twenty armed soldiers' and ran the tender alongside the *Maria*.

> [F]inding the people obstinate, orders were given to fire, which they did. The pilot (then at the helm) and two other men were killed instantly, and several others were so dangerously wounded that two of them died shortly afterwards.

As a consequence of this overwhelming truculence:

> The town of Poole was in a state of uproar; Lts Glover and Phillips, together with all on board the tender, were taken into custody and an inquest was held on the body of the pilot, when a verdict of wilful murder was returned.

The local partiality was doubtless occasioned by the pilot's death, rather than the murders and mortal woundings of the seamen, and Glover and Phillips, having been removed from Poole, probably escaped justice, though their subordinates may have paid the price.[25]

It was always a risk for a master to bring his ship into a naval port, notwithstanding it was also a commercial harbour. Plymouth answers this description and in January 1800 the naval authorities were picking up seamen for service in the fleet. At about 02.00 on the morning of the 17th a boat carrying armed seamen ran alongside the *David*, just then anchoring in the Sound carrying a cargo of wine from Oporto. Having boarded the *David* and discovered the nature of her cargo, the press-gang seized the vessel's mate and two men on deck, went below and 'started two butts', drinking their fill until, thinking to remove themselves and cover their tracks, they returned to their boat and deposited each of their captives on a buoy where they remained clinging on for their lives until daylight when they were rescued by the skipper of a barge on her way to the Cattewater. The wretched men survived their freezing ordeal, but their assailants got clean away.

Matters came to a head within weeks when a case of murder was brought against Midshipman John Salmon of HM Sloop-of-War *Dromedary* and Lieutenant William Wright was arraigned as accessory. In the trial before the Admiralty Court on 21 March, it was stated that on 19 February Salmon had boarded a transport lying in the Thames with the intention of pressing men. A seaman named William Jones had resisted arrest and in the struggle Salmon had stabbed Jones with his dirk. In defence Lieutenant Wright produced his Impress Warrant leading to his acquittal, while the verdict brought in against Salmon was 'Not Guilty'. This was a crucial judgement, removing from the common seaman any right to resist impressment.[26]

Although difficult to resist at sea where the victims were invariably outnumbered and under the guns of a man-of-war, impressment was often violently opposed ashore where the odds were less favourable to the naval authorities and the intended victim conceived himself to be at liberty. In Liverpool in 1794 prior to joining the *Thetis*, Samuel Kelly's:

> lodgings were near one of the naval rendezvous, which gave me the opportunity of witnessing an unpleasant transaction. A carpenter had been impressed and was lodged in the press-hole at the bottom of Water Street. This circumstance being communicated to the shipwrights, a large body of the trade assembled at night with a long spar which they used as a battering ram against the prison door, which soon burst asunder and all the men were liberated. They then proceeded to the rendezvous in Strand Street which they broke open and literally gutted the house, the feathers of the beds were emptied into the streets and the furniture broken to pieces or carried off as booty, in which business a number of women assisted, as well as in drinking the beer and liquors, and even the windows were demolished. At last a magistrate made his appearance and dispersed the mob.

Given the notorious reputation of the port for disorder and riot, the bold effrontery of the press-gangs is the more remarkable, though contemporary evidence suggest the men employed ashore by the Impress Service were of a particularly unpleasant stamp and probably seamen any decent first lieutenant would be glad to see the back of. On a Friday evening in October of the same year, one Felix M'Ilroy, master of the small sloop *Ann* of Newry was accosted in Redcross Street by a press-gang. In the ensuing argument one of the gang 'drew a pistol and shot the captain dead on the spot. The murderer got on board the [Impress] tender [lying in the Mersey], but was arrested next morning'. Although the coroner's jury brought in a verdict of murder, when the case came before the Lancaster Assizes the accused, though found guilty, 'got off with one month's imprisonment'. This palpable injustice so enraged the seamen in Liverpool that on the Saturday evening following they attacked the Impress rendezvous and 'completely gutted' it.

The personal hardships undergone by individuals during these wars were numerous, often occasioned by circumstances as bizarre as the consequences. Difficulties arising from the sovereignty of Malta, removed from the Knights of Malta by the French and falling into the hands of the comparatively enlightened British – which the population generally endorsed with enthusiasm – aroused a frenzy of effrontery in the disturbed mind of Paul, Tsar of all the Russias. As the Grand Master of the Order – that extraordinary relic of anti-Turkic medievalism – Paul issued an embargo on British shipping in 1800. Although it was soon lifted, he renewed it on 6 November when it became known in St Petersburg that the British ministry had decided to possess the Mediterranean island. While the Tsar's actions caused alarm in Whitehall over an inevitable shortage in hemp, the second embargo had a most unfortunate effect upon a large number of British merchant seamen isolated in Russian ports. Not content with immobilising their ships, the Tsar ordered their crews to be removed and marched inland, 'some hundreds of miles, many as far as Siberia'. Among the vessels detained was the Hull whaler *Enterprise* which was carrying out a trading voyage at the end of the whaling season. Her master, Captain John Camp, died in Moscow, while another master, a Captain Pixley, having his son on board, 'bribed the captain of a Swedish vessel, then on the eve of sailing, to smuggle me away at night'. The young William Pixley 'was therefore carried on board and concealed between the bed and the sacking of the captain's berth, and although a rigorous search was made I fortunately escaped detection'. Meanwhile the Russians had emptied the holds of the British vessels, along with the hemp stored in the warehouses of the British merchants and re-rigged the Russian fleet at no expense to their own exchequer. Such was the Tsar's pique that he had also removed many of the senior officers of his fleet who were Britons in Russian service.

As the arrested merchant ships were being iced-in by the onset of winter, the outrage roused a widespread indignation in Britain. The Russia Company raised a subscription for the relief of the seamen, although the whereabouts of many were unknown. William Pixley was ship-wrecked on his way home and spent the winter at Christinansand in southern Norway. He did not arrive home until the following spring when he learned that on 26 March

1801 the Tsar had been assassinated by a palace coup in which the Tsarevitch Alexander was at least complicit. As Alexander I, the new tsar was anxious to placate Great Britain and matters were soon resolved after Nelson's victory at Copenhagen on 2 April, when the admiral headed for the Gulf of Finland with orders to show the British flag off Reval (modern Tallin), and to open communications with Saint Petersburg. Writing to Nelson from Kronstadt, whither he was sent with the admiral's dispatches in May, Captain Thomas Fremantle informed his friend and senior officer that 103 merchantmen were detained there with a further eighty-eight at Riga and ten other Russian ports. The 'Sails of the English ships are quite decayed and unfit for use having been so long without air', Fremantle reported. Tsar Alexander sent Admiral Paul Vassilievitch Tchitachagov to negotiate and the dispute was quickly resolved, though the British right to search neutral vessels for war contraband capable of helping their enemy remained – and would remain – a disputatious issue for the Baltic countries.[27]

There was by now a general war-weariness throughout Europe, and peace negotiations began. Hostilities ended – at least for a while – on 12 October 1801, to the jubilation of the populace who in some places drew the horses from the shafts of the mail coaches carrying copies of *The London Gazette* and pulled them into the coaching-inn yards amid cheers and hurrahs. Over the following months, many men-of-war came home to be laid up in ordinary, their crews paid and discharged. In Plymouth one immediate consequence was the paying-off of the officers and men of the Impress Service among whom Lieutenant John Newton had been 'forty-one years a lieutenant in the Royal Navy' and consequently received a generous – and highly partial – encomium in the *Naval Chronicle* which stated with some distortion of the truth, if we consider what happened to the mate and two seamen of the *David*:

> it is but justice to state there never was a more orderly set of men than the seamen and landmen belonging to Lieutenant Newton's rendezvous; the gallant veteran has raised for naval service…nearly three thousand seamen and landmen during a period of nine years.

For the merchant seafarer, peace meant a return to normal trade or, if he had been forcibly converted to the King's service, unemployment. William Pixley's father who had himself eventually reached home, ordered a new ship to be built at Great Yarmouth. On its completion young Pixley, still no more than fifteen, was sent to sea in her. The vessel was placed on charter to a French company, Messrs Marescaux Frères & Cie., of Dunkerque, to whom young William was sent to learn the business of acting as a shipping-agent.

Mme Marescaux, in whose household he was lodged, befriended him and it was here that Pixley was introduced to Mme Bonaparte. The town was full of troops which, it was common knowledge, were being readied for the invasion of England and when the First Consul was inspecting his assembling legions in the Pas de Calais, the soon-to-be Empress Joséphine, also became a guest of M. et Mme Marescaux. Charmed by and charming the English youth, she dubbed the young Englishman *'Milord Anglais'*, a soubriquet that stuck to Pixley during what was to be a long sojourn in enemy hands.

Although the fifteen-month Peace of Amiens was in the event nothing more than a truce, it did not prevent the authorities from impressing seamen before a formal declaration renewing the war had been made in May 1803. Even as Lord Whitworth, the British envoy in Paris, endured the very public and provocative insults of First Consul Bonaparte over British reluctance to relinquish Malta that would end the short-lived peace, the press was again stirring. Although the fleet was in part demobilised, some frigates were recommissioned and their captains found it expedient to resort to this traditional method of recruiting which was easy on their purses. Sending their own men ashore under junior officers and sometimes, as we have seen, mere boys of midshipmen, they swiftly rounded up any unwary seamen. An unnamed frigate lying in King Road off the mouth of the Avon despatched her boats upstream to raid Bristol as early as late March. Although the regular Impress Service had been disbanded, soldiers were drawn up across the street, barring the escape of 'upwards of 200 men'. Not all were seamen, however, and those of no value to the frigate commander were released next morning, a Sunday. The pressed men were moved under the escort of soldiers and the naval party to Lamplighters' Hall, prior to being shipped out to the frigate, but an angry mob in Hotwell Road flung stones and abuse at the soldiers 'which so irritated the military that they fired among them and killed a boy and wounded several others'.[28]

Elsewhere it was the same. On 8 March in the Tyne 'we had a rumour that set all Shields in an uproar. The ship *Desdemona* came in with the woful newse that two large Frigates lay in the Swin [in the Thames Estuary] impressing ev'ry man protected or not'. Thus wrote John Wetherell, 'protected carpenter' of the *Jane*, just then leaving for London. Off Orfordness on the 19th the *Jane* was boarded and her company mustered aft.

A grim looking fellow took up the ships Articles, Turning to Nicholson [the master] 'Where is your carpenter?' 'There, Sir, at the helm.' 'Relieve him and put his things in the Boat.' 'WHY SIR, HE IS PROTECTED.' 'That is the reason we want him in our carpenters' crew. Come, make haste.' This was all in five minutes transacted, away they bore me on board the *Hussar* Frigate. In a little while Capt Nicholson Anchor'd the ship and came on board after me but it was all

in vain…I was called aft to be stationed and told truth that I was no carpenter;
they put me in the top.

Within hours Wetherell fortunately escaped a flogging on the accusation of
'Obrian a Master's Mate' and began his sojourn in the Royal Navy, his only
explanation coming from 'Mr Wallace the first Lieutenant [who] smiling at
me says you collier Carpenters are the verry boys we want in our tops…'
Of the three dozen men quartered in the main top '24 were impressed from
those unfortunate affidavits [press exemptions] which in the late war was the
strongest protection granted'.

Further plundering of colliers took place and on 1 April the *Hussar* and
two other frigates, including Sir Sidney Smith's *Antelope*, anchored on the
Shelf, off Harwich. Here they sent their boats ashore with orders 'to fetch
ev'ry man…that was able to Serve his King and country' and in the evening:

> in great pomp made their landing good in Harwich. They commenced their Man
> plunder as I term it. The Market house was to be their prison, where a lieutenant
> was station'd with a guard of Marines and before daylight next morning their
> prison was full of all denominations, from the Parish Priest to the farmer in his
> frock and wooden Shoes. Even the poor Blacksmith cobbler taylor barber baker
> fisherman and doctor were all drag'd from their homes that night…
>
> *April 2.* A crowd of Women soon assembled round the prison… Wives
> demanded their husbands, children their Fathers and aged parents their
> Son[s]… The first salute was a shower of stones…[but] by parties of 12 or 15
> they marched all those unfortunate men down to the Boats and left the shore
> crowded with hart broken wives and parents. One brave Young Man, William
> Wright, the Fisherman…sprang from the boat as she left the strand and ran…
> pursued by a number of marines firing at him most furiously but all in vain; he
> crossed a mud bank and gain'd the other bank of a large inlet where he stood
> and wav'd his hat in defiance. The marines and officers return'd to the boats all
> mud and dirt, swearing vengeance against the next Man that made attempt to
> desert… Next day was appointed as regulating day on board the…[*Antelope*],
> the *Monkey* Brig and a Small cutter, to…receive all on board such as were pro-
> nounced able to serve by Sea. All such were cram'd on board the *Monkey* and
> se[n]t up to the Nore there set on board the Guard Ship… Those not able to
> serve [which would have weeded out the priest and doctor among others] were
> sent directly back to the Shore…[29]

Wetherell calls this 'The horrid outrage in Harwich' and it was followed by
boat expeditions against coastal shipping in the Swin against which Wetherell
inveighs at length.

On Saturday 7 May two boats rowed up stream from the Tower of London, where the Impress Tender *Enterprise* lay at her moorings. Each was commanded by an officer and these led their gangs ashore at Hungerford Stairs in pursuit of seafaring men. In a display of solidarity:

> they were resisted by a party of coal heavers belonging to the wharf adjoining, who assailed them with glass bottles and coal, when several of the gang were cut in a most shocking manner. The impressed men, for whom there was no room on the *Enterprise*, were put in the Tower and the gates shut to prevent their escape.

On the 16th the British Government signalled their intention to declare war on France and issued Letters-of-Marque-and-Reprisal all of which had lapsed with the peace. The Admiralty order went out for a 'hot press' and on the 18th the formal declaration — that made by King George III himself — was communicated to Paris. Bonaparte's reaction was swift and unparalleled: without preamble every Briton in France and anywhere France held sway was arrested and detained. British ships suffered the same fate. The four unarmed Post Office packets at Helvoetsluis awaiting the mails for Harwich were included, not even the Post Office agents having the slightest intimation of the action which was carried out by the French army. Two King's messengers on their way from the Hague to join a packet were also taken by surprise, though one escaped by hiring a fishing boat at Scheveningen.[30]

The hot press instituted in May 1803 swept up a great number of seamen, many of whom had been unemployed since the end of the previous conflict. In Dunkerque young William Pixley was 'made a prisoner on parole' and, on hearing of war his father wrote, requesting M. Marescaux sent him to a good school with a view to improving his French. He was sent to the Ecole Militaire at St Omer where he 'attained a great proficiency in the art of fencing and use of small arms. Our number amounted to about 40 English and 70 French youths'. This extraordinary start in the maritime life of a man we shall meet again is in stark contrast to the main stream of seafarers now embarked on the decisive phase of the Anglo-French struggle.

The Peace of Amiens and consequent lifting of the British blockade had allowed the French to get ships to sea, one consequence of which was to re-infest the West Indies with corsairs, while another was to see several large vessels sent out to the Indian Ocean. While the former again threatened British shipping in the Antilles, the latter presented British privateers with a few new opportunities for rich prizes as the Indiamen — French and Dutch — returned home. The out-bound Guineaman *Margaret and Eliza*, armed with a

Letter-of-Marque and under Captain Barry, took a Dutch vessel named *Maria Alletta* heading for Amsterdam from Batavia on 5 September 1803. She was valued at £45,000, and in October 1803 Captain Every of the *Ainsley* brought *L'Aimable Lucile* into the Mersey having seized her as she approached the Gironde after a voyage from Île de France. Every's prize was valued at £80,000 while Captain Sellers of the *Sarah*, and Captain Baldwin of the *Ann Parr*, shared the lesser prize of the *Ville de Lyons*, a smaller ship than the *L'Aimable Lucile*, but still worth a handsome £26,000. The deliberate and provocative attack and capture by Commodore Graham Moore and his frigate squadron of the annual Spanish *flota* commanded by Commodore Bustamente in 1804 made an enemy of Spain.[31] It also made Moore a rich man, for Bustamente's men-of-war bore the annual consignment of silver from the mines of Potosí for the exchequer at Madrid. A rich Spanish prize was the wardroom toast of British gunrooms but a few British privateers scored the desired jack-pot too, for there were other less well-armed Spaniards at sea.

In March 1805 the privateer *Lady Frances*, Captain Hawkins, took one of these, homeward from Vera Cruz and Havana loaded with logwood, sugar and 60,000 silver dollars; and the *Westmoreland*, Captain Goodall, took a second similarly loaded. Goodall also recaptured an Irish coasting vessel out of Waterford which had been taken by a Spanish privateer, but within months the *Westmoreland*, on another cruise under Captain Reed, was engaged by the *Napoleon*, a 14-gun Spanish privateer from St Sebastian. Reed's vessel was captured after an action in which he was mortally wounded.

Such desperate affairs were commonplace and many masters made reputations as fire-eaters. Captain Lutwidge Affleck of the *Juno*, though grossly out-numbered and out-gunned, fought a French national corvette. On 14 August 1803 the *Juno* was badly shattered when, after an action of two hours, she surrendered to the *Poursuivant* whose commander attempted to dispose of her at Charleston, but the American authorities would not permit him to enter their waters with a prize. Instead the captors plundered the *Juno* then burnt her, releasing her crew. For his gallantry Affleck was presented with an inscribed bowl by the *Juno*'s underwriters and owners; such tokens becoming common by way of encouragement for ship-masters to protect their owners' property, while the Letter-of-Marque such ships bore offered an additional chance of augmented profit. Affleck, in command of the *Harmony* in October 1805 made an attack in his ship's boats on a Spanish ship of force lying off Tenerife. Both vessels were becalmed and Affleck's bold attack was beaten off but was remarkably determined, none the less.

Captain Richard Sherrat fell foul of two French corsairs cruising 200 miles east of Guadaloupe on 8 March 1804. He had sailed in the *Caldicott Castle* from Demerara laden with cotton and sugar ten days earlier and now found himself in trouble as the enemy closed in after dark. The *Caldicott Castle's* men drove off the smaller of their two attackers after about fifteen minutes of heavy firing, but it took a further hour before the larger, a ship-rigged vessel that turned out to be *La Grande Decide* from Guadaloupe, lay-off within sight while the protagonists repaired the damage, particularly in their rigging. Action resumed at daylight, the ship-rigged corsair coming 'within pistol shot' whereupon she 'opened a tremendous fire of great guns and small arms' and in fifteen minutes shot away the *Caldicott Castle's* wheel, hulled her, and severely cut up her rigging. Sherrat was wounded, along with two of his seamen, while his second mate was hit mortally. Sherrat was soon exchanged, informing his owners from Barbados that he had noted protest against the loss of his ship and that he was:

> nearly well of my wound; it was a musket ball which entered my right hip, and came out near my backbone. I have nothing more to inform you of, but hope…there will not be any blame attached to either my men or me, as they all to a man behaved in a very gallant manner.

Such sugar-carriers coming from Demerara were well-armed, but were vulnerable from the predictability of their passages and enemy corsairs lay in wait in the approaches to the Irish Sea. It was here in August 1804 that Captain Thomas Phillips ran into the *Général Augereau*. Phillips's ship, the *William Heathcote*, bore 20 guns but her crew of thirty men was insufficient to ensure she brought home her cargo of cotton and sugar. Though armed with only a dozen guns the privateer was full of men and her commander dashed her against the *William Heathcote's* side and boarded 'with nearly their whole force'. Phillips was killed in the first, desperate *mêlée*, dying of multiple stab-wounds but exhorting the mate, named Shepley, to fight on. He too was mortally wounded and so fierce was the onslaught that 'the captain's son, a lad about twelve years old… was mortally wounded, and thrown overboard before he expired'. Phillips's second mate, a Mr Kewley, was afterwards reported by the prize-master from HM Sloop-of-War *Nautilus* which recaptured the *William Heathcote* on the 9th, to have 'killed three men with his own sword' and it was afterwards lamented that Kewley remained a prisoner aboard the *Général Augereau*, which he was 'very sorry for, as his brother was a most particular friend of mine'. Conscious of having secured so valuable a ship, the *William Heathcote* was escorted into the Mersey by HM Sloop *Cockatrice* where her 'average was settled for the recapture, by the [prize-]agents for the *Nautilus* and the underwriters, at £36,000 for the cargo, and £8,000 for the hull, stores, guns and tackle'.

The complexities of resolving disputes over prize money were occasionally pettifogging, often involving a good deal of legalistic work. In July 1807 a special jury was sworn in the Court of King's Bench and a case involving the owners of the privateer *Eliza* of Liverpool versus Captain the Honourable Henry Blackwood of HM Frigate *Euryalus* was brought before Lord Ellenborough. The case centred round the impressment of four of the *Eliza*'s crew by Blackwood which had diminished the owners' share of her prize money. A few days after Blackwood's recruitment drive, the *Eliza*, Captain Keene, had taken a Spanish vessel, *La Dos Amigas*, of 24 guns and 700 tons burthen. The Spaniard had been bound from Peru to Cadiz and had put up a fight lasting and an hour-and-three-quarters, but had struck to Keene and yielded up a large quantity of worked silver, wool, cascarilla, 'sea-wolf skins', indigo, drugs – probably cinchona bark, or quinine – a huge quantity of cocoa, pewter and copper. Besides all this she had on board 179,935 silver dollars, the whole of which, after condemnation in the prize-court, paid a net sum of 'upwards of £151,000'. In accordance with the practice of the day, the owners were entitled to three-quarters of this sum, the crew the remainder, but on this occasion Blackwood's removal of the four men diminished 'the *Eliza*'s share of prize-money…proportionally less by upwards of £3,000, to recover their dividend of which, the plaintiffs claimed £2,888 10 shillings and 6 pence. Ellenborough's summing up heavily underlined Blackwood's duty and his zeal for the public service, but the jury found in full for the plaintiffs.

However, the Royal Navy did not always take advantage of a vulnerable British merchant ship lying under their guns, though in the example about to be related the officer concerned, Samuel Hood, was an outstanding sea-officer and a man of real sensibility. Having three times driven off the notorious corsair *Général Erneuf* in July 1804 when homeward-bound from the West Indies in the *Britannia*, Captain Leavy was nursing his ship's and his crew's wounds. The *Britannia*'s 'masts are full of small shot. We were obliged to bend an entire fresh set of sails, but [I] am happy to say the ship is not much injured in her hull'. He had lost one passenger, his boatswain and carpenter, all of whose deaths he lamented, besides having a number of wounded. The following day Leavy reported, 'we were spoke by Commodore Hood in is Majesty's Ship *Centaur*, who very politely sent his surgeon on board to examine the wounded, and also supplied us with medicines we were in want of'.

The depredations of enemy privateers in the Channel awakened the Government to increase its vigilance. The rigorous rooting out of corruption in the Royal Dockyards embarked upon by Earl St Vincent after he assumed the office of First Lord of the Admiralty almost jeopardised the efficiency of the Royal Navy at a crucial period and this situation required some interim measures to throw off the lobbying of angry mercantile constituents who felt the navy was failing in its fundamental duty to protect trade. One such was 'a system of alarm gun signals, intended to serve as an intimation to the [cruising] men-of-war that a privateer was on the coast, and to point [out] the very place where it might be found'.

Although the Royal Navy's record on trade-protection was historically patchy, it was not invariably inefficient or at fault. Nor were the few losses occurring among the convoyed ships always to the disgrace of the naval escort. Unfortunately however, when confronted with overwhelming forces, an escorting man-of-war was unlikely to immolate herself, invoking the notion of 'he who runs away, lives to fight another day'. Nevertheless, such abandonment did little to endear the navy to the mercantile ship-owners, let alone the masters, mates and their men who were already subject to the navy's appetite for man-power and might in consequence lose their liberty. However, after the resumption of the war in 1803 there were two gallant attempts at convoy defence which, if they did not entirely succeed, frustrated the attackers so that losses were minimised.

In the early spring of 1804 Commander Henry Gordon of the sloop-of-war *Wolverine* was on passage towards Newfoundland with a small convoy of eight sail under his wing. The *Wolverine* was not a regular naval vessel, but an experimental craft mounting a dozen guns.[32] Although bearing only two long cannon, her main armament consisted of heavy-calibre carronades on special slides all set upon a hull that had begun life as a collier. Although she had proved her usefulness in inshore operations, the *Wolverine's* very low freeboard militated against her in the open ocean when heeling under a press of sail in anything like a moderate sea, and it was precisely under these conditions that she and her convoy found themselves being pursued by two French privateers on 24 March.

Seeing 'two vessels of force' coming down with the wind upon the rear of the convoy, Gordon manoeuvred to interpose the *Wolverine* between them and their quarry. In the ensuing action, obliged to tack to fire from the weather side because the sea ran too high to open the lee ports, Gordon found one of his long 18-pounders, which was designed to be run across the deck and swing to fire on either side, jammed in its grooves. After some preliminary manoeuvring, the two vessels lay hove-to firing into each other. Despite putting up a gallant fight, the more formidable of the two vessels prevailed. She turned out to be the 30-gun corsair *Blonde*, commanded by Capitaine Aregnaudeau, himself a member of a consortium of *armateurs* based in Bordeaux. The *Blonde* had the previous year made a cruise into the Indian Ocean wherein she had taken ten prizes. She was a formidable vessel of 500 tons, owned by Gramont et Cie., Chariot et Garaigne, and manned by a crew of 180. After an action lasting fifty minutes, with his rigging cut to pieces, his wheel shot away and his ship badly hulled and sinking, five killed and ten wounded out of a total crew of seventy-six men and boys, Gordon was compelled to strike his colours. The *Wolverine* sank as he and his men were taken into captivity. With his consort achieving nothing and with his first lieutenant mortally wounded and five men slightly wounded in the action, Aregnaudeau made sail to take two vessels out of the convoy before it passed beyond his reach.

Gordon and his men had behaved with a gallantry the inadequacy of their ship could not support. In a typically dismissive account of the action in the *Annual Register*, their courage was traduced, the *Blonde* being referred to as 'a paltry privateer', obloquy which was intended to ensure a smear upon Gordon's reputation. In fact he was made a post-captain in April while in captivity, and exonerated by court-martial upon his eventual exchange in November 1811. The *Blonde*, refitted by Chégaray Frères of Bayonne, was herself taken on 17 August 1805 by Captain Frederick Maitland of HM Frigate *Loire* after 'a long running fight in which the *Loire* had 6 and the *Blonde* 7 wounded, 2 mortally. The prize was disguised as an Indiaman, and had been a serious annoyance to British trade.'[33]

To some extent Gordon had been let down by the grand strategy of the Commander-in-Chief of the Mediterranean station. Lord Nelson's technique of distant blockade before Toulon was intended to draw the French fleet out to sea where they could be destroyed, but unfortunately this required a number of frigates to be retained as lookouts and to maintain a chain of communication from Toulon out to Nelson's waiting battle-squadron. In a theatre where such cruisers were in chronically short supply this left Nelson woefully short of convoy escorts. Like others assigning men-of-war to trade-protection, Nelson entrusted 'the trade' to his weakest and otherwise most useless vessels, notwithstanding his appreciation of the duty as among the most important of his responsibilities.

In January 1805 two of these inadequate men-of-war, the experimental sloop *Arrow* and the bomb-vessel *Acheron*, left Malta bound for England with a convoy.[34] At almost the same time, taking advantage of favourable winds, Vice Admiral Pierre Villeneuve broke out of Toulon with his entire fleet in the first tentative move of a campaign that would culminate off Cape Trafalgar in October. Villeneuve intended heading for the West Indies where he was to gather up isolated French and Spanish men-of-war before returning across the Atlantic, relieve the blockaded Brest fleet, enter the Channel and dominate it long enough for Napoleon to throw his forces onto the beaches of Kent and Sussex.

Having escaped Nelson, who went looking for him in the opposite direction, Villeneuve headed for the Strait of Gibraltar and ran into bad weather, only to return to Toulon until another opportunity offered. However, two of his cruisers, which had been sent to drive off the British lookout frigates, had become separated from the French fleet. After the gale had dropped the two

French cruisers stretched to the west in search of Villeneuve, unaware that the admiral had returned to Toulon. Hampered by failing winds they were making little headway in their quest until at daylight on 3 February, when off the Algerian coast, they came in sight of the British convoy.

Commander Richard Vincent of the *Arrow* sighted the two strange sails which turned out to be the powerful French frigates *Hortense* of 40 guns, Capitaine La Marre La Meillerie, and the 38-gun *Incorruptible*, Capitaine S. Billiet. Signalling the convoy to make all possible haste for Gibraltar and casting off the tow of a slow merchantman unable to keep up in the light conditions, Vincent ordered his colleague, Commander Arthur Farquhar of the *Acheron*, to close-up. During the remainder of the day the two small British sloops placed themselves between the fleeing convoy and the approaching predators, a task frustrated by a complete calm during the afternoon, evening and first part of the night. However, in the small hours of the 4th, a breeze springing up from the WSW, the French frigates, with all sail set, bore down upon *Arrow* and *Acheron*, opening fire at about five in the morning at a range the two British ships, both of which carried only short-range carronades, could not match. At this time the convoy was no more than four miles away.

There followed a long and desultory engagement off Cape Caxine, both sides affected by the light airs, but the advantage lay with the French, favouring their longer-ranged guns. For a while both *Hortense* and *Incorruptible* hammered the *Arrow* until, at 08.30, with his rigging shot to pieces and his ship sinking under him, Vincent struck his colours. Farquhar attempted to escape but the *Acheron* was not built for speed – her only chase guns as a bomb-vessel being stern chasers – and she was soon caught by the *Hortense* and obliged to follow the *Arrow*'s example and submit. She was so battered as to require burning and the delay this caused La Meillerie and Billiet in the pursuit of the convoy resulted in only three ships, 'the *Duchess of Rutland* and two others', falling into the enemies' hands.

Although both Vincent's and Gordon's defence of their convoys did not lack courage, and to some extent mitigated the inevitable losses of merchantmen that followed their respective capitulations, the two vessels assigned the task of convoy-escort were fundamentally inadequate. Both *Arrow* and *Wolverine* were experimental, while *Acheron* was clearly totally unfit for purpose, Nelson himself admitting she 'was not the equal of a strong privateer'. There was nothing exceptional about Vincent falling in with two powerful French frigates, nor of Gordon encountering a relatively well-armed corsair. It is clear that during this pre-Trafalgar phase of the war, before the economic sanctions of the years that followed the pivotal battle began to bite, trade-protection was not taken as seriously as it should have been by commanders-in-chief on foreign stations and, it has to be said, by the Admiralty itself. This was a lesson still to be learned and even in the fateful year of 1805, experimental vessels – for which there was little real need elsewhere in the service – were customarily assigned to convoy duties, as will be seen from the following.

On 29 March Villeneuve broke out from Toulon a second time, again deceiving Nelson. Augmented by Gravina's Spanish squadrons, the Combined Fleet successfully reached the West Indies, though with Nelson by then in hot pursuit. Once the news of Villeneuve's escape reached London in May the Admiralty issued an order for a general embargo on shipping. This was in part to prevent ships poised to leave British ports from falling into the hands of the Combined Fleet, but also in anticipation of an invasion. Since the renewal of war in May 1803 the French had been gradually building up their forces in the Pas de Calais, mustering and exercising a flotilla of invasion-craft and notwithstanding Admiral Earl St Vincent's assurance in Their Lordships' House that he could not say that the French would not come, only that he was certain that they would not come by sea, the country and Government were jittery. Napoleon had hubristically dubbed the massing troops *L'Armée d'Angleterre* – whose assembly was witnessed by young William Pixley from Dunkerque – in anticipation of victory. He awaited only the arrival of Villeneuve – who was to liberate the Brest squadron as he had released Gravina's Spaniards from Cadiz – and who was due to appear in the Channel within weeks.[35] All the Combined Fleets had to do was to make themselves masters of La Manche for a week, and Napoleon and *L'Armée d'Angleterre* would make the French 'the masters of the world'.[36]

'Invasion fever' gripped Great Britain. The volunteer forces were augmented and the whole south coast was thrown into a posture of defence. Old seamen were recruited as Sea Fencibles and defences were erected by public subscription in major ports. In London the East India Company armed a force of their riverhoys and the Elder Brethren of Trinity House commissioned ten naval frigates which were laid up for want of men and moored them as a cordon of armed vessels across the Lower Hope below Gravesend. The force manning them was formally commissioned as the Royal Trinity House Volunteer Artillery and the Corporation's Master, the temporarily out-of-office William Pitt, became its colonel. The Elder and many Younger Brethren assumed commissioned military rank and a force of some 1,200 men was raised at the Brethren's expense – about £10,000. The frigates were joined by the Royal Yacht, *Royal Sovereign*, commanded by Captain Sir Harry Neale and was serviced by the Trinity House Yacht.[37] The men manning these 'blockships' were mostly seamen, including a number of lascars, all of whom received press-exemptions. These were among the very few respected by the Impress Service which had been ordered by the Admiralty, following the embargo of shipping, to institute a very hot press, a matter it found easy under the circumstances.

The attitude to impressment in general and in these particular circumstances among commercial and middle-class circles was expressed by an editorial of 13 May 1805:

> The immediate augmentation of our naval forces is thought a matter of such pressing necessity, that all consideration of personal suffering must, for the present, give way…and during the whole week, the press gang had been indefatigable in their exertions… Persons of all professions, as well as seamen, have been occasionally taken; though many have been released, on proper application being made… The embargo extends to all vessels bound to foreign parts, including Ireland and the Isle of Man, with the exception of ships belonging to foreign powers, provided they have no British seamen on board. It extends, likewise, to coasting vessels of every description, except such as are laden with coals and grain [that is to say those largely employed on the east coast of England whose food and fuel was needed in London].

Although the embargo undoubtedly saved a number of ships and served the Royal Navy's man-power deficiency very well, it did not protect those ships in foreign parts or on the high seas, fifteen of which became embroiled in the great events then unfolding. On 11 August the former chief mate of the *West Indian*, one Mr Joseph Whidbey, wrote home from Oporto whither his ship had been sent as a prize. They had, he said, had the misfortune on 8 June to have been captured by the Combined Fleet.

Having replenished his men-of-war in the West Indies, Villeneuve prepared to return across the Atlantic in accordance with his imperial master's orders. He had captured a fortified rock off Martinique which had been held for some months by a Royal Naval detachment landed by Samuel Hood, but Villeneuve was dilatory in setting off to raise the British blockade of Brest. Off Antigua on 8 June, he learned from an American schooner that a homeward-bound British convoy lay to the northward having departed from Antigua the previous day: making sail, Villeneuve went in chase. The Combined Fleet fell upon the convoy before sunset and took fifteen prizes, driving off the escorting British men-of-war the *Barbadoes*, 28 guns, Captain Joseph Nourse, and the experimental schooner *Netley*, Lieutenant Richard Harward, which prudently ran.[38] Taken under convoy of the French frigate *Sirène* the prizes were ordered to Guadaloupe.

The only good to come out of this loss from a British perspective was that Villeneuve was informed by his captives that Nelson was after him and had already reached the West Indies. Indeed the naval historian William James claims that 'the merchant masters did, most probably, exaggerate the British force under Lord Nelson, in the hope to drive the French admiral back to

Europe. If so, the plan produced its effect…' So much so that an alarmed Villeneuve was led to make a series of decisions that, in due course, set in train events fatal to himself, his Combined Fleet and Napoleon's Grand Design.

Whidbey corroborates James's claim and takes up the tale:

> The French finding the prizes could not beat up to Guadaloupe, and fearful of Nelson overtaking them, they the next morning dispatched 5 frigates (having troops on board) to destroy them and afterwards land the troops at Guadaloupe, which they effected, putting my captain [Dunn] and others on shore with them. It was a distressing sight to see our ships and cargoes burnt and sunk, when two English frigates were bearing down on them, but too late, the 5 French frigates returning at the time to join [the Combined] fleet. We were stripped of everything but the cloaths we had on.

Although the French did not benefit from their prizes, the loss to the British economy was considerable, amounting to £200,000 in cargoes alone. Whidbey was among a number of men from the British prizes who were retained among the ships of the Franco-Spanish fleet and was aboard Villeneuve's flagship, the *Bucentaure*, when, on 22 July in mid-ocean, the Combined Fleet ran into a squadron under Vice Admiral Sir Robert Calder which had been sent out by the First Lord, Admiral Barham, to block the approach to the Channel.[39] An engagement was fought until nine that evening when, as Whidbey attests, the weather 'being very thick', or foggy, it was broken off. Thereafter, 'the French made the best of their way to Vigo Bay, where,' Whidbey concludes, 'we arrived three days after, and landed the prisoners, which were marched into the Portuguese dominions, where I now am, sufficiently distressed'.

He was not the only one. Calder had taken two Spanish ships-of-the-line but he did not renew the action in the thick mist next morning, and history has tended to censure him for this apparent lack of zeal ever since. He went home to condemnation and demanded a court-martial on his conduct which, in due course – and following Nelson's apotheosis in October – rapped the unfortunate Calder's knuckles. In fact, although tactically inconclusive, what became known as 'Calder's Action' sufficiently broke Villeneuve's resolve so that he abandoned his advance on the Channel and entirely dislocated Napoleon's plans. Instead of continuing north-west, towards Brest, Villeneuve scuttled south from Vigo to have Nelson slam the door on him in Cadiz until he emerged in October in an attempt to regain Toulon but suffer annihilation off Trafalgar.

The death of Nelson, mourned in England, accounted for scenes of jubilation among the French. In St Omer the French boys at the Ecole Militaire rejoiced while the English lads, among whom Pixley was ranged, were affected by an 'equal chagrin'. There was an appalling battle arranged 'at the back of the monastery, which was contiguous to the schoolrooms' and from which the British emerged victorious despite the disparity in numbers, probably because they were better fist-fighters than the French. Nevertheless William Pixley 'was cruelly disfigured' in this rough-and-tumble and did not regain his sight 'for more than a fortnight afterwards'. Despite the severe reprimand handed down by the school authorities, there were two duels consequent upon the affray, fought by English youths against subalterns in the French army.[40] Later, 'at M. Mareschaux's splendid château near St Omer' where his vacations were spent, Pixley was to meet Napoleon on five occasions, twice as First Consul Bonaparte, and three times as the Emperor Napoleon. Pixley had become a firm favourite of the new Empress with whom he 'frequently had the honour of dancing…as she took particular notice of me'.

Pixley's privileged experience was unique among the many hundred of imprisoned seamen on both sides who would endure incarceration in French fortresses or British prison-hulks. The latter acquired a terrible reputation among the wretched French, while Verdun and Bitche became notorious among the British. The British Government built a new gaol on Dartmoor for the accommodation of prisoners of war and in which, in March 1815, 6,000 Americans rioted at their over-long confinement following the end of the brief war between Britain and America.

Although the Battle of Trafalgar effectively put an end to widespread attacks on British trade by the French national navy, it did not end the *guerre de course*. As we shall observe in more detail in the Indian Ocean, the French again proved their adaptability in this form of warfare and derive their maritime heroes from their corsairs, all men from the littoral regions whose dash and expertise at sea became legendary, even among their enemies. These dangerous antagonists were in turn joined by other Europeans – particularly the Dutch and Danes – and, in due course, by the Americans, hence their presence in Dartmoor gaol.

In the years following Trafalgar the Royal Navy was to continue to expand, reaching its greatest extent in 1812 when slightly under one thousand men-of-war of all classes were in commission, manned by 140,000 seamen and marines. Much of this naval puissance was increasingly involved in trade-protection, either cruising in critical locations – such as off the Barbary coast – or escorting convoys. Their Lordships were in no doubt of the importance of this task, rubbed in by the eighth Article of War which emphasised its importance, but in their own execution they continued to fall far short of expectation. For the naval officers charged with the duty, a convoy must be defended, its private property respected and every care taken of it. Such orders were, in the main, faithfully discharged by naval officers whose professional regard for trade and its importance had increased, notwithstanding the frequent inadequacy of the means at their disposal. Nevertheless, the level of losses to enemy privateers continued to run high and the Committee of Lloyd's wrote a letter of remonstrance to the Admiralty over this. The response by the Admiralty Secretary, John Wilson Croker, was 'a long apologia' made on 14 March 1809 analysing:

> for the previous six months, figures for convoyed ships and independents and for capture and recaptures of merchant ships in the Channel. The proportion of losses was, from these figures, 1.5 per cent of sailings. In the same period thirty-three men of war or privateers were captured from the enemy.[41]

This was a shrewd reply, both politically and bureaucratically, sampling only the Channel, where the situation had improved since the establishment of the coastal signal stations referred to earlier and where the percentage of losses came out at roughly half the global figure. To further play-down the reality, which was all too well-known to the Lloyd's Committee, and to mitigate the navy's responsibility, Their Lordships 'emphasized the importance of convoy discipline'. But it was not enough to throw the blame upon the hapless, impotent and convenient merchantmen, not by a long chalk, especially when war broke out with America.

There were exceptions on both sides of this argument. In the Mediterranean the new Commander-in-Chief and successor to Nelson was Cuthbert Collingwood, who had so boldly led his own column into action at Trafalgar as Nelson's second-in-command. Following the battle in October 1805 and without remission until his death at his desk aboard his flagship *Ocean* in March 1810, Collingwood's battle-squadrons dominated the Mediterranean. As Piers Mackesy summarises:

> British trade flowed in its accustomed channels; to the new warehouses of Malta, to Smyrna and the Levant, to the Adriatic and the Black Sea. But the protection of this volume of trade weighed heavily on the navy. Fortunately the main trade-route lay along the African coast, far from a raiding force coming out from Toulon. The convoys sailed from England escorted by frigates; were seen through the Gut [of Gibraltar] and past Carthagena by ships of the line detached from [the blockading squadron investing] Cadiz; and at Malta found the shelter of a safe harbour... Four times a year, on 1 February, 1 May, 1 August and 20 October, the convoys reassembled at Malta for the return voyage to England, the last bringing the perishable fruit-trade from Zante and the coast of Greece. They could be seen past Ferrol by a frigate, and then left to the protection of a small cruiser across the Bay [of Biscay] to the Channel.[42]

The strategic situation was eased after the Spanish revolt of May 1808 but this did not allay Collingwood's anxiety in respect of the 'runners', largely from Malta, whose owners would not accept convoy and these ships became the quarry of the small corsairs 'which swarmed in the Mediterranean... concealed in creeks...till a merchantman was signalled from the hills'. Collingwood, bereft of sufficient cruisers to cover the expansion of trade emanating from Malta, protested the folly of sailing independently. His pleas fell on deaf ears; Malta was enjoying a bonanza and this in turn attracted the enemy. By 1807 French corsairs were operating out of Tunis and Algiers and what lay concealed in the anchorages of the Barbary coast was once more a direct threat to British trade. This in turn now inhibited Maltese commerce, a situation worsened in 1808 with the arrival in Naples of Marshal Murat. As the newly crowned King Joachim, Napoleon's brother-in-law began issuing privateering commissions, aggravating the problem: now not only the North African coast harboured these pests, but the heel and toe of Italy and the barren island of Cerigo were added to their list of safe havens. Although Collingwood's cruisers enjoyed some successes in seizing a number of small but agile privateers 'the losses continued'. The Admiralty estimated twenty frigates and thirty sloops were required as cruisers in the Mediterranean; Collingwood had sixteen frigates and nineteen sloops and the want of frigates that had vexed Nelson was to plague his successor. Almost on the eve of his death and as the French Toulon squadron seemed reanimated and reprovisioned, poor Collingwood lamented: 'My distress for frigates and small vessels is extreme'.

Facing confrontation with the whale of British sea-power after Trafalgar, Napoleon conceived the elephantine project of barring imports from Britain into a Europe which, by 1807 was either allied to, or part of, the French Empire. The ban, known as the 'Continental System', of course excluded not only goods of British origin and manufacture, but commodities garnered in British merchantmen from all parts of the world and re-exported from Britain – items such as silk, coffee, sugar and other luxuries much in demand by the very bourgeoisie that Napoleonic Government had created and by which it was sustained.

Initially these measures seriously affected British exports, but the development of avoidance combined with the Spanish revolt of May 1808 'soon blew an enormous hole in the Continental System, opening not only Spain and Portugal but their entire colonial empires to British trade'.[43] However, it was not all plain sailing, not least because the English harvests were poor in 1809 and 1811. Despite the best efforts of British entrepreneurial skill and cunning, French control over the European economy caused trade with Europe to slump and British exports fell from £61 million in 1810 to 39.5 million in 1811, so to this extent the Continental System succeeded. Moreover, inflation began to run away and depreciated the pound sterling, while imports of gold were necessary to support the Peninsular War which had begun in 1808. It is important to note in this respect that the British army under the future Duke of Wellington paid for what it used, unlike the French army which looted its supplies from the country in which it campaigned, thus making it fairly obvious which was the more popular to the native Spaniards. It is equally important to point out that regular Portuguese troops, equipped, trained and in the greater part commanded by British officers, also had to be kept supplied, as did the regular and irregular Spanish forces being backed by London. All had to be paid for by Great Britain and the supplies and arms shipped in her merchant marine.

Against the Napoleonic declarations from Berlin and Milan which established the Continental System, the British Government issued a number of Orders in Council intended to oppose it by hampering neutral shipping seeking to trade with enemy ports. The core of the Orders declared that any vessel carrying a cargo to French port – or a port in a country allied with France – would be obliged to discharge its lading, pay a duty and purchase a special re-export licence from the British. The short-term result of these measures was to further encourage an already vigorous smuggling trade across both the English Channel and the North Sea and to foster a more licit system of circumventing the system by means of licenses. Faced with financial ruin, rectitude among the honest was easily eroded, while those opportunists who profited from every war prospered easily. In the longer term the interference with the free trade of sovereign nations inevitably brought about war with the United States.

However, this was of little actual importance to the struggle between the whale and the elephant, for by such means the impact of the opposing systems were ultimately of far greater effect in Europe than the Napoleonic ban on trade with Britain. Indeed, the bad harvest in England in 1809 was offset by Napoleon himself who 'was more concerned to sustain the French economy that to attempt the starvation of England…[and] licensed export of the surplus French crop' was followed by the same thing in 1811.[44] Not that the British sailed breezily through all this unaffected. On the contrary, when a further dearth of corn followed in the winter of 1812–1813 rising bread prices in the towns of northern England combined with increasing industrialisation and widespread unemployment, to foment serious social unrest. Gangs of Luddites smashed machinery, bankruptcies became commonplace and most of the British army's light cavalry were deployed not in Spain, but in support of the civil power.

British Military Transports by the usually **Anglophobic** Baugean. These were merchant ships chartered by the Admiralty Transport Board and each given a number, here Nos 61 and 12. These vessels kept Wellington's Anglo-Portuguese Army supplied during the Peninsular War. Note the 'yard-and-stay' tackles forming a union-purchase to discharge a cannon into the local small craft alongside for landing. Note also the sacks of horse fodder hung in the fresh air along the taffrail. (Private Collection)

The enemy: a French frigate after Baugean. Such men-of-war, often bearing 40 guns, regularly escaped the British blockade in 'flying squadrons' of three or four to prey on British merchant shipping. (Private Collection)

The enemy: French flying squadrons usually included a smaller corvette. This example, a brig-corvette of 16 guns is shown hoisting out a boat. Such vessels were dangerous to British merchantmen and were used as both national cruisers and private corsairs. After Baugean. (Private Collection)

The enemy: a variety of craft were used by the French as privateers, or corsairs. From large ship-rigged frigates such as is shown here on the left, to swift luggers, or *chasse marées*, on the right: all were well armed and full of men. After Beaugean. (Private Collection)

On the Continent matters were no better. The very real British naval blockade was strangling commercial centres like Bordeaux, Rouen and Lyons; internal trade fell off and there was a run on the Paris banks. Of considerable significance as a processor of a highly desired commodity, the thirteen sugar refineries that Amsterdam possessed at the beginning of the war were reduced by this time to a mere three.[45] From its inception, the Continental System was open to fraudulent abuse, corruption and all manner of scams, all of which ultimately played into British hands for the crisis of 1811 precipitated a shift in policy by both belligerent parties.

The British effectively abandoned their long-cherished Navigation Acts. The carriage of goods hitherto reserved for British bottoms was now allowed to any ship-owner sustaining a trade-route essential to the British economy and – through duties – her war-chest. Clandestine trade was therefore tacitly encouraged and port of discharge, rather than flag-state, was the issue at stake. To some extent this was forced upon Britain by the taking up from trade of her own merchant ships as military transports, a situation which allowed the Americans in particular to fill a large void once a British army was operating in the Iberian Peninsula and required all its supplies from home to avoid alienating the local population. To enforce this new policy shipping in general was allowed to flourish, provided such shipping sailed to and from British, British-colonial, or British-friendly ports. As a consequence neutral-flagged vessels were seen in greater numbers in British ports than ever before and, from time-to-time, even enemy ensigns might be observed as vessels operated under the protection of licenses. Meanwhile British men-of-war had standing orders to take under convoy *any* ship requesting protection, irrespective of nationality 'notwithstanding all the documents which accompany the ship and cargo may represent…[them] to be destined to any neutral or hostile port, or to whomsoever such property may belong'.

On the enemy side – and enmeshed in this – regulation in the form of licenses issued by various competent authorities merely added to the many shady practices already established. One such was for ships bearing Letters-of-Marque to masquerade as privateers while actually carrying illegal cargoes; other bore false manifests passed by bent *douarniers*, while the demand for luxuries had long-since corrupted even the highest echelons of the Napoleonic establishment, so that Marshals of the Empire like Marmont amassed enormous wealth at the expense of undermining the First French Empire. Expedience and survival also played their part. Even during their 'English War', referred to later, the Danes were obliged to obtain licences for the trans-shipment of grain from the fields of Jutland to the hungry population of Norway – then a part of Denmark – whose population depended upon it. These licenses were paid for by exports of Norwegian timber, eagerly swallowed by the ship-building yards of Britain.

Despite the vast resources of the Canadian forests, the varied nature of 'naval stores' compelled the British to maintain their guard over their traditional Baltic trade. The British rape of Copenhagen in 1807 when the Danish capital found itself, in the Hon John Fortescue's phrase, caught ''twixt the hammer and the anvil', had deprived the Danes of most of their fleet. However, in what became The English War, they carried out relentless hostilities against British shipping as it passed to-and-fro through the Danish archipelago, either by way of the Øresund, or the Great or Little Belts. This mosquito war was not insignificant, the Danes manned heavily armed gun-boats which in a calm could swiftly reduce a man-of-war, allowing her convoy to be attacked with impunity. To counter these attacks, the British sent Admiral Sir James Saumarez to the Baltic in HMS *Victory* and, during the ice-free seasons between 1808 and 1812, Saumarez established and maintained a largely effective convoy system. Despite the constriction of the three channels leading in and out of the Baltic and the proximity of small Danish ports, all of which supported squadrons of gun-boats which could be manned at short-notice, convoys as large as 1,000 sail of merchantmen regularly made the long passage through the Danish archipelago. This was not accomplished without loss, however, and not only to Danish gunboats. In January 1809 a delayed convoy was ruined in the ice off Malmö. In July 1810, five brigs which, stationed in Danish Norway, had avoided the destruction meted out at Copenhagen three years earlier, fell upon and captured an entire convoy of forty-seven sail. This triumph, commanded by Kaptein Lorenz Fisker, occurred off The Skaw, when Saumarez's escorting men-of-war had retired to leave the convoy proceeding unescorted.

A worse disaster occurred in November 1811 when appalling weather struck the last convoy of the year as it, along with the British Baltic squadron itself, returned home to winter quarters. Even before it was clear of the Baltic thirty of the seventy-two homeward-bound merchantmen were lost off Nysted at the eastern entrance to the Great Belt. Finally clearing the Skagerrak the vast concourse of loaded ships ran into worse weather, the convoy was scattered and in hurricane-force winds the destruction was fearful. Besides HM Ships *St George* and *Defence*, a number of merchantmen were wrecked, while further south another convoy of 120 ships was dispersed, many were overwhelmed and driven ashore as far as the Dutch coast while the escort of HMSs *Hero* and *Grasshopper* also foundered. Several thousand seamen of both sea-services were drowned in the disaster.

In spite of all this, the Danish interdiction, ice, wind and Tsar Alexander's abandonment of his British alliance in favour of a short-lived entente with Napoleon embarked upon at Tilsit, the British never ran out of hemp. This essential commodity, alone of the naval stores, could not be sourced from anywhere other than Russia and was held in such stocks in 1810 that further imports were allowed only against Russian purchases of British goods of equivalent value.[46] Such inducements the Russians found irresistible, leading to their flouting of the Tsar's *ukase* against trade with Britain, a breaking of the sacred agreement of Tilsit in which Alexander had pledged himself to Napoleon in 1807. In 1810 Alexander was therefore obliged to issue another *ukase* permitting trade with Britain, a measure that precipitated Napoleon's reciprocal *volte face* and fatally misjudged march on Moscow two years later. With Alexander changing sides the situation in the Baltic was transformed.

To force goods into Europe, the British established trading stations to out-flank the Continental System and better bend it to their will. Some places were readily to hand in Gibraltar and Malta, but others were seized and exploited, most notably in the south at Lissa on the Adriatic. This became a both a source of some hemp and a naval base off which a celebrated action was fought in 1811. In the north a most important post was established at Helgoland in the German Bight. This small island had been Danish, but was taken as part of the expedition against Denmark mounted in 1807. It served a number of purposes, being an intelligence-gathering 'listening post' but also acted as a recruitment centre for young Hanoverians eager to join George III's King's German Legion, a mixed force which fought with great distinction under Wellington in the Peninsular War. Helgoland's most important function, how-ever, was as a forwarding depot for proscribed goods, which were brought thither in British ships and carried up the Elbe to Altona – then in Denmark – and the old Hanseatic city of Hamburg beyond. The smuggling of sugar through Hamburg was of particular importance and numerous British trading houses petitioned the Foreign Office for licenses to establish warehouses on Helgoland, sending their ships to the island where they discharged into open boats and stored their cargoes in the wooden warehouses they had erected.[47] Local coasting craft from Hamburg, Hanover and Oldenburg reloaded the goods and slipped into the several adjacent estuaries and their small ports to spirit all manner of commodities to their ready markets and eager if clandes-tine consumers.

During Bourienne's time as governor of Hamburg he admitted 'The Trade of Oldenbourg was carried on as uninterruptedly as in time of peace, English letters and newspapers arrived on the continent, and those of the continent found their way into Great Britain…' Only when, towards the end of the war, Napoleon appointed Marshal Davout to govern the old Hanseatic city was this route dislocated. Davout, a fiercely loyal, incorrupt-ible and ruthless Bonapartist known to his troops as 'the Iron Marshal', adopted a zero-tolerance policy towards smuggling. Learning that it had become the practice to carry sugar into the city in coffins, he interrupted one such phoney burial and had the pall-bearers shot in an attempt to put an end to the ruse. Such efforts were pointless. Even Davout's imperial master connived at defying his own laws as we have noted; indeed Napoleon is even said to have imported boots manufactured in Northampton in which, it is supposed, that some of the Grand Army marched to Moscow in 1812. More certainly licenses signed by the Emperor for the export of French wines, paid for imports of sugar and coffee. As Nicholas Rodger eloquently points out: 'Behind the official façade, the Continental System was dissolving the political glue of the Napoleonic regime'.[48]

The effect of all this on the far side of the Atlantic began to store up trouble in America. 'Our commerce at this moment, is like a poor flying fish, pursued from below by a couple of dolphins, and above from a couple of hawks.' Incidents between British and American men-of-war, in which shots had been exchanged, had further raised the temperature, though conciliation had – for the moment – prevented a complete rupture. The serious disruption in Anglo-American trade had its effect upon the ports most directly serving it in Great Britain: Glasgow and Liverpool, where the latter lost one quarter of her trade. However, fortunately the British found a ready redemption, for eventual military successes in the Iberian Peninsula soon reopened the whole of Portugal to commerce and Liverpool was saved. In due course, as we have touched upon, American shipping would also benefit from this, though not immediately and not soon enough to stem the growing hatred of British maritime policy and the constant slights to the American flag.

The post-1811 period saw a remarkable and rapid recovery in the British economy, putting ministers in bullish mood. In 1812 Lord Bathurst, the President of the Board of Trade and Plantations wrote: 'France, by her Decrees had resolved to abolish all Trade with England: England said, in return, that France should then have no Trade but with England'. That year British exports rose by 28 per cent, just as Napoleon embarked upon his disastrous Russian campaign. The destruction of the *Grande Armée* by Marshal Kutuzov and 'General Winter' was followed by the ruinously expensive necessity to raise more armies and fend off the growing and increasingly united alliance of mighty continental powers. Under-written by British subsidies the dead Pitt's policy of a Grand Coalition began to bear fruit in the aftermath of the Russian Campaign.

By issuing licenses – 18,000 of them in 1810 alone – to regulate commerce the British abandoned the old Navigation Acts. This was a major shift in British policy and it was caused in part to win the support of the United States by encouraging her trade. This bidding for the hand of the United States had been undertaken by both protagonists, but while the French could do little more than greet American ships running the British blockade and arriving in French ports with open arms, the British could enforce their policy with all the ruthlessness at the Royal Navy's command. American shippers and ship-owners, enjoying the high freight-rates of wartime, readily embraced the protection afforded by the Royal Navy, even if Britannia levied a swingeing cut of their man-power to do so. However, irrespective of the British Government's intent, in the manner of enforcing its policy towards the Americans, the Royal Navy utterly failed to woo them. Quite the contrary, its high-handedness directly precipitated a final rupture in 1812.

The ships of countries like Prussia, under the heel of the French and therefore technically enemies, were not only encouraged to trade with Britain, but offered convoy. The ambiguity was not lost on President Madison wrestling with a decision whether to declare war on Great Britain in 1812. Madison believed that Great Britain wished to encompass the destruction of America's trade not because it interfered with her belligerent rights, nor that it supplied her enemies' wants, but because the trade of the United States interfered with:

> the monopoly which she covets for her own commerce and navigation. She carries on a war against the lawful commerce of a friend that she may the better carry on a commerce with an enemy – a commerce polluted by the forgeries and perjuries which are for the most part the only passports by which it can succeed.

The British were aware of the delicacy of their relationship with America, but the announcement of the suspension of the Orders in Council, announced to parliament by the Foreign Secretary, Lord Castlereagh on 16 June 1812 came too late. Backed by Congressional hawks who coveted Canada, Madison took the United States to war. It was to be a humiliating decision, despite some largely illusory but hugely psychologically encouraging victories of American frigates over their British counterparts, and American victories on the Great Lakes. America's long and indented eastern coastline eventually came under a loose blockade by the Royal Navy which, in Nicholas Tracy's phrase, amounted to 'a *guerre de course* campaign [conducted] from a position of strength'. In the interim, however, American vessels bore grain from Chesapeake Bay south to the West Indies from whence it supplied Wellington's dusty battalions in Spain, all of which was enabled by some necessary documentation consisting of about 500 'forgeries and perjuries'. Later, in May 1813, Congress outlawed the use of British passes, thereby simply diverting cargo from American bottoms to British ships under neutral flags. Thereafter the Chesapeake was invested by a close blockade while wheat arrived in Britain from the Baltic and Lisbon where warehouses had been filled with the produce of America.

A large, 22-gun American schooner built specifically to attack British merchantmen in the War of 1812–1814. After a drawing by Baugean. (Private Collection)

The Royal Navy could neither mew up all American shipping, nor inter-cept all her privateers, though the blockade forced up American insurance rates, particularly in their coasting trade. It also left 200,000 bales of cotton – over a year's supply to Britain – clogging up the warehouses of Carolina, while in England Lancashire starved for want of it. As in their war for independence, the Americans embarked upon an effective private attack on British trade which, as before, 'drove up insurance rates [on the eastern side of the Western Ocean]... and produced a storm of protest in parliament'. The impact of American hostil-ity might have been greater had not the Spanish and Russian revolts against Napoleonic policy occurred, but the fact that they did, not only mortally wounded Napoleon's Continental System but permitted a diversion of naval power westwards to blockade the United States. Furthermore, in addition to liberating trade with Portugal, the markets of Spain's crumbling South American Empire were re-opened, allowing trade with both the Spanish colonial settlers and the growing rebel factions then emerging. And as if the trick had not been won by a handful of aces, it was trumped in that it aided British military assaults on France's West Indian possessions.

As for the war with the United States, the competing balance sheets for this unnecessary conflict are difficult to determine. The British navy far out-numbered the American, despite its world-wide commitments, but was unable to prevent – according to several computations – 'from eight hundred to a thousand English [for which one should read British] merchant ships...[being] taken by the American privateers and ships of war'. This contemporary British authority, Edward Baines, adds that 'at least an equal number of American merchantmen were taken'. On the other hand the American privateer commander, Captain Coggeshall, reckoned that American frigates and privateers captured, burnt or sank about 2,000 British bottoms, well over two-third of which were taken by the latter.

As in the previous war the Americans ranged along the coasts of Scotland and Ireland, producing 'so strong a sensation at Lloyd's' that it was difficult to get policies underwritten, except at exorbitant premiums. It is said that 'thirteen guineas for £100 was paid to insure vessels across the Irish Channel'. In 1810 Liverpool cleared 6,729 entered merchantmen but two years later, upon the outbreak of war with the United States, this number had dropped to 4,599, 'a fall in tonnage of 287,603 tons, meaning a loss in revenue of £21,379'.

For merchant ship-masters the war offered more anxiety. Men like the redoubtable William Affleck endured the added burden of another enemy with something like fortitude. Informing his owners of the safe arrival of the *May*, 14 guns and fifty men, at St Lucia in August 1812 he described how he had been chased by a large schooner which had run into the *May*'s wake under British colours on the evening of the 3rd. Having sent his men to quarters, Affleck fired his stern guns to keep the stranger at a distance and was soon afterwards hailed. As it grew dark and the wind dropped there began a charade in which the American commander affected an English accent and claimed to be a British man-of-war, ordering Affleck to send his boat across with his ship's papers. Both vessels had by now come broadside to broadside and Affleck told his interlocutor to come no nearer or he would fire into him, but the stranger insisted a boat was sent, so Affleck despatched his mate, Samuel Hazelhurst, with two seamen in the jolly-boat. Upon Hazelhurst gaining the stranger's deck, a boat came across from the schooner with an officer, Mr Thomas Yorke, and a full boat's crew; Yorke explained that the schooner was in fact a British privateer from Bermuda commanded by Captain Taylor, and if Affleck would but step across with his papers all could be swiftly resolved. It was not a trick Affleck was prepared to fall for and he ordered the intruding Yorke out of the ship. The farrago continued for a while until Affleck was hailed and warned to submit or be fired into, to which he responded: 'Fire away!'

The two vessels commenced an action lasting ninety minutes, Affleck beating off every attempt the schooner made to throw his men into the *May*. Captain Taylor at last sheered off with, according to his log, 'the intention of lying by all night within gunshot'. The action was renewed at daylight when the schooner was hulled several times, a gun was dismounted and Taylor 'received a ball in his left temple which instantly terminated his existence... About the same time a shot struck under the larboard fore-chains...which caused the vessel to leak badly...' The schooner, the *Shadow* of Philadelphia, was thus 'obliged to haul off in the greatest confusion,' Affleck concluded in his own letter, 'nothing could exceed the coolness and bravery of the few people I had the honour to command'.

Other American privateers were vastly more successful. One, the *General Armstrong* of New York, mounting eighteen 18-pounders and one 44-pounder on a swivelling carriage, engaged and captured the *Queen*, a 16-gun ship with a crew of forty men outward-bound for Surinam. The commander and first officer were killed in the action and the prize was afterwards lost on the shoals off Nantucket, but the *Queen* represented a loss of a cargo to her underwriters of 'from £70,000 to £100,000 sterling'. Another, the *True Blooded Yankee*, an 18-gun privateer manned by 160 seamen, boldly lay off Holyhead, between the Skerries and South Stack, where she took the *Fame* of Belfast, the *Margaret* of Hull, the *George* of Kinsale and four other vessels. 'The *True Blooded Yankee* was formerly the *Challenger* gun-brig [captured off Brittany in March 1811], and her crew were said to be chiefly British'. According to Coggeshall she belonged to an American named Preble resident in Paris and although she had an American commission and flew the American flag, she was:

> always fitted out and sailed out of French ports, viz. Brest, l'Orient and Morlaix. This vessel was very successful. She cruised the greatest part of the war in the British and Irish Channels and made a large number of rich prizes... During one cruise of thirty-seven days, she captured twenty-seven vessels, and made two hundred and seventy prisoners...

Unfortunately, the furious assault by these American vessels coincided with the high-point of the French *guerre en course*. To the merchants in their counting houses it seemed like a repeat of the late 1770s and early 1780s. Where the opinion of many had been expressed by *The Statesman* in June 1812 which had dismissed the impudence of Madison's declaration of war with the contemptuous statement that 'America certainly cannot pretend to wage war against us; she has no navy to do it with!' the London newspapers were of a different mind by the end of the year. Referring to the large size of the Royal Navy on 27 December 1812, *The Times* thundered: 'O miserable advocates! In the name of God, what was done with this immense superiority of force?' Two days later it lamented 'Oh. What a charm is hereby dissolved! What hopes will be excited in the breast of our enemies!' All this excited a great deal of anger in the breasts of the mercantile classes who, having endured the losses of a further twenty months of war held a meeting in Liverpool on 29 August 1814. Here they resolved to petition the Prince Regent, sweeping aside a resolution by the ship-owner John Gladstone that they address the Lords of the Admiralty on the grounds that they had already tried this on a previous occasion and received from the Secretary to Their Lordships' Board, Mr Croker, the dismissive retort that as much was being done as was possible. They had had enough of the Admiralty and the following day sent off their memorial to the throne, in which 'humble address' they censured Their Lordships. However, that day there was another meeting, organised by Gladstone, from which a petition was sent directly to the Admiralty. It laid out the precise detail of the petitioners' complaints and was signed 'very numerically'. As predicted by Gladstone, Croker responded in similar vein, enumerating the dispositions of His Majesty's Ships and Vessels of War – not fewer than three frigates and fourteen sloops were stationed in the approaches to the Irish Sea. On 7 September Glasgow followed Liverpool's example, stating:

> That the number of American privateers with which our Channels have been infested, the audacity with which they have approached our coasts, and the success with which their enterprise has been attended, have proved injurious to our commerce, humbling to our pride, and discreditable to the directors of the naval power of the British nation, whose flag, till of late, waved over every sea, and triumphed over every rival. That there is reason to believe, that in the short space of less than twenty-four months, above eight hundred vessels have been captured by that power, whose maritime strength we have hitherto held in contempt. That…when the mercantile and shipping interests pay a tax for protection, under the form of convoy duty, and when, in the plenitude of our power we have declared the whole American coast under blockade, it is equally distressing and mortifying that our ships cannot, with safety, traverse our own Channels; that insurance cannot be effected but at an excessive premium; and that a horde of American cruisers should be allowed, unheeded, unresisted, and unmolested, to take, burn, or sink, our own vessels, in our own inlets, and almost in sight of our own harbours.
>
> That the ports of the Clyde have sustained severe loss from the depredations already committed…renders the necessity of prevention more urgent.
>
> That from the coldness and neglect with which previous remonstrances from other quarters have been received by the Admiralty, this meeting reluctantly feels it an imperious duty at once to address the Throne, and that therefore a petition be forwarded to His Royal Highness, the Prince Regent, acting in the name and on behalf of His Majesty, representing the above grievances, and humbly praying that his Royal Highness will be graciously pleased to direct such measures to be adopted, as shall promptly and effectually protect the trade

on the coast of this Kingdom, from the numerous insulting and destructive depredations of the enemy.

This was strong and measured stuff. It was the more pointed in that Napoleon had fallen that spring and although the adventure of the Hundred Days had yet to accomplish his final destruction on the bloody field of Waterloo in June 1815, the vast resources of the Royal Navy ought – in the opinion of the Lord Provost of Glasgow and the supporting merchants, manufacturers, ship-owners and underwriters of that city – to have been brought to bear upon the acute problem. It never was; on Christmas Eve 1814 the articles of the Treaty of Ghent were signed and the American war was over, officially at least.[49]

Napoleon's first abdication in April of 1814 was a direct consequence of his defeat by Britain's allies: Russia, Prussia and Austria whose guns commanded Paris from the heights of Monmartre. The armies of these powers were in no small measure under-written by British subsidies paid from the war-chest of a Great Britain that gathered the wealth it drew from foreign trade in its shipping. Furthermore, coincident with the investment of Paris, a British and Portuguese army had crossed the Pyrenees and had in turn assaulted Toulouse. This was the army that the Duke of Wellington had, after many vicissitudes, brought from Portugal where it had been landed by British ships years earlier. On his flanks throughout five years of grinding campaigning the Royal Navy had harried the enemy, supported Spanish regular troops and supplied the guerrilla bands that had struck terror into the hearts of the French soldiery. In his rear with a con-stant regularity a succession of convoys of chartered merchant ships, escorted by cruisers of the Royal Navy, had maintained his supply train. Even before he had landed, the first expedition to the Iberian peninsula had been rescued from its retreat to Coruña by the transports mustered under Rear Admiral James Bowen, himself a former sailing master and a Devon man whose family had served in merchant ships. In the great ria to which General Moore fell back, the transports acquired a somewhat tarnished name. Panic was said to have infected the masters as the French shot, fired from the surrounding hills, plunged among them. The disparagement was familiar; no one seemed to recall that the master of a merchant ship, entrusted with someone else's property, is not supposed to have it knocked to pieces under his feet. The plain fact is that the transports gathered by Bowen extricated and saved Moore's precious army.

There is no doubt but that convoy duty could be infuriating to a naval officer and instances of escorts firing into merchant ships not obeying their instructions with the speed expected of them are numerous but there were occasions when the escort was at fault, as in 1804 when the frigate *Apollo*, Captain John Dixon, with a West Indies convoy got so far out of her reckoning in bad weather that she and forty of her charges drove ashore near Cape Mondego on the Portuguese coast. As late as November 1813 a most efficient officer, Captain John Cumby, was escorting a convoy of thirty-seven merchant ships loaded with salt cod from Newfoundland towards Portugal in support of military operations. Cumby, in the frigate *Hyperion*, had in support the sloop *Muros*. On the 20th the thirty-five vessels still with the *Hyperion* were scattered by bad weather which persisted until 1 December when only thirteen remained in company. Ordering the *Muros* to take onwards the four sail bound for Lisbon, Cumby headed for Oporto with the rest, six of which were to be discharged in that port but the masters, having sufficient experience to doubt the bar could be crossed with the heavy swell then running, advised Cumby to haul for Coruña, only to be hit by another gale. When it abated on the 6th the *Hyperion* was alone. Shortly afterwards Cumby fell in with an outbound convoy whose escorting frigate, the *Iris*, had with her only two dozen of the 200 that had left St Helen's Road with her Such were the consequences of keeping the sea all year round.

While these difficulties were serious, losses in convoy were, as we have already noted, trifling and the maritime supply train was sustained to the complete satisfaction of the Commander-in-Chief in the Peninsula: 'If anyone wishes to know the history of this war,' Wellington afterwards stated, 'I will tell them that it is our maritime superiority gives me the power of maintaining my army while the enemy are unable to do so.'

Throughout the long conflict the state had had recourse to private ships for its own strategic purposes. There was only a finite supply of obsolete men-of-war no longer fitted to lie in the line of battle or be cut down into heavy frigates which could be turned into transports. These, commanded by ageing lieutenants and armed *en flûte*, supplied the fleet with victuallers, storeships and transports, upon occasion serving the state itself as in resupplying Botany Bay. However, military enterprises such as Christian's ill-fated expedition to the West Indies, Gambier's descent on Copenhagen, the evacuation of Sir John Moore's army from Coruña, the Grand Expedition against the Schelde, or the supply of Wellington's forces in the Peninsula required many, many ships. These were all taken up from trade, placed under the direction of the Transport Board and allocated to their tasks. It was easy money for the ship-owner whose investment was better looked after by escorting naval forces than in a trade convoy. Unfortunately to some extent these Government charters became the refuge of the less able and enterprising mercantile officers, many of whom were of advanced age and deliberately placed in such relatively safe vessels by their owners. These craft became store-ships, victualling tenders to the squadrons on blockade duty and military troop-transports, in which latter rôle they bore identifying numbers.[50]

There was, however, one way in which merchant ships assumed their old traditional function as men-of-war, albeit auxiliary to the main units of the fleet, and in which they were not commanded by commissioned officers but retained their own masters and mates who were, in contrast to privateers, subject to naval direction. This was as 'armed-ships', a rather equivocal title prefiguring the armed merchant cruiser of the twentieth century. The armed-ship was invariably a well-appointed vessel that bore a Letter-of-Marque and had been selected for her task. There were not many of them and they were usually used for trade protection, to beef up a convoy escort, following the practice noted in earlier wars where a naval officer in charge of a convoy would appoint select masters as 'whippers-in', whom he thought capable of supporting him if confronted by an enemy. Such vessels could carry cargo, or be ballasted if directed to cruise independently as happened upon occasion. One such was the *Swallow* of Liverpool which had been issued with a Letter-of-Marque-and-General-Reprisal against the French dated 12 July 1796. The *Swallow* was owned in Liverpool by Thomas Twenlow, Samuel McDowall, Peter and Iver McIver and her commander, Captain John McIver. She was brig-rigged, of 256-tons burthen and mounted eighteen 6-pounder carriage guns, no swivels and bore a crew of thirty-six, of which one third were permitted to be landsmen; a light armament and complement in the circumstances. In January 1797 a new Letter-of-Marque was issued against Spanish interests in which her armament has been increased considerably to a total of twenty carriage guns, some of 6-pound and some of 12-pound weight-of-shot, a brace of cohorns with swivel guns and a crew of eighty officers and men. In December of the same year she was hired as an armed-ship and received direction from – significantly – William Huskisson, the President of the Board of Trade who directed Captain McIver to place himself under the orders of the officer commanding the escort to a West India-bound convoy. On arrival at St Domingue, McIver was to obey the orders of 'the Officer commanding His Majesty's Troops there...'

This, it will be recalled, was a sensitive time for British arms in St Domingue and the *Swallow*, on arrival, was required to cruise in the Bight of Léogane and keep it clear of enemy shipping. Here McIver took 'a large brig and schooner, laden in America, with French property on board, and saved the *Fame* of Liverpool', sending his prizes in to Port-au-Prince.[51]

Nor was the Royal Navy in this, its era of greatness, able to carry out its duties without not merely the manpower it poached from the merchant service, a fact of which we have become all too familiar, but also its technical experts. As master of the *Thetis*, then anchored in The Downs and awaiting convoy to the westwards, Captain Samuel Kelly went aboard the escorting man-of-war, the *Hawk* of 20 guns. He was:

introduced to the captain (an uncommon circumstance). After he had asked me a few questions, he left me on deck to order my instructions. The sailing-master having a little recollection of old times when he was in the Merchant Service was attracted towards me and invited me to the gun-room for refreshment. One of these sea animals from the Merchant Service is required for every serviceable ship in the Navy, and his responsibility is very great, as there are few transactions in the ship but what he has something to do in. The ship's carcass, clothing, accoutrements, provisions and seamen are under his immediate care. He berths the ship in the harbour, navigates her at sea and directs all her movements in battle. After all [this], he is only considered as a Warrant Officer, and is often looked on with disdain and contempt by his superiors who are honoured by commissions.[52]

Kelly's 'uncommon circumstance' of meeting the *Hawk's* captain was a measure of the social gulf that yawned betwixt the two sea-services. Whereas the relative distinction made among 'the quality' between a naval post-captain and an East India commander might be blurred, resolved by the difference between the prize-money made by the one and the profitability of his private ventures by the other, no such equivocation existed with the ship-masters of more run-of-the-mill merchant ships. Such men were regarded by naval captains as co-equal with own ships' sailing-masters, from whom they were recruited and such as Kelly had met aboard the *Hawk*. Despite their value to the Royal Navy, these experienced men were standing warrant officers and it was to be 1805 before an Admiralty order gave them status to mess in the ward-rooms of HM Ships with the commissioned lieutenants. Summing up the situation, which would – in only slightly modified form – dog the relationship of the Royal and Merchant Navies of Great Britain for its entire history, Kelly wrote: 'I knew it was customary for Naval officers to treat masters of merchant [ships] with hauteur and contempt…' Given the origins of the Royal Navy, this was an unfortunate irony.

Musing on his submission to Captain Frederick Maitland aboard HMS *Bellerophon* after the disaster of Waterloo, Napoleon said that 'If it had not been for you English I should have been Emperor of the east; but wherever there is water to float a ship, we are sure to find you in our way'. He specifically referred to men-of-war, but behind them lay a vast invisible merchant fleet without which Great Britain would not have had the resources to out-do the French.

But what of the farther regions of the world, the northern and southern extremities of the Western Ocean, the high latitudes lying on the navigable limits of the polar seas; how had the titanic struggle affected British shipping in such remote waters?

The so-called Greenlanders went north every year, in pursuit of their quarry, and even before the war the Greenland whaling ships were targeted by the navy as a source of seamen. That veteran of the Polar Seas, HM Sloop *Racehorse*, was stationed in the Humber to collect men, picking up 400 at the conclusion of the 1790 season as the whalers came home, in order to man the fleet in anticipation of war with Spain. Shortly after the declaration of war with France in 1793 the whalers were obliged to venture north well-armed and manned, for it was known that the French had sent six frigates to cruise between Newfoundland and Spitsbergen. Ironically the first victim to fall to the French was a South Seas whaler, the *Chaser* of London, whose master, having been warned of the outbreak of hostilities, had taken a northerly route on his way home. The *Chaser* was taken by an 18-gun corsair off the Orkneys on 19 July, but was soon afterwards retaken by her second mate and three boys who had been left on board. Similar losses and recaptures occurred to the Hull whaler *Raith* and the *Dundee* of Dundee before the privateers were caught by a British cruiser. The French frigates were a different matter, taking three dozen Dutch whalers on the Spitsbergen ground and one British ship, the *Cave* of Hull. Other casualties followed: the *Tuscan*, Captain Dring, was taken, as was the *Ann*, Captain Greathead, and as time passed there were others.

The whalers' private 'war' with the Royal Navy went on too. The men of the outward-bound *Blenheim*, when approached by boats in search of men from the Humber guard-ships *Nonsuch* and *Redoubt*, locked up their ships' officers, fought off the press-gang and killed two of them. They then grounded the *Blenheim* within the Spurn Head and disappeared ashore. Rewards offered for their recapture proved fruitless but on 13 March 1801 Captain Mitchinson of the *Blenheim* was brought before York Assizes charged with the death of the two seamen from HMS *Nonsuch*. The case aroused great interest among the whaling fraternity and the court was crowded as the prosecution contended that Mitchinson had been restrained for purposes of deception. In contradiction the defence witnesses attested that the master had been physically over-powered, hand-cuffed and locked in his cabin, evidence that persuaded the jury to return a verdict of 'Not Guilty' amid scenes of jubilation. The *Blenheim* afterwards sailed for the Arctic.

Nothing stopped the navy's want of men, however, and Kearsley's laden and homeward *Henrietta* was stopped off the Orkneys on 22 July 1804, thirteen men were pressed out of her by HM Cutter *Prince of Wales*. Despite the mutual hostility between the whalers and the navy, the latter were obliged to escort them clear of home waters and naval cruisers kept up a relentless war against enemy privateers. The ending of the brief Peace of Amiens in May 1803 caught the whalers napping when war resumed. The ships were dispersed in the Arctic, ignorant of the turn events had taken and the Hull merchants fitted out a privateer, the *Minerva*, to sail north to meet, warn and protect the home-coming vessels. Later she took the Dutchman *Jonge Ary* off the Humber. Men-of-war were also sent north but the season had been disappointing, with bad weather and a paucity of whales.

The ascendancy of British whalers in the Arctic now made oil an export and, on the conclusion of their northern voyages, many whalers made commercial voyages into the Baltic before the ice formed in that sea, while others were taken out of whaling altogether and put into the Archangel trade. Such was the Admiralty's concern over the numbers of privateers seeking to prey on British shipping in the North Sea that a number of the stoutly fitted Hull ships were taken up as armed-vessels and used for trade protection. However, in 1805 the *John* and *Enterprise*, with the *Centurion* of Bridlington, were captured off Flamborough Head by corsairs, and on 8 January the *Gipsy* of Sunderland was seized inside the Spurn Head by a *chasse marée* from Dunkerque. On the 12th, two Leith smacks running south for London with mail and passengers were attacked off Flamborough Head by a privateering brig, *La Vengeur*, which was beaten off.

The approaches to the Humber proved a favourite cruising ground for enemy privateers but it was from the Arctic that rumours of numerous sightings of enemy frigates began to percolate south as the laden whalers arrived home at the end of the 1806 season. In due course the news was confirmed: a squadron of French frigates led by Commodore Armand Leduc in the 40-gun *Revanche* and accompanied by *La Guerrière*, 40 guns, Capitaine Paul Hubert, *Syrène*, 36, Capitaine Alexandre Lambert, and the 16-gun brig-corvette *Néarque* had left L'Orient on 28 March to cruise in search of British and Russian whalers. Leduc had himself been a-whaling and brought his expertise to the chase, but soon after leaving port he lost the *Néarque* to HM Frigate *Niobe*, Captain John Loring, off Île de Groix.

Far to the north, the pack had drifted south, exposing open water farther to the northwards but creating extensive fog-banks to the south-west of Spitsbergen and driving most of the whalers southwards. Leduc sighted Spitsbergen on 12 June but then in dense fog *La Guerrière* became detached. Leduc now discovered the whaling fleet and, hoisting Swedish colours, bore down and seized a number of prizes which he burned. Meanwhile *La Guerrière* came upon the London whaler *Dingwall* on 21 June which Hubert set on fire three days later. On the 30th he took the *Simes* of Leith, towing her for twelve days while she was plundered, before burning her too. Next *La Guerrière* took the *Boyne* of Yarmouth, Captain Read, on her voyage to Archangel; Hubert set her on fire before discharging his prisoners into a Danish ship. He then destroyed a number of other British whalers, including the *William* of Greenock, but by now Hubert's crew were in a bad way with thee dozen officers and men affected by scurvy.

By this time the petitions of the ship-owners had prompted the Admiralty to order a frigate squadron into northern waters. It consisted of the 38-gun *Blanche*, Captain Thomas Lavie, the 36-gun *Phoebe*, Captain James Oswald, and the *Thames* of 32 guns under Captain Bridges Taylor. Oswald's and Taylor's ships were lying in Leith Roads and without waiting for Lavie, who was coming up from The Downs, they hurried north, heading for Lerwick. Here they met the crews of the burnt whalers landed from the Danish ship and learned that a single frigate, *La Guerrière*, was not far away. Unwilling to tarry for Lavie, they went in search of her. Lavie arrived three days later and picked up the same intelligence. Judging the Faeroes a probable cruising ground at this time of the year when the first whalers would be homeward-bound he made sail north. On the late afternoon of 18 July, *Blanche*'s lookouts reported a strange sail. It was *La Guerrière*. Hubert had been obliged to make for the Faeroes to obtain water but on seeing the approaching man-of-war he endeavoured to escape. *La Guerrière*'s hull was foul and at about two the next morning *Blanche* overhauled her and, after a brief action, Lavie's gunners shot away *La Guerrière*'s mizzen topmast, receiving little damage from Hubert's enfeebled crew, and Hubert stuck his colours.[53]

Leduc's other cruisers, *Revanche* and *Syrène*, had meanwhile made for Cape Farewell hoping to pick up the whalers from the Davis Strait. Moving towards Iceland they took the *Ruth*, a merchantman bound for Newfoundland; a Russian vessel; the *Hope* of Gravesend and the *Rose* of Peterhead before landing for water on 13 July. A few days later they were chased by *Phoebe* and *Thames* but escaped by separating. On the 18th Lambert in *Syrène* took and burned the *Molly* and on the 23rd, having rejoined Leduc, the two watched the Greenock privateer *Minerva* – not to be confused with the Hull vessel bearing the same name – bear down upon them. The misty weather deceived the commander of the *Minerva* into thinking the two French frigates to be Prussian whalers, only to fall into Leduc's hands. Leaving Iceland on the 27th, Leduc transferred all his prisoners into the *Rose* and *Hope*. Captain Sadler of the *Molly*, arriving in Hull aboard the *Rose* on 18 August reported the condition of the French crews as poor and, as a consequence the Admiralty ordered three more frigates out in search of Leduc, for there remained several whalers unaccounted for.[54] There was a sighting off Malin Head on 28 August and then Leduc's ships were seen and reported cruising off Cape Clear, but on 14 September he could keep the seas no longer and headed for home.

At the beginning of October the ship *Eddystone* arrived at Plymouth with the final intelligence of Leduc. The *Eddystone* had been taken off Newfoundland by *Revanche* and *Syrène* and on reaching home her chief mate swore an affidavit that the transfer of men and plunder out of his ship had been accomplished in whale-boats bearing the name of one of the missing Hull whalers, the *Blenheim*. Both she and the *Holderness* had been seized in mid-ocean, making a total of three Hull whalers taken by Leduc on a cruise in which he had lost two of his squadron but taken and destroyed twenty-nine British whalers and merchantmen. The chief achievement of the *Thames* and *Phoebe* was to remove seamen from several whalers, taking eight men out of the *Lottery* of Hull and substituting them with thirteen foreign seamen out of a Prussian sealing brig.

The following years were good for the fishery which was increasingly moving into the Davis Strait. Most years the whalers left for the whaling-grounds in convoy, Scoresby in *Resolution* being furnished with a Letter-of-Marque and acting as commodore. Although enemy privateers continued to plague the east coast of England, the navy was increasingly active against them, employing numerous small vessels and some numbers were captured. The Admiralty also sent a sloop-of-war north to escort the homecoming ships in the North Sea, but Captain Mitchinson, now in command of the *Samuel*, had his crew captured off Norway. However, by rising against their Danish captors, Mitchinson and his men secure their freedom and made their way home by way of Göteborg.

In 1810 the frigates *Belvedere* and *Nemesis* cruised in northern waters to protect the fishery and other minor men-of-war captured Prussian and Dutch whalers and sealers. In 1811 and 1812 attempts by the remnants of the Danish fleet in Norwegian waters, assisted by privateers, were made against the British whale-fishery, but these were largely frustrated by the navy. However, in 1812, the Aberdeen whaler *Elbe* beat off a Danish cutter-privateer which attacked her off the Firth of Forth and the *Latona*, also of Aberdeen, was attacked when outward-bound. The *Latona* fought her attacker for forty minutes until the London whaler *Experiment* came up and joined-in, driving the Dane off.

In 1813 a more serious threat arose from the United States frigate *President* which was reported having taken victuals at North Bergen. Commodore John Rogers was said to have orders to attack the whale-fishery and the Archangel trade. The *President* was joined in the latter by the privateers *Rattlesnake*, Captain Maffit, a 16-gun brig, and the schooner *Scourge*, Captain Nicol, which 'took a severe toll' of it. The *President* seized three ships, the last of which, the whaler *Eliza Swan*, he captured on 24 July, ransoming her for £5,000 and using her to take the three crews off his hands, for Rogers was wary of expending provisions. His frigate was also being hunted by a large number of British men-of-war, but that did not save the whaler *Linn*, of Liverpool, captured by Rogers on 2 August, but afterwards released as her large crew was too burdensome to maintain. In the meanwhile the two privateers, *Rattlesnake* and *Scourge*, were at Hammerfest, landing 180 seamen from their numerous prizes taken in the Barents and Norwegian Seas. They had captured more than twenty prizes, including the Hull-registered *Hope*, Captain Kirkus, which had put up a stout resistance off the North Cape. Maffit, it was rumoured, had sold his prizes for over a million dollars in Norway.

By the following year of 1814 only the *Scourge* remained, command of her having devolved upon her chief mate, now Captain J.R. Perry. On 1 April off Cape Wrath, Perry took the ships *Symmetry* and *Winchester*, and the brig *Union* as the three Liverpool vessels emerged from The Minch. Shortly afterwards the *Scourge* encountered the London whaler *King George* which was running into Stromness in Orkney to repair a leak. Perry engaged the whaler, Captain Gordon receiving ten broadsides before a naval sloop emerged from the shelter of the islands and gave chase. Perry escaped and after a hard passage in which he lost several spars and one man overboard he arrived off Cape Cod after an absence of a year and with a tally of twenty-seven British merchantmen to his name. The appearance of American ships in northern waters prompted the Admiralty to allocate more cruisers to the fisheries; HM Frigates *Sybille* and *Caroline* were sent to cruise off Spitsbergen, and the 74-gun *Victorious* was detached from St John's, Nova Scotia to cover the Davis Strait. She was almost lost herself after striking a rock off Disco but, after fothering a sail over the leak, she was brought safely home. By the time the whalers went north again in 1815 the Great War was over.

The number of British whalers venturing north during the wars of 1793–1815 was far fewer than at an earlier period, but the quality of the ships and the quantity of their catches rendered the trade vastly more profitable, the latter rising threefold. In 1811 Captain Kearsley returned to Whitby with 230 tuns of whale blubber, the *Resolution*'s boats having taken twenty-eight whales in a catch considered by a contemporary to be 'the largest quantity ever imported into Whitby in any one ship and probably the greatest quantity ever brought from Greenland by any ship of a like burden'.

The *Resolution* of Whitby was a lucky ship; she had been purpose-built at a cost of £7,791 by Fishburn and Broderick and had made her first voyage north in 1803 under William Scoresby, senior. Scoresby was a highly professional master-mariner who had gone to sea on a voyage to St Petersburg in 1780 after studying navigation on his own initiative. He then shipped in a transport and was briefly captured by the Spanish on a voyage to Gibraltar, after which he began whaling, rapidly rising to harpooner and in 1791 he was appointed master of the *Henrietta*. His first voyage in her was a disaster; he was faced with a mutiny which he suppressed by brute force and personality and he brought the *Henrietta* home 'clean'. However, he retained the confidence of his owners and, having chosen his own mates, his next voyage began the

William Scoresby, Junior, 1789–1857, son of an equally distinguished father of the same name under whom he served, reaching an extreme northerly latitude in 1806 in the whaler *Resolution*. Afterwards Scoresby studied at Edinburgh, served briefly in the Royal Navy and commanded his own whalers. A scientific sailor, Scoresby became a Fellow of the Royal Society and Anglican Divine. (© Courtesy of Whitby Museum)

successful phase of his career. In 1798 he transferred to the *Dundee* of London, in which he made five voyages and fitted her with his own invention, the crow's nest, returning to Whitby ships with his appointment to the *Resolution* in 1803 in which he had a share of eight sixty-fourths and in which his eldest son, also William, was an indentured apprentice. The younger Scoresby possessed an intellect as keen as his father's and an ability to match. Once out of his 'time' he rose rapidly and in 1806 at the age of 17 was appointed the *Resolution*'s chief officer. Aware that the grounds were becoming over-fished and the ice had moved south, Scoresby senior pushed further north, finding the sea ice-free. The *Resolution* ascended to a Latitude of 81° 30' North in a longitude of 19° West that summer of 1806, her captain quite oblivious to the fact that far away to the southward, Leduc's frigates were loose among the pack-ice, or that on her return with her holds full of blubber, the *Resolution* passed the Faeroes only a day after the capture of *La Guerrière*.

At the conclusion of this voyage the younger Scoresby took part in the expedition against Copenhagen in 1807 in which he appears to have commanded one of the hurriedly constructed gun-boats employed against the Danes. That winter and the following year he attended Edinburgh University where he studied philosophy and chemistry, awakening a powerful scientific interest. On completion of his studies Scoresby Junior was approaching his majority and on his twenty-first birthday in 1810 his father handed him command of the *Resolution*. With his future secured the young William married Mary Lockwood, the daughter of a Whitby ship-broker, and began his own career as a whaling master. For his own part, the elder Scoresby now took over the *John* of Greenock, commanding her successfully until 1817 when, for the following season, he entered the *Fame* of Hull.

His son commanded the *Resolution* until the end of the 1812 season. Scoresby Junior had become deeply interested in the natural sciences and had acquired a religious conviction, so-much-so that he refused to lower his boats after whales on Sundays – often to the annoyance of his crew who were obliged to attend divine service while whales spouted temptingly in the vicinity – but who was nevertheless extremely successful. In the ten years she was under the two Scoresbys' command the *Resolution*'s people slew '249 whales, yielding 2,034 tuns of oil'. In 1813 William Junior took command of the ship-rigged *Esk*, purpose-built at Whitby by Fishburn and Broderick at the enormous cost of £14,000. Measuring 354-tons, the *Esk* bore a complement of forty men and carried seven whaleboats, one of which was spare. Great difficulty was experienced in getting her to sea owing to her draught and she was the last of the Whitby ships to leave on Thursday 18 March 1813, following the *Aimwell, Henrietta, William and Ann, Lively, Resolution* and *Volunteer*. Scoresby had had to use two lighters as 'camels,' half filled, then lashed either side of the *Esk* and pumped out to lift her bodily over the shallows. It proved worthwhile, for 1813 was a good year for all the Whitby fleet, Scoresby's catch being valued at over £10,800.

In 1816 the *Esk* was beset by ice and suffered considerable damage. By superb seamanship William saved his ship, heaving her down on a floe to get at her damaged planking and repairing her with help from men from six other whalers. By now Scoresby's interests had widened and he was sending in observations about natural phenomena and studying magnetism, a consequence of which was his election to the Royal Society of Edinburgh in 1819. The following year he published *An Account of the Arctic Regions with a History and Description of the Northern Whale-Fishery* after which he superintended the fitting out of the *Baffin* at Liverpool, which has received an earlier mention. The ship was built at a cost of £9,500 and in the season of 1822 in company with his father in the *Fame* and a relative, Captain Jackson, in the *Mercury*, the three ships lay west of Spitsbergen. It was to be an extraordinary voyage. In addition to catching whales and studying magnetism, Scoresby found the coast of what was called 'Lost' Greenland on account of the surrounding ice-fields which was, this year, unusually ice-free. He also found his charts woefully inadequate and accordingly combined his fishery with carrying out an extensive survey of the coast, naming a deep indentation Scoresby Sound, after his father.

On his return home, however, Scoresby learned of his wife's death and consequently gave up the sea. In 1823 he published his *Journal of a Voyage to the Northern Whale-Fishery*, before going up to Cambridge where he studied divinity prior to taking Holy Orders. This was the same year that his father was anchored in Stromness in the early summer of 1823 when the *Fame* caught fire. Following his daughter-in-law's untimely death, the old man took this as an omen and he retired from the sea to settle at Whitby where he died six years later. He had made thirty voyages as master between 1793 and 1823, during which he is supposed to have made a profit of £90,000 shared between himself and his owners.

In 1824 the younger William was elected a Fellow of the Royal Society and although he served for some years as a parish priest, he soon gave it up for an intellectual life. He was to marry twice more, to travel extensively, particularly in connection with his researches into magnetism, and to publish scientific and religious papers. In 1856 he took passage to Australia and back aboard the ill-fated *Royal Charter* on her maiden voyage, and he was to die at Torquay in the March following.[55]

The Scoresbys were not exceptional, though their expertise was based on scientific observation and they were the doyens of their craft. They could be matched in skill by other, rougher men of equal dynastic tendency. Such were the Sadlers of Hull, the senior of which, Captain Peter Sadler, commanded the *Manchester*, owned by Stainforth & Foord, for twenty-five Arctic voyages and died at sea in his ship in July 1794. His two sons, Angus and Joseph, rose to command whalers, Angus first commanding the *Molly* in which he made seven voyages between 1796 and 1802, catching 126 whales; and the *Aurora* in which between 1804 and 1817 he took 289. Angus was believed by his crews to possess mysterious powers, not least because a whale followed the *Aurora* on her homeward voyage when every cask was full. Guyed by the great fish, Angus ordered the boats away, the whale was caught and its blubber stored in the whaleboats. His brother Joseph, a less colourful and charismatic figure, commanded the *Gilder* and the *Jane* for Gilder & Co.[56]

The complexities of ship-owning ensured that other families were involved with whaling, not least the Grays of Peterhead who have the distinction of being longest associated with the fishery. The senior of this dynasty, Captain David Gray, assumed command of the *Perseverance* in 1811. Despite these individual successes, during the war the fishery generally suffered from over-capitalisation, the expense of fitting out expeditions and the uncertain and slow recovery of costs. Nevertheless, other ports besides Whitby, Dundee, Peterhead, Hull, London and Liverpool sent whalers north at this period, including Leith, Dundee, Montrose, Aberdeen, King's Lynn and Berwick-on-Tweed.

The Tyne fleet, reduced in the first years of war to one ship, the old *John and Margaret*, began a slow revival, peaking at a dozen ships in 1803 but thereafter dropping to eight venturing northwards every year. So much depended upon the skill and experience of the master; when Jacob Jameson of the *John and Margaret* died his replacement in 1804, Ralph Crawford secured only two whales and heavy fiscal losses ensued. Even though the economy of the day was inflating thanks to the war, losses could be crippling and the Hurry Brothers, owners of the *John and Margaret*, went bankrupt. Their fleet was sold, the *John and Margaret*, *Norfolk* and *Howe* remaining in Tyneside ownership, the *Prescott* going to William Lee & Co. of Hull. It was this port that was to increasingly dominate the Arctic whale fishery, though an owning-master, like James Boswell of Newcastle who bought his ship *Euretta* in 1804 when she was already twenty-nine years old, made a success of her. Scoresby calculated that the *Resolution* earned an average of £6,810 per season; Boswell's *Euretta* made £6,376.

The Southern Fishery fared better until the end of the war, when it attracted the attention of the United States Navy. Chief among the companies whose ships headed south was that of Enderby & Co. of London. In 1808 their whalers *Saxon* and *Otter* rediscovered Bouvet Island but no landing was possible and they, like other ships in the fishery, took what whales they could and raided the seal colonies in the Falklands and South Georgia.[57] Others doubled the Horn in search of the Sperm Whale and exploited the waters about the Galapagos as is detailed in the following chapter.

Throughout this long struggle the Post Office packets had criss-crossed the ocean facilitating the intercourse of the nation with its trading partners. The mails consisted of official, private and commercial correspondence and these broad categories included bills of exchange, letters of credit, bank drafts and all those instruments necessary to commerce. Besides the mails, specie and passengers were also carried and while diplomatic and military dispatches of the first order were usually borne in a man-of-war, Post Office packets frequently conveyed duplicate documents and other papers in addition to personnel of importance to the state and to the war. Packet-commanders were encouraged to observe and report on matters of commerce and politics, as mentioned in the foregoing and they were often men of local status and substance.

There were three dozen ship- or brig-rigged packets employed in the overseas mail runs, most of 170-tons burthen and built to a standard design by Marmaduke Stalkaart, with four larger packets retained for the service to

Brazil. After the surrender of the *Despatch* to a corsair at the beginning of the war all packets were armed, but those on the ocean routes which were based at Falmouth had always borne a small armament of specially cast 9-pounder brass 'Post Office' cannon. These packets were manned by twenty-eight men – thirty-six in the larger Brazil packets – all of whom held press exemptions and they were all privately owned and commanded. Superintended by a Post Office Agent resident in Falmouth, the packets were engaged on seven-year charters by the Post-Master General whose office bore all losses. The remote distance from London and laxity in their supervision led to their commanders earning a reputation for absenteeism, a matter not greatly troubling the distant Inspector of Packets until – as we shall shortly observe – he grew anxious on his own account.

The services were regular: weekly to Lisbon; monthly to the West Indies and North America; packets left for Gibraltar and the naval squadron off Cadiz every third week in the month and this service was extended to Malta in 1800, with a monthly service to Madeira and Rio de Janeiro. A round voyage to Lisbon took four weeks and the trip to Rio de Janeiro and back occupied four and a half months, consequently postal rates were high.

Besides the Falmouth packets, there were other services: six 70-ton schooners were engaged on the Harwich to Cuxhaven, Helvoetsluis and later Helgoland runs, and from Harwich a twice-weekly departure served Göteburg.[58] Smaller packets shuttled between Dover and Calais or Ostend. Both the Harwich and Dover services were interrupted by war and the Harwich packets were transferred to Great Yarmouth while the Dover service was suspended. A number of cutters ran between Weymouth and the Channel Islands, with others – often ship-rigged – plying between Liverpool and Dublin; to Ireland from Port Patrick, Holyhead and Milford Haven; from Liverpool to Glasgow, and between Whitehaven and the Isle of Man or across to Donaghadee. The character of these more parochial services was rather different, less troublesome and more punctiliously overseen than that of the Falmouth packets.

The dangers run in wartime by the Falmouth packets were considerable. Their commanders were not only obliged to sail the instant the mails were on board, irrespective of the weather, but to run rather than fight when being chased. However, the search for speed by privateersmen produced some fast sailing vessels and Stalkaart's traditional design was not always capable of out-running pursuit. If attacked and committed to defending the integrity of the mails, a packet-commander was obliged to jettison them, but the fact that such vessels, which flew a distinctive defaced red ensign and pendant, were known to carry specie and bullion acted as a magnet to predators. Commanders entrusted with such valuable freight – from which, like naval officers, they made a personal bonus – were faced with a difficult decision, not least because of the small numbers in the complement of a packet and the large crews carried in privateers. Unsurprisingly there were some fiercely contested actions between Post Office packets and their would-be plunderers, not all of which ended in glory for the British.

Early in the war, on 1 December 1793, the *Antelope* had fought off an attack by the French corsair *Atalanta* in which her acting commander, Edward Curtis, was killed and her mate severely wounded. The defence of the vessel devolved upon the boatswain, John Pasco, who so furiously counter-attacked that he succeeded in seizing the Frenchman and carried her, a prize, into port. The action was rewarded by a sub-committee of Lloyd's called The Society for Encouraging the Capture of French Privateers, but the Post-Master General disparaged the capture on the grounds that Pasco – who perhaps might be forgiven in the heat of action and was not schooled in the responsibility – had neglected his primary duty of disengaging once the mails were safe. Pasco's success was followed by a series of disasters: the *Arab* was taken homeward-bound from Coruña by the French national frigate *L'Insurgente*; the *Princess Augusta* caught fire and burnt in the Tagus; the *Expedition* was chased and captured by a French frigate and taken into Brest; and the *King George*, Captain Yescombe, was overwhelmed. Having run from one French frigate squadron, Yescombe fell under the guns of another, 'whereupon he sank the mails and despatches and struck his colours', all of which entirely dislocated intercourse with Lisbon for a while. Also a victim to numbers was the *Antelope* herself which, in September 1794, was caught on her way to Halifax by thick fog on the Grand Banks. Here she found herself in the midst of a French squadron and her commanding owner, Captain William Kempthorne, was obliged to haul down his colours. Four days later the packet *Thyme* encountered the same squadron with identical result. The following year was little better, a further four Falmouth packets being taken by French corsairs 'in each case without a fight'.[59]

Three further packets were taken by the French in 1796, and one was seized in Coruña upon Spain's declaration of war, but the *King George* – which had been ransomed, though her captain had died of a fever – was successfully defended by her sailing-master, Bett, while the *Portland* was compelled to fight two actions at the end of that year. Leaving under the acting command of her sailing-master, Mr Nathaniel Taylor, the *Portland* was a month out from Falmouth on 1 October when, off Barbados, she beat off an unknown vessel. Sixteen days later, becalmed off Guadaloupe, she was approached by a schooner which was pulled out of a creek under sweeps. A light breeze sprang up and enabled Taylor to draw away but at daylight on the 18th the schooner came up, again under sweeps. Taylor sent his men to their quarters, hoisted his ensign and fired a gun. This was promptly answered as the French tricolour was hoisted 'surmounted – in strange companionship with the ensign of a great and honourable nation – by the bloody flag, which signified she would give no quarter in the coming fight'.

Enlisting the help of his passengers which consisted of four army officers, a military surgeon and five West India merchants, Taylor prepared to defend the *Portland*. Having lost one man in his first action, Taylor had forty-one men and boys to pitch against sixty-one who, in a surge of strenuous activity, brought the schooner rapidly alongside, running her jib-boom over the packet's deck. Taylor promptly lashed this and there followed a desperate hand-to-hand fight in which the French were slaughtered to the number of the British crew and in a frenzy of destruction after the death of Taylor which the passengers were unable to stem.

In the face of a dozen losses Taylor's action had little effect. In the City of London 'the voice of discontent was loud and menacing', no less than eighteen consignments of mail had been lost. 'The inconvenience was immense, and the merchants grew restive under it'. This anger was exacerbated by the grounding off Calais of the packet carrying the dispatches of Lord Malmesbury, just then fruitlessly attempting to negotiate peace. Despite the protests of the British Government and the claims of diplomatic privilege, the packet was seized and claimed as lawful prize. Moreover, among the intelligence garnered by the packet-men was the news that there were forty corsairs from Nantes alone cruising between the meridians of 20° and 30° West. Worse was to come, one of these privateers, *L'Actif*, took the *Princess Elizabeth* homeward with the West India mails of 28 February 1797, while three outward mail consignments to the Antilles were taken within weeks with the captures of the *Swallow* and *Sandwich*. The folly of sending out multiple shipments in the same vessel drew more opprobrium upon the head of the Post-Master General, while the numbers and huge complements of the corsairs rang further alarm bells – all of which added to the anger of the merchants which frequently boiled over into strong remonstrance to Government as we saw earlier. The Post-Master General's defence that the packet crews were insufficient and that the service already ran at a loss of £12,000 per annum – excluding the liabilities for captured packets then amounting to £34,000 – only increased the ire of the merchants, who naturally transferred their attention to other ministers whose responsibilities included the protection of merchant shipping and for whose services they were paying hitherto unprecedented levels of tax. In short the impasse over the mails was the entire mercantile war at sea in miniature, not least because there was now an abatement in losses and the country was faced with greater crises in the mutinies of the Royal Navy at Spithead and the Nore. The aftermath of readjusting the navy's pay and conditions enabled the matter to be dropped.

It was June when the *Grantham* was taken off Barbados, though her crew were soon afterwards liberated by HM Frigate *Tamar*, but all this was obscured amid the turmoil of a fleet mutiny. Far from spreading the mails, the shortage of packets was worsening the situation, the service was disrupted and further chaos was caused by the rapid taking of the outward-bound *Prince Edward* in December and of the *Prince Earnest* and the gallant *Portland*, both homeward. All had been carrying the West India mails and, in the words of Arthur Norway: 'This was more than the merchants could bear… The inconvenience was mounting to a intolerable pitch' and the merchants sought another meeting during the progress of which came the news that the *Roebuck*, homeward, and the *Swallow* outward for the Leeward Islands had both been captured by the Nantes corsair *La Liberale* armed with eighteen 18-pounder guns and over 200 men. It was clear, the merchants argued, that the packets were too slow and that their armament was too light. Their request for a naval cutter to be lent to supplement the packets was granted but she too was shortly afterwards captured, followed by the seizures of the *Prince of Wales*, heading for Jamaica, and the *Prince Adolphus*, on her way to Lisbon.

While Captain Boulderson and most of his crew were taken out of the *Prince Adolphus*, the surgeon named Bullock was left with four men and the prize-crew. Bullock persuaded the prize-master to carry the packet into Lisbon on a promise of £4,000 ransom, but the Post Office agent, Mr Gonne, refused to countenance the transaction on the grounds that it was, by a recent Act of Parliament, a capital offence to treasonably remit money to the enemy. Fortunately for Bullock the matter was referred to London where a decision was given in favour of modifying the act and paying the French.

It seemed that these disasters might have ended on 22 June 1798 when the Halifax-bound *Princess Royal* was chased by a brig *L'Aventurier* of Bordeaux. Captain Skinner cleared his ship for action but light winds drew the day out and the brig got out her sweeps in order to catch the *Princess Royal*, coming up with her that evening. On deck, in addition to her crew, the passengers mustered under General Murray. A few broadsides were exchange, whereupon the corsair lay off until three the next morning when she suddenly swept up astern, being met with discharges from the *Princess Royal*'s stern chasers. One of these destroyed its carriage axle, an accident that befell two more of Skinner's engaged broadside guns as the enemy came alongside, drastically reducing the packet's fire-power but enabling the remaining guns to be plied to deadly effect and for Murray and his fellow passengers to keep up a hail of musketry. Skinner manoeuvred the *Princess Royal* so as to prevent the larger corsair from getting close enough to board, continuing his defence for two hours, long enough to take a toll of their assailants until at dawn *L'Aventurier* sheered off. Unfortunately the news of this gallant action was off-set by the accompanying intelligence that the *Duke of York* had submitted on her way out to Jamaica and in April 1799, the *Chesterfield* and then in July the *Carteret* were also captured.

The impact of these losses, particularly on the West India trade, was complex. There were insufficient packets to keep up the service, even though substitutes had been hurriedly chartered by the Post Officer agents. Lord Auckland was now appointed joint Post-Master General[60] and with an able Secretary in the person of Francis Freeling, carried out a reform of the service. However, before any remedies could be applied, that November the *Lady Harriet* was taken on her way to Lisbon and the *Halifax* homeward from the Leeward Islands succumbed a few days later. By now the precaution of sending duplicate, and even triplicate, copies of despatches was well-established, but all those sent from the Leewards were lost in the *Westmoreland* when she was captured on 7 December. Ironically the triplicates disappeared when ditched from the *Adelphi* on the 22nd when she fell foul of *Le Grand Buonaparte* of 22 guns and 200 men.

News of more captures came in: Captain Skinner and the *Princess Royal*, having escaped *L'Aventurier*, were taken on 27 February; ten days later the ransomed *Carteret* was captured a second time by the formidable, 30-gun corsair *Bellona* and on 12 March the *Jane* was boarded 'after a sharp engagement'. Although she was recovered a few days later by a British cruiser, the mails were irrevocably doomed, as were those in the *Princess Charlotte*, lost on 4 May, those aboard the *Marquis of Kildare* taken on the 6th and those aboard the *Princess Amelia* captured on 11 May, all by French corsairs. To add further bitterness to the cup Auckland and Freeling were quaffing, a Spanish privateer took the *Duke of Clarence* a few months later, but by this time the two men were drawing some painful conclusions: it was not only the West India mail that was most affected – obvious in terms of a supportable *guerre de course* from the French perspective – but it was homeward packets that were mostly targeted. From this it could be reasonably deduced that the vulnerability of these vessels arose from proximity of enemy bases combined with the ready transfer of intelligence as to their schedules. But there was also the quirk that, with the exception of officers like the young Skinner in *Princess Royal*, only *Antelope* and *Portland* had offered resistance – at least successfully. Did the injunction not to lose the mails result in a commander giving-up once he had sunk his weighted mail-bags? If so it was counter-intuitive that British seamen would prefer a French gaol, for the opportunities for prisoner exchanges were uncertain and had not the handful of men left aboard the *Marquis of Kildare* risen upon their prize-crew and carried the reclaimed packet back into Falmouth? The two men began to smell several rats.

Others were finding the business stank. Colonial governors were instructed to send their duplicate and triplicate copies of correspondence *per favour* of the masters of well-armed merchantmen 'which appear to have a better chance of arrival than the regular Packets'. It was a sorry state of affairs. Auckland, for whom the Colonial Secretary's instruction was more surprise than embarrassment, discovered that packet-commanders were not subject to enquiry over their vessels' loss; they and their officers merely had to make a conventional sworn statement before a notary, known as a 'protest', and nothing remotely resembling the court-martial that sat to judge not merely the commander of a naval ship, but the conduct of the whole crew. It began to dawn on Auckland and Freeling that the case of a packet commander was entirely different and that this was due to the ownership of the packets themselves. If their vessels were not their own outright property, each commander had an interest in her or held his command under the direct patronage of the packet's owners. Moreover, upon receipt of the protest by the Inspector of Packets, the loss to the packet's owners was made good by the Post-Master General's office. Deeper digging by Freeling revealed that the method of compensation was modelled upon that pertaining in the loss of an ordinary merchant ship. This, the Inspector of Packets maintained, was the time-honoured system at Lloyd's because, in the final analysis, a packet was a private and chartered ship. But, Freeling realised, whereas a ship-master had to answer to owners and to underwriters whose closely-guarded pockets were touched by any loss and who would pursue any hint of perjury to the destruction of the perjuror, no such rigour was applied to the case of the packet-commander. Finally, whereas a merchant ship-master faced a long period of confinement of one sort or another in the case of being captured, packet-masters were almost invariably quickly exchanged.

There was also the vexing question of a packet's value to her captors. She was not supposed to carry cargo and what cargo she carried did not match the value of a regularly laden merchantman. Once the mails had been dumped, the only value lay in the vessel herself, and this was scarcely bait enough to tempt a privateer looking for profit. While a dislocation of the mails so severe as to disrupt trade was a laudable objective in time of war, it was not an objective attractive to a corsair, for no direct funds arose from it. Of course, if the packet carried specie, the situation was dramatically altered, but insofar as the letter of regulation was concerned, no cargo was carried. However, Freeling and Auckland discovered that cargo was carried quite openly in the Falmouth packets and had been since time immemorial. Furthermore, it was widely known officially that such cargoes were set down as 'provisions' and that officialdom recognised the practice to the extent that an instruction had been issued at Falmouth that the quantity of 'provisions' carried should not put a packet out of sailing trim. The few efforts made thus far to interrupt the traffic and apply the letter of the law had been met with both private and official indifference: the vested interests were Byzantine. Indeed to some extent, in the absence of a more secure system, trade itself – if only to the extent of comforting the traders – required the law to be flouted. And if this was true on the Lisbon service, it was the more so on that to the Antilles.

> The West India boats carried out cheese, potatoes, boots and shoes, and, curious addition to the list, fighting-cocks, for which there was a brisk demand. The Lisbon packets exported every kind of manufactured goods, often to the value of £4,000 on a single voyage. These were by no means the speculations of the captain or of the officers alone. The seamen traded, each on his own account. Every man had his own stowage space…and no one claimed to interfere… Sometimes the seaman's ventures consisted of goods entrusted to him by some merchant, to sell on commission… sometimes he had purchased them himself; for not a few of the seamen were capitalists on a small scale… The goods once sold in foreign ports, others were of course purchased there. Silks, wines, tobacco, numberless things which by a little ingenuity could be smuggled into Falmouth duty free…[where] a whole corps of female pedlars was in existence, locally named 'troachers', who trudged the country and hawked about the goods of Jamaica or New York from farm house to country mansion…To most it formed the a chief inducement to enter the service; for the wages were very low, and would not of themselves have attracted men away from the Revenue Service or the Royal Navy.

It had not escaped the notice of those interested in the mails – but not in the mailmen – that it was profitable to be captured and the packet-commanders were often rich enough to appoint and pay substitutes in order to themselves enjoy a higher standard of life than comparable ship-masters in their station. Under enquiry it emerged that an ingenious scam was being worked whereby insurance was claimed on goods sold at the end of the outward passage which were declared to have been lost to the enemy. The bills of exchange on the goods sold were sent home in other ships – those well-armed merchantmen – but this fiddle, whilst corrupt and dishonest, seemed scarcely sufficient to justify the risk of a French prison: the Inspector of Packets, when asked, declared the fraud impossible. Matters rumbled on and on, and were unresolved as the War of the French Revolution drew to its unsatisfactory close. Nevertheless, in June 1801, the homeward Lisbon packet *Earl Gower* was intercepted by the corsair *Télégraphe*, a cutter mounting 14 guns and carrying a crew of seventy men. Captain Deake defended his ship vigorously but, at the crucial moment, his men deserted the deck and the *Earl Gower* was taken, a circumstance that seemed motivated only by a desire for submission.

Matters came to a head after the outbreak of the Napoleonic War when another packet homeward from Lisbon fell in with a privateer on 18 September

1803. The wind was light, the sea slight and night was drawing on. The *Duke of York* was under an acting commander who evinced his indecision by consulting with his surgeon as to whether to defend the ship. The surgeon advised not to and, just before it grew dark to ensure there was no mistake, a boat was lowered and pulled over to their pursuer. At first the loss of the *Duke of York* was reported in the regular manner but Auckland had had enough. By his order a court was assembled at Falmouth, consisting of all available commanders under the presidency of the agent. Unfortunately, the court had no power to administer oaths, nor were its judges indifferent to the outcome, for the assembled gentlemen so phrased their questions as 'to shield the culprits as far as possible; and finally stultified themselves by finding that all the [*Duke of York's*] officers did everything possible to save the ship'. Auckland and Freeling were stumped. However, the Inspector of Packets who seems hitherto to have considered his post a sinecure and good only for mulcting, was sufficiently shaken by events as to institute enquiries of his own, and discovered the personal gains by individual members of the *Duke of York's* crew. The surgeon had made £250, a further £750 had been made by three members of the crew, with others admitting lesser sums. The Inspector also discovered that several of these men, including the surgeon, had been captured several times. The Inspector's report produced a damning indictment by Auckland upon the case of the *Duke of York* and although no further proceedings were undertaken, an implicit condemnation of the greater part of the thirty-two packets lost in previous years.

Besides this enquiry in 1800 a private complaint made direct to William Pitt had produced a clamp-down upon private trade in respect of the West India packets. These measures provoked an immediate and dissenting reaction, for they deprived the packet crews of income and the companies of several packets refused to sail until their pay was raised. This however proved insufficient compensation. As the war dragged on, worse was to come. Despite a simmering resentment which died down as the seamen stealthily resumed their private but illicit trade in a modified form, the conduct of the packets in the succeeding years began to change. Freeling's reforms provided for widows and orphans of masters, and levied mulcts on commanders shipping proxies. In return a rising generation of new commanders seemed imbued with a different spirit. The regulation to run rather than fight remained, but if an attack was inevitable, defiance not submission was looked for. One commander, aptly named John Bull and himself the son of a packet captain, fought a number of actions and became the doyen of his compeers, though the odds these men faced were staggering. These improvements took some time to manifest themselves, however, for hardly had the war resumed than on 30 July 1803 the *King George*, Lisbon for Falmouth under old Captain Yescombe, was taken by a corsair named *Le Reprisal*. The Falmouth men were outnumbered four-to-one and were carried by boarding, Yescombe being killed and the prize taken in to Vigo. Here some of her crew escaped in a hired Swedish vessel and afterwards fell in with the homeward packet *Auckland* into which they transferred. A second loss occurred when the *Grantham* foundered while anchored off Barbados, from an unknown and unexpected cause, though the mails were saved. This ship was entirely owned by her young commander, John Bull, who was hard-hit by the disaster, but he persuaded the island's merchants to petition the governor to allow him to charter a privateer then in the island and carry the mails home in her. This was approved, the *Caroline* set sail and shortly afterwards ran into a gale in which she leaked so badly that Bull was obliged to run her ashore, again saving the mails. He and his people now took passage in an armed merchantman, the *Thomas*, but in mid-Atlantic they ran into and fought a French national corvette. Happily they shot away her mizzenmast and escaped and in so doing established Bull's reputation, for the mails, though delayed, arrived safely.

Back home Bull was soon in command of a new packet, the brig *Duke of Marlborough* and in April 1804 she was chased by a strange sail when 75 miles east of Barbados. Bull ran until the distance closed and in mid-afternoon an engagement commenced. The day wore on, the enemy had a score of marksmen in her tops and Bull himself was picked off, taking a bullet through both cheeks. Meanwhile the broadside guns, five to three in favour of the enemy, shot away the *Duke of Marlborough*'s rigging until her opponent, the *Général Erneuf*, ran alongside and Bull was obliged to order the mails overboard, the private signals torn up and his colours struck. They were carried into Guadaloupe where the *Duke of Marlborough* was converted into a corsair. The *Général Erneuf* engaged another packet a few months later in which Captain Patterson and the men of the *Eliza* drove her off, but in the May following Captain Mudge, having fought for two hours, surrendered the *Queen Charlotte*.

That Post Office packets could give good account of themselves when determined to do so was demonstrated by Captain Dyneley of the *Duke of Montrose* who was caught-up in a French expedition mounted from Guadaloupe against Dominica. This operation had been prompted by the defection of the crew of HM Cutter *Dominica* which had been carried over to the enemy by the mutineers. Taken over by the French she was remanned and renamed *Napoléon*. This vessel and her consort, *L'Imperial*, were both engaged by Dyneley who captured the latter and chased the former under the guns of a British cruiser, HMS *Wasp*. In the following November, however, outward-bound with the mails and approaching Barbados, Dyneley's *Duke of Montrose* fell in with a corsair mounting besides her normal carriage guns, a heavy 12-pounder on a midships, traversing carriage. This formidable weapon played havoc with the packet and although stubbornly defended, when Dyneley fell alongside his wounded mate, the exhausted and out-numbered crew capitulated.

Better luck attended Captain Anthony of the *Cornwallis* who was attacked by six heavily armed Spanish gunboats off Tarifa on 28 July 1806 when carrying the mails on the extended service to Malta. Unable to secure an escort through the Gut of Gibraltar from Admiral Lord Collingwood, the *Cornwallis* drove off her pursuers with the loss of one man. The following spring, on 28 May 1807, the new *Duke of Marlborough* was approaching Barbados when she was chased by a schooner and her acting-commander, Mr James, cleared for action, triced up boarding nettings and brought the mail-bags on deck to be weighted with shot. Just after ten o'clock in the evening the schooner approached with the obvious intention of boarding and overwhelming James's small crew. At the critical moment James put his helm over, crossed the enemy's bow and raked her with his starboard broadside, causing carnage among the assembling boarders. Another attempt to board was foiled and the two vessels drew apart until after daylight. At about eight o'clock the corsair was again in range of the *Duke of Marlborough* and a running fight of over two hours commenced, but it ended with the two parting and the packet continuing on her way.

On 2 July a similar action occurred when the *Cornwallis* was chased in the Bay of Biscay by a *chasse marée* flying British colours. When within pistol shot she:

> ran up the Spanish flag at the mizzen, and the French ensign, topped with a red flag, the signal for no quarter, at the main. In the same moment, without hail or summoning-gun, a broadside roared out, followed by a rattling volley of small arms.

Captain Anthony met this with two double-shotted and grape-loaded 12-pounder carronades which cleared the gathering party of boarders with terrible effect. The corsair then hauled off and attempted to knock the *Cornwallis* to pieces but after some time gave up the action and allowed the wounded packet to resume her passage.

The waters off Barbados were one of the richest hunting grounds for the French and here, on 1 October, the most celebrated defence of a Post Office packet took place. The schooner *Le Jeune Richard* was a successful corsair. Only two months previously in the same waters she had taken the brig *Pope* after an all-night chase which culminated in a furious action at sunrise on 2 August. *Le Jeune Richard* was armed with eight 9-pounders and a heavy traversing long

Left: Acting Commander William Roger of the Post Office packet *Windsor Castle*. (Author's Collection)

Below: Rogers leads a counter-attacking boarding party after beating off a furious attack on the *Windsor Castle* by a French corsair on 1 October 1807. W. Ward after S. Drummond. (Author's Collection)

18-pounder amidships which wrought fearful destruction. Captain Masheter responded with his twelve 6-pounders but in the cannonade he lost his right leg and his left arm, while several of his men were severely wounded so that when most of the enemy crew of 120 men stormed aboard the *Pope*, the dying Masheter was almost powerless, though he defended himself until finally cut down. By now both the mates and a number of seamen were dead, while others were wounded. With the remainder overwhelmed, the French carried the day and bore the *Pope* off to Guadaloupe. On this cruise *Le Jeune Richard* had taken 'no less than six fine running ships, viz. – the *America* and *Clio* in company, the *Margaret*, the *Pope*, the *Portsea* and one other…' It was this formidable corsair that, on the 1 October when six days out on a new cruise and with a crew of eighty-six men, came up in the wake of the Leeward Islands packet *Windsor Castle*.[61]

The packet was commanded by William Rogers in the absence of Captain Sutton. She was brig-rigged and armed with six guns, manned by a crew of twenty-six men and boys, besides her acting-commander, and bore three passengers. Rogers manned his guns, hoisted his boarding nets and awaited events. He was not left long in doubt of the enemy's intentions; after a broadside that killed three men and wounded seven, *Le Jeune Richard* was run aboard the *Windsor Castle*'s starboard quarter and her crew attempted to cut through the nettings. Their first attempt to board was swiftly dealt with: before the enemy could cut through the nets the *Windsor Castle*'s people drove boarding pikes into their bodies, or cut them down with cutlass strokes, several falling between the two hulls and into the sea. An attempt to sheer off by the commander of *Le Jeune Richard* was frustrated by the entanglement of the rigging of the two vessels.

> Thereupon our pikemen again flew to their muskets, pistols and blunderbusses, our gallant captain all the while giving his orders with the most admirable coolness…encouraging his crew by his speeches and example in such a way as there was no thought of yielding… At every discharge we began to hear them scream, which so inspired our gallant crew that many of …[our] wounded returned to their quarters.

It was now about three o'clock and, although demoralised, the French were not finished. There was a brief lull; on *Le Jeune Richard* the men were remustered; on the *Windsor Castle* a 6-pounder was 'crammed with double grape, canister, and one hundred musket balls' and at the critical moment, as the Frenchmen rushed the side, Rogers discharged the over-loaded and brutal weapon. A second was discharged in its wake. Another letter written by a passenger winds up the account:

Captain Rogers...was left with only ten men about him for the last half hour, rallying them to their duty, with a determination to carry the prize, which repeatedly endeavoured to clear the packet, but was too fast lashed by her bowsprit to escape, and he boarded her at the head of four men, and charged her decks with a gallantry never excelled and seldom equalled.

The final scuffle ended with the death of *Le Jeune Richard*'s commander – whose name, sadly, is lost to us – upon which the remainder of her crew gave up and were driven below. A summary of this minor but notable action is given by the same correspondent:

.... such was their gallantry, that they carried the privateer, after killing 26, wounding 30, and making prisoners of 30 not wounded, in all 60 prisoners, almost treble the number we had left for duty. We have therefore...had little comfort for the last three days, not having had our clothes off, and being obliged to sleep on deck in order to secure the prisoners... I cannot enter more into detail...and can only say that if any man has deserved a token of merit from Your Underwriters, Captain Rogers deserves it in the highest degree.

Rogers was immediately advanced to the command of a packet and showered with encomiums, plate and money. He received a presentation sword from the merchants of Tortola and was made a Freeman of the City of London. Cash was also distributed among the surviving crew which had been further whittled away by the wounds of many proving mortal. Many might have been saved but official parsimony denied the *Windsor Castle* a surgeon, the remuneration being insufficient to tempt young surgeons willing to go to sea to join the Packet Service. Nevertheless, the value of the prize was paid to the General Post Office and divided among the officers and crew, for although the packets carried no Letter-of-Marque authorising them to take prizes which – given their reputation for venality would have proved too great a temptation and place the mails at further peradventure – it was clear that in the case of the *Windsor Castle* her crew were forced to fight for their very lives.

Some further notable actions followed. On 19 March 1808, Captain Petre of the *Prince Ernest*, defended his packet off Barbados, forcing a privateer-schooner away after a ferocious assault by having a marksman shoot her helmsmen until she yawed away and lost her appetite. In September, with a considerably enhanced armament of a dozen guns, Captain Anthony of the *Cornwallis* fought off *La Duquesne*, but John Bull, now himself commander of the new *Duke of Marlborough* was, that November taken with his packet by the brigantine *La Joséphine* mounting fourteen 24-pounders and sixty-eight men. Happily both brig and crew were soon afterwards ransomed.

Some time later, on 26 July 1810, the *Duke of Marlborough*, again under the acting-command of Mr James and when homeward from Lisbon, fought and beat off a French brig in the first of two actions. On 1 October that year when back under John Bull, the same packet was within sight of home, having rounded the Lizard when she was intercepted by a strange sail. The wind was now light and as the two vessels drew together Bull discharged a heavily loaded gun and cleared the boarders, deterring his attacker who hauled off, subjected the *Duke of Marlborough* to an ineffectual bombardment and retreated on the approach of armed boats coming out from Falmouth. The packet now stood in for Carrick Roads where a furore had already erupted.

The grievances over the deprivation of their private trade in the West India packets had simmered for years and came to a head in 1810. The poor pay in the Packet Service was not only below that in the Royal Navy – and well below that in the merchants' service – but with the rising prices caused by the dwindling harvest and the economic sanctions of the Continental System had driven the packet-men's wage below the level of subsistence. This was a widespread problem among the nation's poor, but few were in a position to exploit it as they were. The inequity of allowing only the Lisbon packets to retain their trade had rankled mightily, but had been offset to a degree by the gradual, subtle and stealthy recommencement of their own former but illicit trade by the seamen in the West India packets. Although the amount of goods carried was much diminished, their scarcity value had raised prices, facts which only encouraged a steady increase and an exposure to public rumour among the jealous. Following Freeling's reforms, the Post Office had instituted a 'searcher' who undertook to clear all packets of any imputation of breaking the new rules, but the crews had become adept at concealing goods from this worthy whose probity, though never publicly questioned, may be privately doubted. However, confronted with trade-goods discovered aboard the *Townshend*, the searcher was obliged to report it. An example would have been made by placing the packet's company on oath to reveal whose venture it was, had not Auckland intervened, his lordship ruling that he would not 'place a whole ship's company in the alternative between worldly ruin and a perjury'. The discovered goods were disposed of at public sale and the matter quietly dropped with a small – and inadequate – pay-rise. This was accompanied by a warning to all and a coercive reminder that the crews were, by their protections, exempt from impressment. Against this the men argued that these papers were not respected by men-of-war entering Falmouth, the documents being readily torn in a scuffle or left in their homes. As for the warning as to their future conduct, this, of course, went unheeded.

Earlier in the year of 1810 the privilege of trade had finally been removed from the Lisbon packets and, as the Falmouth agent Mr Saverland reported to

London in August, a mood of 'uneasiness' permeated the packet crews. In due course a memorial was submitted by the combined crews who besieged Saverland's office and on 15th sent in two men from each vessel to deplore the low wage rates which did not permit the men to feed their families and pay their rents. The matter was referred to London, causing a frustrating delay which was exacerbated by the Post Office taking the view that responsibility for this entire matter lay with the packet-owners and commanders who, as part of their charters, received a fixed sum for the hire of packet and crew. How these worthies distributed the actual monies was a matter for them, so nothing had been resolved when the men returned in a body before Saverland's office to demand an answer to their memorial. On being told an answer was awaited for London, they dispersed, but Saverland thought many would leave the service if something was not done. A pay review was held, discovering that, in fact, the men were marginally better off than seamen in the navy and had, besides their press exemptions, better conditions and a regularity of intercourse with their families. So matters might have been left had not a punctilious Customs officer intervened.

On the morning of 24 October the officer boarded the *Prince Adolphus*. The mails for Malta were on board, the sails loosened and Captain Boulderson was about to weigh his anchor. Nearby, the *Duke of Marlborough* with the Lisbon mails, was ready to weigh and join her consort for the run across the Bay. At this point the zealous revenue man ordered the seamen's chests opened for inspection. Discovering some prohibited articles intended for sale abroad, he confiscated them, then had himself pulled across to the *Duke of Marlborough* where the scene was repeated. The crews of both packets immediately refused to weigh the anchor and Boulderson was obliged to signal for the agent while Bull set off in his own boat to consult with Captain Slade of the Falmouth guardship. Attempting to coerce the men Saverland reminded them that they endangered their press protections, threatening them with forfeiture of this privilege. Bull meanwhile consulted Captain Slade and an attempt was made to impress men from the *Prince Adolphus* while Bull went back to his ship to persuade his own crew to return to their duty. While the refusal to obey orders was mutiny, like any other merchant seamen, the packet-men were not bound by the Mutiny Act that governed the Royal Navy. Slade's blustering on board the *Duke of Marlborough*, whither he hied himself after ordering the *Prince Adolphus's* seamen carried aboard his frigate, only increased resentment to the point where one seaman drew his knife against Slade, who wisely withdrew.

The following morning every sailor in Falmouth and from the surrounding villages gathered outside Saverland's establishment, demanding the release of the pressed men. Amid an uproar the Riot Act was read by the magistrates and in the following disturbed days the packet-men, lumpers and riggers made the Seven Stars tavern their headquarters and there resolved to appoint a deputation to proceed to London. Meanwhile Saverland, Slade and the packet-commanders sought help from Sir Robert Calder, now the Port Admiral at Plymouth. A naval detachment arrived and attempted to arrest the rebels holed up in the tavern but on breaking in found it empty. A furious Slade demanded the mayor called in troops and forcibly enter the homes of the ring-leaders to arrest them. This the mayor refused to do, there being great sympathy for the plight of the packet-men in Falmouth and the detachment of the West Essex Militia which shortly afterwards arrived was quietly billeted in the town with a sergeant's guard sent to nearby Flushing. Two cutters despatched by Calder were anchored in Carrick Road, but the rebellious seamen had melted away.

They had, however, sent their representatives, Messrs Parker and Pascoe, in the coach to London, but the conveyance was overtaken by an express carrying a warning from Saverland which arrived ahead of the mail. This ensured that the Admiralty raised an impressment warrant signed by the Lord Mayor – since the arrest would take place within the boundaries of the City of London – and alerted the City Marshal to execute it. Forgetting nothing, Their Lordships also warned the Regulating Officer at the Tower of London to expect the arrested malefactors. Pascoe and Parker arrived at the General Post Office in Lombard Street on the afternoon of the 29th to meet Freeling and the City Marshal, who promptly took them into custody. Unfortunately for their cause, the two men were known to the authorities as trouble-makers: Parker was an American and Pascoe had been dismissed from the Excise Service for 'seditious and treasonable expressions'. However, before the men were brought into the Mansion House for examination, legal opinion had been sought and the Lord Mayor was advised that he had no powers to impress, particularly as neither man had committed a crime in the City of London: the two men were consequently remanded.

Back in Falmouth, in order to defuse the situation and induce the men back to work by intrigue, Saverland had misguidedly started a rumour that if they did not swiftly return to their duty the entire operation of the packets would be transferred to Plymouth. Almost immediately enquiries, tentative at first, but gathering momentum as the ripples of disturbance spread outwards, were made of Mr Saverland. Perceiving the restorative effect, Saverland elaborated his disinformation in order to accelerate the process which he heartily wished concluded. The men began to drift back to their duty and Saverland was induced to encourage this by a public notice restoring the protections from impressments for all except a few who had distinguished themselves in the days of riot.

Alas, however, the seamen had flown in the face of fate. There was no appetite for conciliation and where Government was powerless to protect the mails at sea, it could secure the mode of their going. The same solution as had been bruited abroad by an imaginative Saverland was, in fact, being decided upon in the General Post Office. Moreover, when Freeling took this news to Whitehall on 31 October, he too discovered great minds thought alike and orders were already on their way post-haste to order Calder to take over the packets and move them to Plymouth. Accordingly, to the consternation of the inhabitants of Falmouth, on 6 November Commander Thomas Coe brought HM Sloop *North Star* into Carrick Roads. Taking charge of the packets with their skeleton crews of loyalists augmented by drafts of seamen from HM Ships, the little flotilla proceeded to Plymouth where Saverland was put up in the Fountain Inn.

Within a fortnight the deficiencies of Plymouth were revealed. The anchorage was poor, the bottom strewn with so many abandoned anchors as to foul the ground, the lack of concentration of passenger mustering points and confusions over the delivery stations for the mails all resulted in chaos. The ridiculous nature of the shift of location was made manifest when packets encountering heavy weather before clearing the Channel ran into the traditional haven of refuge on the coast: Falmouth! In due course the heavy lobbying of forty-four Cornish Members of Parliament induced the Ministry to return the Packet Service to its traditional station in January 1811, while after a fruitless attempt to receive compensation for their three-day imprisonment, Pascoe and Parker fade out of the story.

While that might have been that, a year later the American War broke out. This was a misfortune, for the Royal Navy was – at last – turning the tables on the French corsairs and a number of frigates were proving themselves able privateer-hunters. But in June 1812 the *Princess Amelia* was taken after a stiff running fight by the American privateer *Rossie* of Baltimore and commanded by Captain Barney. In the action, of the packet's crew of twenty-eight, Captain Moorsom, Mr Nankivel, the sailing-master, and three men were killed and eleven were wounded. Among these was Mr Ridgard the *Princess Amelia*'s mate, and he ordered the mails hove overboard and the colours struck. In November another packet was lost when the *Townshend* approached Barbados and instead of running into Bridgetown she ran into two American privateers, the *Tom*, Captain Thomas Wilson, and the *Bona*, Captain Damaron. Grossly out-gunned and out-numbered it was inevitable that Captain James Cock and the *Townshend* would be overwhelmed as the contest was quite unequal. Nevertheless, Cock and his crew fought gallantly in the hope that the gunfire would be heard in Bridgetown and some measure of assistance afforded them. Damaron and Wilson intended to knock the packet's rig to pieces in order to preserve her hull and then board. Their first attempt having been repulsed, they stood off and rendered the *Townshend* immobile by bombardment. With the hulled packet filling beneath his feet, Cock ordered the colours down and fell to weeping with anger. Wilson gave Cock a certificate as to his gallantry and that he had not struck until the *Townsend* 'was unmanageable' and indeed she proved so worthless to her captors that she was to be burnt. On hearing this Cock pleaded his cause and negotiated a ransom against a bill for £1,200, and struggled into Carlisle Bay with all hands at the pumps. Cock set off home in the New Year, the *Townshend* imperfectly refitted. On 18 January he had the double misfortune to be chased by another American privateer-schooner. With the enemy coming up in his wake, Cock manned his stern chasers and succeeded in shooting away his pursuer's foreyard. Taking advantage of the confusion, he yawed and discharged a broadside before, a few minutes later, with a hard squall coming on, the two parted.

This small triumph failed to outweigh the seizure of two packets by an American frigate squadron under Commodore Rodgers. On 15 October Captain Stevens, on his way to Malta, had deceived an enemy privateer into thinking he commanded a man-of-war brig by his bold handling of the *Lady Mary Pelham*. A similar aggressive use of a packet off Georgetown, Demerara, in November, drove off a pair of American privateers, one of which was the *Rattlesnake*. The two were lying in ambush for an expected convoy and Captain Kirkness, embarking a detachment of troops, stood out in the packet *Queen Charlotte* to the discomfiture of the enemy.

A lucky escape is recorded by Captain Hartney of the *Montagu* who fought off an American privateer on 1 February 1813. The *Montagu* had on board the mails and £16,000 of bullion and as the enemy sheered away after a three-hour fight, Hartney's gunner reported all the powder expended. Captain Elphinstone in the *Manchester* was not so lucky, surrendering to the privateer *York-Town* when he could resist no longer for lack of ammunition. Elphinstone's action lasted a whole day, but even this was exceeded by the desultory, three-day fight put up by Captain White and the crew of the *Princess Charlotte*. The American tactic of standing off and wrecking a victim before boarding was helped by the increasing use of traversing guns of a heavy weight-of-metal. The packet *Mary Anne*, Captain Caddy, was overwhelmed by the *General Tompkins*, a privateer carrying a long 24-pounder mounted in this way, which demolished the brig by degrees. At about the same time as Hartney's escape, the *Duke of Montrose* had also avoided capture in similar manner but on 9 June, on her way to Halifax, she ran into another privateer. Blewitt handled his brig brilliantly, raked his enemy twice and escaped. However, he shortly afterwards sighted a large frigate which gave chase and proved to be the USS *President*. This time there was no escape and Blewitt sank the mails and hauled down his ensign. Treating his prisoners well, Rodgers released ship and crew on condition that they returned home under the direction of an American officer and then returned the packet under him manned with an equivalent number of American seamen then imprisoned in Dartmoor. The Government repudiated the undertaken given upon Blewitt's word-of-honour and the American officer was sent home empty-handed while the *Duke of Montrose* was perfidiously returned to service.

Another desperate affair was that of the *Express* and the *Anaconda*. Returning from Rio de Janeiro and west of the Cape Verde Islands on 23 March 1813, the *Express* was subjected to a long chase by the American privateer *Anaconda*. Captain John Quick had on board mail, despatches and £20,000, and decided to make a run for it. When eventually the *Anaconda* ranged up close and pressed the *Express* to action, her masts and rigging were severely shot away and, with water filling the hold, Quick struck his colours. The Americans seemed content to seize only the gold and let the devastated packet go, paroling Quick and his company, so the following hours were spent in hoisting up some spare spars, repairing the rigging and bending new sails, after which the *Express* set off and after several anxious weeks she arrived in Falmouth with the mails intact. The same year the *Lapwing* was twice taken, the second time after a bloody fight, but the loss of mails was not to be set against the sacrifice and gallantry of the dead and wounded.

These various disruptions to the mail services were complicated by an outbreak of plague in Malta which required the quarantining of inward packets in the Thames estuary, a matter that further frustrated the merchants who began another agitation that was linked with their representations to the Admiralty about the ineffectual nature of Their Lordships arrangements for the protection of commerce against the Americans. They argued that both the crew and armament of the packets should be increased, while the Post-Master General countered with an assertion that doubling both would not have prevented the taking of the packets seized by Rodgers' frigates. He was able to point out Captain Bell's spirited defence of the *Francis Freeling* against an American privateer which had preserved not only the lives of her passengers and the Lisbon mails, but 130,000 silver dollars. Unfortunately, the delays in the mails in general occasioned by the shortage of packets and the time taken to effect proper repairs was telling, while the loss of the *Hinchinbrooke* during a West Indian hurricane and the wrecking of the *Lady Emily* on a reef off Bermuda only added to the general disorder and ailing reputation of the Packet Service.

Some measure of relief was effected by chartering, on a temporary basis, the brig *Morgiana* commanded by Captain James Cunninghame, formerly Earl St Vincent's sailing-master. The brig was despatched towards Surinam when, approaching her destination early on the morning of 26 September 1813, a strange sail was sighted. The day was calm and the stranger put out her sweeps, rapidly closing her quarry. Cunninghame exhorted his crew and cleared for action; then the wind rose and there was a long running fight until the enemy ranged up and boarded. Cunninghame threw his helm over, which left numbers of the boarders clinging to the nettings as the vessels sheered apart, from which they either dropped voluntarily, or were shoved from by pike and cutlass. However, after further exchange of gunfire the *Morgiana* was badly damaged, immobilised and, with a third of her crew down, outnumbered. As the enemy crashed alongside the larboard bow, Cunninghame, who was wounded himself in four places, gave orders to ditch the mail and lower the colours. With seventy men in possession of his foredeck the sight of the mail going over the stern afforded him 'a secret relief'. As he gave his ship over to the enemy he was informed that she was the *Saratoga* of New York, Captain Thomas Adderton, a vessel of very superior force to the *Morgiana*. Taken below, Cunninghame was next told that his thigh wound was mortal. The prize was sent in to Newport, Rhode Island where, after many months convalescence, Cunninghame eventually confounded the quacks and recovered. Sent home he appeared before a court of inquiry which honourably acquitted him the loss of his vessel.

When possible the practice of sending packets in pairs for mutual support was clearly sensible, but their simultaneous departures were not always possible. However, where most packet-commanders were by this stage of the war, of proven competence, there now transpired an extraordinary case of folly and misjudgement. On the eve of his departure for Brazil in the *Lady Mary Pelham*, Captain Stevens was told that he had been promoted to the Holyhead station and immediately appointed a substitute commander in his own place. However, rather than promoting his sailing master Carter, the man who would have normally stood in his stead, Stevens took the extraordinary step of obliging a man to whom he had some moral debt by appointing a retired lawyer who was also a yachtsman. Saverland objected to this folly, but claimed there was no time to argue and defended his decision with the twin argument that the gift was in Stevens' hands and in any case Carter was on board to keep an eye on things. Thomas Carter had been acting third lieutenant aboard the line-of-battle-ship *Thunderer* at Trafalgar, but he had received no further advancement and he had been obliged to seek employment in the Packet Service in the hope of better things to come, in which case he was to be disappointed at this turn of events.[62] The *Lady Mary Pelham* sailed on 13 October and was followed on the 19th by the *Montagu*, commanded by Captain John Norway.

Norway was also a former naval officer and conducted his ship swiftly to Madeira, arriving in advance of his colleague, landing the mails there on 1 November by boat and standing off until this returned with the onward mail.[63] That evening the *Lady Mary Pelham* hove in sight but did not answer Norway's signals. During the night a strange schooner was also seen approaching the *Montagu* and Norway called his men to quarters. Hardly had he done so than the enemy opened fire with a broadside; Norway returned fire and the stranger sheered away. Next morning a boat came across from the *Lady Mary Pelham* in which Carter, who had heard the firing, concerted matters with Norway. The enemy privateer remained in sight and was clearly awaiting the packets outside territorial waters. That evening the mails came off for both packets and they made sail together. The following morning the privateer-schooner was again seen approaching and the two packets formed a rough line, the *Lady Mary Pelham* ahead of and slightly to starboard of the *Montagu*. As the enemy ranged up, the *Montagu* fired a few shots from her stern chasers, which were replied by the privateer's bow chasers before her bowsprit was run over the *Montagu's* deck, fouled in her starboard rigging and a score of boarders dropped onto the packet's deck.

The enemy attempted to clear the packet's deck with grape and langridge from an 18-pounder, at the same time swinging her main boom over the *Montagu's* deck. Norway was hit in the thigh but the enemy were driven back, a number of them being lost overboard. As the privateer sheered off, a chain shot almost severed Norway's body and he fell into the arms of Ure, the surgeon. At this instant a shot took off Ure's head and both men fell in a weltering fountain of blood. The deck was taken over by Watkins, the *Montagu's* master, whose work was now cut out: in addition to the loss of the *Montagu's* commander, two seamen had been killed and four wounded and Watkins still had to face over 100 men in the privateer. Having dropped astern, she was now pressing up on the larboard quarter, galling the *Montagu's* deck with a hail of musketry from her tops and bows. A musket ball shattered poor Watkins's hand and a moment later he was shot through the body and carried below. The mate and the carpenter were both wounded and the gunner was summoned from the powder-room to take command of the deck.

Throughout this desperate affair the *Lady Mary Pelham* had been subject to a battle of will upon her own deck. Seeing that their inexperienced commander stood steadfastly on, Carter and Pocock, the mate, remonstrated that Carter should support the *Montagu*; however, as soon as this had been agreed and Carter gave an order, the helmsman countered it. Carter drew his pistol and ran to the helmsman, thinking it evidence of cowardice in the face of the enemy, but the terrified man pleaded the yachtsmen-commander had countermanded Carter's order. At last a furious Carter had his way and the packet was put about, engaging at some distance.

Aboard the *Montagu* Mr Hensell, the gunner, came on deck to see the bow of the enemy, infested with men, looming over the *Montagu's* quarter.

Ordering the mails overboard Hensell summoned all who could to repel boarders. Only four of the enemy got across, one of them being recognised as a deserter from the packets and he was run through, as was a second; the other two, one of which was the privateer's first lieutenant, were secured as prisoners and the attempt to board thus failing, the privateer sheered off. Although the two packets chased her, she was too fast for them and escaped.

There was, of course, an aftermath to this sorry and sanguine business. The lawyer, who was rewarded with a ball in his thigh, 'made many charges against most of the persons concerned in this affair' and later induced an interested Member of Parliament to deprecate the dead Norway. Happily Freeling opposed any defamation of a dead and gallant officer, while a merchant who had been held aboard the privateer when she put into the Canaries, later revealed to Freeling that the packets' assailant had been the *Globe* of Baltimore, Captain Moon. He also corroborated the facts and added that of the thirty-nine men who had boarded the *Montagu*, not one had returned to the *Globe*.

These events, whatever their merits, continued the disruption of the mails and increased the packet crews' desire for better pay. The risk of attacks provoked a disinclination in some men to serve, and on 12 July a number of the crew of the packet *Speedy*, just on the point of slipping her moorings, asked to be put on shore. They were led by the gunner and refused the agent's blandishment of a month's wages in advance, going instead into a tavern. Soliciting assistance from the guardship, the agent sought his men in vain: they had disappeared. So too did the replacements engaged at a premium rate by Captain Sutherland of the *Speedy* who gave out a generous advance only to find the men failed to muster aboard the packet. Faced with this, Sutherland proceeded to Plymouth where he quickly made up his crew and sailed, but the incident effectively ended the Falmouth Packet Service, as we shall see.

There were more losses and damages in 1814: the *Townshend* was chased and brought-to under the guns of the French national frigate *La Clorinde* whose captain ordered her scuttled. Taken on board the frigate Captain Cock – who had dumped his mails – and his crew were liberated when *La Clorinde* was herself captured by HM Frigate *Eurotas*. Cock died shortly afterwards, honoured by the Regent of Portugal but ignored by his own principals, for 'Whitehall had no distinctions for officers of the Packet Service'. In May James, now promoted to command the *Hinchinbrooke*, fought a long action against an American privateer off the Azores on his way home from St Thomas. The *Hinchinbrooke* was badly damaged in her hull, but was kept afloat and reached Falmouth, the mails intact. In the early summer the *Walsingham* fought off an American, but the hired packet *Little Catherine*, Captain Vivian, was taken by the French national frigate *Le Sultan*. A week or so later *Le Sultan* took the *Duke of Montrose* into which Vivian and his crew were put and the ransomed packet was sent on her way.

Among the last action of the packets, and the penultimate action of the war in the Atlantic, was fought by Captain Furze who had recovered from wounds sustained in the taking of the *Lapwing* to be appointed into the *Chesterfield*. The packet sailed from Falmouth for Surinam in December 1814, almost on the eve of the signing of the peace treaty at Ghent and had sighted the peak of Madeira by the morning of 4 January 1815 when a strange schooner was reported and a running fight of nearly four hours duration began. One man was killed and two wounded aboard the *Chesterfield* before the American bore away. The last act was less glorious, though infinitely more bloody and ought never to have occurred in the new year of 1815 after the end of hostilities, for it resulted in the loss of the *Windsor Castle*, so gallantly defended by Rodgers but lost to the American privateer *Roger*, Captain R. Sutton and his crew fought until the packet lay unmanageable and entirely at the mercy of the large American crew, so the mails were ditched and the colours struck.

The most regrettable affair, however, affected the *Duke of Marlborough* which had been off Cape Finisterre on her way to Lisbon on the night of 12 March when she encountered the 18-gun British brig-sloop *Primrose*. Neither ship properly acknowledged the recognition signals and Commander Phillott of the *Primrose* complained afterwards that he had not been able to distinguish the packet's pendant or ensign. The *Duke of Marlborough* was commanded by the redoubtable John Bull, who fired his stern chasers, outmanoeuvred Phillott in the *Primrose* and inflicted casualties. Unfortunately, the *Marlborough* had received two 32-pound carronade balls in her hull and was taking water before the error was discovered and the action ceased. One passenger, an army officer named Andrews on his way to join Wellington's army, had been killed and Bull and ten of his men were wounded, but the packet struggled into Lisbon and was not lost – nor were her mails. The subsequent court-martial censured Phillott, though to be fair he afterwards took the American privateer *Pike*, while Bull – who at the enquiry produced a pendant 30ft in length and an ensign 9ft 4in in the fly and 4ft 6in in the hoist which his packet had been flying on the fateful night – was presented with a sword by the passengers he had had on board.

This was a whimpering end to a 'long and dangerous' war in the Atlantic and its adjacent seas, in sharp contrast to the glories associated with the legend of Nelson: an inglorious encounter and an exchange of – that curious expression – friendly-fire. And yet there is an odd symbolism to this protracted account of the Post Office packet service in these years of warfare and the manner of its end, and that is the inner national conflict between private aspiration and the perceived imperatives of the state, ending with unintentional but a determined internecine warfare.

In the closing months of the war the questions of pay and impressment caused trouble elsewhere. There were several strikes among merchant seamen on the banks of the Tyne which resulted in civil disturbances and the reading of the Riot Act. Finally, at the end of hostilities, as a demobilising Royal Navy threw men ashore by the thousand, the labour-market was flooded, to the further detriment of the common sailor. Three years after the end of the war the Post Office mail service was – at least for some years extending beyond the limits of this present volume – taken over by the navy. The unreliability of an undisciplined workforce and the objection to a vital public service being in private hands, was one reason given by the Government to which Their Lordships added another: that the Packet Service would prove a worthy employment for some of the numerous naval officers placed on the half-pay list at the end of the war. As for the Cornishmen, they reaped the whirlwind they had sown. Not for the last time, the dangerous truculence and self-deception of the British seaman had proved a fatally self-harming act.

NOTES

1. Those registered in 1792 as being owned in Ireland numbered 250, with colonial bottoms amounting to 103; by 1814 these totals had changed to 84 and 203 respectively. See C. Ernest Fayle's essay *The Employment of British Shipping* in C. Northcote Parkinson's compilation *The Trade Winds*.

2. See Grocott, pvii.

3. Henry Greathead's lifeboat *Zetland* may still be seen at Redcar on the north east coast of England. The Royal Humane Society, HM Coastguard and the Royal National Lifeboat Institution were all established as an indirect result of the movement to save life at sea. Much impetus was given to the design of lifeboats by the very public wrecking of the merchantman *Adventure* which went to pieces off Tynemouth in front of an impotent crowd of 300 spectators who watched as, one-by-one, her crew were washed off the wreck to their deaths. The raising of a public subscription prompted a competition for a boat-design capable of succouring such distressed vessels.

4. They could be as difficult and delinquent as their detractors insisted. In 1792 several masters of British ships lying in the Tagus were imprisoned at Lisbon on account of shooting a Portuguese boatman 'in a drunken frolic'.

5. Kelly, p244.

6. See, among others, C. Northcote Parkinson, *Britannia Rules*. Lord Howe's victory on 'The Glorious First of June', 1794, had crippled the French National Navy's Brest Fleet, but it did not stop a detached squadron safely escorting a huge convoy which arrived safely in a starving France with cargoes of American grain, thus saving the Revolutionary Government. At the symbolic level, the Peace of Amiens resulted in the removal of the *fleur-de-lis* of France from the

British Royal coat-of-arms and with it the relinquishing of the rather fatuous claim on the French crown.

7. A brilliant campaign led by General Simcoe to hold Saint-Domingue was in vain and the island was evacuated and left to the armies of Toussaint l'Ouverture. St Nicholas Mole was held until 1798 by which time the black rebellion under Toussaint l'Ouverture and his successors Dessalines and King Christophe, although denying the British control of the Bight of Léogane, created problems for the French.

8. Unlike other measures such as the window tax, income tax was to become permanent after the renewal of the war in 1803. At the time it was life-saving, although it fell short of diverting a tenth of the income of the citizenry into the Government's coffers.

9. Sugar imports almost doubled, while the influx of coffee increased nine-fold.

10. This accounts only for those in registered ships. Another 30,000 are thought to have been employed in the fishing industries, small coasters, lighters, hoys, wherries and so forth. The increase in merchant seamen between 1792 and 1802 was about 11,500; whereas the Royal Navy, although partially mobilised thanks to the crises with Spain and Russia– mentioned elsewhere – had stood at 16,613 in 1792 and had risen to 126,279 by 1802. Of the combined national resource of approximately 300,000 seamen in the entire population – including fishermen – only 4,000 were in enemy prisons in 1798.

11. Kelly, p312.

12. Not to be confused with the French line-of-battle-ship *Duguay Trouin* captured after her escape from Trafalgar by Sir Richard Strachan and renamed HMS *Implacable* and whose figurehead and stern galleries are in the National Maritime Museum at Greenwich.

Calvert enjoyed more success with the ex-Indiaman *Tartar*, also mentioned earlier, which he bought from Wilkinson who had had her converted into a whaler and later chartered for a voyage to Calcutta. Calvert purchased her in 1795 and hired her to the Transport Board for trooping in a familiar echo of the practice common in the American War and an alternative to chartering vessels for the carriage of convicts.

13. Gué also took a third vessel and the result of his foray was valued at 1.5 million *livres*.

14. Though the notion of inducement was not held to, and such swords were presented to naval officers for other distinguished services, rather diluting their original purpose.

15. See below, Note 34.

16. Quoted Wareham, *Frigate Captain*, p64 *et seq*

17. Laird Clowes, Vol.4, p291.

18. Barton later lengthened the *Harriet* and by January 1798 she had 'taken and retaken some vessels, and rescued others…an instance of commercial expedition, we believe, scarcely to be paralleled'.

19. Some of these so-called French privateers were reported by some jaundiced British masters encountering them as wholly American in all but flag.
20. 'On a creen' means 'ready to turn either way on receiving an impulse'.
21. The position of Speers's ship – or Spiers, as the *Naval Chronicle* calls him – was 03° 30' South, 022° 00' West at the time of the encounter.
22. Shovell was lost with his flagship, HMS *Association* and three other men-of-war. Ironically Shovell had been among the handful of survivors of Beaumont's disaster off the Goodwins in 1703.
23. In response to a generous reward, Frazer's body was recovered some miles distant and interred at Inch.
24. Essington's letter was published in *The Times* in 1810. He rose to flag-rank though was on half-pay after being present at the attack on Copenhagen in 1807.
25. The only Lieutenant John Glover in the Navy Records Society's list of *The Commissioned Sea Officers of the Royal Navy, 1660-1815* that fits the dates seems to have escaped trial and execution, dying, still a lieutenant, in 1798. Phillips is less easy to identify; despite there being a number of officers by the name of Phillips, none answers the dates as a lieutenant and the offending officer might well have been acting only. There is, however, a John Philips who was a lieutenant in 1794. He was made post-captain in 1797 and died in that rank in 1813.
26. The *Dromedary*, Commander Bridges Taylor, sailed for the West Indies and was wrecked near Trinidad in the following August.
27. Earlier in 1800 the Danish frigate *Freya*, escorting a neutral convoy through the Strait of Dover had resisted attempts to have the merchant ships in her charge searched by the Royal Navy. She had been fired into, surrendered and been carried into The Downs. The fury this had caused in Denmark had revived the armed confederation of the Baltic states and at first this had been defused by an embassy led by Lord Whitworth to Copenhagen backed by a naval squadron. The issue had not gone away, hence the descent of Hyde Parker and Nelson the following Easter.
28. *The Times*, 30 March, 1803, quoted Grocott, p144.
29. *The Adventures of John Wetherell*, edited by C.S.Forester, p27 *et seq*.
30. The wholesale rounding up of Britons included many of the well-to-do who, after years of war, were eager to visit Paris again.
31. Moore's action was deliberate and intended to force a war with Spain owing to Madrid's supine attitude to Napoleon in allowing French men-of-war shelter in Spanish ports where British warships could not attack them.
32. The *Wolverine* was largely the brain-child of Captain John Schank a Loyalist American, who, among other innovations, advocated 'sliding keels' or what we should today call centre-boards.
33. Laird Clowes, *The Royal Navy, A History*, Vol.V, p348.
34. Bomb-vessels were only fitted with their mortars when intended for bombardment, a detachment of artillery specialists being attached to them for the purpose. Until required for such service, they mounted only six or eight carronades, were classed as sloops-of-war and used, as was the *Acheron* on

this occasion, for very inadequate convoy escorts. The *Arrow* was constructed on entirely new principles to a design by Samuel Bentham, brother of the philosopher, combining shallow-draught with immense – but close-ranged – fire-power. Her sister-ship *Dart* did much better properly employed in inshore work, specifically off Boulogne in July 1800 when she attacked and captured the much larger French frigate *Desirée*.

35. On 2 December 1804 First Consul Bonaparte had, after a plebiscite of the French nation, been crowned Emperor of the French in Notre Dame.

36. Napoleon struck a triumphal medal which was somewhat prematurely marked as having been manufactured in London.

37. The yacht *Royal Sovereign* should not be confused with the line-of-battle-ship of the same name that was Collingwood's flagship at Trafalgar.

38. Another of Bentham's experimental craft, fitted with sliding keels, capable of being disguised as a harmless Dutch galliot and being rowed to windward at 3 knots. Later in the war the *Netley* proved better at trade-protection off the coast of Portugal, capturing numerous small corsairs. One experimental man-of-war built by the navy in 1809, the *Transit*, was designed by Captain Richard Gower of the Honourable East India Company. She had an innovative fore-and-aft sail plan.

39. Barham had replaced St Vincent as First Lord of the Admiralty on the change of Ministry.

40. The weapons were foils with their buttons ground to a point. Messrs Young and Bendex pinked their opponents who were both cashiered by a disgusted First Consul Bonaparte who offered Young and Bendex commissions in the French army, 'accompanied by most complimentary encomiums'. These were 'respectfully declined'. See *Short Autobiography of Captain William Pixley, and Elder Brother of the Trinity House*, W.H. Smith & Son, 1916, p11 *et seq*. My thanks to Captain Joshua Garner for drawing Pixley's life to my attention.

41. See Richard Hill, *The Prizes of War*, Sutton Publishing, 1998, p62

42. Mackesy, P,. *The War in the Mediterranean, 1803 -1810*, p115.

43. Rodger, *Command of the Ocean*, p557.

44. Having installed his younger brother Louis as King of Holland, Napoleon was afterwards obliged to remove him from the throne on account of Louis' sympathy for his subjects' desire for goods. King Louis himself broke the Continental System by allowing the licensing of proscribed goods to get out of hand and thereby angered his elder brother. That the Emperor adopted the same policy was unfortunate for his younger sibling.

45. See Tracy, N., *Attack on Trade*, p73 *et seq*. Despite the intermittent food shortages, as Tracy points out 'Food shortages were in fact of so little consequence during the wars against France that the population of the British Isles rose by an unprecedented 14.3 per cent between 1801 and 1811.'

46. This is not quite true; hemp could be had from ports in the Adriatic, especially Lissa, but the product of the Illyrian and Dalmatian provinces of the French Empire were somewhat inferior to the best 'clean' Russian hemp. Despite huge stocks the

cost of hemp was volatile. The Navy Board had had to pay £35 per ton in 1798 which rose to £42 a year later, £61 in 1800 and reached £86 in 1801, falling to £43 that year after the Battle of Copenhagen, when Nelson's squadron was in the Baltic. During his period as Commander-in-Chief in the Mediterranean, Nelson had sourced hemp, spars and beef from the Black Sea, sending Lieutenant Henry Frederick Woodman with two chartered transports to undertake this task. I am indebted to Professor Roger Knight for drawing this to my attention.

47. Helgoland remained a British possession until handed over to the Kaiser's Germany in 1890 in exchange for territory in South East Africa.

48. See Rodger, *Command of the Ocean*, p558.

49. Owing to the time taken for the news to travel, fighting went on in America, the Battle of New Orleans being fought early the following year.

50. A score of such vessels were taken up from trade in 1809 to provide fire-ships and explosion vessels for Captain Lord Cochrane's raid – under the unenthusiastic eye of Admiral Lord Gambier – the French squadron anchored behind a boom in Aix Road.

51. Another armed-ship was the 12-gun *Active*, Captain Teed, which appears to have been sent in 1808 to cruise off Demerara to protect the trade there. Here she fought a Spanish privateer, neither having in July heard of the Spanish Uprising and the affairs in Europe that made Spain an ally of Great Britain. The *Active* also engaged and drove off a large French corsair.

52. Kelly, p262.

53. Extraordinarily for what appears to have been an easy victory, the action earned Lavie a knighthood and his first lieutenant promotion. A powerful frigate, *La Guerrière* was taken into the British fleet.

54. The three frigates were HMSs *Amethyst*, *Diana* and *Princess Charlotte*.

55. See Vol. 3 of this history for the fate of the *Royal Charter*.

56. A third brother, Peter, was when but a youth impressed into the navy out of a fishing coble. He rose to serve as boatswain of HMS *Orion* at the battle of the Nile.

57. The island, sighted by Bouvet on 1 January 1739, was thought to have been a headland – named Cape Circumcision – of the great and unknown southern continent. It is the loneliest spot on earth, no land – uniquely – being within 1,000 miles. It was visited again in 1822 and 1825 by sealers who managed to land in the latter year, but not finally accurately fixed – though not landed upon – until the German Deep Sea Exploration voyage in the *Valdivia* in 1898.

58. The Continental System greatly interfered with both the European pick-up ports and the regularity of the sailings, but the service was maintained across the North Sea using, in addition to the ports mentioned in the main text, Altona (then a Danish port on the Elbe) and Tönning.

59. Norway, A.H., *History of the Post-Office Packet Service, 1793 – 1815*, p61.

60. With Lord Gower.

61. Gomer Williams says *Le Jeune Richard* bore eight 12-pounders yet a letter he quotes from written by a passenger on the *Windsor Castle* says she bore

six long 6-pounders and the traversing long gun was a 32-pounder. Arthur
Norway agrees with the carriage guns numbering six, but writes the traversing
gun down as an 18-pounder, which seems more likely and would, in any case,
have been a fearful weapon against a small brig. There is equal confusion over
the *Windsor Castle*'s armament, which was a matter of official establishment
but subject to individual commanders taking action to beef-up their guns. All
authorities agree on the broadside guns being six, three a side, but their weight
of shot was either 4 or 6 pound, with two long chase guns, which are agreed
to be of 6-pound weight-of-metal. The complement of *Le Jeune Richard* is also
unclear but I have stuck to the head-count made by the witnessing passenger,
rather than the inflated figures favoured by the newspapers issuing encomiums
on Rogers's conduct. Further confusion arises from this engagement since the
distinguished artists Robert Dodd and Thomas Whitcombe whose paintings
were invariably etched as prints for the popular market of the day, attribute the
name *Le Genie* to the French corsair. However, there is no doubt that this was,
in fact, *Le Jeune Richard*.

62. The *Thunderer*'s captain had been called home to stand a witness before the
court-martial of Sir Robert Calder and she was commanded by her first
lieutenant, hence Carter's position of acting-up in his train. He had been made
lieutenant in 1801.

63. Norway appears to have joined the navy from the merchants' service as a mate.
He was promoted lieutenant after distinguishing himself in the action between
HMS *La Nymphe*, Pellew, and *La Cleopatre* off the Start, following Sir Edward
into the *Indefatigable* as second lieutenant and being present at the destruction
of the *Droits de l'Homme* in 1797. He remained with Pellew until invalided
home. After convalescing, Norway was given command of a cutter on the Irish
station, being made commander in 1802; in 1806 he was again invalided, but on
recovering solicited the Admiralty to no avail and joined the Packet Service.

Chapter Five

'Hot Action'

War in Eastern Seas, 1793–1815

Upon the outbreak of war in 1793 the East India Company found itself in possession of the French posts of Chandernagore, Karical and Mahé, all of which surrendered without a struggle. A brief but bloody siege of Pondicherry by Crown and Company forces, at which three of the Company's cruisers were present, ended on 23 August, and the captured colours were sent home in one of them, the *Scorpion*. Unfortunately she was captured in the Chops of the Channel by a superior French man-of-war and her crew were taken to the United States where they endured six months detention before being repatriated. Upon the capitulation of the French at Pondicherry, Rear Admiral The Hon. William Cornwallis withdrew from the Indian Ocean, leaving only a small 20-gun cruiser on the station, exposing 'the valuable interests of the Company...to the ravages of the enemy'.[1]

The French 'hoisted the New National Colors (sic) for the first Time at Whampoa on 18 October 1791', but little changed in the Pearl River. On 18 July 1793 the Country-ship *King George*, in ascending the river towards Whampoa with a cargo of cotton, sandal-wood and myrrh, was struck by lightning and caught fire, being burned to the waterline, but the great event of 1793 in China was the arrival of Lord Macartney's embassy.[2]

Superseding Cathcart's failed mission, this was to be more elaborate, with a guard of infantry and a display of pomp designed to impress the imperial court at Beijing. Macartney's objectives were similar to Cathcart's: a Chinese port-of-access closer to the sources of tea and silk but without any territorial claim; an easing of the restrictions imposed at Canton and a better channel of communication between the trading principals; a reduction of duties and their use to reduce debts owed by the Hong merchants; a raising of the status of the English merchants to that of the Portuguese, with the allocation of similar rights; a removal of the liability for British merchants and supercargoes to stand forfeit for the crimes and malfeasances of their employees; better regulation of the criminal laws and, most importantly, to increase the imports of British manufactures and furs in order to close the trade deficit between Britain and China. The expanding volume of trade with Britain and India was to be adduced as evidence of the importance of an agreement, and if a port was not forthcoming Macartney was to 'turn [his] principal attention to the relief of our present embarrassments at Canton.'

On the troublesome question of opium the British Government's instructions to Macartney were both explicit and pragmatic. Should the subject be raised by the Chinese:

> it must be handled with the greatest circumspection. It is beyond a doubt that…Opium raised within our Indian Territories actually finds its way into China; but if it should be made a positive requisition (requirement)…, that none of that drug should be sent by us into China, you must accede to it rather than risk any essential benefit by contesting for a liberty in this respect, in which case the sale of our Opium in Bengal must be left to take its chance on the open market, or to find a consumption in the dispersed and circuitous traffic of the Eastern Seas.

The embassy was not entirely supported by the Company's Court of Directors in London. The Chairman, Francis Baring, rightly detected the poking of the government finger into the Court's own pie, particularly as Macartney's large salary and the entire cost of the embassy was to be borne by John Company. Some idea of the extent of these expenses may be gauged from the presents which were designed to impress the Son of Heaven. In addition to subsuming those returned by Strachan in the *Vestal* from the previous failed embassy under the late Cathcart which were valued at £2,486, a further £13,124 was disbursed.

Macartney and his train of ninety-five persons were to be carried to China in His Britannic Majesty's 64-gun ship *Lion*, Captain Erasmus Gower, attended by the HCS *Hindostan*, Captain William Mackintosh, and the tender *Jackal*. The ships weighed from Spithead on 26 September 1792 and anchored off the Kwantung coast on 20 June 1793.[3] From here Macartney sent his deputy and secretary with Mackintosh in the *Hindostan* to Macao to determine the latest situation. Notice of the embassy had been passed to the Viceroy of

Kwantung from Baring by way of the Select Committee, initiating a flurry of anxiety among the Hong merchants. Gower weighed *Lion*'s anchor on 23 June, arrived off Chusan on 3 July and proceeded north to enter the Gulf of Po Hai and anchor on the Taku Bar at the mouth of the Peiho River not far from Tientsin on 25 July. Landing on 5 August, Macartney was welcomed by the local Viceroy and conducted with due ceremony to Beijing where he found himself cut off from all outside news until he returned to Canton overland and empty-handed on 19 December.[4]

From Taku the embassy had enjoyed a leisurely progress, Macartney finally being received by the Emperor at his residence at Jehol on 14 September. He received a second audience and retired to Beijing to await the Emperor's return to his capital on 30th. On 3 October Macartney formally presented a note of his requests and a letter from George III, receiving a reply on 7 October, the day he was ordered to depart. The embassy proceeded to Canton by way of Hanchow in the company of the new Viceroy of Kwantung province, Shun Lung. Macartney's 'modest Charter of Rights for the English Trade' foundered on Chinese indifference,[5] though he himself had suffered no lack of respect, while his tact had glossed over the cultural chasms that occasionally gaped between visitors and hosts. Sadly, however, absolutely no progress had been made, a tragedy that was going to increase British prosecution of the opium-trade and would erupt half a century later in a war which secured all Macartney's requirements by force of arms in a world in which the British were immeasurably stronger and cared less about sensibilities than in 1793, while the Chinese were proportionately weaker. For the time being therefore: 'The Embassy failed…and the procedure under which the foreign trade was conducted became even more fixed and regularized'.

On the outbreak of the European war in February 1793 the East India Company began to lose its monopoly. The merchants of the declining port of Bristol and the growing one of Liverpool had long railed against the oligarchs of London, provoking a new Act which, while extending the life of the Company's existing charter, admitted others to the trade. The Company was now obliged to allow 3,000 tons of shipping to be provided by free-traders at 'reasonable rates' of £5 per outward and £15 per homeward ton. At the time the Company's regular, chartered fleet consisted of thirty-six Indiamen of the 1,200-ton class and forty of the 800-ton class, to which must be added a number of smaller ships, between 480 and 520 tons, used for the carriage of 'gruff' or bulk goods, that is cotton, rice, sugar, pepper, hemp and saltpetre, all the natural produce of India. Although these ship were nominally 'East Indiamen' this additional tonnage, known as 'Extra-ships', was chartered-in from outside the closed inner circle of the Marine Interest.[6]

However, another crisis was looming as the demand for ship-building timber caused a severe shortage in British yards. This decline in the construction of Indiamen was accompanied by a loss to the Company of six Indiamen which, in 1795, were transferred to a Royal Navy short of hulls. A further eight then nearing completion on the stocks were also promised to Their Lordships, an obligation throwing light upon the semi-establishment status of the Honourable East India Company, standing in sharp contrast with the reciprocal contempt with which naval captains regarded the plunderable asset of an Indiaman's crew.[7] If this sacrifice was not enough, in March the Court of Directors also voted to raise 3,000 men for naval service in the hope that this would curtail interference with their own man-power. It did not. Then, in July, a further fourteen Indiamen were taken up by the Transport Board, producing a major short-fall of tonnage for the Company itself. This was solved by the expedient of shipping home cargoes of rice in twenty-seven Indian-built Extra-ships, but since these were offered at low freight rates, it further weakened the Company's monopoly. Many of these teak-built Country-ships had been put forward as a speculation, their owners believing that freights would offer for the return voyage to India, but this did not prove to be the case and the consequent disappointment only increased the Company's enemies.

All shipping sailed in convoy under the escort of a frigate or two. Those bound east of the Cape of Good Hope carried this escort to St Helena and thereafter protection depended upon the state of hostilities and availability of men-of-war. Where possible, vessels of the Bombay Marine supplemented naval weakness, but the Company's cruisers were still required to carry out some of their traditional duties. In 1796, after returning from his fruitless survey of Tasmania, Lieutenant John Hayes was sent in the 6-gun *Vigilant* to recover a merchantmen seized on the coast of Baluchistan. During the operation he was wounded when fighting a furious action against an overwhelming force of Sanganian 'pirates' in the Gulf of Kutch, losing part of his upper jaw and the lobe of his right ear. In 1799 Hayes was on active service ashore against Tippoo Sultan, after which he was actively employed in the *Alert* in releasing some local merchantmen from confinement by the remnants of the Angrian freebooters at Kennery. A resurgence of this piracy along the coast south of Bombay called for his services in the 10-gun brig *Fly* in 1800. Once again the coastal trade was being interfered with by freebooters based on Gheria, Melundy Island and Vingoria, and Hayes, with seventy-five men in the *Fly* actively securing the release of local shipping together with substantial compensation. Thereafter he and his colleagues were closely associated with the conduct of the wider war, for losses began to be experienced by British owners trading in eastern waters soon after the outbreak of hostilities.

The first Indiaman to be caught by war in far eastern seas was the 30-gun *Princess Royal*. She had made two voyages to India and was off Anjer in the Sunda Strait on her third when she was attacked and taken by three French corsairs on 29 September 1793. One of these was the notorious privateer *Général Malartic*, another, the privateer-frigate *Orpheus*. After a furious action which lasted over an hour – during which the *Princess Royal* lost forty men killed, including her chief officer and carpenter, and sixty men wounded – Captain James Horncastle struck his colours. The Indiaman was recommissioned as a French Third Rate and renamed *Duguay Trouin*.

Meanwhile, rumours of the outbreak of a European war arrived at Canton simultaneously with Macartney's landing at Taku and were confirmed on 8 September, having been passed overland to Basra and forwarded from Calcutta, where despatches had arrived on 7 July. (British men-of-war made occasional visits to Fort William, usually conveying specie from Bombay or, as in the case of the *Leopard* and *Thetis* in February 1791, they arrived in need of help 'with their crews suffering severely from scurvy, and in need of immediate fresh provisions'.) But the return from North China of the *Lion* and *Hindostan* providentially placed Gower's ship in Kwantung waters when the news of hostilities was confirmed. All foreign men-of-war were forbidden to pass the outer bar and the narrows of the Pearl River – known to westerners at the time as the Bocca Tigris – where forts existed, but on 4 November 1793 a French ship 'of about 300 tons was chased by HMS *Lion* off Macao and ran for protection under the guns of the Bar fort'. The *Lion* embarked Macartney and escorted eighteen sail of laden Indiamen home, one of which was Mackinstosh's *Hindostan* which arrived in the Thames on 10 September 1794.

The establishment of the penal colony at Botany Bay attracted outward freights for some of the Company's chartered ships, like Calvert's *Active*, or the small, 350-ton *Indispensible*. Originally a French West Indiaman, she had been taken by the Guernsey privateer *Tartar*, Captain Peter Le Lacheur, and purchased for the Company's service by D. Bennett. Under the command of Captain William Wilkinson she reached Botany Bay, discharged her cargo:

> and left New South Wales the 8th of July and endeavoured to make a passage thro' the Straits of Macassar (being the nearest route to Bengal) but strong Westerly winds & an easterly current prevailing, I thought it most adviseable (sic) to bear away for China & there to wait the change of the Monsoon. Since my arrival in Macao Roads [1 January 1795]…I have applied to the China Pilots to carry me to a place of safety and they inform me they dare not take charge of the Ship unless she goes up to Whampoa.

This, of course, meant Wilkinson incurring Measurage and its attendant dues, so to make a virtue of necessity the Selectmen arranged for the *Indispensible* to be loaded with tea and sent directly to London.

Such circuitous voyages, though unusual, were not uncommon and the homeward ships which left the Pearl River on 7 May 1795 'struck soundings on the Macclesfield Shoal', passed east of Sulu and then by way of the Macassar Strait ran west through the Java Sea to reach Batavia and thence the Indian Ocean via the Sunda Strait. The outward-bound vessels underwent similar diversions, the new 1,200-ton HCS *Cirencester*, Captain Martin Lindsay, having also to pass through the Macassar Strait. Also outward-bound the equally new and large HCS *Arniston*, Captain Campbell Marjoribanks, having called at Madras for 600 troops to garrison Malacca – just then captured from the Dutch – was then obliged to effect her passage 'by the Eastern Route' along the west coast of Borneo and the Philippines. The *Belvedere*, which had earlier been in company with the *Cirencester* but was delayed a week off St Helena, had the worst of it in the South China Sea. Captain Charles Christie was obliged to beat 'against the South West Monsoon between [Macao] and Formosa (Taiwan) ever since the 10th of …[March and] was fearful I should not have got up till an easterly wind sprung up yesterday…' The *Belvedere* arrived at Macao on 25 March.

The *Cirencester* sailed for home in July 1796 taking as a passenger Mr Titsingh, the Dutch Ambassador who had recently arrived from Beijing after leading an embassy on behalf of the Dutch government as fruitless as Macartney's. The over-running of the Seven Provinces and their transformation into the Batavian Republic by the French had resulted in the British capture of – besides Malacca–Capetown, Pondicherry, Ceylon, Amboina and Banda. The most significant of these was the taking of the Cape, greatly easing operations in the southern and eastern oceans for both the Royal Navy and the East India Company. East Indiamen had been used as military transports in all of these expeditions, while the Company's cruisers acted in support of the Royal Navy. Commodore Picket in the then brand new 38-gun Company cruiser *Bombay* acted under the orders of Rear Admiral Rainier in HMS *Suffolk*, 74 guns, during the capture of Ceylon in August 1793 and immediately prior to the reduction of naval forces in the area. Later, in 1797, the *Bombay*, by then commanded by Lieutenant Henry Frost, assisted in the capture of Timor, surrendered by the Dutch governor – the same man who had rendered assistance to Bligh of HM Transport *Bounty*, Edwards of HM Frigate *Pandora* and McCluer's expedition in *Panther* and *Endeavour*.

As yet these were the chief events of the war in the east and they affected trade in the adjacent seas generally to the advantage of the Honourable East India Company. However, whilst the navy could count upon the Company's support, the Company could not always rely upon the Royal Navy's and it had, in some measure, to provide much of its own defence. It had suffered its first war-loss in the east soon after the news of its outbreak reached Macao in September 1793, and more would follow as time passed. The exposure of the East India Company's trade following the withdrawal of Cornwallis's squadron and news of the loss of the HCS *Princess Royal* in September galvanised the admiral's elder brother, the Governor-General at Calcutta. He ordered the formation of a squadron of Indiamen to act in defence of the trade in the China Seas. Accordingly the *William Pitt*, Commodore Charles Mitchell; *Britannia*, Captain Thomas Cheap; *Nonsuch*, Captain John Canning; and the Bombay Marine's 14-gun brig *Nautilus*, Captain George Roper, were sent east and on 2 January 1794 lay off the eastern extremity of the Singapore Strait where Mitchell heard of three French men-of-war to the southwards off Palembang. Sailing south to anchor off Anjer, the squadron was joined by the *Houghton*, Captain Robert Hudson.

On the 22nd two strange sails were chased by the *Britannia* and *Nonsuch*, with *William Pitt* and *Houghton* following. The strangers were the French privateers *Vengeur*, Capitaine Corosin, and the *Résolu*, Capitaine Jallineaux, and a running fight ensued. At about noon, when Corosin and eleven of his men had been killed and a further twenty-six wounded, his first officer struck to Cheap's *Britannia*, which had herself lost one killed and two wounded. With the two other Indiamen coming up fast, Jallineaux surrendered to the *Nonsuch*.

Unbeknown to Mitchell at the time, five days earlier the two French privateers had attacked the Indiaman *Pigot*, Captain George Ballantyne, which lay at anchor in a sheltered anchorage off Rat Island near Benkulen. Early in the morning of the 17th the *Vengeur* had forced the narrow entrance to the basin, anchored and engaged the *Pigot*, whose crew her own greatly outnumbered. Having taken punishment, Corosin cut his cable and withdrew, leaving the field to Jallineaux in the *Résolu*. Jallineaux stood his ground for only twenty minutes before following his colleague out to sea, where the two licked their wounds and repaired the damage sustained from the *Pigot*'s 32 guns.[8]

Ballantyne's highly creditable defence had cost him one man but his ordeal was not yet over. Meanwhile, Mitchell's squadron broke up, the *William Pitt* and *Nautilus* in chase of strange sails with the remainder of the ships anchored off Bantam. Canning in the *Nonsuch* had anchored off the Zuften Islands in the Strait with his two prizes, *Résolu* and *Vengeur*, when shortly after dawn on the 24th four ships were seen beating up from the southwards. These were the French frigates *Prudente* and *Cybèle*, the brig-corvette *Vulcain* and the *Duguay Trouin* – formerly the *Princess Royal* – all under Capitaine Renaud of the *Prudente*. Having established the strangers as enemies, Canning gave orders to weigh anchor and after noon made sail to the north east with the French in chase. During the night, which proved blustery, the British became separated and the *Duguay Trouin* almost overhauled the *Résolu*, but the pursuers were otherwise thrown off the scent. Next morning *Nonsuch* and *Vengeur* were joined by the *Houghton* whose commander, Hudson, informed Canning of the whereabouts of the Commodore and the *Nonsuch*, *Houghton* and *Vengeur* then sought him out. The three vessels rejoined Mitchell the following day, finding the *William Pitt* anchored with *Nautilus* and *Britannia*. Shortly afterwards the *Résolu* was seen still trying to throw off the enemy who were all heading for the anchored Indiamen.

Cutting their cables, the *William Pitt*, *Nautilus* and *Britannia*, joined *Nonsuch*, *Houghton* and *Vengeur*, with the *Résolu* running down between *William Pitt* and *Britannia* and drawing her pursuers between two fires. The leading French vessel, the *Cybèle*, now came under attack and tacked to the southward. As she did so *Houghton* fired into her stern. Canning, meanwhile, clewed-up *Nonsuch's* mainsail, backed her mizzen topsail and luffed-up to exchange fire with the French frigate, a shot from which killed one of *Nonsuch's* crew. Renaud then withdrew to an anchorage and Mitchell:

> having distributed among his ships a greater number of French prisoners than the amount of their united crews, and each ship, from assisting to man the prizes, having scarcely hands enough to work her guns, considered it best to make no attempts to renew the action. Nor did the French commodore seem more hostilely disposed.

Mitchell proceeded to Batavia where he took in powder, guns and men, and was reinforced by the 36-gun Dutch frigate *Amazone* and an armed Dutch Indiaman.[9] The combined squadron cruised in the area until 8 February but Renaud had disappeared, so the British headed for Benkulen, leaving the *Amazone* to sail east to Sourabaya where she afterwards captured two French corvettes. It was to Benkulen that Renaud had headed and on the 9th his squadron, including the quondam East Indiaman *Duguay Trouin*, entered Rat Island basin and succeeded where Corosin had failed, taking Ballantyne's *Pigot* as she completed her repairs. Renaud's demand for the surrender of Fort Marlborough was rejected and he stood out to sea with his prize, heading for the refuge of the Île de France. Here, off Port Louis on 4 May 1794, he was engaged by a naval squadron coming out to reinforce the British East Indies squadron. In the fierce engagement that followed the *Duguay Trouin* was recaptured by the British 32-gun frigate *Orpheus*, Captain Henry Newcome. Taken to Madras, she was judged a prize and sold for £2,900 into the Indian coastal trade as the *Catharine* until October 1798 when, on arriving at Bombay under the command of a Captain Henry Flubister, she was renamed *Princess Royal*. She continued as a Country-ship and, for the last time, fell into the hands of a French privateer in November of the following year when captured off the Sumatran coast.

After the invasion of the United Provinces of The Netherlands in the winter of 1794–95, the ships of the Dutch East India Company, the VOC, were exposed to seizure by the British. Almost immediately the *Prins Frederik* was captured on her first voyage by the Royal Navy and, having been condemned as a prize, she was sold to J. Scougall who anglicised her name to *Prince Frederick* and chartered her as an Extra-ship. When homeward-bound under the command of Captain Peter Ramage, she fell in with the French National frigate *L'Insurgente*. Ramage and his ship's company fought a ferocious action in which the *Prince Frederick* was so badly damaged that she afterwards sank.

In March of 1796 the French sent a powerful flying-squadron consisting of six frigates into the Indian Ocean under Contre-Amiral Sercey. On the way out Sercey had some success, capturing a British whaler and an East Indiaman, an American merchantman and a Portuguese Indiaman. Having left Île de France after storing and watering his ships, Sercey headed for the Coromandel coast, detaching the schooner *Alerte* in quest of intelligence, only to have her and her papers fall into the hands of Captain James Alexander of HM 28-gun Frigate *Carysfort* who thus spread the news of four enemy frigates in the offing. Sercey himself lay for a while off Dondra Head, the south point of Sri Lanka, before heading north to raid the coastal traffic along the Coromandel coast between Pondicherry and Madras. Here and at Tranquebar a few prizes were taken, among which was the Country-ship *Tazbux*, owned by Pestonjee Bomanjee of Bombay. With her master, officers and sea-cunnies removed for transfer to Port Louis, the *Tazbux* followed her captors. However, she was found to be so leaky that her prize-crew blew her up and abandoned her forty lascars and fifteen passengers in the ship's boats. Luckily, these were seen from the Indian-commanded Country-ship *Bombay*, whose *nacoda* ordered his ship hove-to in order to rescue them.

The depredations of Sercey's ships prompted the Governor-General to write to London from Fort William, stating that: 'Notwithstanding your intention to furnish us with a strong naval force, we are actually at this moment in a most defenceless state and six French frigates parade in the Bay of Bengal in triumph'. But Sercey was frustrated: the expected Indiamen were nowhere to be found, for Captain Alexander left false intelligence – picked up by Sercey from the captured ships – that a larger British naval force was on the coast than was, in fact, the case. In consequence of this, Sercey made off to the east, in search of easy pickings in the Strait of Malacca and intending to destroy the British factory at Penang.

Arriving off Pulo Weh in early September, the French squadron captured Country-ships trading off Aceh among which was the *Favourite*, laden with rum and rice. Plundering the prize at daybreak on the 8th prior to sending her to Port Louis, Sercey's *Forte* with five other frigates, *Cybèle, Seine, Vertu, Prudente* and *Régénérée*, came in sight of two British 74-gun line-of-battle ships, *Victorious* and *Arrogant*. In the succeeding hours the two forces fought a bloody and inconclusive action – for the British retired to Madras with the *Arrogant* towing her consort – and the French withdrew to the Mergui archipelago off peninsular Thailand. Having refitted, Sercey cruised briefly off eastern Sri Lanka before heading for Batavia to replenish, thereby missing the passage of the large trade-convoy from China, so to that extent the otherwise inconclusive action off Pulo Weh was to the advantage of the British.

But the French were not the only danger in eastern waters, for piracy thrived off the coast of China. In June 1796 the Country-ship *Kennett* was attacked by a fleet of armed junks off the Ladrone islands.[10] After a fight of several hours all but four of the *Kennett's* company were killed and, having been plundered, she was set on fire. Only one of the prisoners survived, Richard Ramwell being later restored to his countrymen after being liberated by a mandarin. Piracy was to be a continual problem throughout the war and for long afterwards, but in December news of Sercey's six frigates cruising on the track of the China trade encouraged the Secret Committee at Macao and composed of the most senior Selectmen to correspond with the new Commander-in-Chief of the East Indies station, Rear Admiral Peter Rainier, to settle on a homeward route to be followed by the Company's ships. Rainier arrived at Macao on 30 December in his flagship, the *Suffolk* with the sloop-of-war *Swift* and two transports, intending to escort the so-called 'China-fleet' for the first part of its homeward voyage.

In the event, however, Rainier left the Pearl River on 30 December 1796 with only four laden Indiamen, those it seems bound for India, escorting them clear of the Straits of Malacca and giving neither thought nor provision for the remaining six East Indiamen ready to depart for London. Instead the senior Company commander, Lestock Wilson acting as commodore, was given specific routeing instructions to carry his six charges clear of Sercey's squadron, which was thought to be on its way from the Île de France. The French admiral was admirably prescient in anticipating such a diversion of the Indiamen and succeeded in intercepting the convoy on 28 January 1797 off the Strait of Bali, to the east of Java. The convoy consisted of HCSs *Exeter*, Lestock Wilson; *Woodford*, Charles Lennox; *Ocean*, Andrew Patton; *Taunton Castle*, Edward Studd; and two other ships.[11] Wilson, 'with as much judgment as presence of mind', hoisted a blue admiral's flag at the mizzen truck and the convoy followed with the pendants of so-called 'private ships'.[12] All hauled down the grid-iron colours of the Company and wore instead blue naval ensigns. Thus disguised as the absent Rainier and his squadron, Lennox's ships formed line-of-battle and boldly stood on.

Lennox further extended this masquerade by ordering his two leading ships to crowd on sail and reconnoitre the enemy. Sercey had done the same: the *Cybèle* under Capitaine de Frégate Thréouart advancing, only to take alarm as he approached the aggressively handled British Indiamen. Flying the signal that the enemy force was superior to the French, she went about and fell back upon *La Forte*, Sercey's flagship, whereupon the entire French squadron turned away, the French admiral's 'intelligent plan being ruined by an excess of imagination'.[13] Lennox's ships did not push their luck, even when *La Forte* lost her main topmast under the press of sail she was carrying, a fact that ought to have moved Sercey to reconsider his action. Unfortunately for him, however, in passing his commodore, Thréouart had hailed Sercey and informed him that the British squadron consisted of two line-of-battleships and two frigates, 'facts' which sufficiently alarmed Sercey. It was to be a month – by which time he was back at Port Louis – before a mortified Sercey learned that Rainier had been nowhere near the east point of Java, but at anchor off Penang.

By July there remained sixteen ships at Whampoa, all loaded and ready to depart but now the south west monsoon had set in. This convoy was under Charles Drummond in the HCS *Glatton* (third of that name, the second having been one of the Indiamen purchased into the Royal Navy in 1796). News of a squadron of Spanish men-of-war being at Manila persuaded the apprehensive Selectmen to order Drummond to take a wide sweep. This proved wise, for the Spanish squadron of two line-of-battle ships and four frigates were at sea, and although their primary objective was to cover the arrival of the Acapulco treasure ship, their secondary was to seize homeward-bound British Indiamen. Unfortunately Drummond's convoy ran into a typhoon which caused Captain George Palmer to run back to Macao in the *Boddam* to refit. With him went the damaged despatch vessel *Crescent*, which was later driven out to sea from Macao Road by a second typhoon.

Meanwhile the battered convoy had passed through the Bashi Channel between the northern tip of Luzon and Taiwan into the Pacific where, on 2 July, they too were caught in this second typhoon. The *Canton*, Captain Abel Vyvyan, and the *Glatton* were badly damaged and turned back. It was 7 September before the *Canton* finally found refuge and Vyvyan did not long survive his own ordeal. His report makes grim reading: On Saturday Evening 1 July it had begun to blow:

from the N.East hauling round to the westward of North and so round to the N.W. At sun set...the Commodore [Drummond in *Glatton*] bore S by W distant about two miles – The *Duke of Buccleugh* (Captain Thomas Wall), *Taunton Castle* (Captain Edward Studd) and *Cuffnells* (Captain Charles Cotton) in Company – we made the Ship as snug as possible before night and was scudding under the foresail and close reef'd Main Topsail, The sea getting up very fast and it blowing quite a Storm – At midnight took the Main Topsail in and not chusing (sic) to run the risk of heaving her too (sic) till day light, we kept scudding…four Quarter Masters steering with the utmost difficulty – At day break found the Main rigging had slackened very much in consequence swifted it [re-tightened it] and when in the act of taking the Mainsail in the ship broach'd too, and shipped a prodigious Sea on Deck which…carried all the Boats and everything clean overboard and carried away the Foretopmast – in this situation the Tiller broke in the rudder Head and before we could get the rudder chock'd it tore all the braces and Gudgeons off the Stern Post and went adrift – during this time the Mainmast [was] working very much and fearful of its safety while the Maintopmast was standing, got a few people up in the Main Top who had cut away all the rigging but perceiving the Mainmast to open about 30 Feet above the deck called the people down, who had just time to reach the Deck when the mainmast went away and carried the Mizen mast with it, the wreck[age] striking very hard… In the Evening the Foreyard broke… We had now nothing left standing but the Bowsprit and Foremast…it is impossible to describe the rolling and straining of the Ship – Daylight could… be perceived thro' the seams… Great quantities of Water having been taken [in]… All the Pumps were from the commencement of the Gale constantly going which just reduced the Water in the Hold to 3 Feet, and as it came out discolor'd I am under serious apprehensions that great quantity of your tea is damaged… It was with difficulty we could keep the Guns fast, everything else breaking adrift, and all the water stowed on the Gun Deck was obliged to be stove to save the People…and was under the immediate necessity of going to an allowance of a quart a man per day…

There is a great deal more in similar vein. Quite incredibly Vyvyan and his crew avoided being driven ashore, though the ship was blown to the northeastward of Taiwan. He had fifty-six men down with sickness and was burying men at a rate of 'two or three a week'. The crew eventually managed to fit a jury rudder – no mean feat of seamanship – and on 6 August 'got a Chinaman on board who…ran us into a very secure harbour close to the Continent…' somewhere in the approaches to Foochow. Here they were refused help by the local mandarin but 'built a small Boat out of some Deal Plank large enough to bring off a Butt of water at a Trip' and refitted their rudder sufficiently to put to sea. Unfortunately they again ran into trouble, losing the jury fore topmast, and putting into Amoy for assistance. Again they were told they had no business there and Vyvyan was ordered to sea, but the following day a relative of the Hong merchant Puankequa gained them a reprieve and a respite. Upon an easterly wind springing up on 30 August Vyvyan got under way and finally arrived at Macao.

The damaged ships had to be careened and refitted, the Canton's cargo dis-charged and sorted, all in the teeth of opposition by the impractical Hoppo for whom this was an unprecedented situation, so-much-so that the *Canton* was refused entry into the river and had to anchor in Anson's Bay, an unsafe roadstead in the prevailing south-west monsoon. All but the *Canton* left with the last convoy in December; the *Canton* finally departing in late March under her chief officer, for poor Vyvyan had died the previous October. The repairs cost the *Canton*'s owner, William Lushington, 18,000 dollars while the Company's costs included demurrage, the labour of discharge and reloading, plus the value of some 700 chests of damaged tea. No further lading was taken up owing to the threat of enforced payment of both import and export duties on the discharge and loading of the *Canton*'s cargo.

Like the Indiamen they had been seeking, the Spanish men-of-war had suf-fered in the first typhoon, but the predictability of the China fleet's departure, regulated by the monsoon and tea crop, made every departure from the Pearl River vulnerable. Consequently the eleven homeward-bound Indiamen of January 1799 were afforded the escort of three men-of-war by Rainier. With the convoy assembled at the Second Bar the sudden appearance of a Franco-Spanish squadron off the mouth of the river caused a flurry in the anchorage. Captain William Hargood of HMS *Intrepid*, 64 guns, immediately gave chase, and was swiftly followed by HMS *Arrogant*, 74, and the frigate *Virginie*, 38. The enemy consisted of the Spanish 74-gun battleships *Montanes* and *Europa*, the frigates *Lucia* and *Fama*, and the French frigate *Brûle Gueule*. The British formed line and gave chase but the enemy declined battle and ran into the sunset. That night the Allies anchored among the Ladrones while the British observed them from Lark's Bay, but the following day the Franco-Spanish squadron had vanished. Returning to the Pearl River, Hargood:

> began to bombard the Committee with urgent appeals to get the Indiamen away without any delay, in order that the convoy might make its way south with the strong north-east monsoon before the enemy should return; but the Committee decided…that it was their duty to have the bills of lading signed, their reports to the Court of Directors and the Secret Committee written, and their secret sailing orders communicated to the commanders…on February 4th, and the fleet sailed without further incident.

Elsewhere other losses among ships engaged in this eastern trade had been sustained. On 20 February 1798 the small Extra-ship *Zephyr*, Captain John Scott, was taken by the French corsair *La Vengeance* when running from

Bengal to the Cape and sent in to Île de France. On her way home in the North Atlantic on 3 March another Extra-ship, the *Sylph*, Captain White, was captured in the North Atlantic by the corsair *Buonaparte*. She had made a round voyage typical of this additional shipping, outwards to Botany Bay with supplies for the penal colony there, then on to Whampoa to load a homeward cargo of tea, silk and nankeens.

Nor were ships safe on the Indian coast, despite the presence of the Company's armed cruisers. On 20 April 1798 both the *Raymond*, Captain Henry Smedley, and the *Woodcot*, Captain John Hannay, were loading cargo out of lighters in Tellicherry Road when they were attacked by the French national frigate *La Preneuse*, commanded by Capitaine Jean L'Hermite. Both ships resisted, Smedley's men putting up a smart fight for about an hour before being overwhelmed, while the *Woodcot* was so badly damaged that – unusually – she sank. In fact nowhere was safe. The Country-ship *Pearl*, owned by Joseph Harding of Bombay, had been captured by the corsair *Dumouriez* in the Malacca Strait in 1793, although later being retaken by part of her own crew who had been left on board and who rose and overwhelmed the prize-crew, taking the ship into Benkulen. Harding's anxiety for his ship which, with her cargo, was worth a fortune, was understandable, though the naval authorities were too preoccupied to offer him much assistance to recover her. Six years later, commanded by a Captain Fowles, or Fowler, she was chartered by the East India Company for service in the Persian Gulf at the instigation of Samuel Manesty, the Company's resident there. The voyage was to prove eventful for, leaving Bombay bound for Basra with a general cargo at the end of May, she ran into the onset of the south west monsoon. The heavy weather compelled her crew to jettison 'all the timber from our upper deck with some large logs of teak belonging to the Hon. Co. in order to secure our boats and to prevent the violent strain upon our upper deck'. Driven south, Fowles and his officers avoided being cast ashore on the Maldives and drove their ship down to the equator beyond the reach of the monsoon, stretched across to Ras Hafun on the African coast and then north by what was then known as 'the Western Route' up the Omani coast and into the Strait of Hormuz. Approaching Basra on 5 August the *Pearl* ran aground, Fowles blaming the Arab pilot, and several dhows were required to lighten her. Fowles and his mates noted protest to the Company that wind and weather were responsible for the loss of cargo.

The *Pearl* left Basra and proceeded to Bushire (Bûshehr), sailing again on 4 October and made a good passage south so that by mid-morning on the 7th Fowles was within sight of Jazira Tumb, off Qeshm. The forenoon was hazy and, as the *Pearl* approached the isolated rock, a ship appeared ahead of them which hauled up her courses and fired a broadside accompanied by musketry.

Leaping to the helm and ordering the weather tacks hauled aboard so that the *Pearl* was hard on the wind, Fowles attempted to escape, but a round-shot struck him in the chest while another carried-away the main topsail tye and the ship was caught aback. At this juncture 'the crew, mostly lascars, sepoys horse-keepers and sea-cunnies, all quitted the deck'. Having suffered, besides the captain, five killed and several of those remaining at the guns wounded, the senior surviving officer, John Cramlington, threw the official mail overboard and surrendered. He was taken on board the enemy, which turned out to be the 22-gun corsair *Iphigéne*, Capitaine Malroux. Malroux had observed the *Pearl* coming down from the north from Jazira Tumb the previous evening and rightly judged her to be a rich prize. Next day Malroux transferred the bullion and valuable freight into the *Iphigéne* and also withdrew the surviving members of the *Pearl*'s crew.

He now made to quit the Gulf with his prize and return to his base at Île de France, but fell in with HM Sloop *Trincomalee* and the Company's armed brig *Comet*. Hailing the *Pearl* and not receiving a reply, the two British cruisers fired at her, whereupon Malroux put about, thinking his prize lost. However, the next morning he made the *Pearl* out in the distance and she seemed some distance from the protection of the two strange enemy men-of-war which were some leagues away, so he closed with her. The winds were light, the air hazy and any manoeuvring was extremely slow so that although a few shots were exchanged, nothing was resolved for several days. At ten o'clock on the 10th, the British ships approaching, Malroux ran alongside the *Trincomalee* with grappling irons lashed to the ends of his extended studding-sail booms and a fierce engagement between the *Iphigéne* and the British sloop began. As Malroux mustered his much larger crew to board, the *Trincomalee* exploded with a terrible roar, only one English sailor and a lascar seaman surviving. Because the two vessels were alongside each other, one side of the *Iphigéne* was stove-in, the main and mizzen masts were 'forced clear of the ship' and she began to fill with water:

Mr Cramlington was then on the orlop deck [of the *Iphigéne*], which was reserved for the wounded and prisoners, He therefore had two decks over his head with the hatchway choked with lumber, at this time the *Iphigéne* was going forward [in the water] but Mr Cramlington and about thirty Frenchmen managed to jump overboard through the wreckage of the ship which foundered about four minutes after the explosion, the men in the water supporting themselves on pieces of the wreck. The *Pearl* and the *Comet* were in the meantime firing at each other which precluded their sending immediate relief to the sufferers and boats from the *Pearl* picked up the survivors.[14]

Cramlington was lucky; 'A Jewish passenger whom the *Pearl* had received on board at Bussora (Basra)' and several of the *Pearl*'s crew went down in the *Iphigéne*. This extraordinary affair ended in Muscat on 15 October, whither Malroux's first lieutenant took the survivors in the *Pearl*, some sort of compromise having been worked out in the aftermath of the explosion with the commander of the *Comet*. Malroux, his surgeon and boatswain were among the 115 men lost from the *Iphigéne*. Along with Cramlington, the *Pearl*'s prize-master landed all the Indians on board – who presumably had assisted working the guns against the *Comet* – before sailing with the French survivors for Île de France.

The appearance of numerous French privateers in the Indian Ocean had by now become a grave concern to the Indiamen. Earlier in the year of 1799, on 3 February, the small Extra-ship *Echo*, Captain William Catline, which had made the round trip out to Botany Bay and then China, was homeward-bound from the Cape of Good Hope to London when taken by *La Confiance*. This was commanded by Robert Surcouf who had been menacing British trade in the Indian Ocean for four years, having first arrived at Île de France on a slaving voyage in 1795. Governor Malartic had despatched him in the *Émilie* to secure foodstuffs for the island, but Surcouf had other ideas. Although intending to load a cargo of rice on the Burmese coast, in December 1795 he had encountered a British ship, the Country-brig *Penguin*. The *Émilie* was not flying colours and the master of the *Penguin* had fired a shot intended to force the stranger to reveal her nationality, but this was just the notional provocation Surcouf wanted and he immediately engaged the astonished *Penguin* which was, with her cargo of timber, sent into Île de France as a prize. Emboldened by this success Surcouf now sailed to the head of the Bay of Bengal, rightly judging that off the Sand Heads at the mouth of the Hughli he would be able to prey on British shipping – inward or outward-bound – around the pilot station there.

At first light on 19 January 1796 the twenty-three-year-old Surcouf had spotted the pilot brig leading two outward-bound and loaded Country-ships clear of the shoals. Within an hour all three were his prizes. The two Country-ships were sent on their way to Port Louis and since both were full of rice, Surcouf had the satisfaction of having fulfilled Malartic's orders and saved the Île de France from starvation. His conscience thus clear, he transferred his crew into the pilot-brig *Cartier* and sent the *Émilie* back to Port Louis. He was now able to lie in wait in a vessel not only familiar to all regular traders in the Bay but actively sought out by them for pilots. Under this deception, on 28 January Surcouf took a third rice-carrying vessel, the *Diana*. Having dispersed several prize-crews and being now short of hands Surcouf accompanied his newest prize on her way south, only to find the HCS *Triton* lying in Balasore Roads near the mouth of the Hughli, awaiting a pilot.

On 29 January 1796 the watch aboard the *Triton* spotted the approaching pilot vessel and soon afterwards she rounded-to and lowered a boat which, on approaching, hailed them in English. Naturally assuming the pilot was about to embark, the boat was allowed alongside and a moment later the boat's crew were on the *Triton*'s deck, their weapons revealing them as French corsairs. Captain Philip Burnyeat was among those killed in the smart fight that followed between 'full two hundred stout fellows' taken by surprise by eighteen bold Frenchmen led by Surcouf himself. Although the *Triton* was later recaptured by the Royal Navy and arrived at Madras in June 1798 – whereupon her former mate, David Dunlop, assumed command – the initial loss of this ship was a major blow to the Company's prestige.

Surcouf was now embarrassed by the number of prisoners on his hands and released the *Diana* in exchange for a ransom promissory-note guaranteed by her master. Sending the *Diana* into the Hughli full of news of the French corsair's audacity, Surcouf took command of the *Triton* and arrived triumphantly at Port Louis, only to learn that in his absence the *Cartier* had been captured by HMS *Victorious*. This was not the only bad news he received, for his daring exploits had been carried out without any Letter-of-Marque-and-Reprisal and Governor Malartic was furious. Unimpressed by the young man's audacity, Malartic confiscated Surcouf's prizes and initiated a legal wrangle which later continued in Paris. The beneficiaries of Malartic's action were the British, for Surcouf took passage to France to fight his case with a claim of 1,700,000 livres against the governor. This he won after a process lasting over a year, tactfully remitting two-thirds of his award into the Directory's coffers. The case, however, had attracted the notice of an *armateur* at Nantes named Félix Cossin. Of the fifty-seven privateers sent out from Nantes in 1797, no less than ten belonged to Cossin, who had been successfully fitting-out and operating corsairs since the beginning of the war. Now he offered the 14-gun ship-rigged *Clarisse* to Surcouf, an offer that was accepted and Surcouf, accompanied by his older brother Nicolas as first lieutenant, travelled to Nantes. At the end of July 1797 the *Clarisse* slipped down the Loire and escaped to sea, evading the British blockade.

Cossin's investment nearly ended three weeks later when, a little south of the equator, the *Clarisse* ran into a British slaver. In the sharp engagement which followed Surcouf received a superficial but painful wound in the face, but he shot the commander of the slaver and was rewarded by having the *Clarisse*'s fore-topmast carried away. These two events terminated the engagement; the two ships drew apart, disengaging to repair the damage. Surcouf now proceeded directly for Port Louis, securing one prize – a brig – which accompanied him to Île de France where the *Clarisse* arrived on 5 December.

Surcouf left again early in January 1799, heading first for the Sumatran coast. Off Benkulen he took two prizes following a savage action in which brother Nicolas led the boarders, but the loss of men and damage to the *Clarisse* persuaded Surcouf to accompany his prizes back to Port Louis where he refitted his ship and recruited his crew. He sailed next on 17 August, heading again for the Sunda Strait were he took a Danish interloper on charter to British merchants, and a Portuguese merchantman. He now made for the Sand Heads and seized a large Country-ship, the *Auspicious*, which was bound for Bombay with a valuable cargo that realised, after condemnation as a lawful prize, over one million francs.

Cruising in the offing the *Clarisse* encountered the *Général Malartic*, a French privateer owned in the Île de France and commanded by a Mascarene named Jean Dutertre. The two men dined together and in the course of an over-convivial evening fell out, starting a feud that was to have consequences of some moment. Having taken his departure of Dutertre, Surcouf watered off Mergui before approaching Balasore Road again on 30 December 1799. That night the *Clarisse* gave chase to a large merchant ship and almost ran down another vessel in the darkness; she was the British frigate *Sybille* and she now gave chase to the little *Clarisse*. Obliged to run, Surcouf knocked the wedges from his masts' heels and threw all but six of his guns overboard: the *Clarisse* led the chase all night and all the following day. During the night, as the wind dropped and favoured the corsair, he was able to give the *Sybille* the slip.

On New Year's Day 1800 Surcouf took the Country-ship *Jane*, owned by Bruce, Fawcett & Co. of Bombay, as she was outwards from Bengal laden with rice. Captain John Stewart had spoken to the American ship *Mount Stewart* and been warned by her master that a French corsair lay in the offing. Stewart had therefore prudently decided to keep company with the homeward-bound Indiamen *Manship* and *Lansdown* and next day, the 31st, Stewart spoke with the *Sybille* which was returning to the Sand Heads from her fruitless chase of the *Clarisse*. This only confirmed the corsair's presence. At daylight next morning the *Jane* lay 5 miles astern of the two Indiamen and at this moment:

> we saw a strange sail…who on perceiving us bore down with great caution, because, as Monsieur Surcouf afterward told me, he took one of the Ships to be either *Sybille* or *Nonsuch* seeing the other two ships safe into the Sea.

Stewart himself was more certain of the situation.

> When I saw the strange sail altered her course, I took it for granted that she was the Privateer which the American had given intelligence of and immediately ordered a gun to be fired as a signal to the Indiamen. We continued the signal till about 8 o'clock when the Privateer saw that the ships a-head paid no atten-

tion to our firing, she hoisted English Colours – up studding-sails and royals and came on with more confidence – at ½ past 8 she gave us a shot, hauled down the English Colours and hoisted the French National Flag. We returned her fire from a 6-pounder which we got off the deck into a stern port in the great cabin, at the same time carrying every sail after the Indiamen, anxiously hoping that the constant firing would bring them to our assistance, but we looked in vain, for they never made the smallest movement to assist us. At 9 the Privateer having got very near us, they began to fire grape shot from 2 brass 36-lb cohorns [small grenade-firing mortars] which they had mounted forward. At this time it came on a light squall from the southward which brought the Indiamen directly to windward of us. During the squall we carried on [a] press of sail and the firing ceased on both sides [but] the superior sailing of the Privateer soon brought her up again when she commenced a smart fire from musketry and grape shot from one of the 36-lb cohorns – the other having been disabled early in the action; at 11 our powder was wholly expended, the last gun we fired being loaded with musket cartridges. The Frenchman then prepared to board us. They triced up graplins (sic) to their main and fore yardarms, and Surcouf gave orders to board, animating his men with a promise of liberty to plunder. Seeing that we were incapable of resisting the force that was ready to be thrown on board of us, I was under the necessity of ordering the Colours to be hauled down and we were taken possession of by an officer of the *Clarissa* (sic)...

On boarding his captor Stewart learned that the *Clarisse*'s armament had been much reduced by the necessity of throwing overboard seven of her carriage guns and all her spare spars in running from the *Sybille*. Her men had begun to cut away the upperworks when the wind fell light and enabled Surcouf to escape the *Sybille*. Stewart goes on to state what happened to his own ship and men after their capture:

Surcouf sent on board the...[*Jane*] one officer (by trade a taylor), sixteen Frenchmen, and ten lascars. They were employed until sunset shifting prisoners, and so refitting the rigging of the prize, which had been shot away during the action, and cutting out a double-headed shot which had entered near the stern post just above the waterline.

In his report Stewart records a further insight, inveighing with Surcouf against the Company commanders who had deserted him and pointing out the consequences:

All this time the Indiamen were in sight to the S.W. At sunset when Surcouf was viewing them from the poop thro' a telescope he requested I would tell

him upon my honor whether they were Indiamen or not. I repeated what
I told him before that they were two Company's ships with whom I had kept
company ever since we left the pilot. He replied they were two *Tritons*, alluding
to the easy capture which he made of that ship, and said that the commanders deserved to be shot. This was the universal opinion of the French officers.
I fear their conduct will be attended with bad consequences to the Hon'ble
Company's ships as it has given the Frenchmen a very contemptible opinion of
them and will subject them to many attacks which a spirited behaviour would
have freed them from…

The senior of the officers concerned was John Altham Cumberledge of the
Manship who subsequently became a principal managing owner and captain of the HCS *Neptune* as late as 1826. The other is less easy to identify,
the *Lansdown* not being listed as a Company ship after 1788, though she was
undoubtedly a chartered Extra-ship. However, it is inconceivable that they
were ignorant of the *Jane's* plight and one can only assume that if they were
not cowards, their zeal to avoid risking their own ships was excessive. Clearly,
a bold front would have rescued Stewart from his fate.

Happily, the worthy Stewart was not held long, being landed at Bemblepatam
to report to Calcutta, revealing what he knew of Surcouf's intentions – a good
example of merchant masters contributing to the intelligence picture:

> Surcouf does not mean to come any more near the Sand Heads, being very
> much afraid of the *Sybille* and the *Nonesuch* (sic), but intends to cruize in the
> latitude of 19 and 20 degrees…the trade of Bengal will be entirely cut off until
> they have surfeited themselves with prizes and returned to the Mauritius to
> recruit their crews. I have written to Lord Mornington (the Governor-General)
> a similar letter to this…

Three days after taking the *Jane*, Surcouf ran across two American merchantmen, the *Mercury* and *Louisa*. At the time the United States and France were
in a state of quasi-war (as a result of French seizures of American ships trading in defiance of the blockade declared by the French government's First
Consul Bonaparte). Surcouf immediately chased and engaged the *Louisa*,
which fired back with her stern-chasers while the *Mercury* attempted to cross
the *Clarisse's* stern and rake her. Seeing himself overtaken, the master of the
Louisa put his helm over and tried to cross Surcouf's bow, intending to rake
from ahead, but he failed to avoid a collision and as the *Clarisse's* bowsprit
rode over the *Louisa's* deck and entangled in her rigging, over the battered
bow of the French corsair swarmed a boarding party at the head of which
were the Surcouf brothers. A bloody fight concluded in the capture of the

Louisa. Putting Nicolas in command, Surcouf headed after the *Mercury*, but the *Clarisse* was so knocked about that he had to abandon the chase and follow his brother back to Port Louis.

On survey, the *Clarisse* was found to be both damaged and strained, requiring an extensive refit. Surcouf therefore accepted an offer to command *La Confiance*, a ship-rigged corvette with a fine reputation for speed. In raising a crew for her, however, he found himself in competitions with Dutertre, just then returned from a highly successful cruise and himself recruiting. The two men again fell out, this time over an escalation of bribes offered to likely seamen, and Surcouf challenged Dutertre to a duel. At this Malartic intervened and, after pointing out the only beneficiaries from the death of one of them would be the hated British, the two men embraced and decided to choose their crews by lot.

La Confiance sailed in mid-April 1800 but her cruise got off to a bad start, Surcouf sailing initially for the Sunda Strait where the convoy system denied him any prizes. Surcouf then made for the Seychelles, took aboard wood and water and headed for the east coast of Sri Lanka, where he arrived in August. Here he carried off several prizes before evading British cruisers by falling on the Coromandel coast until, at the end of September, he again met the *Sybille*. Some measures had been taken to disguise the frigate to look like a merchantman and a deceived Surcouf was unable to avoid a close encounter, though he approached her wearing a British red ensign and with an Englishman standing alongside him masquerading as the ship's master.

Through his 'interpreter' Surcouf began a complex explanation of his plight, sending a boat over with instructions to the young ensign in charge of the boat to pull out the plug when half-way between the two ships. As the boat sank Surcouf made sail, calling out to the *Sybille* that he had no other boat to pick up his men, a subterfuge that succeeded in giving him sufficient of a start to again throw off his pursuer. Having lost the *Sybille*, Surcouf headed north, capturing two vessels, one of which was the Calcutta Country-ship *Armenia*, Captain Thomas Meek, before *La Confiance* arrived off the Sand Heads in early in October. At daybreak on Tuesday the 7th Surcouf's lookouts spotted a large Indiaman. Issuing a ration of spirits, he treated his men to an exhortation in which he reminded them of the horrors of a British prison-hulk and promised them the pillage of the ship in the offing. They then went to their stations and ran down on their quarry.

It will be recalled from the previous chapter that in May 1800 the HCS *Queen* had caught fire off Brazil. Her survivors were taken up by other Indiamen with which the *Queen* was in company, most of them – including several women and a detachment of troops under General St John – ending up aboard the *Kent*.[15] Owned by Henry Bonham, the *Kent* was commanded by Captain Robert Rivington and bound for Bengal and Benkulen. From Bahia Bay to Bengal her passage, though hampered by the numbers on board, had been untroubled. With its end in sight, she was making up for Balasore Roads when Rivington altered course towards what he took to be the pilot vessel, hoisting the appropriate signal. As the two ships closed one another, Rivington backed his main-topsail and lay-to in anticipation of the pilot's arrival. Deceived to a point, Rivington now noticed the absence of colours flying from the approaching vessel which was not the expected schooner but a ship. He summoned his men to quarters, loaded his guns and fired a warning shot as the stranger passed on the opposite tack. Immediately, the other vessel's helm went over and she came about to range up alongside the *Kent*, firing into the large, overcrowded Indiaman.

Rivington found himself embroiled with Robert Surcouf in *La Confiance* which, according to the *India Telegraph* of 18 October 1800:

> then shot ahead, and passing round the bow of the *Kent*, renewed her engagement on the other side… She afterwards made sail ahead…of the *Kent* [when] she was…observed to haul her mainsail up and wear round for the *Kent*, and for the first time hoisted her national colours. *La Confiance* then fired a broadside and a volley of musketry from every part of the ship, which was returned by the *Kent* for as long as her guns would bear; the privateer then wearing around her stern, ranged close up alongside and received a full discharge from *Kent's* starboard guns; at this moment the privateer fired a whole broadside and threw a number of hand-grenades from her tops…some of which penetrated the upper deck and burst on the gun deck, at the same time a fire of musketry was kept up from her tops, which killed and wounded a number of the passengers and recruits that were on the quarterdeck and poop; when the ships were completely locked…Captain Surcouf entered at the head of about one hundred and fifty men [who] jumped by scores from their fore shrouds, fore yard and top, upon the poop and mizzen of the *Kent*.

Surcouf, 'in the dress of a seaman that he might not be distinguished, was one of the first that boarded'. Along with Rivington, twenty-one others died on the *Kent's* bloody deck, including a wealthy passenger named William Cator who left a widow and an orphaned daughter, a young writer named Thomas Graham, an officer of the Bengal army, the *Kent's* third and fourth mates and Mr Findlay, her carpenter. By the time the Indiaman's colours came down concluding an action that lasted for about an hour and three-quarters, the last twenty minutes of which had been hand-to-hand on the *Kent's* deck, forty-four persons had been wounded. Among these were Captain Pilkington, aide to General St John, and thirty-four of the *Kent's* crew. Hickey recounts the end of the affair:

Surcouf sent the whole of the surviving passengers, together with the wounded men, under the care of the surgeon of the *Kent*, to Bengal in a Country merchantman which he captured while conducting his prize to the Isle of France [Mauritius], about fourteen days after taking the *Kent*. He had behaved with the tenderest humanity to the wounded and with the utmost liberality to the British prisoners in general, especially the ladies whom he treated with every possible degree of respect and generosity.

The Country-ship was Arab-owned and Surcouf's arrangements were under cartel, the passengers and wounded being exchanged on promise of the release of his own men he had left in their scuttled boat to the *Sybille*'s tender mercies. Surcouf, meanwhile, retired with his immense prize to the Île de France. The news of this second major loss of an Indiaman to the charismatic corsair provoked the Governor-General to offer a *lakh* of rupees for the capture of Robert Surcouf.[16]

In Port Louis Governor Malartic insisted on a consignment of gold dust and ingots in the *Kent*'s lazarette being a *droit* of the French state, a development that left the young Surcouf indignant with rage, so-much-so that he had the gold flung overboard. Surcouf was consequently ordered home, leaving in January 1801. After evading all British attempts to catch him *La Confiance* arrived at La Rochelle on 13 April and in the following month Surcouf – who appears to have avoided any consequences of his defiance of Malartic – married and settled down in St Malo to enjoy his wealth. Here he remained quiescent for six years.

Surcouf was lucky; his brother Nicolas was less so, having been captured when emulating his sibling off the Sand Heads on 13 November 1800, in command of the *Adèle*. Captain Webster of HM Sloop *Albatross* sent his captives up the Hughli to Fort William and Nicolas was afterwards sent to England to be incarcerated in the prison-hulk *Hero* at Chatham. That same month Surcouf's old rival Dutertre attempted to seize the HCS *Phoenix*, Captain William Moffat, when the Indiaman was outward-bound. As the Indiaman approached the privateer a suspicious Moffat sent his men to quarters and, as the *Général Malartic* attempted to run alongside, her men swarming into her rigging to board the larger ship, Moffat's gunners poured in a broadside and Dutertre was compelled to strike his colours and be carried a prize into the Hughli which, but a few days before, he had almost succeeded in blockading by capturing upwards of a dozen Country-ships.

Another corsair commander of notoriety was Constance, commanding *L'Eugénie*, 'a large American schooner, expressly built for privateering and of extraordinary swiftness'. In 1801 Constance was also cruising on the pilot station off the Sand Heads, able to pick off vulnerable shipping but outrun serious pursuit. Having once been given the slip by *L'Eugénie*, Captain Frost disguised the Company's man-of-war *Mornington*, determined to rid the mouth of the Hughli of this second nuisance. '[A] false poop, to resemble that of a Country-ship, was hastily constructed, the painting changed, patches of old dirty canvas were put into the topsails and courses, and every other expedient adopted'. It was not long before Constance took the lure, falling in astern of the *Mornington* as night fell whereupon Frost, in emulation of a cautious but unsuspicious master, shortened sail. *L'Eugénie* came up hand-over-fist, hailing what Constance considered an easy quarry. As Constance called for the *Mornington* to bring-to, Frost swung the Company cruiser athwart the approaching corsair's bow and opened fire, his gunners aiming high to disable *L'Eugénie* and prevent her escaping again. After an action of three hours, Frost had the satisfaction of capturing the badly hammered *L'Eugénie* and she was taken into the Company's service as the *Alert*, her command going to Frost's first lieutenant.

As for Contre-Amiral Sercey, his offensive fizzled out. Although he had the use of the Dutch dockyard at Batavia, he enjoyed little such co-operation from Malartic at Île de France where revolutionary politics, disorder among his crews and a lack of man-power, created problems for him. Sercey remained ashore at Port Louis while his former flagship, the powerful frigate *La Forte*, enjoyed a brief spate of prize-taking in the Bay of Bengal under the aptly named Beaulieu le Loup. Half a dozen Country-ships, including Captain Eastwick's snow *Harrington* and the Indian-built Extra-ship *Chance*, were captured. The *Chance* had barely left Balasore Roads on her first trip to London early in 1799 when *La Forte* pounced on her. However, her prize-crew had almost reached the safe-haven of Île de France when they hove in sight of a British squadron consisting of HMSs *Tremendous*, *Jupiter* and *Adamant*. Recaptured, the *Chance* resumed her voyage and might well have lived up to the promise of her name but she struck a reef off St Mary's, Madagascar, to become a total loss. Another of Le Loup's victims was the HCS *Osterley*, Captain John Piercey, when on her way to Madras, though she too was afterwards recaptured. In due course, however, *La Forte* encountered Captain Edward Cooke's *Sybille*, herself a captured French frigate, and on the night of 28 February 1799 the two ships fought a furious action during which Le Loup was killed amid over 100 dead and sixty wounded. Cooke too was mortally wounded along with five of his own men killed and seventeen hurt.

The action ended when the senior surviving officer aboard *La Forte* begged Captain Robert Eastwick, then a prisoner on board, to hail *Sybille* and declare *La Forte* yielded.[17]

The surrender of *La Forte* effectively ended Sercey's operations. All his other ships had been sent home to France, except for the *Prudente*, which was sold at Port Louis and converted into a corsair, and L'Hermite's *La Preneuse*, which was caught on 11 December 1799 by HMSs *Adamant* and *Tremendous* in the Baie du Tombeau, Île de France. Run ashore, she surrendered and was set on fire by her captors.

The capricious nature of war is further exemplified by the case of the Extraship *Britannia* which was taken by the French corsair *Herion* on her way home from Bengal but, within days, had been retaken by HM Frigate *Endymion*. Built by Wadia at Bombay in 1767 to the Company's own account for the coastal trade, the 400-ton *Cartier* – not to be confused with the pilot-vessel of the same name – was captured after war had broken out again in 1803. Renamed *Caravan* she was put in the Javanese coastal trade and retaken six years later by HM Frigate *Fox*, whereupon she reverted to her original name.

Henry Meriton, whom we met previously as the only officer to survive the loss of the *Halsewell*, was one of the most distinguished of the Company's commanders. In May 1800 Meriton took command of the HCS *Exeter* on her fourth voyage to China direct, part of a convoy of eight Indiamen which left Torbay on the 27th under the escort of HMS *Belliqueux*, 64 guns, Captain Rowley Bulteel. At daylight on 4 August a squadron of three French frigates was seen to the north-west.[18] These were the 40-gun *La Concorde*, along with the *Médée* and the *Franchise*, both of 36 guns. The French commodore, Jean-François Landolphe, signalled his ships to intercept, and a chase ensued, continuing throughout the morning. At noon, however, as the French frigates closed the convoy, the Indiamen appeared more formidable, and Landolphe broke off the chase 'and by signal separated'. At this turn of events Bulteel crowded on sail to intercept the heaviest Frenchman, *La Concorde*, signalling to the four largest 1,200-ton East India Company ships to join the chase. The HCSs ships *Exeter*, *Bombay Castle*, *Coutts* and *Neptune* consequently hauled round and made after the retreating enemy. By sunset *Belliqueux* had engaged *La Concorde* and, after a sharp action, Landolphe struck his colours; meanwhile Meriton in *Exeter*, with Captain Archibald Hamilton in the *Bombay Castle* astern of him, was hard upon the heels of *Médée*.

It was nearing midnight when the *Exeter* had drawn up on the *Médée*'s quarter and Meriton hailed her, demanding she surrender to superior force. Capitaine Jean-Daniel Coudin, thinking by his enemy's bold handling and two rows of open gun ports, that his pursuer was a two-decked line of battle-ship with a powerful consort coming up fast to her support, hove-to and hauled down his colours. The *Exeter* also laid her main topsail to the mast and Meriton ordered a boat out to pull over to the prize and bring off her captain. Half-an-hour later Coudin stood on the *Exeter*'s quarterdeck and offered Meriton his sword then, catching sight of the smallness of the quarterdeck guns, asked sharply to what ship he had surrendered. Relishing the moment,

Meriton drily replied, 'to a merchant ship', provoking an outburst of indignation from the hapless Coudin.

Capitaine Pierre Jurien was more fortunate: the *Franchise* escaped in the darkness by throwing overboard several guns, spare spars and boats; meanwhile the two prizes were secured and the convoy resumed its passage. Unfortunately for their captors, neither *La Concorde* nor *Médée* was condemned by a prize-court before the signing of the Peace of Amiens and therefore both ships were returned to the French.

The chief duty of the Bombay Marine's men-of-war was trade protection, two of the Company's cruisers being stationed off Penang, two in the Bay of Bengal, while convoy escort was also undertaken, though rarely outside eastern waters. However, in 1800, the 58-gun Company cruiser *Cornwallis*, Captain Isaac Richardson, carried out this task all the way to The Downs, returning to India with an outward convoy. More common were actions in defence of the coasting trade, typical of which was the engagement fought on 22 November 1800 between the small 10-gun snow *Intrepid* and a 12-gun French privateer off Muscat. The *Intrepid* was covering commerce in the Persian Gulf and the action was a fierce, close-range duel. The enemy threw a heavier broadside, which mortally wounded the *Intrepid*'s commander, Hall, and killed five of his crew. On Hall's fall, Lieutenant Thomas Smee took over and drove off the enemy, sustaining a wound himself. The *Intrepid*'s crew was mixed, consisting of about forty Europeans – of whom two dozen were Marine Society boys – and forty lascars and sepoys, twenty-two of whom were wounded.

On her return to Bombay the *Intrepid* was ordered to the China Sea with another Company cruiser, the *Comet*, to search for the HCS *Talbot* which had gone missing. At this time the *Intrepid* was commanded by Captain George Roper – late of the *Nautilus* – and the *Comet* by Lieutenant William Henry, who had among his junior officers the son of Richardson of the *Cornwallis*. Neither vessel was heard of again, while the fate of the *Talbot* also remains a mystery.

Elsewhere vessels of the Bombay Marine assisted the Royal Navy, the 20-gun *Swift* under Captain Hayes and the brig *Star* under Lieutenant Scott co-operating in attacks on the Dutch in the Moluccas in 1801. Admiral Rainier left the two vessels to blockade Ternate but Hayes, not content with this and having some Company troops available, mounted assaults on the Dutch forts. Driven back several times and with the native population reduced to a state of famine during the fifty-two day investment, the force prevailed and the island of Ternate surrendered. Although the commander and crew of the *Swift* were debilitated by 'a malignant fever' after this service, Hayes received a warning that the Company's resident at Amboina was threatened by a large force of 'pirates'; the rapacious *orang laut* were the sea-people of the islands who

Above: An early steamer, the little *Comet* passing Dumbarton Rock with passengers on board. Watercolour by an unknown artist dated 1812. (From the British Mercantile Marine Memorial Collection)

Left: The *Comet*'s engine. (Author's Collection)

had burned the chief town on the Sangir Islands and abducted some of the inhabitants. In a bold action Hayes engaged and destroyed a fleet of forty large praus, after which the *Swift*, supported by the *Bombay* and the *Star* remained for some time in the vicinity of Sulawesi to suppress the so-called pirates who 'swarmed in those seas'.

The Bombay Marine also took part in military operations, assisting General Baird's army from Bombay to Kosseir, from whence the French Expeditionary Force which had invaded Egypt under Napoleon Bonaparte – and was subsequently abandoned by their commander-in-chief – was finally expelled. But it was the protection of trade that was its chief duty and at the resumption of the war in May 1803, Hayes was promoted to commodore of the Marine and maintained a squadron of the Company's cruisers in the Bay of Bengal. During this period, Hayes reasserted the Company's authority on the coast of Sumatra where the war had eroded it. The resources of the Bombay Marine did not extend to Chinese waters and when convoy was not available, which was not infrequently, Indiaman were obliged to take wide sweeps east of the Philippines and often sailed alone, as we have seen. This was the case with the *Thames* in 1800; having arrived at Whampoa late in the season, her loading lagged behind the 'fleet', so she sailed unaccompanied, obliging Captain Robert Williams to use Pitt's Passage, still an ill defined but generally understood route through 'a variety of channels…between New Guinea on the east, and Gilolo or Celebes (Sulawesi) on the west…'

As far as possible, however, naval protection was supposed to be available, but this was difficult by the absolute exclusion on the part of the Chinese of any foreign men-of-war within the sheltered waters of the Bogue. All that could officially be offered Royal Naval vessels requiring a refit after storm-damage was the open road at Lintin. Even such anchorages as Lark's Bay and Anson's Bay at Chenpui were usually denied to men-of-war arriving to escort convoys or bringing quantities of silver for the Company treasury. Their exclusion added a further difficulty in the security of such consignments of specie and negotiations for improvements sank under a weight of protocol and the competing sensibilities of the Hoppo and the Viceroy. In January 1800 Captain John Dilkes of HMS *Madras* arrived with ninety-five chests of silver. With the *Madras* came HM Schooner *Providence*, intended to act as a tender to visiting men-of-war and to operate as a small cruiser to lie off shore and give warning of any Spanish warships in the offing. Although boats from the Indiamen were sent downstream to pick up the chests of treasure from the *Madras*, the weather was bad and, fearing its loss, Dilkes had it put aboard the *Providence* for carriage above the second bar where it was to be transferred to the long-boats for onward transport to the Company's factory at Canton. This was done and the *Providence* returned down river but later anchored at Whampoa where, on the night of 11 February, she was surrounded by several sampans. On three previous occasions attempts had been made to cut the schooner's anchor cable, and blank pistol shots were regularly fired from her deck to warn off these boats but when one made a determined move, a live ball was fired into her from a musket. The sampan sheered off and the *Providence*'s boat went in chase, taking off a wounded Chinese and carrying him aboard the HCS *Earl of Abergavenny* where the surgeon treated his wound. Another man was said to have gone missing after jumping over the side of the sampan and reparations were soon sought by the angry Chinese.

The implication of the *Earl of Abergavenny* led to the Selectmen denying the incident had had anything to do with any Company ship other than on humanitarian grounds, although they pleaded the dangers to the *Providence* of having her anchor cable tampered with. The Viceroy agreed, but stated that impartial justice required he initiate an enquiry into the circumstances and required that the *Providence*'s commanding officer, a Lieutenant Mayo, should be called to give evidence. At this point Captain Dilkes remonstrated that he would be happy to be received by the Viceroy and explain the situation but that neither he nor Mayo could 'consent to enter into an explanation…with any person but an Officer of Government'. Moreover, neither the Hong merchants nor the Selectmen could act as go-betweens as they 'were all in the Mercantile line'. He 'as a King's Officer could not therefore submit to their interference or mediation'.

The Selectmen under their President, Richard Hall, were dismayed at being set aside so cavalierly, and a stalemate ensued until, a month after the incident, Dilkes was allowed ashore at Canton to meet the *Anchatze*, or Provincial Judge. Required to leave his sword at the city gate and accompanied by a Company interpreter, Dilkes was received by several Chinese officials. In addition to the *Anchatze* these were the *Kwangchow Fu*, or Prefect of Kwangchow (Canton), the two magistrates responsible for the area in which the factories were situated and his colleague responsible for the Whampoa area. In preparing the ground for this encounter the Viceroy had 'had a breadth of vision which was not common among the officials of the Empire'. Having agreed that the man lost overboard had jumped of his own accord, and therefore his death was not attributable to Mayo's sentinels, Dilkes was now told that there was no case to answer if the wounded man survived forty days after being shot. This was 'a magnificent olive branch, designed to put an end to the incident in such a way as to save the face of the Chinese authorities and yet not to bring any Englishmen before the court of enquiry', but there were yet ten days to go before this period expired.

Unfortunately Dilkes failed to see the true nature of this, seeing in the transaction only the devious, dubious and contemptible practices of those 'in the Mercantile line'. According to George Staunton who acted as his interpreter, Dilkes 'refused to accept the substance and persisted in reaching after the shadow, and engaged in an acrimonious discussion with the Judge on the question of admitting evidence on the charge of cutting the cable.' Dilkes attempted to take over the proceedings but the Judge ordered him and Staunton out of court, leaving the proceedings hanging upon a promise that the seaman who had fired the shot would return to Canton in ten days 'if required'. Mercifully the wounded Chinaman survived and although 'the English Sailor was still punishable by the Laws of China…the Viceroy's confidence and benevolent disposition towards the English had induced him to dispense with the strict execution of the Laws in this instance'.

Such conflicts, though usually associated with the drunken affrays of seamen enjoying shore-leave, became acute when naval vessels were involved. The presence of men-of-war in Chinese waters as puissant manifestations of a foreign power were deeply resented by the Chinese authorities, who regarded them as an affront, a point-of-view beyond the grasp of men of Dilkes's stamp. The *Providence*, having executed her purpose of bringing the silver upstream and passing it into the boats of the HCSs *Earl of Abergavenny*, the *Hindostan* and the *Duke of Buccleugh*, had in fact returned to Lintin where the *Madras* lay at anchor. She should have remained there but she had returned to Whampoa for no better reason than 'for the convenience of some of the Officers of HM Ship *Madras*', probably a shooting party on the adjacent islands where wild-fowling was known to be enjoyed by the East India Company officers.

Fortunately, the affair fizzled out: Dilkes lacked the practiced finesse of the Selectmen and said so, misunderstanding the great condescension of the Viceroy, a fact which was properly appreciated by Staunton and his principals, particularly as the Viceroy made it clear that any repetition of such an incident would have a different outcome. On the other hand the lawlessness of the river population which threatened the safety of a small vessel like the *Providence* remained unchecked. In the end printed copies of the Laws of China were circulated insofar as they affected conduct between people of the two nations where their respective systems came into conflict. This was the moot point when on the one side the British held to the principle that a ship, and especially a warship, should be regarded as an extension of the territory of her flag-state, and on the other death or injury occurred to a national of the host state in whose territorial waters the ship lay. Such incidents were to pepper relations between the two trading partners.

As early as 1796 a serious lack of silver currency had been felt in Canton, 'notwithstanding the large quantities constantly introduced to finance the foreign trade of the port…occasioned not solely by the demand of the country dealers to some portion of the price of their teas in silver', but to a considerable extent by the call for hard cash in paying Customs duties and in *cumshaw* to the Hoppo and other officials – these payments being invariably sent away in specie and not through the channels of trade. This prompted the Selectmen to request from London 'an ample remittance of Bullion'. Although vacillating and far from constant, this imbalance of trade would, in the end, lead to the forcing of opium through the flimsy and permeable defences of the Chinese Empire, but opium remained absolutely forbidden as any part of the lading of the Company's ships, a prohibition reinforced in December 1799. This was honoured in principal by the Company, but not in Macao 'where the Opium Trade is carried on by the Portuguese on an extensive and uninterrupted Scale and is the principal source whence we (the Select Committee) draw our Supplies of Bullion for Bills upon Bengal'. In 1802 the annual demand of the market at Canton for the drug was estimated at 3,000 chests. British self-interest in Macao was increased by the French threat to the place which escalated in 1801 after the invasion of Portugal by Franco-Spanish forces. The notion of reinforcing the Portuguese was delicate, for Macao was only nominally Portuguese, sovereignty still being Chinese, and neither power wished for British armed forces anywhere near the place. Nevertheless on 18 March 1802 HMS *Arrogant*, Captain Edward Osborn, arrived with three fully armed Indiamen, the *Dover Castle, Asia* and *Rainier*, each with 'a Company of European Infantry and a proportion of European Artillery' under Lieutenant Colonel Robert Hamilton. The ships were later joined by HM Ships *Orpheus* and *Fox*, and all waited outside Chinese jurisdiction at Lintin, the only place a supply of fresh water was available to the men-of-war. The Selectmen advised Osborn that neither the Chinese nor the Portuguese would sanction intervention, while they themselves feared for the impact upon trade that any high-handed action by him or Hamilton might provoke, but in the end all was brought to a conclusion by the Peace of Amiens and the cessation of hostilities between Great Britain and France, at least for the time being.

Notice of the resumption of the war reached Canton on 23 July 1803 and the fate of homeward-bound Indiamen troubled the Selectmen and the ships' commanders. A suggestion to increase the armaments borne by the ships would, it was deprecated, necessitate an increase in man-power and a consequent increase in running costs and loss of profit. Moreover, the Selectmen's fears for the reputation of the British which would follow increased numbers of sailors roistering ashore were not to be contemplated:

the abused name of liberty by which these days of Riot are distinguished seems the signal of permission for every kind of enormity. The horrid liquor to which they have easy access and which the Chinese mix with ingredients of irritating and stupefying qualities causes a state of Inebriety, more maddening and ferocious than that occasioned by any other Liquor… It would be disgusting to particularize the scenes we are witnesses to, it is only [a] matter of surprise to us, that they do not more frequently end fatally and we are convinced that the unfavourable opinion entertained of the Europeans by the Chinese was first occasioned and has since been kept up by the scenes of brutal violence and beastly intemperance.

This was not the only problem confronting the senior representatives of John Company in China. In addition to apprehensions of French cruisers, warnings of piracy were given by James Horsburgh, while the return of British men-of-war to act as escorts to the Company' ships did little to mollify this anxiety as Admiral Rainer 'apologised' for the regrettable necessity to send out a 'hot press' and poach the legal maximum of seamen from Indiamen, which varied between twenty and thirty according to tonnage. For some years the complements of homeward-bound Indiamen had been made up with a clandestine recruitment of Chinese sailors, encouraging Chinese emigration – especially to the Company's new station at Penang – but the case of the HCS *Walmer Castle* was too conspicuous to be ignored by the Hoppo. With her crew reduced by the press, desertions, accidents and disease, Captain Essex Bond had been driven to embarking a large number of Chinese on the eve of sailing with the China fleet on 1 January 1805. The ship's security agent, Puiqua, reported to the Selectmen that he was in serious trouble for condoning this action since it contravened the imperial prohibition against emigration. James Drummond, the Select Committee's president, suggested to the other Hong merchants that they approached the Hoppo and explained that the sailors were not emigrants and were engaged as seamen for the round voyage, a compromise by which, after protracted negotiations, a satisfactory solution was found.

More worrying was the uncertainty of naval escort which, at this early stage in the new war, was far from perfect. Indeed such was the anxiety on this subject at Fort William that it had been decided to refit two of the Company ships, the *Calcutta* and *Lady Castlereagh*, and arm them as 40-gun 'frigates' to act as armed escorts to its convoys. However, no such expedient was ready for the departure of the China fleet from Whampoa on 31 January 1804 and so the convoy, the constituent Indiamen of which had left the Thames before the renewal of hostilities, sailed from the Pearl River without naval escort. The 'fleet' consisted of sixteen Indiamen of the largest class, eleven Country-ships, the Extra-ship *Rolla* from Botany Bay, a Portuguese vessel and the Company's armed-brig *Ganges*, amounting to a valuation of £8 million sterling. The fleet was under the titular leadership of the senior Company commander, Nathaniel Dance, flying his commodore's broad pendant aboard the HCS *Earl Camden*.[19]

At dawn on 14 February 1804 the convoy was off Pulo Aur, bearing down upon the eastern entrance to the Singapore Strait, which in turn led to the Strait of Malacca. The ships were in good order, running before the north-east monsoon which had blown hard during the previous night. As the light grew they came in sight of a French squadron lying in ambush. Under Contre-

Sir Nathaniel Dance,
1748–1827, East India
Company Commander and
Commodore of the China
Fleet during 1804 when, on
its homeward voyage it drove
off an attack by Admiral
Linois. The action off Pulo
Aur in the South China Sea
earned Dance a knighthood.
(Private Collection)

Amiral Linois this consisted of the 74-gun *Marengo*, the 40-gun frigate *Belle Poule*, the 36-gun frigate *Sémillante* and the 22-gun corvette *Berceau*. Linois had taken a number of prizes on his way out to the Indian Ocean (see below) and had refitted and replenished his squadron at Batavia where he had been joined on his cruise by the Dutch brig-of-war *Aventurier* of 16 guns. Linois knew of the departure of the China fleet early in the year and had gleaned specific details from several sources, including an American merchant ship, two Portuguese vessels and an English brig from Macao, all of which informed him to expect two dozen British-flagged ships.

On their own part, the Company ships' commanders had agreed prior to their departure that the renewal of war meant that they would benefit from sailing in a single convoy with the Country-trade under their wing; a larger force than Linois was expecting. None were, however, carrying guns on their lower decks and even the largest bore nothing heavier than medium-length 18-pounders popularly called 'cannonades' in ironic emulation of the heavy-calibre, short-range carronade carried by men-of-war; most carried nothing weightier than 12-pounders. Neither the Indiamen, nor their commodore was particularly fitted for encountering a powerful French squadron.

Up to this date the fifty-six-year-old Nathaniel Dance had had an undistin-guished if steady career, going to sea as a captain's servant in the HCS *Clinton*

Commander Henry Wilson, a seaman with four years in
the coasting trade, served five years in the Royal Navy
and was then second mate in a merchantman trading
to the Mediterranean. After two years in the East India
Company as an able seaman, he was made fourth mate in
the HCS *Triton* in 1768, rising to third mate of the HCSs
Sea Horse and *Worcester*. Leaving the Company's service
to become master of the *Adamant* trading to Nova Scotia
and Quebec, he reverted to second mate on appointment
to his old ship, the *Worcester*, in which he rose to first
mate. In 1781 he was appointed to command the *Antelope*
and survived her wrecking when surveying, after which
he was appointed mate of the *Earl Talbot* and finally
captain of the *Warley* from which he retired after seven
voyages in 1805. His work on surveying in the Pacific was
published in 1788. (Private Collection)

The homeward China fleet under Dance consisting of East Indiamen and Country-ships
encountered Admiral Linois and a French squadron off Pulo Aur in the South China Sea on
15 February 1804. The Indiamen formed line-of-battle and opened fire, driving off Linois
and pursuing him. From a painting by Thomas Buttersworth. (© Courtesy of the National
Maritime Museum, Greenwich)

in 1758 followed by a second voyage as midshipman in the same ship. He had
then shipped in an ordinary merchantman, the *Lord Halifax*, as a seaman, rising
to second mate in the *Warner* on a trip to the West Indies, before rejoining the
Company's service as fourth mate of the former *Lord Camden*, in which ship he
rose to second mate. In 1777 he secured posts as first mate in the *Mountstuart*,
the *Royal George* – in which ship he had the experience of being captured by
Cordoba's squadron in 1780 – and the *Warren Hastings* before being appointed
to command the new *Lord Camden* in 1786. This was unsurprising, for his eld-

erly father owned her. In 1802 Dance transferred to the *Earl Camden*, herself a new vessel built for John Larkins and on her maiden voyage. As they encountered the French on that February morning, Dance's reputation was little more than that of an officer noted for ill-luck in his private ventures.

There was a scattering of naval officers among the Indiamen, including Lieutenant Robert Fowler, late commander of HM Armed transport *Porpoise*. In the previous August both the *Porpoise* and the Extra-ship *Cato* had been in company when both were stranded and wrecked on the Great Barrier Reef off the Queensland coast. The two had been on their way from Botany Bay with survivors of Matthew Flinders's *Investigator*, herself wrecked in the course of her surveying voyage on the Australian coast. Both crews got ashore and were rescued later by the *Rolla* and Fowler was accompanied by a young midshipman and future Arctic-explorer named John Franklin. Much has been made of the presence of a handful of junior naval officers in the action that followed, but the credit for what happened resides with Dance and his fellow Company commanders. The Company's ships, though not addicted to exercising for action, nevertheless possessed a battle-worthy signals system and practised the occasional manoeuvre.[20] Moreover, the collective naval and active experience among the Indiaman was impressive: Farquharson of the *Alfred* had led the deception of Sercey in 1797; Timmins of the *Royal George* had seen two fierce actions as a naval midshipman and served as a lieutenant in HMS *Indefatigable*; his first mate, Nisbet, had served as a lieutenant in HMS *Monarca* against de Suffren, and his second, Robert Hay, had been in the HCS *Pigot* when she fought and was taken by a French frigate-squadron led by *La Sybille* off Benkulen in 1794. Captain Torin of the *Coutts* had fought in the same action, while Moffat of the *Ganges* had captured a French privateer when commanding the HCS *Phoenix*; Pendergrass of the *Hope* had also been in action. Apart from Meriton in *Exeter* and Hamilton in the *Bombay Castle*, both of whom we have met in action earlier, Captain Clarke of the *Wexford* had previously served as a lieutenant in the Royal Navy, and John Boyce, first mate of the *Coutts* was an experienced privateer officer. So, as Northcote Parkinson points out, 'the China fleet had no great need of the advice of Lieutenant Fowler'.

It was the *Berceau* and *Aventurier*, scouting to windward of the French squadron, who were the first of Linois's ships to spot the approaching British convoy against the dawn. They fell back on the *Marengo* signalling first that four, and finally that twenty-eight sail were in sight running down towards the strait. Linios sent Capitaine Bruilhac to reconnoitre in *Belle Poule* and received a rather confusing report, the nub of which was to persuade him that the convoy was accompanied by a powerful escort, a deception easy to understand as even Pellew had once informed the HCS *Royal George* that she looked very like a British frigate. It was in fact from the *Royal George* that Linois's squadron was first seen – she was a very smartly run vessel – and Timmins hoisted the signal for an enemy in sight.

Dance at once sent Timmins, supported by *Alfred*, Captain Farquharson, *Bombay Castle*, Captain Archibald Hamilton, and *Hope*, Captain Pendergrass, to investigate. Lieutenant Fowler also volunteered to go and Dance had him transferred into the Company's armed-brig *Ganges* which chased after the Indiamen. In the mean time Dance signalled the remainder of his colleagues to form line while shepherding the Country-ships into a loose formation on the side of the Indiamen away from the approaching strangers. About noon Dance received a signal from Timmins that the 'strangers are suspicious' and later that they consisted of one ship-of-the-line, three frigates and a brig. Dance immediately hoisted the recall, sending the *Ganges* to pass instructions to the Country-ships. As the sun set the China fleet hove-to, waiting for the Country-ships to form up behind them – which was accomplished after dark – and for Linois to reveal his intentions. During the night the *Earl Camden*, *Hope* and *Royal George* hoisted lights to simulate a man-of-war's battle-lanterns, indications to Linois that they were prepared to accept action. Despite the preponderance of numbers, it was a bold move given the essential relative weakness of the Indiamen.

Linois was nervous; the best he could do was to work to windward during the night, in order to hold the weather gage next morning. When the following day dawned, Linois was about three miles to windward of the convoy in a light breeze. The three British ships seen to have borne lights overnight now hoisted blue ensigns, as did the armed-brig *Ganges*; the remainder of the fleet still wearing red. Still Linois appeared to dither and at about 09.00 Dance made sail and resumed his course as if making for the strait but hoisting the signal to the Indiamen to 'form the order of battle in two columns' thus, as Christopher Biden asserts, 'avoiding confusion when the decisive moment came'. In fact Linois had taken advantage of the light airs and had summoned his captains to explain that he intended to cut off the rear of the enemy formation. However, from the French perspective:

> Though near enough to distinguish the vessels of the fleet, the Admiral could not ascertain their real force. Twenty of the vessels had the appearance of two-deckers. We thought we could distinguish a frigate. A brig-of-war and three ships had blue ensigns. The latter formed part of eight ships which seemed to be more particularly appointed for the protection of the convoy…

Linois now came on in pursuit and at about 11.00 it was Dance who wavered. He was leading one column of Indiamen but was not far distant abreast of the other. This was led by Captain Timmins in the *Royal George* and it was he who took the initiative. Hauling *Royal George* out of line and edging towards the weather division, Timmins hailed Dance, calling out: 'I am of the opinion that the enemy menace our rear and that we should tack to their support!' to which Dance gave his assent. Timmins put the *Royal George*'s helm over, 'the yards were all braced round together, it was a haul of all...'

The signal for the headmost ships to tack in succession ran up the *Earl Camden*'s signal halliards and: 'At 12.10 the enemy opened their fire on the *Royal George*, *Ganges* and ourselves [*Earl Camden*] which we returned...' Seeing the five leading Indiamen bearing down upon him, passing the other ships whose crews cheered them, Linois altered course to engage. As the *Royal George* approached the French flagship, the *Marengo* bore up to rake the approaching Indiaman but was foiled by Timmins also putting his helm over so that the two ships came to action broadside to broadside. The *Ganges*, *Earl Camden* and *Warley* were quickly involved and there followed 'a hot action [which] was kept up for half an hour'. The *Marengo* fired 380 rounds to little effect initially, but was unable to determine the inferiority of her enemy and, after about forty minutes, 'suddenly the *Marengo* and squadron crowded all sail in flight'.

The *Royal George* suffered some minor damage aloft and had two men wounded, one of whom 'died under amputation', but as the enemy withdrew Dance hoisted the signal for a General Chase 'and the whole convoy made sail after the retreating foe'. This continued for two hours, when Dance made the signal to tack and to resume their westwards passage. 'As long as we could distinguish the enemy, we perceived him steering to the eastwards under a press of sail'. The action, insignificant in itself, had by its bold handling, the initiative of Timmins and the rapid support given him by Dance, entirely fooled Linois. No one was killed aboard any of the French ships, although the *Belle Poule* suffered some damage. The entire business hinged upon the fact that Linois 'observed that seven or eight of the ships fired from both their decks'. And the key to his self-deception is given by this 'observation' that: 'It was obvious that they wished to induce him [Linois] to attack them, as they did not show their lower-deck-guns until after the action began...'

Thus Linois, who had lain in ambush with everything blowing in his favour, had been deceived by a simple misunderstanding. The Dutch commander of the *Aventurier* stated later that only Linois and his chief-of-staff, Capitaine Delarue, believed in those lower deck guns. When he knew of the incident, Napoleon was scathing. As for the China fleet it eventually met its naval escort of HMSs *Albion* and *Sceptre* in the Malacca Strait and was accompanied by them to St Helena, but the crisis of its homeward passage was over. While Dance later publicly paid due tribute to Timmins and all the commanders received lavish rewards from the Company, Lloyd's Patriotic Fund and the Bombay Insurance Company (including Fowler who received £300

The Honourable East India Company's Ship *Warren Hastings*, Captain Larkins, under attack from leeward by the French National Frigate *Piémontaise*, Capitaine de Frégate Epron, off Réunion in the Indian Ocean on 21 June 1806. Aquatint by J. Jeakes after a painting by Thomas Whitcombe. (© Courtesy of the National Maritime Museum)

for a piece of plate and a fifty-guinea sword), it was Dance as commodore and senior officer who received a knighthood.[21]

Linois was to have another encounter with Indiamen on 6 August of the following year when the outward China fleet under the convoy of the *Blenheim*, 74 guns, met the *Marengo* and *Belle Poule* 'some hundreds of miles to the east of Mauritius'. The *Blenheim* was carrying Rear Admiral Sir Thomas Troubridge out to Madras and the convoy consisted of ten Indiamen. With the British to windward in a heavy sea, the *Marengo* opened fire on the Indiamen, approaching the *Exeter*, *Preston* and *Hope*, the commanders of which, Meriton, Sturrock and Pendergrass, bore down upon the French. The hot-headed and jealous Troubridge was unhappy with the Indiamen going into action – later censuring them for 'their seeming boldness' – and carried the *Blenheim* towards the enemy. Aboard HMS *Blenheim* a passenger had been killed and the Indiamen had lost a single soul. With ten men wounded aboard his own ship Linois broke off the action and although he remained in sight until the 7th, he failed to take any prizes. On his way home Linois, a disappointed man, proved that whatever his deficiencies as a tactician, he was no coward and fought gallantly with severe losses before the *Marengo* and *Belle Poule* were taken by Sir John Warren's squadron in 1806.

With her fore and main-masts destroyed and the braces to her main topsail shot away, the HCS *Warren Hastings* lies at the mercy of Epron's *Piémontaise*. After a four-hour fight during which his ship and men suffered greatly Larkins was obliged to surrender. Unfortunately, even though his colours had been struck, Larkins was wounded by a drunken French lieutenant as he gave up his ship. (© Courtesy of the National Maritime Museum)

Later that year, in August, the Extra-ships *Union* and *Eliza Ann*, together with the HCS *Sir William Pulteney*, fell in with a French brig-corvette, the *Vénus* (not to be confused with the large French frigate of the same name which appears later). The *Vénus* at first flew British colours, but then tacked and hoisted the tricolour, whereupon the closest of the British merchantmen, the *Union*, opened fire and after a sharp action lasting about twenty minutes, the *Vénus* struck to her.

Less successful defences of Indiamen were carried out, notably that of the *Warren Hastings* which was intercepted by the French national frigate *Piémontaise* on 21 June 1806 when homeward-bound from China on her second voyage.[22] The Indiaman was off the Mascarene Island of Réunion, running before a stiff north-easterly breeze, when a strange sail hove in sight. It appeared that the stranger was a frigate flying British colours, so Captain Thomas Larkins hoisted the recognition signal. On receiving no reply, Larkins prudently cleared for action. Although bearing 36 guns, Larkins had only sufficient men to man two-thirds of his lower battery, having had men pressed out of the *Warren Hastings* at Whampoa.

The *Piémontaise*, on the other hand, mounted 40 guns, most of a heavier calibre than her quarry, and she was well-manned, with 385 men eager for a rich prize. Capitaine Jacques Epron swung his frigate round to range up on the larboard quarter of the *Warren Hastings*, breaking out French colours. By engaging from leeward Epron sought to catch Larkins at a disadvantage as the *Warren Hastings* heeled towards him while his own frigate, the faster ship, swept past firing into the Indiaman's rigging aiming at disablement. Larkins's gunners returned fire, but the *Piémontaise* raced by, tacked and came back again, so close that the yardarms of the two vessels all but brushed. The *Warren Hastings* had suffered damage to her rigging and her ensign halliards had been shot away when Epron again tacked under the Indiaman's stern. Taking in sail as Larkins ordered his colours rehoisted, the *Piémontaise* again ran up on the larboard quarter of the *Warren Hastings* and Epron passed along his victim's side for a third time. Having tacked ahead, Epron ran again past the Indiaman and wore round for the second time under the *Warren Hastings's* stern before he loomed on the larboard quarter and proceeded to wreck his opponent by shooting away her bowsprit and masts until only the main was left. The tangle of fallen spars and rigging hampered the working of the Indiaman's upper deck guns, a fire was started in the gunroom and the surgeon's instruments were swept away by a round-shot as he tended the wounded. While the *Warren Hastings* had inflicted some damage to her enemy, it was insignificant and, after an action of four hours in which every upper-deck gun had been disabled, the steering shot away and the *Warren Hastings* rendered helpless, Larkins ordered his ensign struck. He had lost seven men killed, including the purser, John Edwick, and thirteen of his crew were seriously wounded. Significantly these included First Mate James Coxwell, Third Mate Edward Davies, the sixth mate and the surgeon's mate.

Unfortunately, as the *Piémontaise* lowered a boat to take possession of her prize, the *Warren Hastings* ran athwart the French frigate. Although completely unmanageable, the boarding officer interpreted this as an act contrary to the rules of war after the lowering of colours. Infuriated and, according to witnesses, intoxicated, Lieutenant Moreau ran Larkins through the body with his sword and a spate of bloodshed followed as Second Mate John Wood, Surgeon John Barnes, Midshipman James Boyton and the boatswain's mate were all wounded in a vicious fracas. Larkins survived this atrocity, though with a damaged liver, to command the ship's successor, but the *Warren Hastings* was triumphantly towed into Port Louis by the *Piémontaise*. Here the Indiaman was used as a prison-ship, incarcerating the numerous British seamen captured by the French national frigates and privateers then operating from the island. Owing to their remote situation the French actually derived little profit from their prizes beyond the contents of their holds and quantities of ship's stores and chandlery, which supported their war on British trade, but against which the cost of the subsistence of the imprisoned crews had to be offset. Along with the other prizes, the *Warren Hastings* was recovered on 28 August 1810 when the island finally fell to British forces.

Having secured his loot at Île de France, Epron resumed his cruise and on 24 September ran across the HCS *Fame* on her way to Calcutta from Bombay. Captain James Jameson put up a spirited defence, killing seventeen of Epron's men at the cost of seven of his own, but he too was overwhelmed and compelled to submit. The *Fame* joined the *Warren Hastings* at Port Louis. Eighteen months later the luck of Epron and the *Piémontaise* ran out. Following the taking of the *Fame*, Epron's frigate had captured a number of Country-ships but on 20 January 1808, the *Piémontaise* was sighted by Rear Admiral Drury as he was making for Madras. Thus alerted, Drury passed orders to his cruiser commanders to intercept her while Epron, hearing that three unescorted Indiamen had made a late departure from Bombay, headed for Cape Comorin to catch them. On 6 March his lookouts spotted the Indiamen but, to Epron's alarm, they were escorted by a frigate and Epron made sail in flight.

Captain George Hardinge, himself the son of an East India commander and ship's husband, commanded the escort, His Britannic Majesty's 36-gun frigate *San Fiorenzo*.[23] He too crowded on sail in hot pursuit and in an intermittent running action over the succeeding days Hardinge pursued Epron towards the coast of Sri Lanka. The action was hard fought, Epron constantly firing high to disable the *San Fiorenzo* and using numbers of lascars retained on board from his several prizes to work the *Piémontaise*'s pumps after Hardinge's gunnery repeatedly hulled her. Finally at nine o'clock on 8 March 1808 the *San Fiorenzo* again bore down upon her enemy. The waterlogged *Piémontaise* was no longer able to escape the faster British frigate and Epron accepted battle. The ensuing action was furious. The twenty-five-year-old Hardinge fell in *Piémontaise*'s second broadside and command of the *San Fiorenzo* devolved upon her first lieutenant, William Dawson, who fought the ship for a further hour and twenty minutes. At the end of this period Epron's ensign fluttered to the deck; he had suffered forty-nine men killed and ninety-two wounded. The length of the action had emptied the *Piémontaise*'s magazines of all but shot for his 36-pounder carronades and he had little alternative but to surrender.

Besides her captain, *San Fiorenzo* had lost thirteen killed and twenty-five wounded. Having secured his prize, Dawson accompanied her towards Colombo until next day, when all the *Piémontaise*'s masts went by the board and Dawson was obliged to tow her into port, his own colours at half-mast in honour of the *San Fiorenzo*'s dead.[24]

The French plan of getting flying squadrons of frigates through the British blockade mentioned earlier, had its successes, hence the presence of these formidable ships preying on the British trade routes in the Indian Ocean, but its double-objective in restocking France's overseas possessions was just as important. Decaen, now governor of Île de France, was no less troubled by the prospect of famine in the Mascarene Islands than his predecessor Malartic but in 1808–09 four big frigates and some lesser ships reached the Indian Ocean. These were the *Manche* and *Caroline*, both of 40 guns, and the *Vénus* and *Bellone* (neither of which should be confused with corsairs of the same name), both of 44 guns. Having resupplied Decaen they then cruised on the enemy's trade routes, the *Caroline* being off the Sand Heads in February 1809. Here Captain Billiard had some successes against Country-ships, alarming the Calcutta merchants and adding to Rear Admiral Drury's burden. By May Billiard had shifted his cruising ground athwart the approaches to the Sunda Strait and on the 31st he captured the HCSs *Europe*, Captain William Gilston, and the *Streatham*, Captain John Dale. Unfortunately, although 'both ships fought well', neither was well-manned and neither was close enough to support the other. 'The *Europe* was in almost a sinking state, when she struck her colours, and three days were occupied in refitting the two ships'.[25] A third vessel, the Country-ship *Lord Keith*, escaped.

Following Billiard, Commodore Hamelin in *Vénus*, joined by *Manche* and the corvette *Creole*, slipped past the British cruisers watching Port Louis and headed for Sumatra, destroying the Company's small factory at Tappanooly before intercepting the HCSs *Charlton*, Captain Charles Mortlock, and the *United Kingdom*, Captain William D'Esterre. Both ships were taken on 18 November 1809 when off the Sunda Strait and heading for Cocos Keeling Island. Like so many of their sisters they were spirited away to Île de France, but liberated later.[26]

Perhaps more fortunate was Captain John Stewart's *Windham*, captured by the same French force on 22 November 1809, but retaken by HMS *Magicienne* five weeks later, on 29 December, whereupon she resumed her interrupted voyage. The French frigate *Bellone* also escaped the British blockade off the Île de France on 18 August and later, in the Bay of Bengal, Capitaine Duperré captured the sloop-of-war *Victor* and the large, 52-gun Portuguese frigate *Minerva*, which was later commissioned as a French cruiser.

While the heavy French frigates were formidable in the right hands, the sheer numbers of corsairs accounted for the greater number of losses. Not being national men-of-war, their accomplishments tend to have been overlooked but, when in the hands of a Surcouf, they proved extremely dangerous and they seemed to be everywhere. Only three months after the resumption of hostilities, on 14 August 1803, the HCS *Lord Nelson* was attacked off Cape Clear, Ireland, by a powerful 28-gun French privateer, confusingly named the *Bellone*. Captain Robert Spottiswoode, assisted by his passengers, put up a gallant defence for an hour-and-a-half but with Spottiswoode, his brother – a man 'who had been in the medical line in Bengal and was returning with a handsome fortune' – the fourth mate, one seaman an army officer and two other passengers dead; the ship's first mate, Robert Ramage, her second mate, James Masson, two midshipmen five passengers and eighteen of her company wounded, the ship disabled and the mizzen mast overboard, she struck her colours. The *Bellone's* commander, Jacques Perraud – who had taken three prizes during the earlier war in the Indian Ocean – headed for Coruña with his prize, but on the 27th the two ships were chased by HM Brig-of-War *Seagull*. At five in the afternoon a running action began, lasting until half-past eight when, upon the appearance of the 74-gun *Colossus*, Perraud abandoned his prize and ran for Passagès, leaving the battered but recaptured *Lord Nelson* to be escorted home.[27]

Perraud was to be among the French corsairs to reappear in the Indian Ocean in the post-Trafalgar period and a brief notice must be taken of these events which affected both Indiamen and Country-ships. Perraud captured the Bombay Marine's cruiser *Viper* and unsuccessfully fought the *Teignmouth*, Lieutenant Hewitson. Along with Perraud was Surcouf, whom we left in St Malo with his bride in 1801. There he might have remained, fitting out his own privateers as an *armateur*, had the fate of his brother Nicholas not reignited both his patriotism and his Anglophobia which, combined with his acumen and cupidity, was to prove potent. Nicholas Surcouf had endured his confinement amid the assorted horrors of the prison hulk *Hero* at Chatham and in August 1801 he had been exchanged by cartel. Having by his incarceration conceived such a hatred of the English, when hostilities were renewed in May 1803, Nicholas impetuously accepted a new command, the 38-gun *La Fortune*. Reaching the Indian Ocean he made two successful cruises from Port Louis in one of which he captured the Company's 14-gun brig *Fly*, Lieutenant Mainwaring. However, before the Company could retaliate, Nicholas Surcouf again fell into the hands of his enemy, *La Fortune* being taken by HM Frigate *Concorde*. Hearing of his brother's second incarceration, Robert threw up the business of an *armateur* – in which he was squandering his fortune – and returned to sea in a newly built vessel, the 18-gun *Revenant*. Surcouf had refused a commission as a commodore of a frigate-squadron offered by Napoleon himself, preferring profitably independent command on his own terms.

He arrived at Port Louis in June 1807 and left again in September to cruise off the Sand Heads and in the Bay of Bengal. Here he snapped up Country-shipping, preying upon the rice-trade between Bengal and Madras in order to keep the Île de France supplied with a staple. For part of the time he operated in company with the frigate *Piémontaise* prior to her capture while other corsairs were never far away, seeking rich pickings among the merchantmen traversing the bay. The *Revenant* proved exceptionally fast, enabling Surcouf to evade British cruisers sent against him and so successful was the combined effect of all of this enemy activity that after a loss estimated in excess of £300,000, trade was suspended and 'an embargo of traffic in and out of Calcutta was maintained for sixty-seven days'.[28] In the end, however, Surcouf was obliged to return to his base on 31 January 1808 having dispersed so many of his men in prize-crews.

After refitting, Surcouf sent the *Revenant* to sea under his first lieutenant, Joseph Potier de la Houssaye. She had a specific mission: to intercept the large, 64-gun Portuguese man-of-war *Concecão de Saõ Antonio*. It was known that this ship had struck her lower deck guns into her hold and was loaded with a valuable cargo which she would bear home from Goa to Lisbon. While Surcouf remained in Île de France, De la Houssaye caught and fought the *Concecão de Saõ Antonio* in June, taking her after a bloody action. Despite the value of the *Concecão de Saõ Antonio's* cargo, it was valueless in Port Louis and Surcouf was anxious to get it and what remained of his other captures – including the sums realised from the rice he had seized – through the British blockade of the Mascarene Islands and home to his bankers. However, in Port Louis Governor Decaen was an embittered man, jealous of Surcouf's wealth and reputation, all of which he disapproved of, but he was a dutiful governor and sought to strengthen the islands' defences against the attack he felt certain would be mounted against them.[29] To this end he requisitioned *Revenant*.[30] There was an ugly confrontation between the two men, the upshot of which was that Surcouf agreed to give up his ship if he took command of the frigate *Sémillante* which had been so damaged in an action with HMS *Terpsichore* that she had been condemned as a warship and bought by the merchants of Port Louis. Renamed the *Charles*, she would be loaded with the loot from the *Concecão de Saõ Antonio* and the proceeds of other seizures, including his own, and sailed to France by Surcouf. Thus seduced by wealth Surcouf, the doyen of French corsairs whose *croiserie en guerre et marchandise* had been so troubling to Indian trade, withdrew from the Indian Ocean. After several narrow escapes from British cruisers, he reached home to enjoy a wealthy retirement. Fortunately the privateers Surcouf managed were far less successful than those he commanded and, by 1812, the Royal Navy had turned the tide against the *armateurs* and their investments. However, for some time yet French privateers cruised in the Bay of Bengal and its approaches: the *L'Intreprenante* took the Country-ship *Clyde*, Captain McGall, off Sumatra on 15 July 1809; the *Gazelle* was in the Indian Ocean twice, in 1807 returning to St Malo in 1808, and again in 1810; while the *Général Junot* and *Fântome* were also active, all making captures. But the threat was diminishing; resources at Port Louis dwindled while the burden of British and Indian prisoners increased.[31]

Nor did the corsairs always have it quite their own way, for in 1804 Captain George Saltwell of the HCS *Admiral Gardner*, mounting 26 guns and 120 men:

> beat off the *Bellona* [of 36 guns and 200 men], maintained a brisk action, and skilfully repelled so superior a force. Captain Saltwell dressed some of his crew in soldiers' clothing, and put on a shew of resistance.

Similarly, in 1808, the Bombay Country-ship *David Scott*, owned by the Parsee Ardesir Dady – but also a partner of Alexander Adamson – frightened off a French privateer by a bold *ruse de guerre*.

> The *David Scott*…in company with several smaller vessels from Bombay to China, fell in with a large French privateer at the entrance of the China Seas. By great presence of mind by dressing the top-men (her crew were all lascars) in red jackets, showing a blue ensign and pendant, and hauling out from the fleet, the privateer sheered off. The *David Scott* and most of the Country-ships, during the war, were in high order. This ship had a tier of quakers, or sham guns, and presented a most imposing appearance.

Not all Country-ships were so passively equipped and several bore a formidable armament, particularly those operating into the Persian Gulf, though they were often pierced with more ports than bore guns. Nor was all prize-taking straightforward, for the complexities of ownership and chartering arrangements combining with a tortuous legal process often frustrated the corsairs and their backers. One such oddity is the *John and James*, an American vessel which was chartered by the East India Company and was sent out to Bengal in 1795, only to be taken by the French when off Madeira. The capture sparked a prize controversy in which she was eventually condemned.[32]

Some individual ships' fates were curious. The Calcutta-built *Calcutta*, owned and commanded by Captain J. Haggey, was taken up by the Company as an Extra-ship and on her second chartered voyage she was captured by the French privateer *Syrene* off Madeira on 17 December 1799. Within hours she had been retaken by HMS *L'Aimable*, after which event Haggey took her back to London, later completing the voyage to Bengal. The *Calcutta* was then employed in the coasting trade and in September 1809 was captured a second time by the French corsair *Hirondelle* – one of several so-named. Haggey must have been ransomed or exchanged when the *Calcutta* was taken back to France to become a naval transport. His old ship became one of Captain Lord Cochrane's victims and blew up when he attacked the French squadron anchored in the Basque Roads in 1809. Haggey himself seems to have had little better luck, for he was building a second ship and, upon her launching, having by then lost the *Calcutta*, he gave his new ship the same name. She too became an Extra-ship and on a round-voyage from London to Botany Bay and then on to Whampoa, was wrecked on the poorly charted coast of New Guinea in 1807.

Retaining the same name was a commonplace among owners of Indiamen and Country-ships. Among the latter, the *Highland Chief*, owned by Lennox & Co., was chartered as an Extra-ship but was captured while on her second voyage under Company colours on 30 March 1802 by the French corsair *Bellone*, Capitaine Jacques Perraud. Captain Scott led a 'most determined resistance' but paid for his courage with his life, after which the *Highland Chief* was taken into Île de France. Having lost his ship, Lennox now laid down a second *Highland Chief* and she too was accepted as an Extra-ship. However, on her maiden voyage in October 1807 Captain Makepeace fell in with the French national frigate *La Piémontaise* and the second *Highland Chief* was also sent in to the Île de France to join her namesake. Here both vessels and their wretched crews languished until the island fell to the British in 1810. Among Perraud's captures on this cruise was the HCS *Porcher*, Captain Benjamin Blake, which arrived at Île de France on 9 April. She was sent home to Bordeaux where she arrived the following February to be sold to local owners who renamed her *Ville de Bordeaux*. Fortunately she was recaptured in 1804 and, restored to her original name, continued trading to India as a Licensed-ship.

The crews of the captured ships at Port Louis were kept in many of their own vessels, one of which was the Calcutta-built *Althea* of 800-tons.[33] Captain Roberts lost her in the Indian Ocean on 17 April 1804 to overwhelming force, the frigates *Belle Poule* and *Atalante*, both part of Linois' squadron. But not all the prizes taken in the Indian Ocean were recovered after the capture of Mauritius in 1810. Another seizure by Linois was the 1,500-ton Country-ship the *Countess of Sutherland* which had been built on the Hughli and then chartered as an Extra-ship. In November 1803 she was outward from London when she fell in with Linois's squadron in the Gulf of Guinea as the French admiral was himself heading for the Indian Ocean. Later in his cruise, Linois took the 560-ton Extra-ship *Hope*, owned and commanded by Captain Henry Elliott. Both prizes were sent in to Île de France, but whereas the *Hope* was there in 1810 when the island was taken by the British, and although the *Countess of Sutherland* arrived a month after being captured, no trace was found of her. Another unaccounted for vessel was the Extra-ship *Stirling Castle*, Captain Thomas Henchman, taken by a French corsair when on passage between Calcutta and Colombo in 1804.

During his cruise Linois' success against isolated merchantmen was marked. He took the *Lucy and Maria*, Captain Walter Dawes, in the Indian Ocean in February 1804, sending her in to Amboina where she was in due course retaken by the Royal Navy and returned to her owners, Gilmore & Co., of Calcutta. The *Marengo*, Linois' flagship, seized the *Admiral Aplin*, on 9 January 1804 after Captain John Rogers – a survivor of the ill-fated *Halsewell* – had 'sustained a long action', his vastly superior enemy keeping at a distance favourable to his long guns. Other captures included the *Upton Castle*, which had become a licensed ship and was taken on 18 August 1804 by Linois in

Marengo; and the *Brunswick*, Captain James Grant, taken off Pointe de Galle on 11 July 1805 by both *Marengo* and *Belle Poule*.[34]

The ubiquitous nature of the French *guerre de course* could catch a ship inward from India within sight of the English coast. One such victim was the 217-ton Indian-built *Flora*, Captain Ferguson, which was taken off Folkestone in September 1799 and carried into Boulogne. She was lucky, being cut-out by the boats of a British man-of-war a few days later, but this was unusual. Some ships – and their crews with them – suffered violent swings of fortune and an extraordinary tale attaches to the 520-ton French ship *Modeste* which was refitting at Chittagong on the outbreak of the war. Taken as a prize, she was sold to Hogg, Davidson & Co. of Calcutta, renamed *Coromandel* and placed under the command of Captain J. Robertson. In early 1800 she took up a charter for London and made a voyage as an Extra-ship before resuming employment in Indian waters. On 15 March 1805 she fell foul of the corsair *Henriette*, whose commander sent her as a prize into Île de France. Here she remained until the island fell to the British, whereupon she was restored to her owners in December 1810. Within two years she had gone ashore in the Karimata Passage, but was salved and repaired. Then, on 2 August 1814, having left Batavia for London, she had almost reached her destination when she was taken by the American privateer *Yorktown*. Ten days later she was recaptured in home waters by HM Frigate *Eridanus*. Long after the war, in 1821, she finally foundered off the Indian coast.

After the outbreak of hostilities with the United States in 1812 American privateers were found far from the North Atlantic and British home waters. The Extra-ship *General Wellesley* was taken in the South Atlantic towards the end of the war when outward-bound from London towards Batavia; sent in to Charleston she was wrecked on the bar. The Licensed-Ship *Clarendon* was taken off the Cape of Good Hope in January 1815 by the United States privateer *Young Wasp*. Despite the fact that the war between America and Britain was over, in a particularly partial and harsh judgement the *Clarendon* was condemned as a prize when she arrived in Baltimore in April 1815.[35]

Wartime conditions produced enemy privateers, but in Chinese waters the problem of piracy was perennial. The Portuguese maintained an armed brig and a *grab* at Macao which were effective at policing Macao Road, but beyond, among the islands and the anchorages to the east and west, and along the coast of Hainan, literally hundreds of armed-junks awaited whatever pickings they could seize. Indeed, so bold did these 'Ladrone Junks' become that they actually convoyed native Chinese traffic, in particular the craft carrying salt, which enjoyed a government monopoly. Since foreign naval vessels in Chinese waters invariably created huge diplomatic problems, the Company's

Selectmen debated whether to fit-out two armed ships themselves under the pretence that they were surveying vessels. The problem was vexing enough, particularly as a naval escort was considered indispensable to the homeward China fleet and in September the frigate *Phaeton* further complicated matters when, having taken a rich Spanish prize off Mindanao, she sent this in to Macao only to have the vessel wrecked on the coast to be pillaged by the Chinese, who also interned the prize-crew. The brig-of-war *Harrier* was sent to remonstrate and both captains sent letters to the Viceroy at Canton while the Selectmen attempted to distance themselves from the affair on the grounds that it was none of their business. The matter descended into a farcical argument over protocol: Captain John Wood of the *Harrier* refused to stand in the presence of the Imperial Viceroy and the latter refused Wood a chair upon which to sit.

By ascending the river, Wood had broken the imperial edict forbidding foreign men-of-war entry into Chinese waters and the Viceroy now took his displeasure out on the wretched Hong merchants whose intermediary function put them at the mercy of both sides. Next a letter of remonstrance was accepted from Captain Ratsey of the *Phaeton*, Wood's senior, by a mandarin of lower rank than the Viceroy. This did not end matters for, while the Royal Navy pressed for the return of its prize's cargo and crew, the Viceroy objected to the presence of warships within the Bogue. The matter was left unresolved.

For its own anti-piracy protection and the betterment of the charts of the Chinese coast the Company agreed to send out a survey vessel, the *Discovery*, and build a second one at Bombay. This was yet another *Antelope*, an armed brig which arrived at Macao on 5 May 1806 under the command of Lieutenant Daniel Ross of the Bombay Marine. Ross, however, found the Portuguese hostile to his activities, even though on 20 October a large fleet of 'Ladrone boats' passing through the waters of Macao were driven off by a few shots from the *Antelope*'s guns. To support the *Antelope*, a small Country-ship named the *Prime* was acquired to act as an armed-tender to keep her supplied and act alongside her when necessary. Notwithstanding the presence of these two vessels, piracy flourished in many forms, one favourite being abduction for ransom.

On 7 December 1806 the chief mate of the Country-ship *Tay*, a Mr F. Turner, was being rowed ashore by five lascars to arrange for a pilot when his boat was attacked and all were kidnapped. A ransom of 3,000 dollars was demanded for Turner's release and when this was turned down, it was increased to 10,000; later, in mid-January, it rose to 30,000 dollars. The negotiations dragged on until May 1807, when Turner and his boat's crew were liberated at a cost of 6,000 dollars made up from 2,500 dollars in cash, three chests of opium and

5,000 pieces of matting. Turner and the lascars were brought back to Macao by the Company's surveying cruisers *Antelope* and *Discovery*.

For those Chinese seamen retained aboard Indiamen to make up for the losses of white sailors to disease and the Royal Navy, London had little hospitality to offer. The long periods in between the seasonal voyages of Indiamen meant that many were thrown ashore. Gradually, generated by that quiet patience and stoic acumen that westerners too easily characterised as 'inscrutability', small Chinese communities grew round and out of the boarding-houses which accommodated them. Among the most prominent of these was 'John Anthony', a man who learned English, married an English wife and by 1799 was running what amounted to an agency on behalf of Chinese seamen stranded in London. Based in Shadwell this remarkable man appeared in court, acting as go-between and interpreter when Chinese sailors were involved in affrays or disputes against the boarding-house runners, landlords and ladies who sought to defraud them by trickery. He changed money and acted as banker, adviser and friend, and thereby amassed a considerable fortune from commission while his pastoral and domestic services offered to his fellow countrymen earned him warm approbation. In 1805 John Anthony was naturalised by Act of Parliament, taking the English name he has left to posterity and assuming, at least nominally, the Anglican faith. His death occurred not long afterwards and his cortege was accompanied to Shadwell church by hundreds of mourners, not only Chinese, but many of east London's poorer citizens to whom this remarkable man had become a friend.

In addition to the Chinese seamen engaged for homeward voyages the Company had for some time been conducting skilled Chinese artisans to Penang. As already mentioned this was, strictly speaking, illegal. In late 1804 Lord Wellesley, Governor-General at Calcutta, had intimated to the Selectmen that further emigrant labour would be useful in Trinidad, which had been annexed to the British crown in 1797. While there was no shortage of those willing to sign up as indentured labour for a small cash advance and a better life, the difficulties of circumventing the imperial edicts seemed insuperable, despite the Selectmen's enthusiasm for the project. The affair of the HCS *Walmer Castle* was still remembered and the Hong merchant involved, Puiqua, had been heavily fined for his transgression. The Selectmen were therefore opposed to using the Company's own ships and not even in favour of sanctioning the traffic aboard Country-*wallahs*, which, it was felt, would compromise the Company's activities and their essential allies, the Hong merchants. However, by shipping the emigrants downstream in junks to Macao and then embarking them in Portuguese vessels for the passage to Penang, a small traffic in indentured labour began. The extent to which this would grow

in the wake of the abolition of the slave-trade will become clear in a later
volume, but in this way people were exported just as opium was imported:
with the connivance of all parties as long as the outward forms of propriety
were maintained for purposes of imperial 'face'.

Despite the war in Europe, trade continued as before, the outbound Indiamen
discharging English woollens to the value of around £1.2 million annually. Both Indiamen and Country-ships coming from India brought huge
quantities of rice and Indian cottons, while fur-traders from the Pacific
north-west of America, both British and American, were now regularly arriving at Whampoa. The deficiencies in the balance of trade, usually – but not
always – in favour of the Chinese, were made up in opium and silver specie,
the former, of course, illegitimate, and none of this taking into account the
volume of private trade 'on adventure'.

   The China fleet leaving the Pearl River in 1805 consisted of about a score
of Indiamen and three times that number of Country-ships, laden chiefly
with tea and silk, the quantities of porcelain loaded as ballast scarcely troubling the compilers of manifests. Such was the commercial activity that here,
as elsewhere, it overrode national enmity and the Selectmen arranged for a
loan to be made to the Spanish merchants on the grounds of a:

> general principle of the propriety and advantage of Foreign Companies trading
> to this Country, mutually accommodating each other in cases of temporary
> exigency and embarrassment...

This did not prevent either the Royal Navy protesting, or the drunken revels
of British jacks ashore culminating in the tearing down of Spanish flags, but
neither did it prevent the mutual accommodations of trading partners.

   Of some significance was the continuing inability of most Selectmen to
speak Chinese, all translations at the commonplace level being in the hands of
Chinese translators whose knowledge of English was rudimentary and confined
largely to pidgin, though several of the Hong merchants were better informed.
Among the British residents only Sir George Staunton was familiar with the
official tongue, Mandarin.[36] This lack of mutual intelligibility failed to ease the
rumbling argument of the *Phaeton*'s prize which resurfaced with the change of
naval command of the East Indies station. Admiral Rainier had been relieved
in May 1805 by Sir Edward Pellew, but that August the Admiralty unwisely
divided the station, conferring command of operations east of Sri Lanka to
a second flag-officer, the irascible Sir Thomas Troubridge, whose plundering
of men from the HCS *Perseverance* has already been remarked. The arrangement was unsatisfactory and in due course the Admiralty saw the error of its

Poor Jack; although a beribboned seaman in the Royal Navy in this drawing by Cruikshank illustrating the patriotic sea-songs of Charles Dibdin, Jack was traditionally trained in, and pressed from, British merchant ships. (Author's Collection)

ways, recalling Troubridge who died in the foundering of his flagship on the homeward passage as mentioned earlier. Pellew now had a free hand and, highly distinguished and competent though he was, he unashamedly declared his chief ambition was to make a fortune on behalf of his two sons. Nor was he shy of lining his own nest and to that end the flag-officer's percentage of prize-money earned on the station was an attraction. Thus the unfinished business over the *Phaeton's* prize required a resolution that would be beneficial to Pellew and, even before Troubridge had left for home in the ill-fated *Blenheim*, Pellew revived the matter on 7 August 1806, sending Wood back to Macao with a convoy under his wing and special instructions in his pocket.

However, before pressing the claim Wood, now in command of *Phaeton* herself, took her on a cruise off the Philippines and returned to Macao with another Spanish prize, the *Prince Fernandez*, with a cargo estimated at 400,000 dollars and from which Pellew would receive a handsome rake-off.[37] Hearing of Wood's arrival the Viceroy despatched three of the Hong merchants to tell him that while he would treat with him personally, he must on no account attempt to bring his frigate into the Pearl River. The discussions rumbled on through intermediaries, the *Phaeton* being joined by a second frigate, the *Sir Edward Hughes*, commanded by Captain Ratsey who also joined in. Although the British warships remained outside the Bogue forts, the Viceroy ensured that they were able to acquire fresh supplies at an anchorage at Chunpee Bay, close-by.

Captain Rolles of HMS *Lion* had no better luck in gaining an audience with the Viceroy when he arrived with the convoy of East Indiamen direct from London. By this time the relationship between the Chinese and the British was coloured by two events, the *Neptune* affair and a shortage of rice. The latter arose first and was the more pressing, arising from a high price being demanded for scarce home-grown rice. Both the Viceroy and the Hoppo were concerned that the dearth of so essential a staple would pro-voke riots in Canton which might lead to more serious rebellion among a population already stirred by news of an uprising in Taiwan. The situation for the Chinese government was acute since the prevalence of pirates along the coast prevented transhipping rice from elsewhere. To remedy this situation the Hong merchants, led by Puankhequa, advised the Select Committee of the situation and, in asking for imports of Indian rice, spoke of the Hoppo having agreed to waive port-charges for a limited period.

Mr Drummond, the President of the Select Committee 'had every wish to place the Chinese authorities and merchants under obligations to the Company, and he sent urgent appeals to the three [Indian] Presidencies'. He also arranged for credit to be afforded to a Captain C.C. McIntosh, a man prominent in the Country-trade, to arrange for the shipment of 20,000 tons of rice before the end of the 1806 season in November. There were some difficulties over the consistency of the price since contrary to predictions it fell, threatening the importers with losses and, as a consequence, Puankhequa fell out with the Selectmen in the dispute but, in due course, all was finally resolved upon an agreed flat rate payment through the Hong merchants.

Unfortunately this mutually beneficial deal was lost amid the disturbances surrounding the liberty-men of the HCS *Neptune*. On 23 February 1806 a party of seamen from the *Marquis of Ely* had:

> been enticed into boats, robbed of their belongings, and flung stripped into the river or on shore, probably stupefied with drink; some were rescued from the river by the purser with difficulty; one had disappeared and was not seen again.

Following this, the seamen allowed ashore next day were bloody-minded. Several affrays broke out, promoted particularly by men from the *Neptune*, who set fire to a customs post. The Hong agent responsible for the *Neptune*, Mowqua, considered matters might be set aright by making a present to the discomfited customs official and, although the mood of the local population was inflamed, this seemed to work.

On the 27th Captain Buchanan of the *Neptune* called on the new chairman of the Select Committee, Mr Roberts, to inform him that a Chinese man, Leau-Ah-ting, wounded in one of the many affrays had since died, which required the striker of the fatal blow to be delivered up to Chinese justice. Such had been the confused nature of the disturbance that it was impossible to ascertain who precisely had committed the offence. The Committee ordered Buchanan to convene a court with two other commanders and examine the *Neptune*'s men. On the Chinese side the Hoppo stopped all commerce while the magistrates carried out an inquiry ashore at the termination of which Mowqua was taken into custody against the production of a culprit from the *Neptune*. Meanwhile Buchanan, unable to find a single defendant, had isolated seven seamen who had proved 'most active in the riots'. This did not suit the Chinese, who wanted the sole culprit and they hinted that Buchanan himself might be arraigned. Matters drifted into a serious impasse and involved a higher judicial officer, the provincial Judge.

A compromise was reached: loading could resume on all ships except the *Neptune* which would be retained at Whampoa until the murderer had been identified and on 28 March an agreement was concluded whereby Buchanan was ordered to bring up to Canton all fifty-two seamen allowed liberty at Canton a month earlier. However, it was not until 8 April that the trial got under way in the old factory. Present on the British side in addition to the Selectmen and Buchanan was Captain Rolles of the *Lion* who attempted to have marines present, though he was dissuaded from this indelicacy by the Selectmen. A lengthy process of questioning produced no more evidence beyond an admission that some of the seamen had carried rattans and had been excessively drunk. However, by this time eleven sailors had been identified as having been the most turbulent and it was clear that the Chinese would be content with any one of them who would satisfy the need for justice to be seen to be done. On the other hand the British required the guilty man to be precisely identified. Once again impasse loomed, and with ten Indiamen awaiting the order to sail, matters teetered upon the edge of a cultural chasm.

Now a second compromise was arranged whereby one English seaman would be delivered up as the nominal murderer upon 'whom would be inflicted a merely nominal punishment'. This was rejected by Roberts and his Committee who feared the worst, but they had perforce to accede to the final Chinese demand that they alone be allowed to determine the guilty man and once again the eleven men were brought into court. Having concluded their deliberations the Chinese judiciary declared that by admitting himself drunk, wounded and in possession of a pipe during the affray on 24 February, Edward Sheen was deemed guilty. He was taken into custody, the rest of the seamen held were released and loading of the *Neptune* resumed. As soon as the imperial pleasure was known, the China fleet sailed.

In the event Sheen's charge was reduced from homicide in an affray to accidental killing. He was fined about £4, a trifling amount after so prolonged a process, but it is clear that just as the Chinese responsible for the trial were essentially seeking a way out of the affair in which they suffered no loss of honour, it was also in their own interest not to render worthless a trade that was of vast pecuniary advantage to themselves personally. The firm stand of the Select Committee, at peril to the annual trade, over a semblance of respect for the individual rights of the common sailor was, in its turn, essentially motivated by their own desire to show the Chinese their own power, as much as an example of English jurisprudence. Behind the scenes, however, there were suggestions that Mowqua had been influential – and probably 'bled white' – while the dead Leau-Ah-ting's relatives had been mollified by a grant of cash. Although Sheen was released into the custody of the Selectmen, he was not allowed to leave China until 4 March 1808 when he was sent home in Captain Pendergrass's *Hope*.

One curiosity of this period was the recapture of the Country-ship *Admiral Rainier*. On 30 December 1806 Captain George Richardson in the HCS *Dover Castle* hove in sight of the *Admiral Rainier* wearing French colours. She had been owned by Hudson, Baker & Co. of Calcutta and had been commanded by Captain Lay when she fell foul of a French national corvette. Retaking her,

Richardson sent her into Calcutta as a prize and had the satisfaction of having her purchased into the Royal Navy as a 5th Rate, to be named *Hindostan*.[38]

The imperial proscription against foreign warships entering the Pearl River complicated many matters, not least the occasional shipments of silver produced at this period from trade with China which were sent from Canton to Calcutta. The chests of specie had to be carried down to Whampoa by the boats of the Indiamen and then on to Anson's Bay by ship. In 1807 the Country-ship *Albion*, in preparing to drop down stream towards the frigate *Modeste* waiting off Chuenpi, caught fire. To save the chests of bullion she carried she was scuttled but the silver was later recovered by divers, amounting to 2,250,467 dollars.

The following year, 1808, the task of bearing the silver to Calcutta fell to HMS *Jupiter*, with a smaller consignment going in the *Belliqueux*. Naval captains were entitled to a small percentage for this work by way of perquisite, usually 1 per cent, but Elliot of the *Modeste* and Baker of the *Jupiter* rapaciously demanded twice this amount, at which the Selectmen baulked. However, the Governor-General, Lord Minto, referred to the orders of the Court of Directors in London which stipulated a 1 per cent payment and with this they had to be content. In 1810 Captain Francis Austen, brother of the novelist and then commanding HMS *St Albans*, convoyed the Indiamen from the Pearl River to London. He was allowed no more than 1 per cent, receiving instructions to share this single percentile when obliged to ship some of the money to Madras in another man-of-war. Notwithstanding this limitation, the Company's payment to naval officers can scarcely be regarded as niggardly, all post-captains concerned doing handsomely out of the business. Further to this perquisite, men-of-war engaged in the escort of the China fleet were paid an allowance – or *batta* – of £500 to the captain and £250 to the wardroom officers when east of Madagascar, an arrangement that must have added some comforts to the hardship of their dreary duty. Other easements to the labours of naval officers were provided by American merchant ships which, when lying at anchor, were as liable as British merchantmen to be raided for seamen.

The presence of men-of-war was, along with the cruises of the Company's *Antelope* and *Discovery*, regarded with suspicion by both the Chinese and the Portuguese, the latter owing to the aborted attempt of the British to occupy Macao in 1802. The naval cruisers were mainly employed attacking Spanish shipping off the Philippines, a profitable exercise for both the ships concerned and their commander-in-chief, Pellew. However, along with the Company's two cruisers, to which a third – the *Retreat* – was now added, HM Brig-sloop *Diana* was tasked with combating piracy and on 8 August 1807, Lieutenant William Kempthorne boarded an American schooner in Macao Roads. The master was killed in defending his vessel which had, according to Kempthorne's despatch 'been committing acts of Piracy under English Colours on the coast of Spanish America'. Kempthorne then jealously escorted his prize to India, foolishly abandoning his prime task and presuming the native Chinese pirates to be quiescent. In his absence they emerged to overwhelm and defeat the Viceroy's 'Mandarine fleet' sent to extirpate them.

In the new year of 1808 a new Hoppo named Chang reiterated the imperial prohibition of opium, repeating those of 1729, 1799 and 1800.[39] Theoretically at least the Selectmen stood aloof from this trade, though everyone knew that both Malwa and Patna opium from Bengal was imported into China in Country-ships and the Company had a good deal to do with it, since it controlled the production of the crop in India. The subject of opium was intruding increasingly into the open because an alarm had occurred in the previous year when American vessels began bringing in Turkish opium which was considered very inferior to the Indian product and was 'used entirely for the purpose of adulterating the product of Bengal', circumstances that disturbed clandestine trade in which numerous Anglo-Indian merchants quietly dabbled. Other developments held out more promise.

British naval operations under Pellew brought the first signs of an easing of the navigation of the eastern seas in the spring of 1808 when a despatch arrived from the admiral then in his flagship, HMS *Culloden*, in the San Bernadino Strait. Dated 14 January, Pellew informed the Selectmen that:

> there now remains no impediment to the [Company's] ships proceeding with the most perfect safety thro' the Straits of Sunda…the whole remaining force of the Dutch in these seas…having been destroyed at Gressee [Griessie at the eastern extremity of Java] by the Squadron under my command early in December last.

The news came too late for the sailing of the homeward ships on 9 March and was promptly rescinded by Pellew on 25 September, when the situation again deteriorated. However, happier news arrived that Spain and Great Britain had been reconciled on 4 July 1808 following the revolt of the Spaniards in May against Napoleonic rule and this information arrived at Manila on the following 28 February. However, while the Chinese failed to suppress piracy and the Viceroy so far finally debased himself as to request the assistance of the Company's three surveying cruisers, the British commanders in distant Calcutta were meditating an altogether different offensive. In the meantime Captain William Dawson of HM Frigate *Dédaigneuse* joined Ross in the *Antelope* and with the *Discovery* and *Retreat*, cruised along the coast to the east of Macao, hoping to smoke out the junks of the piratical 'Ladrones'.

The apparent acquiescence of the higher Chinese authorities in the Viceroy's unprecedented request for British help to rid the coast of piracy excited the revival of an old project, the British occupation of Macao. This was now lent a degree of urgency owing to a number of circumstances not least of which was the situation of Portugal herself, now that French hegemony had extended into the Iberian peninsula following the Spanish uprising of 2 May 1808. French activity based on the Île de France encouraged the spectre of a French occupation of Macao, which was now directly hinted at by secret intelligence that the French had requested the Portuguese to improve Macao's defences, a suggestion that 'can only be with a view to harass our valuable trade…' In Calcutta the Governor-General in Council, having consulted Sir Edward Pellew, was determined to offer the Portuguese enclave the protection of His Britannic Majesty's arms. This reinforcement rather than dispossession of the Portuguese followed a similar accommodation reached at Goa, but the governor of Goa had not informed Macao of his own circumstances and left his colleague uncertain as to how to proceed.

Rear Admiral William Drury was appointed to the task prior to his relieving Pellew as Commander-in-Chief and on 11 September 1808 he arrived off Macao from Madras with a small detachment of about 300 troops. These were landed on the 21st with reinforcements arriving from Calcutta a month later. While the Portuguese were angry at the presumption inherent in this action, the Chinese were incensed: the Portuguese were tenants; Macao remained Chinese sovereign territory and the presence of British forces was regarded as infamous, dishonourable and insulting. The Viceroy did the only thing he could and suspended all trade, a circumstance that placed the Selectmen in an invidious position, but the *Tsontoc*, the Viceroy himself, in a worse one.

If there had previously occurred collisions between the British and Chinese commercial cultures they were scarcely to be compared with that which now pertained between the Royal Navy and the Select Committee. Drury could not understand why the Viceroy refused to see him, misunderstanding the relationship between the Company's Presidential *Taipan*, Mr Roberts, and the Chinese authorities. Neither did he comprehend the traditional low esteem in which military officers were held by Chinese opinion, nor their aloof detachment from – and complete indifference to – events in Europe. Their failure to fear, as Drury considered they must fear, the imminent appearance of the French was all the more lamentable since they had by now landed in Java. As a consequence of Roberts and his colleagues treading their customary cautious if inept way through the circumlocutory quagmire of Sino-British intercourse, notwithstanding the robust stand they made from-time-to-time, Drury – the man of action – found the tedium of negotiation beyond his patience. The situation was, as always, confused by vested interest on all sides, the stern imperative for the maintenance of 'face' and propriety, and the maintenance of trade. There were fourteen large Indiamen then breaking bulk at Whampoa, along with fifteen large Country-ships from Bombay, six from Bengal, five from Penang, and one each from Madras and Negapatam. Failure to discharge the cargo of cotton would ruin the Hong; failure to load tea would ruin the Company; failure to pay duty on imports and exports would ruin the Hoppo and Viceroy, while the unapproved occupation of Chinese territory dishonoured the distant Son of Heaven in Peking. However, the Emperor, most of whose customs' duties went into the Viceroy's pockets, did not much care if either Canton or the foreigners' Company were ruined; while the Portuguese governor, Bernado Alexe de Lemos e Faria, wished to await his own instructions from the Viceroy at Goa. Amid this confusion Roberts and the Selectmen vacillated, confounding Drury with changing advice, fearful that not only would the season's trade be ruined, but the laden ships might be confined by a Chinese blockade of the river's Second Bar.

Drury was now faced with a multitude of concerns: the cessation of trade, the interdiction of the normal supply of produce to Macao from the mainland which threatened the inhabitants with starvation, and a demand from Canton for the instant withdrawal of British troops from Macao. The admiral, regarding his mission as a pacific reinforcement of an ally to head-off the common French enemy, now found himself enmeshed. While he could wave his commission as a King's flag-officer and insist on his over-riding superiority as the sole representative of His Britannic Majesty's government, the troops in his ships were the Company's. Meanwhile the Selectmen, having changed their minds in respect of their relationship with Dom Faria, now decided that Macao *should* be occupied. It was not a happy start as all parties stumbled upon the banks of the Rubicon.

Having landed the Company's sepoys, Drury now moved his men-of-war to Chenpui to take on fresh water, further exacerbating matters by sending two frigates, *Dover* and *Dédaigneuse*, beyond the Bogue to Whampoa 'to receive specie, which was promised to a great amount, both public and private'. He next ordered all British shipping out of the Pearl River, whereupon the Company's commodore at Whampoa, Captain Miliken Craig of the HCS *Elphinstone*, joined by all the commanders present, demurred, arguing that the admiral's orders conflicted with those they had from the Court of Directors in London to whom they were sworn men. The sanction of the Selectmen was necessary and until then they had no intention of moving their ships. Meanwhile, alarmed by reports of impending attack by fire-boats, Miliken and his colleagues began rowing a guard, and Roberts ordered all staff out of the factory at Canton and downstream to Macao. He remained with a secretary aboard the *Walmer Castle* at Whampoa from where 'he exercised dictatorial powers over the Company's affairs'.[40]

The Company commanders, now anxious at the delays occasioned by the presence of the troops at Macao, sent Roberts a round-robin begging that 'any pacific Overture…consistent with the British Character…' might be made to achieve 'a speedy and amicable Adjustment of the present difficulties'. There now prevailed a simmering and hostile atmosphere among the assembled commanders, many of whom disagreed with what they had heard was the Selectmen's plea for the occupation of Macao, hence Roberts' dictatorship. All had had experience of the Royal Navy's high-handed methods which were tolerable only so long as they did not interfere with their own sphere of activity, which Drury was now doing. By 8 December the Chinese compradors had to leave the ships for fear of their lives, all local communication by sampan was cut off and it was announced in Canton that any 'Englishmen' appearing there would forfeit their lives. The Company's officers declined to move, claiming their ships were too deeply laden to do so without pilots, though some of the Country-ships dropped downstream. Drury then:

> Perceiving we were infringing and trampling under foot every moral law of Man, and of Nations, and the poor defenceless Chinese infuriated to Phrenzy, calling forth their feeble means of defence and offence, and still trusting in the superior local knowledge of the Supra Cargoes [the Select Committee], that all would be well if I appeared at Canton, I was at length induced to hoist my Flag in a Frigate, and…to go to Canton, to demand an audience of the Viceroy… which I certainly could have had, from the dreadful alarm of the Chinese at my appearance at Canton with near a thousand armed men in my retinue, were it not prevented by the Supra Cargoes.

This self-exculpatory report of proceedings was for the Admiralty's consumption and threw the blame for what happened on Roberts and his trading partners, playing down the resistance his own 'appearance' had called forth from the 'poor defenceless Chinese'. Drury admitted that in the face of his demonstration in the squadron's boats he had been offered through the Hoppo an enormous bribe to pretend to evacuate Macao. He rejected this, explaining to the Hoppo that such a suggestion, while it might attract the cupidity of the 'Merchants' was offensive to 'An English officer'. He went on to castigate the Select Committee in unflattering terms:

> However Highly the superior knowledge of the select Committee may be esteemed by the Hon'ble Court of Directors…it has failed in every instance throughout this arduous and most complex transaction, and as the crooked, left handed, winding mode of proceeding, is so opposite to the Summary straight line, prompt and vigorous common sense, prudence, justice, and Dignity marked

for an Officer to pursue, I can no longer waste the Services of His Majesty's
Ships, so much required in India, in negotiating where neither party gives the
other Credit for a sentence of truth being uttered.

By this means Drury extricated himself from a situation not of his own making but
that he had aggravated by his own mode of proceeding. In fact what had happened
had been a humiliation – or as the Chinese saw it – a victory over Drury's forces.
The admiral's perception of infringement and trampling on the moral law of men
and nations had arisen from a boat expedition intended, in the first instance, not
to secure Drury an audience with the Viceroy, but the collection of stores – 'liquor
mostly' – for his ships from the Company's factory at Canton. He had accordingly
ordered Captain Dawson of the *Dédaigneuse* to take a number of the squadron's
armed launches upstream for this purpose. At the last minute:

> fearful of the immense mob at Canton provoking our men, and considering too
> great [the] responsibility I was putting on the Shoulders of so young a man as
> Capt'n Dawson, with express order not to risque anything…and viewing the
> immense Stake we were playing for, suspended by a thread, a single musquet
> [shot] would have broken, and the greatest monopoly England and India has in
> the World would be lost for ever! I determined to accompany Capt'n Dawson
> in my Barge…

If, as Professor Parkinson points out, Drury so feared the outcome of things
going awry, why did he allow a single musket to be taken? And were his
frigates so much in want of spirituous liquor that he must hazard the greatest monopoly in the world to obtain some? In fact his demonstration was
intended to intimidate the 'poor defenceless Chinese' for whom he professed
a concern but demonstrated an increasingly fashionable contempt.

Word of the approach of the British boats preceded them upstream and:
'On approaching Canton, their armed Junks were drawn across the River and
[had] myriads of People on board of them…' Ordering Dawson to hang back,
Drury advanced in his barge 'with a man…who spoke Chinese in order to
explain to their Admiral my peaceable intentions'. Then:

> When within about a hundred yards of them they fired a shot over the Boat.
> I still advanced, and one or two shots more passed over us, until I got within
> about forty yards, all this time endeavouring to speak, but in vain. Now all the
> Junks opened fire on my Barge, with stones and God knows what, until one
> of the Marines in the Boat was struck, and the Seamen in all, the other Boats,
> seeing me fired at so furiously, no longer were under control, but pulled close
> up, when I saw the necessity of ordering them all back, or the total annihilation

of their poor junks and Canton must have been the inevitable consequence, had I permitted a single Musquet to be fired, which was most impatiently looked for by every one.

Drury ends his account of this misadventure with a preposterous assumption that, but for his Jovian forbearance, Canton would have been destroyed, casting himself in an heroic role which he had undoubtedly fulfilled in personally confronting such a mob, but which was a little disingenuous in the telling.[41] Withdrawing as soon as the ebb set in, he removed himself to Whampoa where, aboard the *Walmer Castle*, he lectured Roberts, whom he considered duplicitous. 'I gave you quiet possession of Macao,' he remonstrated, expressing his distaste for operations against the Chinese, and indicating his intention of withdrawing. In his report to Pellew, Drury wrote that: 'The Select Committee are directed to be the sole Arbiters in this transaction: and I hope and expect that their next requisition to me may be firm, wise, and final.'

The Selectmen's next requisition on 8 December was indeed firm, wise and final, for they requested Drury to withdraw the troops, which greatly pleased the admiral. 'And thus,' he concluded with a flourish for Pellew's benefit, 'has finished the most mysterious, extraordinary and scandalous affair that ever disgraced such an Armament...' Drury's contempt for the Selectmen was also reiterated, such a weighty matter as 'National concerns' being inimical to 'the hands of Merchants or Supra Cargoes...vesting such men with exalted authority...was offering a mighty sphere to the small and feeble hand...' Nor did Drury trouble himself to carry out the second part of his mission, the suppression of piracy, which he considered 'as a Tale told by the Supra Cargoes of Canton, full of sound signifying nothing'. This is not to say that Drury did not believe in the existence of the Ladrones, but of the impossibility of destroying them and their essentially ineffectual nature against the East India Company's ships, escorted as he assumed them invariably to be by a man-of-war.

All-in-all the whole affair, now blamed entirely on the Selectmen's opinion that in order to forestall the French, Macao should be quietly occupied and that the Chinese authorities would, after a while, accept a *fait accompli*, was held to be 'totally void of Common Sense...' Drury's sarcastic Parthian shot was that he could:

only conclude from the immense sum offered me [400,000 dollars] to withdraw the Troops from Macao, that the object of the Supra Cargoes was by intimidating the Chinese, to have forced them to a Liquidation of the immense debt due by the beggarly Hong Merchants to the Honourable Company – as I cannot attach to Gentlemen standing so high for liberality and honour, any thing so unworthy as selfish motives.

Declaring in a subsequent letter that Macao could be held with a British battalion against all China 'provided no Merchants or Supra Cargoes, India Captains, Parsees, Portuguese Priests or Governors have any thing to do with the plan', Drury ordered the embarkation of the troops on 15 December. It took five days. Drury departed from China on Christmas Eve, the day that trade reopened with the Country-ships. He left HM Ships *Lion*, *Dover* and *Dédaigneuse* to escort the China fleet when it finally completed cargo-work, which in their case resumed on 26 December.

Drury met Pellew at Penang and took over command of the East Indies station. Learning that the China fleet would not leave Whampoa until March, Pellew proceeded in *Culloden* to Galle from where he reinforced the escort of the frigate *Terpsichore* to the homeward-bound Indiamen from Bombay, *Coromandel* and *Bengal*, sailing on 15 February 1809. Off the Mascarene Islands the convoy was dispersed by a cyclone, suffering the loss of the four Indiamen – the *Bengal*, *Calcutta*, *Lady Jane Dundas* and the *Jane Duchess of Gordon*, mentioned in the previous chapter.

Back at Whampoa the resumption of trade for the Company had been granted only upon a petition being submitted by Roberts. This was, in its initial form, unacceptable to the Viceroy who was now fighting for his own position. Although contemptuous of Roberts, Drury remained quite ignorant of the *Taipan's* assiduous efforts not to blacken the admiral's name by the insertion of clauses prejudicial to Drury's reputation. In the end, thanks to the translating skills of Mr Manning, who had joined Staunton as translator, a form of words was found acceptable to the Viceroy through the Hong merchants. This did not save the Viceroy or the Provincial Governor, both of whom were cashiered and demoted for allowing foreign troops onto Chinese soil, circumstances that made their successors more sensitive. Restrictions were laid upon the boundaries of the British factory at Canton and henceforth 'no Sycee Silver should be sold or exported by Europeans'. Nor did Roberts and his Selectmen escape unscathed, for all except Mr J.F. Elphinstone were replaced during the following year.

In the short-term, however, when Roberts and the Select Committee returned to Canton on 8 January, the first matter they had to clear-up was the liberation of Padre Rodrigo who, despite being a disparaged 'Portuguese Priest' had been the man who courageously acted as Drury's interpreter. As in the case of James Flint, the Chinese authorities visited their wrath against the translator – a simple case of making the messenger pay for the privilege of delivering the message. The Selectmen achieved their objective by in turn stopping the discharge of the Indiamen, which expedient quickly procured Rodrigo's release. They received scant thanks, only provoking Captain Heathcote, then in temporary command of the frigate *Phaeton* at Chuenpi, to:

lament the Steps you have taken as subversive of the Arrangement which has so lately occurred under the sanction of Read Adm'l Drury (when in command of a large naval and military Force) for the restoration of our Trade with the Chinese...And I beg leave to recommend as the only efficacious Recourse that every...reconciliatory means be immediately recurred to for obtaining the Release of the said Padre in order that our Commerce with this Nation may speedily be re-established without the necessity of retracting that threat by which you have again resigned it.

To this sanctimonious epistle – for Drury's attitude must have been infectious – the Selectmen were able to respond that the objective had already been achieved and the threat to trade been a mere artifice.[42] Loading now went on apace; on 3 March 1809, the China fleet finally left for London, three months late.

Following the departure of the ships the Selectmen mended fences. In April despatches arrived from Calcutta in which Minto officially approved the removal of the troops. In May Macao was visited by the new Viceroy. Here the *Tsontoc* could waive some of the formal protocols necessary in Canton. Roberts was received and questioned as to why, after so many years of amicable trade, the 'English' should be so offensive as to land troops on Chinese soil? Roberts explained the French threat and the Viceroy 'was most benignant...and, metaphorically, patted them on the shoulder and bade them be good children in the future'. The Viceroy's subsequent report to the Emperor was less conciliatory and involved Roberts and his Committee in a long correspondence that threatened the resumption of trade later in the year when the outbound Indiamen arrived. Happily, however, the uncaring intrusion of Country-ships and a tedious exchange of views had laid the matter in the dust by the autumn of 1809. Whatever the roots of this unhappy affair two facts emerge clearly, that the Portuguese did not own Macao, but had the usufruct; and that 'however much humiliated Admiral Drury may have been, Mr Roberts had to descend much farther into the vale of humiliation'. Such loss of face was of graver consequence to the East India Company's resident agents in China than to the now distant British Commander-in-Chief of the East Indies station.

Alongside such weighty concerns it is surprising that, despite being confined aboard their ships for more than five months, there were only 'some exhibitions of rowdyism, none very serious, on the part of the sailors of the Indiamen'. A few unwisely attempted desertion and a disturbance took place on 31 January when a seaman was involved in a fight, but the affair blew over as no one was killed. On 3 February an officer and some seamen from the HCS *Royal George*, Captain Charles Gribble, returning from Chuenpi in the ship's yawl, were attacked by pirates under the guns of the Bogue forts.

They escaped to sail on 3 March but the piracy problem remained unsolved and one can only regret that had Drury concentrated upon the Ladrones, he might have earned praise from all parties rather than the contrary.

By the time the twelve outward Indiamen arrived from the Thames on 17 September under the convoy of Captain Austen in HMS *St Albans*, it was piracy that had risen to the top of the Selectmen's agenda. Not only had the Ladrones captured a Portuguese brig and fitted it out, they were raiding the coast and penetrating to within five miles of Canton, holding out for ransom and seizing an American ship, the *Atahualpa*, in Macao on 23 August. So bad had matters become that the Hong merchants themselves bought and fitted out a British brig, the *Elizabeth*, intending to use her as protection against these piratical raids. Then, almost immediately after the arrival of the Indiamen, the fourth mate of the *Marquis of Ely*, Mr Richard Glasspoole, who had been sent away in a cutter to embark a pilot, was seized by a pirate junk and held to ransom for 100,000 dollars. This incident heightened negotiations between the new Viceroy and Roberts. The former was desperate to have an assurance that no such incident as Drury had occasioned the previous year would follow any request to help to suppress piracy, for this now threatened the new Viceroy's credibility with Peking.

Roberts, meanwhile, was in the final throes of his humble petition for forgiveness for the previous years' transgressions and while trying to steer this through using his influence as *Taipan*, could not acknowledge that neither he nor the Select Committee had any power over the Royal Navy beyond relying upon it to afford convoy escort. The Viceroy's negotiators thought that the *Dédeaigneuse* might cruise in the Pearl River, north of the Bogue if necessary, to intimidate the Ladrones who had seized laden lighters on the river between Whampoa and Canton and anchored almost within gunshot of Dane's Island. So bold had they become that an imperial customs-post had been burned and the Mandarins' war junks had taken cover amid the foreign ships.

The Hong merchants were now authorised to buy and arm a second Country-ship, the *Mercury*, but Roberts considered her inadequate and, concerned only with the safety of the Company's ships, assured the Hong that the arrival of Captain Austen in *St Albans* would afford sufficient protection. Applications for help in urging the commissioning of a squadron of armed Country-ships from the Viceroy were referred to Captain Austen and a meeting was eventually arranged between Austen and the *Kwangchow Fu*, in Roberts's presence, at the British factory. Austen sensibly pressed for a commission direct from the Viceroy if he was to attack pirates for these were, nonetheless, Chinese citizens. On 2 November Austen, with Captains Pellew (Junior), Bell and Wells, with Roberts and Morrison as translator, all assembled at the Hoppo's *yamen* where he and the Hong merchants awaited them. The Viceroy, however, failed to arrive, sending a message that urgent despatches from the Emperor demanded his attention and the British withdrew, aware that it was the loss of face attaching to a request for help from a foreign power who had so recently occupied Chinese territory that had baulked Viceroy Chang.

The Portuguese had also been commissioned to help and the new governor at Macao, Senhor d'Alvarenga, fitted out six small vessels at the expense of the Chinese government and the Hong. These were manned in part from deserters from the Company's ships, an irony to which was added a request from D'Alvarenga to Roberts for the supply of guns, powder and small-arms. The little fleet set off, cornered a pirate squadron among the islands to the east of the Pearl Estuary, then watched it escape. The only benefit from all this was the ransom in cash, opium and cloth, valued at 7,500 dollars, of Mr Glasspoole and his boat's crew. By the New Year the pirate fleet was as active as ever, capturing a number of Mandarine war junks and, on 29 January 1810, attacking a Country-ship's boat, throwing its crew overboard and carrying off the chest of cash it bore. Desperately the Viceroy now tried bribing the Ladrones, whose junks anchored *en masse* off the Bogue forts while negotiations with the pirate chief, Apo Tsi, went on. He:

> was loaded with gifts of money and robes of honour…it was expected that he and his followers would soon submit; and it must be believed that the silver of the Viceroy was more potent in the affair than the iron shot of the Portuguese.

All this time the Indiamen and Country-ships had been loading and were ready to drop down river on the spring tides needed to carry the deep-draughted vessels over the Second Bar. The Chinese now refused to supply pilots and the ships were obliged to dispense with them altogether. Meanwhile offence had been caused to naval officers ashore at Chuenpi where they had been 'roughly handled' by a crowd of Chinese and on 16 January a Chinese named Hwang Ah-shing was killed near the factories at Canton, allegedly by an English seaman from the *Royal Charlotte*. This, on the eve of the ships' departure was clearly a stratagem, but the allegation against a 'Red-haired devil's imp' – in Chinese parlance an Englishman – required Roberts to make enquiries of Captain Henry Rush who had been ashore in Hog Lane. In fact as many American as British seamen had been roaming the area so, once again, no one could be surrendered for trial and the Hoppo was unable to issue the Grand Chop allowing the China fleet to clear outwards and sail for London.

Negotiations – interrupted by the Chinese New Year – ground on and on. There was no accusation against any individual and no examination could produce the slightest shred of evidence sufficient to identify a culprit, but the Chinese wanted an example made and suggested a compromise and nominal punishment as had been effected in the case of Edward Sheen. Austen said he would convoy the ships clear of the coast, intimating that he would use force if the Bogue forts contested the matter, to which the Viceroy declared that three of the Hong merchants would be imprisoned. A plan to appeal over the Hoppo's head rebounded on the Selectmen and Austen, and matters staggered into another stalemate.

More tedious arguments were batted back and forth until on 21 February, having put up bonds, the Hoppo announced the Chop would be issued. Nothing had occurred by the end of the month so the Selectmen ordered the fleet to proceed, thanking Austen for his 'assistance in the late unpleasant discussions with the Chinese Government'. When it was known that the Company's despatches were aboard and the thirteen Indiamen were ready to weigh, the Grand Chop arrived on 1 March 1810.

There was a curious sub-agenda to this and it had nothing to do with an alleged homicide. It was widely thought by the Selectmen that, arising from their dealings with the Hong merchants, difficulties had been created by the Hoppo, who always had the whip-hand over the rich but wretched and sub-ordinate Compradors of the Hong, subjecting them to 'squeeze' on any items that seemed, in the Hoppo's opinion, to attract exceptional import duties. Since all parties were industriously milking the entire system, the variable inter-personal relationships could cause hitches that had, as with the delay in sailing thirteen Indiamen, mighty consequences. While the Selectmen might not speak Mandarin or understand the subtle intricacies of all this, they grasped the general principle and were expert in handling the delays, prevaricating and turning aside official – if insubstantial – wrath. It was such painstaking skills that Drury failed to comprehend and thought so contemptible, but which the more sympathetic and sensitive Austen seems to have perfectly understood. From these machinations it emerged that the import of clocks, watches and musical boxes, practically the only items of western manufacture that attracted the attention of the superior class of Chinese, were the fundamental cause of the delay in the sailing of the fleet. It was impossible for the covetous-ness of the envious to be expressed by open purchase, without admitting that there was nothing to match them among Chinese manufactures – and with the admission a loss of face. Consequently all manner of convoluted obstacles obstructed the import of these items – many of which were part of private offic-ers' trading ventures – in order that they fell into the right hands. The upshot of this was a series of dutiable hurdles which put up the cost of the Hong's Consoo levy, made irregular and unpredictable the actual sums demanded of the Company, and occasioned a vast and frustrating delay.[43]

It was in the aftermath of this and upon arrival of the next season's outward ships that Roberts received his dismissal, attributed to his handling of the 'rice

imbroglio', his conduct during the occupation of Macao and the risk to which
he had put future trade during the recent difficulties. Although Roberts had
navigated through a most labyrinthine period he had, for some time 'been
in the cold shade of [the Courts of Directors']…censure'. He was replaced
as President and *Taipan* by Henry Browne who, having retired in 1795, was
sent out again and took over at a time when the Hong merchants owed the
Company considerable sums. It is of interest to note that for three years 'large
remittances of specie' had been made to India and that in 1810 the whole was
to be sent directly to London.[44] By order of the Court only £300,000 was
to be left in the Treasury at Canton for the coming season's trade, an indica-
tion of the economic – and particularly fiscal – stresses being felt in Britain
at this period of the war. India, meanwhile, or at least the Company's government there, required the outstanding debt to the Company which should be
secured by 'prudent measures' and sent to Calcutta 'without delay'.

   While the Chinese authorities appeared readier to accept the presence of
men-of-war arriving for the purpose of convoying all British merchantmen,
this may well have been occasioned by the continuing failure of the Viceroy
to either suppress or coerce the pirates. Since they were to remain a problem
to British merchant shipping until the Communists took over China in 1949,
they have a relevance to this history. In April 1810 the Select Committee minutes record that:

> the female Leader of the Pirates has gone up to Canton to arrange with the
> Viceroy the submission of all the Force and she is supposed to possess con-
> siderable influence over Apo Tsi the most formidable of the Pirates in this
> neighbourhood… From all we can learn the Ladrones are very indifferent to
> the proposals of the Viceroy… Apo Tsi requires for himself to retain Eighty
> armed boats under the pretence of employing them against the Pirates that
> remain and thirty or forty more to be employed in the Salt Trade.

On 20 April the Viceroy prevailed at some cost, Apo Tsi accepting an imperial
commission and pension, turning smoothly from poacher to game-keeper and
making 'a state visit' to Canton and then Macao. Lord Minto, meanwhile, sent
the Bombay Marine's 12-gun *Vesta* from Calcutta with a detachment of the
Company's artillery to join the *Antelope* and *Teignmouth*, the two surveying-
vessels then working on the coast. These were to be followed by a veritable
anti-piracy squadron of the 20-gun *Mornington*, the *Numa* and *Nautilus* of 14
guns and the *Ariel* of 12. Hearing of this reinforcement the Viceroy thanked
the Company' Selectmen for this welcome and faithful compliance with their
duty, assuring them that: 'The Pirates of Consequence in Kwantung are all
now…exterminated and at rest, the whole number is reduced to profound

Tranquillity so that there is no need for assistance'. Browne and his colleagues were unconvinced and rightly so, for reports were being received of raids along the coast to the west.

Whether this apparent 'suppression' of the pirates emboldened the Viceroy to increase his extortion of the Company is uncertain but when, on 21 January 1811, the first convoy was ready to depart and the clearance of the Grand Chop was applied for, the Selectmen 'had the mortification to learn that the Mandarins have availed themselves of our anxiety [for the fleet to sail]...to enforce a compliance with their requisition respecting the affair of the Chinese killed last Season'. Having met the Hong merchants, Browne now reported at length on this new 'detention of our Ships' to the Court of Directors.

> [It] was a measure of the Chinese Govt. not directed against us but against themselves in consequence of the absolute inability of most of them and the actual refusal of all to satisfy the extortionate and continually increasing demands of the Hoppo for the purchase of the various articles of Clock Work and Mechanism...which it seems are now become the established vehicle of Corruption between the Officer and his Superiors at the Capital...

As to the matter of a British seamen being guilty of murder, Browne referred previous cases to the Court, none of which could be replicated by the murder of Hwang Ah-shing. For his response to the Viceroy, Browne took unprecedented steps. Mustering a party of gentlemen–clerks from the factory, and ship's commanders and officers from the waiting Indiamen, he ordered the junior Selectman, Mr William Parry, and the fleet's commodore, Captain the Hon. Hugh Lindsay, at their head. Placing in Parry's hand a memorandum rejecting the Viceroy's demands, the whole deputation proceeded to the city gates in defiance of the regulations. Unobstructed here, the party handed the memorandum in at the entrance to the Hoppo's *yamen*. In it was expressed the assertion that submission to the 'present injurious detention of our Ships' was now intolerable, since no law of China had been broken and that they would 'take on ourselves to dispatch the fleet even without the usual permission should the Government by protracted delays absolutely reduce us to that unpleasant alternative.'

Magically the Chop was issued and the ships sailed on 10 February, taking Roberts home; Browne, his work done, followed in the second fleet at the end of March, being relieved by John Elphinstone. Among those leaving China at this time was a Mr Kerr, His Majesty's Botanical Gardener, a plant-hunter who had been in China since 1803 and who was moving on to Sri Lanka, having sent numerous samples home to Kew Gardens.

Cape Colony had been returned to the Dutch as a condition of the Peace of Amiens and its loss increased the difficulties of the passages of the Company's ships after the resumption of hostilities in 1803. It was not until 1806 that an expedition under General Baird retook the 'Tavern of the Seas' and secured the roadstead for British trade. The final step in gaining control over the Indian Ocean was the capture of the Mascarene Islands. Indiamen, Country-ships and several of the Bombay Marine's cruisers – just returned from an expedition to suppress piracy in the Persian Gulf – took part alongside the Royal Navy. While entrance to the islands' ports was easy, thanks to their lying in the Trade Wind belt, the maintenance of a blockade was not. This, mounted from the Cape of Good Hope since its recapture, had never been enforced for periods much above ten weeks at a time, allowing the French a period of unobstructed access, both inwards and outwards. Although the British block-ade was largely ineffective, as we have noted, the captured Indiaman *Windham* was retaken by the newly arrived British frigate *Magicienne* on 29 December 1809. However, the remote isolation of Decaen's colony militated against it and although he now received a final reinforcement of the 36-gun *Astrée*, the harassed governor was increasingly desperate.

By 1810 the attractions inherent in active operations against the enemy to both the Governor-General, Lord Minto, in Calcutta and the naval com-manders-in-chief in India and at the Cape undoubtedly seduced them from the primary business of trade-protection. The whole notion of com-merce was anathema to a certain patrician cast of naval mind and it mattered not that this was acquired and not genetic. Sir Edward Pellew, whatever his considerable and sterling merits as a naval sea-officer, had little interest in the subject. On assuming the chief naval command in 1806 he had writ-ten: 'My objects here were my two sons...' whose opportunities from prize money realised considerable fortunes, while the Commander-in-Chief himself made some £100,000. Although he did not neglect convoys entirely and had only slender resources with which to protect them, Pellew and his successors nevertheless provoked 'the merchants, agents, underwriters and shipowners of Calcutta' to memorialise the Admiralty, complaining that:

> The favourite expeditions against the Dutch...a prostrate, passive and fallen foe, are attended...with no national or public advantage, while at the same time they leave the whole Trade of India exposed to the depredations of an active and enterprising Enemy.[45]

This was the substance of a document borne home by Michael Prendergast and Alexander Steward, fellow passengers with William Hickey in the *Castle*

Eden in 1810. Other copies followed after being sent to Bombay for additional supporting petitioners. It did little good; though Pellew escaped trouble, and criticism of military and naval officers only widened the gulf between them and the mercantile fraternity. Sir Arthur Wellesley, although the recipient of the opprobrium of being regarded as a 'Sepoy General', so disliked the Company that he wrote of 'the most loathsome den of the India House…'

Meanwhile commerce, itself a sinew of the war, went on and remained susceptible to the sorties of the French from Île de France which had yet to be subdued. After his earlier successes it was unfortunate that Henry Meriton should again fall foul of the enemy, but in July 1810 he was in command of the HCS *Ceylon* which was in company with the *Astell*, Captain Robert Hay, and the *Windham*, Captain John Stewart. All were outward-bound, the last named after her short captivity during her the previous voyage, and were in the Mozambique Channel at daylight on 3 July 1810, some 36 miles from Mayotta. The three Indiamen were running before a strong south-south-easterly wind when they saw ahead three sails. These were the French frigates *Bellone* and *Minerve* (previously the Portuguese *Minerva*) and the corvette *Victor*.[46] Commanded by Capitaine Duperré in the *Bellone*, the French squadron had left Port Louis in mid-March, taking advantage of the absence of the British blockading squadron from the station on account of the cyclone season. The Frenchmen had recently taken the Extra-ship *Young William*, Captain James Mortlock, also off Madagascar, and now close-hauled on the port tack gave chase to the Indiamen. Meriton, as commodore, threw out his own signal and the three Indiamen hauled their wind and stood away on the same tack under double-reefed topsails, courses, jib and spanker.

After about an hour, at 07.30 and with the enemy four miles away, Meriton hoisted the private signal which received no reply. The Indiamen cleared for action and two hours later Hay of the *Astell* signalled that he was overpressed. Meriton therefore instructed the three ships to reduce sail and remain in company for mutual support. At about 09.40 Meriton bowed to the inevitable, signalling his two colleagues to the effect that as escape was impossible it would be better to reduce sail still further and force the issue before darkness confused the situation. Stewart in *Windham* responded: 'If we make all sail and get into smooth water under the land, we can engage to more advantage'.

In a rising wind at 10.00 the three Indiamen hove-to and took in the third reef of their topsails. Even with this reduction of sail the ships heeled so much and the sea ran so high that they could not keep open their lee lower-deck gun-ports. An hour and a half later the *Minerve*, now about six miles away from them, tacked in the wake of the Indiamen. The *Bellone*, four miles on their lee beam, and *Victor* about four miles on their weather quarter, also tacked. The *Minerve* was closing on them fast and Meriton ordered Hay and

Stewart to form line abreast upon *Ceylon*. As they attempted to do so the *Victor* and *Minerve* were the closest of the three enemy ships, coming up on the Indiamen's starboard and weather quarters.

At 14.15, the *Minerve* had closed the *Ceylon* with the *Victor* in close company. The *Minerve* fired one shot at the *Windham*, then slightly ahead of the *Ceylon*, afterwards pouring a broadside into *Ceylon*. The *Astell* was astern and to leeward as the action began, with *Ceylon*, under the *Minerve's* lee, receiving most of the damage. Since the three Indiamen had troops on board, these were employed in keeping up a sharp hail of musketry upon the enemy. Finding the fire of the Indiamen too hot, Morice in the smaller *Victor*, bore up and in passing to leeward of the *Astell* engaged her. Captain Hay was now severely wounded, command of the ship falling upon the first mate, Mr William Hawkey. At some point in the action Seaman Andrew Peters of the *Astell* climbed the main-mast and 'nailed the pendant to the maintopmast-head, and was killed as he descended the rigging'. At about 16.00 the *Minerve* gained on the *Windham* and bore down, with the intention of boarding: 'a mode of attack to which the Indiamen, from the number of troops they had on board, were not much averse [to]'. Seeing this Meriton and Hawkey closed their consort which was now knocked about, though instead of boarding her quarry, the *Minerve* crossed just ahead of the *Windham* and passed, for the moment, out of range.

Closing the heart of the action Hawkey now hauled *Astell's* yards sharp up and ran astern of the *Windham* to become the leading and weather-most British ship. The *Windham* was also by now astern of the *Ceylon*. Seeing the *Windham* falling back, *Minerve* rounded upon her and would have fallen upon her had her own main and mizzen topmasts not at this point come down. The respite caused by this set-back to the enemy was short-lived. The *Bellone* now approached and, with the *Victor*, pressed a heavy fire upon the falter-ing *Windham* until Dupperé continued ahead, to engage the lee side of the *Ceylon* and direct one bow-chaser at the *Astell*. Meriton, meanwhile, edged down on the French commodore, hoping to use the advantage of his mus-ketry, ably supplied by the draft of soldiers on board. Unfortunately Meriton was now struck by a grape-shot in the neck and fell, severely wounded. First Mate Thomas Oldham took command but within minutes had been knocked down himself, the command of the *Ceylon* swiftly devolving upon Second Mate Tristram Fleming.

At about 19.00, with the *Ceylon's* rigging shot to pieces, 'all her upper deck and five of her lower deck guns disabled, and her hull so badly struck, that she made three feet of water an hour; and also having sustained a serious loss in killed and wounded, the *Ceylon* bore up and ceased firing'. The *Bellone* remained engaged with the *Windham* whose captain, Hay, repeatedly hailed Hawkey, but having realised the *Windham* was powerless that officer decided to save his ship, extinguished all lights and, under a furious fire from the *Bellone*, crowded on sail to escape.

Finally, twenty minutes later, the *Ceylon's* ensign was struck. The *Windham* continued resisting 'chiefly for the purpose of favouring the escape of the *Astell*' but at 19.45 'having had nine of her guns dismounted, and sustained a serious loss in killed and wounded, the *Windham* hauled down her colours'. The *Ceylon* had lost six dead and twenty-one wounded; the *Windham* six killed and eighteen wounded. The *Astell* had suffered the loss of eight killed and thirty-seven wounded. Among the casualties were, besides Meriton, Hay and Oldham, several British and Lascar seamen, officers and soldiers of the 24th Foot and some Company cadets. *Bellone* lost four killed and six wounded, *Minerve*, seventeen dead and twenty-nine wounded, and *Victor* one killed and three wounded.

The escape of the *Astell* caused some rejoicing and the Directors settled a pension of £460 on Captain Hay, with an *ex gratia* payment of £2,000 to her officers and crew, when she finally arrived at her moorings in the Thames on 28 August 1811. While a successful defence of all three ships against such a force would have been highly creditable, it was not Hawkey's duty to fight to the last, for she was a commercial vessel, not a warship. As one Company officer Thomas Addison wrote, under the Company's regulations: 'having been captured by an enemy or the ship in any way wrecked and destroyed, the captain officers and crew forfeit their pay and wages'. Addison had some reason to expatiate on this subject, for he had been a midshipman in the HCS *Brunswick* when taken by Linois off Pointe de Galle in July 1805. Notwithstanding this and the time it took for the news of the fates of the other ships to reach London, the gallantry of the captured ships resulted in a grant of £500 to each of the captains and 'a handsome remuneration upon the remaining officers and men'. In the short-term, however, they were prisoners, Stewart and the Windhams for the second time.

However, despite Duperré's triumph, it was to be short-lived. Even as he headed for Port Louis with his prizes, an expedition was taking the first of the Mascarene Islands, Rodriguez, along with the corsair *Édouard* of Nantes which had attempted to escape from that island with despatches. The taking of the other two islands was eventually accomplished after some severe fighting but not before the British – making an initial attack with inadequate forces – had taken a drubbing. It was amid this brief French triumph that Duperré arrived with his prizes. The *Victor*, coming into Grand Port with the *Ceylon*, did not realise the situation and Morice ran the gauntlet of attacking British warships. Duperré, instructing his prize-master to take *Windham* westwards, stood inshore and also passed into the harbour to augment its defences. The *Windham* meanwhile was anchored off Rivière Noire where she was boarded and recaptured by the boats from HMS *Sirius*.

The *Ceylon* had perforce to remain in enemy hands as part of the defences of Grand Port until the final British assault in December when she, along with the HCSs *United Kingdom* and *Charlton*, amid several other prizes, including the Calcutta-built *Sir William Burroughs*, 560 tons, Captain Thomas Watkin, taken in the Bay of Bengal in 1806, and numerous prisoners were liberated from captivity. Refitted, the *Windham* and *Ceylon* returned to the Thames on 11 August 1811, less than a fortnight before the *Astell* on the final completion of her dramatically interrupted voyage.

By that time a further French frigate squadron, ignorant of Decaen's surrender, was destroyed off Tamatave, finally ending French naval ambitions in the Indian Ocean. Of the three Indiamen involved in the action with Duperré on 3 July, the *Windham* lasted longest. In 1817 she was sold to the Chileans, became the 52-gun man-of-war *Lautaro* and took part in Lord Cochrane's blockade of Talcahuano; among the three Company commanders, in addition to their fiscal rewards, Henry Meriton was in due course appointed to command the Bombay Marine.[47]

By now at least several vessels were coming out annually to China by way of New South Wales. These took supplies out to the penal colony of Botany Bay and then usually picked up sandalwood in the Fiji islands prior to heading for Whampoa. In 1811 the range of British shipping's cargoes remained impressive: importing into China from Britain quantities of woollens, lead, tin, copper, iron bars and red lead. From India and elsewhere came cotton, sandalwood and pepper. Some sealskins and rabbit furs arrived in British free-traders, though more came in small fast American vessels which also carried ginseng. Homewards nineteen Indiamen and twenty-five Country-ships carried cotton piece-goods, raw and woven silks, nankeen cloth and, of course, tea.[48] The Company also shipped to London 1,158,685 dollars, largely made up of 'dollar silver, partly broken of chopped dollars taken by weight, partly new dollars received directly or indirectly through the [Spanish] Company of the Philippines'. Part of this was sent in HM Frigate *Indefatigable*, the second remittance being conveyed in the Company's own ships being put on board 'as they passed homeward bound through Macao Road on March 3rd'.

Among the exports from China was 'a most interesting shipment' to Batavia. The Selectmen had learned that Batavia had surrendered to British forces on 20 August 1810 and that the conquest of Java was almost completed. Of greater interest than the huge quantity of 'crimson, yellow, light blue, pea-green, and white silks and satins with brocaded flowers of gold, of silver, or of gold and silver', was the consignee. This was a Company servant who, on 21 October had been appointed lieutenant-governor. His name was Thomas

Stamford Raffles and he was a man to watch. In December 1813 a request of his to recruit Chinese labourers was answered by the despatch of 700 coolies to the island of Banka, lying between Java and Singapore. A second consignment of 425 followed in February 1814, each being conveyed from Macao to Pulo Banka at a cost of 30 dollars passage-money.

To this early intimation of a coming trade in humans was that in drugs. It was quite clear to the Selectmen that quantities of opium were now arriving in vessels other than the Anglo-Indian Country-ships. Eighty chests had been recorded as arriving in the HCSs *Woodford* and *Alfred* in 1810, but this was neither on the Company's, nor the commander's accounts, and no investigation appears to have been carried out. Despite its importation being illegal, the matter was swept under the carpet, the Selectmen deciding – by way of a veil over their decision – that it was inferior to Bengali opium and may have been Turkish. American ships had long been importing the drug from Turkey and this was confirmed in October 1812 when the *President Adams* of Boston was wrecked on the coast west of Macao. She had on board besides silver amounting to 170,000 dollars, 'a quantity of Turkish Opium'. While a certain suspicion existed in respect of American vessels after the outbreak of war between Great Britain and the United States, the traffic in opium was less-and-less inconspicuous and chests were habitually 'deposited as collateral security for bonds given to obtain bills on Bengal in advance'. For some time the Select Committee had been reporting the arrival of small, but remarkably fast American ships, the first intimation of the early clippers, one of which, the *Sylph*, arrived off Macao in 1811 loaded entirely with opium. Though of the inferior Turkish variety the discharge of the *Sylph* marks a change of gear in the importation of the drug and the method of its conveyance, a matter that British entrepreneurs – whatever John Company said about it – could not leave in the hands of others, especially the rival Americans.[49]

As Anne Bulley points out:'The paradox of the East India Company's servants in Canton making use of private funds that were generated by contraband cargoes is glaringly displayed in the records until their final exodus...in 1834'. By 1812 the use of chests of opium as a means of establishing security had become common, and this in turn contributed to the trade through Macao 'in whose success, connected as it is with an important branch of the Hon. Co.'s Revenue, we cannot be wholly indifferent'. Indeed not; while the Directors claimed the compulsion under which they overlooked such 'clandestine proceedings' unless they were officially notified of them, they had the grace to admit that 'instances have occurred...of our necessarily resorting to them ourselves when the Balance of Trade in our Favour required a remittance of Bullion to India or England'.

A merchantman of about 400 tons working cargo. With no square sails on the mizzen, this is an early nineteenth-century barque-rigged vessel, as opposed to the bark-*built* standard of the eighteenth. Note the hoisted boat and the long spar rigged as a derrick for cargo-handling. From the drawing by E. W. Cooke who remarks that the vessel is a 'free-trader' and was probably engaged in the Indian trade after 1813. (Private Collection)

Of more immediate concern that year was news of a rupture with the United States. It was rumoured that American frigates were somewhere in the offing and HM Frigates *Clorinde*, *Owen Glendower* and *Doris* were sent to cruise in search of them without success. However, the report seems to have been discounted and the sighting was attributed to the Company's own surveying-cum-anti-piracy cruisers, *Antelope*, *Teignmouth* and *Vesta*, all of which had been east of Macao wearing the Company's distinctive grid-iron ensign.

The greatest dangers to the loading ships remained the arbitrary decisions of the Chinese authorities and the conduct of their own crews. In October 1812 there was yet another affray involving the stabbing of two seamen from the *Marquis of Ely*, but no Chinese were hurt and Captain James Dalrymple was reprimanded for allowing shore-leave near the factory. There was a similar incident the next month involving two officers from the frigate *Phoenix* who were walking ashore at Chuenpi. Fortunately there was an 'immediate redress'. In February 1813 Captain John Collins was assaulted by a Chinese Customs officer when clearing private trade goods, while action had to be taken against some seamen aboard the *Charles Grant* who stole and sold some of the ship's cargo of nankeens. Captain John Lock convened a court of commanders and four of the accused were found guilty and ordered to be flogged, a sentence watched by a boat's crew from each of the other Indiamen.

Oddly the year 1813 closed on the China coast without significant acknowledgement of the profound change in the Honourable East India Company's position, perhaps a measure of the shift in the loyalties and ambitions of its servants. While it retained its monopoly of trade to-and-from China, having reviewed the Company's charter the British Government dispossessed it of its exclusive rights of carriage to-and-from India. It was, however, given a twenty-year extension of its remaining chartered-powers, by which it retained its political and military authority over the sub-continent under the auspices of the British crown. By 1814 Lord Moira[50] had relieved Minto as Governor-General at Fort William and the objectionable Drury had been replaced by the admirable Sir Samuel Hood, an officer with real ability and talent who sadly did not long survive the tropical climate.

As for the war, with the sting drawn from Mauritius, as Île de France was now known, and the British in possession of Java, only the Americans caused concern. Mutual indifference pertained in the neutral waters of China, but when HM Frigate *Doris*, Captain O'Brien, took the American schooner *Hunter* and sent her into the Pearl River this again infringed the neutrality of the Celestial Empire. On the other hand the capture of the Country-ship *Arabella* by the American privateer *Rambler* was smoothed over by the liberation of the commander and some of the hands of a second American privateer, the rather mischievously named *Hyder Ally*, which had been taken by Captain Brian Hodgson in the British frigate *Owen Glendower*. The most dramatic and potentially damaging incident occurred in December 1814 when the Country-ship *Earl Spencer* began to drop downstream on the 28th on completion of her lading. It was observed that the American privateer *Jacob Jones* was unmooring and consequently presumed that she was going in chase, to seize the *Earl Spencer* the moment she was clear of the protection of Chinese neutrality. Word was passed and the armed boats of seven Indiamen were sent downstream to muster alongside the HCS *Wexford* where Captain Charles Barnard held them in readiness to act, after warning the *Earl Spencer*. The Country-ship got clean away and the *Jacob Jones*, along with half a dozen American vessels, left the Pearl River unmolested but empty-handed.

In the vast and lonely spaces of the Pacific no such support was available. The risks attached to the Southern Whale fishery were chiefly on account of its remoteness, although the *Lydia*, Captain Horner, and one other British whaler were take by the Spaniards at Payta in January 1797, their masters being ignorant of the fact that Spain had entered the war. Early whaling voyages were often as experimental as contemporaneous government explorations, one such 'secret expedition' being sent out to the Pacific in 1800 when the whalers *Kingston*, Captain Thomas Dennis, and the *Elligood*, Captain Christopher Dickson, took three whales in King George's Sound near the south-east tip of Australia in August and September. The more conventional outwards passage was round Cape Horn, entering the Pacific by way of Drake's Passage, a long and miserable voyage which was little better on return when the advantages of fairer winds might be offset by the prolonged service of ship and crew.

Nor did all whalers pass directly into the Pacific, many first hunting for seals in the South Atlantic amid the islands of the Falklands and South Georgia. On 4 March 1803 the whaling brig *Thomas*, owned by Broderick & Co. of Wapping and commanded by Captain Gardner, dropped down the Thames and headed for South America. On reaching the Strait of Le Maire, Gardner spent some six months cruising about Staten Island taking about 800 seals for their skins and then, landing the *Thomas*'s longboat on the island, converted her into a tender by lengthening and decking her. On completion of this in January 1803, Gardner ordered his second mate, Robert Scot, to take a few men and follow the brig towards South Georgia, where both arrived safely after eleven days. They resumed hunting seals and sea-elephants until early April when, in company with another brig, the *John* of Boston, they proceeded towards Tristan da Cunha.

On the 14th the three vessels ran into heavy weather and the longboat was soon in trouble. Ducking below to pick up a knife to cut away the rigging, Scot avoided the fate of his crew who were, all three, washed overboard:

> At that time he had on board only three pounds of flour and three and a half of meat, six pounds of bread and two hogsheads of water, which were all more or less damaged by the gale, some whale oil…and a small quantity of salt. On this scanty pittance, and without any means of dressing even that, he prolonged his existence for seventy-five days. He likewise emptied a medicine chest…and got out of it some burning medicine, which he found made his body a little comfortable and warm, as he never got his clothes off. He was almost constantly wet.

When he was picked up Scot was 'shaping a course for the Cape of Good Hope, having missed the island of Tristan da Cunha' wrote one of his rescuers, Fourth Officer Paulin of the HCS *Europe*. Paulin describes Scot's condition:

> His debility was so great that he had been for several days incapable of….[finding] what little sustenance then remained, or of shifting his helm should a change of

wind happen. He then lived mostly on tobacco…both his cheeks were swelled out amazingly with the ruinous quantity he had in his mouth, and which he seemed to suck with convulsive agony. The appearance of this poor wretch when he was hauled up the side (for he could not walk) deeply affected every-one; he had entirely lost the use of his extremities – his countenance was pallid and emaciated; and it was the opinion of our surgeon that he could not have prolonged his existence two days longer.

Scot, a native of Spalding, Lincolnshire, survived, but for how long? His small-boat voyage alone was a minor epic; his lonely survival for seventy-five days quite remarkable.

On the Pacific whaling grounds British-flagged whalers were never so numerous as their Yankee counter-parts with which they were in direct com-petition. However there were enough of them to attract the attention of the United States Navy during the War of 1812–1814 and their favoured hunting ground was known to be in the vicinity of the Galapagos Islands. Moreover, the fact that some of the whalers were managed by former Loyalists did not escape the notice of the Secretary to the Navy in Washington when he issued Captain David Porter with orders to conduct the United States Frigate *Essex* on a raiding cruise, allocating the headstrong young captain with extra stores and sixty men above the *Essex*'s official establishment. Porter's depredations were to be considerable. On his way south he took the British packet *Nocton* off Fernando de Noroñha on 12 December 1812, fol-lowed by the schooner *Elizabeth* off Cape Frio, near Rio de Janeiro on the 27th. Once he arrived in the Pacific he notched-up prizes totalling 4,000 tons, among which was the *Seringapatam*.

As we have observed previously, whalers employed in the South Sea fishery were required to be sea-worthy with long endurance and these qualities were often provided from vessels found redundant in other trades. One example which might in fact hint at a deliberate change of policy was the *Seringapatam*, built of Malabar teak in Bombay in 1799 for P. Mellish & Co. Initially char-tered by the East India Company as an Extra-ship, she brought a cargo home from India, but once in London, she was taken in hand, converted into a whaler and sent into the Pacific. Here, after a decade of whaling, she fell victim to the *Essex*.

The progress of Porter's cruise was complex. He arrived on the coast of Chile at a time when the Spanish colonies of South America were embarking upon their wars of liberation against Spain. Anarchy prevailed in a Chile not yet fully independent, but the American consul was friendly to the rebels and Porter had no difficulty in refitting the *Essex* prior to a foray into the Pacific.[51]

With his extra men intended to form prize-crews Porter made his intentions plain to his men, to whom he issued a written proclamation.

> The unprotected British commerce on the coast of Chile, Peru and Mexico will give you an abundant supply of wealth; and the girls of the Sandwich Islands shall reward you for your sufferings during the passage round Cape Horn.

Alas, Porter's rhetoric was all deception, for his men would receive no prize-money, while the girls of the Sandwich Islands rewarded Porter's sailors with the syphilis their enemy had left behind during their own pleasurable interludes some years earlier. But this lay in the future; the beginning was brighter. Two days after leaving Valparaiso on 23 March 1813 Porter overtook a Peruvian privateer, the *Neredya*, which had been taking American whalers. Disarming her he let her go and three days later he recovered one of the *Neredya's* prizes, the Nantucket whaler *Barclay*. Thereafter the USS *Essex* visited the Galapagos where, by convention, whalers of both nations dropped off their mail in Post Office Bay to be carried onwards by the first vessel bound for home, an agreeable and durable convention. By rifling the 'post office' he learned of recent visits by British whalers and, on 29 April, he took the first of them, the *Montezuma* of London, which surrendered after receiving a volley of musketry. That same day the *Essex* also captured the *Georgiana* and the *Policy*, both of which bore several Nantucketers who had either been serving in British vessels since the American War of Independence or who had been pressed into the Royal Navy and sought employment in these ships when the end of the war in 1783 threw them on the beach. These men and the stores borne by the two ships 'removed all apprehensions of our suffering for want of them'. The *Georgiana* was now armed as a consort, her own six guns being augmented by those from the *Policy*, and she was sent on an independent cruise under Lieutenant John Downes.

With *Barclay*, *Montezuma* and *Policy* in company the *Essex* continued her cruise and on 28 May fell in with another group of whalers on the fishing grounds. Under false British colours the *Essex* first approached the British-owned *Atlantic* and invited her master aboard for a 'gam', or gossip. Captain Obadiah Wyer came across in his boat and was misled by Porter's accent into confiding that he had been born in colonial America, that his wife and children lived in Nantucket, but that he had been born British and would remain so, a confidence he instantly regretted when Porter revealed his proper nationality and his intention of seizing Wyer's ship. Of different stamp was the master of the *Greenwich*, encountered later that same day, who did not submit until *Essex's* guns were employed in firing over him.

With over 100 prisoners and the need to dispose of some of his prizes, Porter and his ships headed for Peru where on 19 June they anchored off

Tumbes. After a few days Downes arrived in the *Georgiana* with three more British whalers, the *Hector*, *Rose* and *Catharine*, all taken on the 24th and bringing the value of their haul to some two million dollars. Porter now armed the *Atlantic* and renamed her the *Essex Junior*, transferring Downes into her with orders to escort the *Barclay* and four of the prizes to Valparaiso where he was to dispose of them and their oil. The *Essex*, with the *Georgiana* and the *Greenwich* – which had also been armed and manned by Porter – resumed their cruise round the Galapagos.

Arriving at Valparaiso Downes now discovered the limitations of rebellion: the Chilean rebels had no money, so he sent the *Policy* with a hold full of casks of sperm oil back to the United States by way of the Horn and left the remaining four vessels moored off the port. He did not stay himself, for he learned from a despatch brought over the Andes from Buenos Aires that a British frigate and two sloops-of-war were on their way to deal with the *Essex*. Downes hurried towards the rendezvous with Porter in the Galapagos.

Here, meanwhile, Porter's ships had continued taking prizes. On 14 July the *Essex* seized the *Charlton*. Meanwhile the *Greenwich* approached the *Seringapatam* whose master exchanged a broadside before lowering her ensign, whereupon a third whaler, the *New Zealander*, capitulated. Sending the *Georgiana* home laden with oil and the *Charlton* to Rio de Janiero with forty-eight of his British prisoners, Porter retained the *Seringapatam* and the *New Zealander*. On 15 September the *Essex* came upon and took the *Sir Andrew Hammond* while her crew were flensing a Sperm Whale. It had all been so easy.

Porter's frigate had now dominated the Pacific for months, destroying the British South Sea fishery by seizing a dozen whalers in succession – about two-thirds of the whole. Porter punctuated these successes with bombastic exhortations to his people. 'Fortune has at length smiled on us, because we deserved her smiles,' he declaimed, adding, with a reference to the political banner under which the American challenged Great Britain at sea: 'The first time she enabled us to display *free trade and sailors' rights*, she put in our possession near half a million of the enemy's property'. Then he concluded that 'we will yet render the name of the *Essex* as terrible to the enemy as that of any other vessel'.

He had already accomplished this, adding to the single-ship victories achieved by the frigates of the nascent United States Navy. In Halifax, Nova Scotia, a newspaper complained that the USS *Essex* had 'annihilated our commerce in the South Seas' doing more damage 'than all the rest of the American Navy', while Washington Irving noted that Porter had occasioned great uneasiness in Great Britain.

The merchants who had any property afloat in this quarter trembled with apprehension for its fate; the under-writers groaned at the catalogue of captures, while the pride of the nation was sorely incensed at beholding a single frigate lording it over the Pacific, in saucy defiance of their thousand ships.

The strength of the Royal Navy in 1812 had almost reached this number, and had, by 1813 declined slightly, but the point was well made. However, while the Royal Navy might be approaching exhaustion after twenty years of war, its quality diluted by its enormity, it was no longer an eighteenth-century institution. The experience of the American War of Independence and the leadership of the generation of fighting officers of which Nelson was the star, had imbued it with a different spirit. Porter might be in distant waters, but the arm of the British Admiralty was long and annihilation was its watch-word. As Porter learned when Downes joined him off the Galapagos on 30 September, his run of luck was over.

Hearing of the approach of nemesis, Porter ordered his improvised squad-ron to Nuku Hiva in the Marquesas where they arrived on 25 October and from where they might have evaded the British hue-and-cry. In a seven week idyll, Porter careened the *Essex* and annexed the islands to the United States. His men, more interested in fornication than imperialism, divided their time between refitting their ship and miscegenating, while Porter embroiled him-self in local politics and tribal war. As Bligh had done after a prolonged period of lotus-eating, Porter found his men mutinous when he passed orders to prepare for sea. Unlike Bligh, however, Porter threatened to blow them all up, himself included, in a dramatic confrontation and they bent to his will. The *Essex* and *Essex Junior* left Nuku Hiva on 13 December and headed east, not for the Horn and home, but for Valparaiso.

The prize-master aboard the *New Zealander* was ordered to proceed directly for the United States, while the remaining four prizes were left at Nuku Hiva under Lieutenant John Gamble of the Marines. Gamble was left to occupy Fort Madison, thrown up by Porter as the hub of America's new colony. The enterprise did not prosper: within months a mutiny broke out among the Americans who joined the British prisoners and retook the *Seringapatam* in which they departed for New Zealand. Faced with this, Gamble set fire to the *Greenwich*, abandoned Nuku Hiva and left for home in the *Sir Andrew Hammond*; he had just seven men with him. The ship was captured by a British man-of-war off Hawaii and Gamble and his small crew were taken prisoner. In the interim Porter had met his own doom in another British cruiser, but not without hubristically attracting this by glory-hunting:

I had done all the injury that could be done to the British commerce in the
Pacific, and still hoped to signalise my cruise by something more splendid before
leaving that sea. Believing the British would seek me in Valparaiso, I determined
to cruise about that place.

Porter and Downes did not have long to wait. On 8 February 1814 Captain
James Hillyar in HM Frigate *Phoebe*, in company with the sloop *Cherub*,
Commander Thomas Tucker, cornered the Americans in Valparaiso. Hillyar
tested Porter's respect for Chile's neutrality, sailing straight at the *Essex*,
defying Porter to rake *Phoebe*. Characteristically Porter afterwards claimed
'The *Phoebe* was completely at my mercy', but Hillyar merely hailed Porter
announcing that he had no intentions of attacking in neutral waters. Porter
responded, shouting: 'You have no business where you are. If you touch…this
ship I shall board instantly!' After anchoring, replenishing stores and water
and indeed meeting Porter at the residence of the American consul, there
followed a week during which the respective ships' companies traded insults
after which Hillyar withdrew and blockaded Valparaiso. This stalemate lasted
a month before Porter ordered the burning of two of the prizes Downes had
escorted to Valparaiso and which had languished at anchor ever since. He then
sallied, testing Hillyar and seeking to let the *Essex Junior* escape. Hillyar fell
back on the *Cherub*. His orders required him to destroy the *Essex* and he was
not going to give up his superiority in fire-power for some quixotic notion.
Then, on 28 March an onshore gale parted one of the *Essex*'s two cables and
faced with this *fait accompli*, Porter resolved to break out.

A few miles outside Valparaiso harbour but still within Chilean waters the
men-of-war engaged. After a while Porter drove the *Cherub* off but in *Phoebe*
Hillyar succeeded in pouring a raking fire into the *Essex*, reducing her to a
wreck in one and three quarter hours, whereupon one magazine exploded.
The carnage aboard the *Essex* was frightful; that aboard the *Phoebe* less so: five
dead in the opening manoeuvres and a handful of wounded. Hillyar was gracious in victory:

> The defence of the *Essex*, taking into account our superiority of force, and
> the very discouraging circumstances of her having lost her main top-mast did
> honour to the brave defenders, and most fully evinced the courage of Captain
> Porter and those under his command. Her colours were not struck until the
> loss in killed and wounded was so awfully great, and her shattered condition so
> seriously bad, as to render further resistance unavailing.

President Madison, too preoccupied with the burning of his capital by a
British expeditionary force, did not share Porter's enthusiasm for colonial

acquisition, though he eulogised Porter's heroism when the latter arrived home in the *Essex Junior*, paroled by courtesy of Hillyar. As to Porter's prizes they, with the other fag-ends of this story, fade into the obscure margins of history. As a testimony to her builders the *Seringapatam*, having conveyed the reluctant colonists and their prisoners to safety, swam on until 1860 when she was reduced to a hulk.

Although the British were to maintain a South Seas fishery, the Pacific was to become increasingly an American preserve, though in the short-term other East Indiamen found employment in the hunt for the Sperm Whale through the more conventional route of old-age. In 1804 the *Telegraph* was sold to H. Swain & Co. of London for the purpose; the *Tartar* – which we have met before in connection with Captain Edward Fiott -was purchased by W. Wilkinson, another London owner. Among the Extra-ships which ended up oleaginous and smoky on the widespread Pacific grounds were the *Boyd, Dart, Elligood, John and James* – which foundered off Cape Horn in 1806 – and James Mather's *Prince of Wales*. While whaling could provide generous returns, each 'expedition' was a risk and depended upon the quality of the master, not all of whom were either lucky or competent. Captain Robert Rhodes of the whaler *Alexander* of London so protracted his laden homeward sailing from a cruise to the 'Great South Sea' that his cargo of seal skins and whale oil was spoiled, much of it having leaked into the *Alexander's* bilge, the rest being rancid. The *Alexander* had picked up a homeward convoy at St Helena on 19 April 1806 and arrived off Gravesend on 26 June where Rhodes found himself in debt to his backers to the tune of £5,000.

The new colonies on the Australian coast also contributed to this harvest, but the vigour of its exploiters soon emphasised the dangers of over-fishing. The vast quantities of seals and whales in the Bass Strait and along the coastal waters of Tasmania drew speculative adventurers. In the early 1800s the newly established settlement of Hobart was increasingly busy 'enriching itself on their oleaginous remains'. Sperm Whales were so plentiful that the master of a whaler claimed in 1803 that they could be taken almost 'without looking,' while gravid female Southern Right Whales actually swam into the Derwent estuary to calve. Oil, blubber, meat, Right Whale baleen and Sperm Whale ivory produced a useful glut, so prodigal that the meat and tried-out blubber was given to pigs and other livestock. But this bounty soon ended and by 1810 the cetacean population of the Bass Strait was exhausted, the local elephant-seal was extinct and the fur-seal so reduced in numbers that extinction seemed imminent. The local whaling and sealing fleet, owned by companies such as Kable and Underwood, had to venture further a-field, going to New Zealand for seals, and for whales ever farther into the South Pacific.

Such, then, were the British-flagged ships and their crews encountered in later years by Herman Melville when a seaman in the New Bedford whaler *Acushnet*, and which make a cameo appearance in the closing chapters of *Moby Dick*.

Hillyar's victory, obscured by that of Philip Broke in HMS *Shannon*,[52] effectively marked the end of the attack on her trade waged on Great Britain by her several enemies during the wars of the French Revolution and Empire. Specifically, the war with America was ended by the Treaty of Ghent, concluded over Christmas 1814, but news of it was not received at Bombay by way of Baghdad until 4 May 1815 and it was 2 July before it reached Canton in dispatches carried by the frigate *Horatio*. By this time the greater world war had ended at Waterloo on 18 June, news of which conclusive event was learned at Canton by a second visit of the *Horatio* on 14 January 1816.

This general easing of tensions was countered by the effects of the end of the Company's monopoly of trade to India which created expectations that the China trade would soon also be thrown open. More immediately, Indian merchants now arrived in China to prosecute the Country-trade with vigour, ignoring the prohibitions against foreigners residing on Chinese soil and deaf to the remonstrance of the Select Committee. In all this they were aided by the British ship-masters in their employ, all increasingly resenting the stand taken by the Selectmen who were still – legally at least – the overall arbiters and organisers of trade on the British side. In May 1815 six British and fifteen Parsee companies based in Bombay memorialised the newly created Lords Commissioners for the Affairs of India, complaining that they should not be placed under restrictions or 'subject to such interference or impediment as is calculated not only to diminish its advantage, but which in its exercise brings inevitable ruin upon the Individuals engaged in it'.

'From this time,' as Hosea Morse points out, 'the Company was forced to combat, not only the rapacity of the Chinese officials, but also the adventurous spirit of independence of the private English and Indian merchants, impatient of the imposition in China of the restraints which it was not now lawful to impose in India'.[53] In short, although the Honourable East India Company was to continue sending its ships out to China for a further twenty years, it was an institution already clinging to a former, bygone age.

More fell at the end of the Great War than Napoleonic France and, while Europe was suffered to retire under the cold shadow of aristocracy, the distant frontiers of commerce were – like frontiers everywhere – subject to the necessary revisions of the frontiersmen. Few of these felt any longer that they owed allegiance to the remains of a joint-stock company established in the days of Good Queen Bess – even its sworn servants.

NOTES

1. William Cornwallis was a brother of Marquess Cornwallis whose surrender at Yorktown effectively ensured American Independence. He was to become a brilliant admiral, known as 'Billy Blue' for his reluctance to tarry in port and his keeping of the Blue Peter – the flag signalling imminent departure – flying at his flagship's foremast-head. He was a fine exponent of blockade when charged with investing Brest from the sea. The Marquess, his elder brother, was twice Governor-General of India, supported Catholic emancipation in Ireland and assisted the negotiating of the short-lived Peace of Amiens. He died in India in 1805 at the beginning of his second term as Governor-General.

2. George Macartney had served as Envoy-Extraordinary to St Petersburg and, after election to the Irish Parliament, was appointed Chief Secretary for Ireland. In 1774 he was elected to the British Parliament for a Scots constituency and was sent as governor of Grenada, being raised to the Irish peerage. In late 1780 he became governor and president of the Council at Fort St George, Madras, arriving in India the July following. He left Madras in 1785 after refusing the Governor-Generalship of Bengal but having so ably administered the Madras Presidency the HEIC awarded him a pension of £1,500 for life. On 3 May 1792 Macartney was appointed Ambassador to China and made a viscount. He was later governor of Cape Colony and died in 1806.

3. The unhurried nature of such voyages is well exemplified here. The ships anchored off the Ladrones Islands near modern Hong Kong after stopping at Madeira, for wine, Rio de Janeiro, Tristan da Cunha, Amsterdam Island, Batavia and Turon.

4. Macartney was not quite empty-handed for, in passing through Kiangsi he had been allowed 'to take up several tea-plants in a growing state with large balls of earth adhering to them, which tea-plants I flatter myself, I shall be able to transmit to Bengal.'

5. The general social and economic benefits of an increase in trade to a nation, then becoming apparent in the thinking of European statesmen and especially the British, ran contrary to Chinese governance. 'In China the emoluments of even the greatest and wisest statesmen were obtained by the methods which involved the taxation of trade and not its encouragement... the Manchu nobility and ministers, and the Court itself...shared in the irregular and unregulated, but not illegal, gains of the Hoppo at Canton. To this dominating party it was obvious that the Hoppo, and his control and his methods, must at all costs be maintained...' In the Emperor's conclusion to his response to Macartney's note and King George's letter, the Son of Heaven stated that: 'As the Requests made by your Ambassador militate against the Laws and Usages of this Our Empire, and are at the same time wholly useless to the End proposed, I cannot acquiesce in them. I again admonish you, O King, to act conformably to my Intentions, that we may preserve Peace and Amity on each

Side, and thereby contribute to our reciprocal Happiness.' See Morse, Vol. II, page 226 *et seq.*

6. The regulations governing qualifications for commanders and officers in Extra-ships were slightly less stringent than in the Regular vessels, particularly in the matter of age. This reflected the dwindling of suitable man-power as the war progressed, time passed and demand increased.

7. The high social grouping of the Company's 'Marine Interest' was intimately acquainted with the daily problems of the Admiralty, largely through the medium of Trinity House. During the period 1793 – 1816 the two influential Deputy Masters of the Corporation were Sir Robert Preston and Sir Joseph Cotton. Preston commanded three Indiamen (HCSs *Asia, Hillsborough* and *General Eliott*) and with Charles Foulis part-owned at least four (*Foulis* – which was lost without trace in 1791, *Cuffnells, Bellmont* and *Pigot* – the last two being lost to the enemy). Cotton, having served in the navy and been commissioned as lieutenant, afterwards commanded the HCS *Royal Charlotte* and part-owned several Indiamen. He became one of the most influential members of the Court of Directors and Marine Interest and with John Woolmore – his successor as Deputy Master at Trinity House – founders of the East India Dock Company. During their tenures of office at Trinity House, Admirals Lord Barham, Sir Hugh Palliser, Earl St Vincent and Lord Hood, together with the First Lords Melville and Spencer and Prime Ministers Pitt and Portland, were all Elder Brethren.

8. Merchant ships' guns were generally inferior weapons to naval cannon and manufactured for merchantmen as 'cannonades', not to be confused with the Carron Company's patent – and potent – 'carronade'.

9. Mitchell was afterwards knighted for his conduct during these days.

10. Not to be confused with the North Pacific Ladrones, or Marianas Islands. Both, however, mean islands of robbers.

11. William James in his *Naval History* attributes this ruse to Lennox, entirely ignoring the presence of Wilson in *Exeter*, though he concedes the convoy consisted of: 'Five (if not six) homeward-bound, richly laden Indiamen…' He also mistakenly states that the *Boddam* and *Canton* were part of this convoy and is followed in this by Cotton and Fawcett; these two ships actually made their departure from the Pearl River later in 1797, both suffering considerable set-backs. The other two ships are possibly the *Alfred*, James Farquharson, and *Bombay Castle*, John Hamilton. Professor C. Northcote Parkinson confirms Wilson as commodore in *Exeter* and Rowan Hackman the *Exeter*'s presence.

12. Rainier was a rear admiral of the blue squadron and therefore flew a rectangular blue flag at the rearmost masthead, the mizzen. Hence he was a 'flag-officer'. Naval men-of-war under a post-captain were referred to as 'private ships' to distinguish them from flag-ships bearing an admiral and they flew a long, thin pendant.

13. C. Northcote Parkinson, *War in the Eastern Seas*, p106.

14. Laird Clowes erroneously puts this action in the Straits of Bab-el-Mandeb on 12 October, following James, who misspells Malroux's name. This makes no sense,

and conflicts with the account published in the *Naval Chronicle* which was based upon the letter written by Cramlington from Muscat on 10 November 1799 and addressed to the Company's Directors in London. C.R. Low makes no mention of the incident in his *History of the Indian Navy*, perhaps because *Comet*'s conduct was indifferent, seeing that she was engaging a Country-ship manned by a prize-crew, though the light winds may have played their part. For the first part of the *Pearl*'s voyage see Bulley, p95, and Cramlington's account is in Grocott, p79 *et seq*.

15. The precise number on board is unclear but some sources indicate as many as 600. General St John was apparently much taken by Surcouf's charm and visited him at St Malo after the war.

16. A *lakh* amounted to 100,000 rupees.

17. Later commissioned into the Royal Navy *La Forte*, with the *Egyptienne*, the most powerful frigate in the French navy, was wrecked and lost in the Red Sea.

18. The French frigates were accompanied by an American schooner which was acting as tender to the squadron and had been captured off the West African coast whence Landolphe had been sent to harry British and American ships there as a consequence of France's quasi-war with the United States. The French had just refitted in the Rio de la Plata.

19. In addition to the *Earl Camden*, the other Indiamen were the *Warley* (Henry Wilson), *Alfred* (James Farquharson), *Royal George* (John Timmins), *Coutts* (Robert Torin), *Wexford* (William Clarke), *Ganges* (William Moffat), *Exeter* (Henry Meriton), *Earl of Abergavenny* (John Wordsworth), *Henry Addington* (John Kirkpatrick), *Bombay Castle* (Archibald Hamilton), *Cumberland* (William Farrer), *Hope* (James Pendergrass), *Dorsetshire* (Robert Brown), *Warren Hastings* (Thomas Larkins) and *Ocean* (John Lochner). The HCS *Ganges* should not be confused with the Bombay Marine's armed-brig of the same name.

20. I have before me Captain Charles Weller's manuscript signals book (see Bibliography) which includes, *inter alia*, single flag signals denominating: '*Enemy in sight, Take and Keep the appointed station either in Line of Battle or Order of Sailing, Prepare for Battle, Engage the Enemy*'. There are also two-flag numerically coded signals that contain such instructions as to: '*Alter the course as I do without further signal, The headmost ships of the Line of Battle or Order of Sailing are to alter course…, Tack headmost and weathermost ships first, but in Line of Battle in succession, etc, etc.*'

21. Lloyd's Patriotic Fund was set up by subscribers at Lloyd's Coffee House on 20 July 1803. Mr Brook Watson was in the chair and the object was 'to animate the efforts of our defenders by sea and land…for the purposes of assuaging the anguish of their wounds, or palliating in some degree the more weighty misfortune of the loss of limbs – of alleviating the distresses of the widow and orphan – of smoothing the brow of sorrow…' It was also intended to encourage the exertions of otherwise disinterested naval officers to properly protect trade convoys, a job not perceived as worthwhile to the increasingly commercially minded warriors of the later phase of the war.

22. The *Warren Hastings* was the second of three Indiamen of the same name all principally owned by John Pascall Larkins, uncle of the ship's commander. After being retaken in 1810, she was retained for some time in the Indian coasting trade before returning to London. She then made four further voyages to China for Larkins and one for a new owner, William Sims, after which she was laid up for three years before being sold in 1829. Her successor, into which Thomas Larkins transferred as commander when new, held the name and made voyages to China concurrently with her and only outlasted her by six years. The two ships encountered each other off Saugor some time later when the older was in the country trade and Larkins hailed her whereupon 'the shouting on both sides was quite deafening'.

23. Sir Richard Hardinge had commanded the *Kent* for fourteen years and had become one of the members of the Marine Interest. Created a baronet in 1801, the family had intimate connections with British fortunes in India.

24. After extensive refitting the *Piémontaise* was purchased into the Royal Navy under her own name and Dawson was made post into her. He was awarded a 100 guinea sword from Lloyd's Patriotic Fund but died at Madras in 1811, only twenty-eight years of age.

25. The *Europe* was retaken at the fall of the Île de Bourbon (Réunion), the *Streatham* seems to have been retaken by the Royal Navy in December and resumed her voyage.

26. Both vessels were used at Port Louis as confinements for the very many merchant seamen held there. After the capture of the island in 1810 *Charlton* was put into the Indian coastal and China trade, being wrecked in the Red Sea in 1812; the *United Kingdom* was taken over by the Transport Board but foundered off Cape of Good Hope in 1815 when bound from Batavia to London. Captain Laird, the chief mate and twenty-five of her crew were lost with the ship.

27. As noted earlier the *Lord Nelson* foundered in an Indian Ocean cyclone along with the *Experiment* and *Glory* in October 1808.

28. Macintyre, *The Privateers*, p127.

29. Decaen was embittered largely because all his contemporaries were gaining glory, titles and wealth in Europe while he was dutifully serving the Emperor of the French on a distant rock, constrained like Prometheus. His antipathy to the 36-year old Surcouf whose war was more a matter of private profit than patriotism is therefore understandable if not admirable. Robert Surcouf was now very wealthy and back home in St Malo continued his interrupted career as an *armateur*. After the war he financed a fishing fleet. He died at St Malo in 1827.

30. The *Revenant* was renamed *Jena* and commissioned as a French national 18-gun corvette under Capitaine Nicolas Morice. On 8 October 1808 she fell in with the British frigate *Modeste*, of 36 guns, which chased her for nine hours and after an action of one, compelled her to strike her colours. Doubtless in the hands of Robert Surcouf she would have escaped. In these waters, the state of the fouling

on a vessel's hull must be taken into account, but it is quite clear that she was an exceptionally fast little ship.

31. Among Decaen's uninvited guests on Île de France was the British explorer and surveyor, Commander Matthew Flinders. Although Flinders had been furnished by the French government with a passport, it was made out in the name of HMS *Investigator*. After wearing her out in a tremendous survey of the Australian coast, he was given the *Porpoise*, the loss of which we have noted as placing some of her survivors aboard the Indiamen engaged under Dance off Pulo Aur in February 1804. Flinders was captured and, his passports not covering his current vessel, Governor Decaen refused to recognise what his master Napoleon had: that Flinders was engaged in a mission from which the whole of humanity would benefit. Flinders's health was already damaged from the privations of his expeditions; it deteriorated still further in captivity which he used to write an account of his exploits. He was liberated by the capture of the Mascarenes and returned home, to die on the eve of the publication of his great work *A Voyage to Terra Australis*.

32. Another American ship taken up by the Company was the *Paragon* of Boston, which made a single voyage to Bengal in 1794.

33. A considerable number of Indian-built ships chartered as Extra-ships were seized by French corsairs perhaps because they were less well-armed as the London-equipped Indiamen, or perhaps because they were less aggressively handled. Another was the Calcutta-built and owned Extra-ship *Suffolk*, Captain John Robinson, taken in the Atlantic in 1805.

34. The *Upton Castle*, Captain John Pavin, was recaptured at Port Louis in 1810 and burnt out at Saugor in February 1817. The *Brunswick* was wrecked near the Cape of Good Hope on her way to France as a prize.

35. Among other prizes taken by the enemy was the *Bellona*, taken in 1811 by the French privateer *Invincible Napoleon*.

36. Sir George Staunton returned home in March 1808 but by then a Mr Robert Morrison had been engaged 'as Interpreter to the Company's establishments in China at a salary of 2,000 dollars a year'. Others, often with a religious mission in contemplation, were by now arriving to learn Chinese. Morrison features in the subsequent volume, *Masters Under God*.

37. The frigate *Phaeton* was, under a series of post-captains, an extraordinarily lucky man-of-war, capturing a great number of rich prizes during the wars of 1793–1815.

38. Teak-built, at the age of 31 she became *Justitia*, a convict hulk, a task she fulfilled for a further 25 years.

39. Morse claims this to have been only the second prohibition on the carriage of opium officially received by the East Indian Company since that of 1729. This is, I submit, a little disingenuous: it may have only been the second minuted at East India House in Leadenhall Street, but the local prohibitions were well known, hence the local ban on Company ships carrying the drug as part of their official

cargo and the burden of the trade being left for the Anglo-Parsee trading houses to exploit.

40. Parkinson points out Drury's lack of pragmatism and his detachment from real life in that he voiced a claim as C-in-C, East Indies, to hold 'the highest official situation in India' out-ranking the Governor-General on the grounds that Lord Minto was, strictly speaking, a servant of the HEIC. See *War in the Eastern Seas*, p320 *et seq*. 'Drury [unlike Pellew, Troubridge and probably Rainier] had come to regard his profession as a superior caste, above the criticism of ordinary mortals but infinitely responsible in the eyes of heaven; a chosen aristocracy with a special standard of honour, worthy therefore, of a very special respect'. In this characterisation, Drury presages the worst form of proto-imperialist. Drury's contempt extended to the commanders of East Indiamen whom he anathematised as 'a mongrel kind of gentlemen,' an attitude that did little to smooth relationships between Britain's sea services.

41. This is a little less fantastic than Sir John Duckworth's exculpation of *his* conduct at Constantinople which takes the biscuit for splendid but circumlocutory evasion of the facts!

42. Heathcote's attitude is a sad comment on the emerging character of naval officers of his generation and was, moreover, liberally demonstrated in the several encounters not merely between the British mercantile fraternity, but with Americans at sea, precipitating the War of 1812. Rodrigo was unpopular with the Chinese and the anti-British faction among the Portuguese at Macao. He was given a grant of 10,000 dollars by the Select Committee and granted a free passage to London from where he went to join the Portuguese Regent in Brazil.

43. The risks actually and corporeally run by the unfortunate Compradors were far worse. Bankruptcies and imprisonment were resorted to by the imperial officials at the slightest infringement of complex regulations, hostage-taking to ensure compliance with the imperial will – official and unofficial – being commonplace.

44. Some 400,000 dollars was shipped home aboard HMS *Belliqueux*, of which Captain Geo. Byng received 1.5 per cent commission on its carriage. This was loaded at Macao to avoid the proscriptions against Sycee being exported from Canton. Among this, according to Morse, 'was doubtless some from the proceeds of the sale of opium'.

45. See Parkinson, p314, *et seq*.

46. Commanded by Morice, late of the *Jena*, ex-*Revenant*.

47. Following his extrication of the *Astell*, William Hawkey was made captain of the *Lady Carrington*, commanding her for one voyage to Bombay and Bengal 1812–1813.

48. The trade was carried on through ten Hong merchants and among the varieties of tea were Congo (126,000 chests), Souchong (5,200 chests), Twankay (36,300 chests), and Hyson (9,000 chests). At this period there were four Selectmen, one of whom remained at Macao to superintend the collection of specie and grant

Bills of Exchange on the Bengal government. Besides these senior Supercargoes there were eight others, all of whom had specific tasks, and six writers of varying seniority. The establishment was completed by five Supernumeraries who included two Inspectors of Tea, two surgeons and Morrison the translator. All were on salaries which ranged from the two Junior Writers on £100 per annum, up to the Selectmen each on £7,124, with Elphinstone as President receiving £8,550. The salaries cost a total of £67,000 to which had to be added Factory charges paid to the Compradors of the Hong amounting to £27,941, making a total of £94,941. Additional to these officials were a number of British nationals, servants of both sexes.

49. The regulation against carrying opium in the Company's ships remained part of the standard charter-party under which they were engaged. This specifically included private trade wherein it was 'possitively (sic) forbidden and serious consequences may attend your [the Commander's] neglect of this injunction'.

50. Francis Rawdon Hastings, Second Earl of Moira, was a soldier who served with distinction in the southern theatre during the American War of Independence. He was to be crucial in securing British supremacy in central India by defeating the Marathas and in the secession of Singapore in 1819 (see Vol.3). An enlightened man – particularly in his conduct towards the Indian population – he was awarded £60,000 by the East India Company but resigned when the Court of Directors annulled his gubernatorial permission to the banking house of Palmer to lend money to Hyderabad.

51. The American consul was Joel Roberts Poinsett, who introduced a Mexican flower into the United States. It was named the poinsettia.

52. The frigate-action between HMS *Shannon* and the USS *Chesapeake* fought off Boston in May 1813 restored some of the battered pride of the Royal Navy after a string of single-ship defeats which in fact had little effect upon the short war with America. Broke's defeat of Lawrence was therefore a matter of propaganda. Hillyar's defeat of Porter was the most significant of these frigate-actions and while it came too late to save the British Southern Whale-fishery, it was a powerful demonstration of British naval sea-power's reach and set the standard for the century that was to follow.

53. I am much indebted to Hosea Ballou Morse, whose rich pages of *The Chronicles of the East India Company Trading to China, 1635-1834*, of 1926, I have plundered at some length. The story is not yet quite over and is dealt with in Vol.3, *Masters Under God*, which includes the end of the Company's trading activities in China in 1834. This event in turn opens a new era wherein the British merchant marine expanded into a still vaster void left by the shrinking power of imperial China. Today, the wheel has come full circle.

POST SCRIPTUM

'AGAINST WIND, WAVES AND TIDE'

1816

When the war ended, the victorious allies assembled in Vienna to divide the spoils and settle the peace of Europe. Although Talleyrand rescued France from dissolution, this was no repeat of the Peace of Amiens: this time the British conceded nothing and gained much. An exchange of territories with the Dutch secured the fringes of the Malay peninsula for them; in addition they took possession of the Cape of Good Hope, Ceylon (Sri Lanka), Mauritius, Guiana, Trinidad, Tobago, Malta and Helgoland. For good measure the troublesome General Bonaparte, stripped of his imperial pretensions and held by the British, was isolated upon the East India Company's staging post of St Helena, ceded to the British Government for the term of the quondam Emperor's life. But among the settling of kingdoms and colonies, there was another matter, that affront to a Europe that thought of itself as Christian: the white slaves of Barbary. The new United States, concerned over the abduction of many of its seafarers, had mounted a naval expedition against Tripoli ten years earlier and, negotiations with the Dey having failed, in 1816 Admiral Sir Edward Pellew was sent to demand the release of all European slaves. On his way, Pellew was joined by a Dutch squadron under Admiral Van Capellen and on 27 August, after a long and furious bombardment reciprocated by massed cannon in the stone casemates of the city's massive defences, a few hundred white slaves were released. This was not the end of Barbary piracy, but Pellew had made a point: a new spirit was abroad and there were many men poised to take advantage of it.

The ending of the East India Company's monopoly of the Indian trade in 1813 had persuaded Thomas Brocklebank to send a ship east. He had tried privateering without much success, finding chartering to the government a steadier form of employment for some of his ships, while others had sailed in convoy to and from the West Indies, brushing with privateers as they did so. But in 1813, the *Hercules* had made a voyage to Madagascar on Government service and in 1816 Captain McKean left Whitehaven for Calcutta in the *Princess Charlotte*, breaking into the Indian trade with a cargo valued and insured at £3,000. McKean's ship wore a distinctive livery, her black topsides divided by a broad white ribband. Her voyage was to be the beginning of a long association with the sub-continent.

MacAndrew's ships were busy too, carrying fruit home from the Iberian peninsula; while the ship-broker John Bibby, who had acquired an interest in the *Dove* in 1801, having made an advantageous marriage, went into partnership with John Highfield and began running some coasting vessels. His ships were soon venturing further afield: by 1810 his brig *Thames* was heading for Brazil and in 1811 the *Lucretia* cleared outwards for Trinidad. Meanwhile, in the West Country city of Exeter, 'a moderately successful watch and clock-maker' of thirty-eight decided to emigrate and in 1816 took ship, crossed the Atlantic and settled in St John's, Newfoundland. His name was Benjamin Bowring and he too would found a shipping dynasty.

In London the grave men of the East India Company made their own plans. Anthony Calvert was dead, but John Woolmore was by now a powerful owning-manager and, along with others of the 'Marine Interest', he was an Elder Brother of Trinity House. The Corporation was acquiring more lighthouses on shore and in 1807, when the lease of the Eddystone expired and it ceased to be a private lighthouse, it too became the direct responsibility of Trinity House. Already running a number of lighthouses on shore, ballasting shipping on the Thames and maintaining the buoys in the Thames estuary and along the East Anglian coast, Trinity House's power was growing. In Scotland the Commissioners for Northern Lighthouses, and in Ireland the Commissioners for Irish Lights, had, with the Elder Brethren, begun adopting the new oil lamps of Argand and the lenses of Fresnel. War, as it always does, had accelerated advances in technology.

The quest for a communications system faster than a man on a horse and more precise than coastal beacons had led in 1796 to the adoption by the Admiralty of the Reverend Lord George Murray's shutter signalling apparatus.[1] But the electro-magnetic age was poised to succeed such crude apparatus, for in 1814 Matthew Flinders, in his *A Voyage to Terra Australis*, noted the effect of iron fittings within a ship on her compass, and devised a compensating bar, now named after him, to correct this deviation. This was to be an important principle once iron and steel were used in the construction of ship's hulls

A bird's-eye view of the great East India Dock. Secured by a high wall to protect it from looting and pilfering, the dock is filled with East Indiamen rigged down and awaiting the new season. The large mast-house with its crane for re-stepping the ships' masts was a wonder of the age, but the idleness of the ships for several months every year was out-dated the instant peace returned. (Private Collection)

By contrast with the previous plate, the dock is now almost emptied, the Indiamen having sailed in convoys on their voyages to Bombay, Calcutta and Whampoa. (Private Collection)

while in the withdrawing-rooms of the rich, experiments demonstrating the magical properties of a mysterious substance called 'electricity' were giving rise to great speculation.

During the latter part of the war, the quest for faster sailing ships had led to advances in hull design which manifested themselves in French corsairs and, more significantly, American privateers. The hull-form sported by the so-called Baltimore 'clippers', of which the *Prince de Neuchâtel* was such a fine example, attracted the notice of the British who – eventually – captured her. Her lines, taken off at Portsmouth dockyard, would later inspire a hull with hollow lines at bow and stern, far faster and more weatherly than anything that had gone before.

While sail had yet a century of profitable refinement to run, its days were numbered, for steam-power had made its appearance on the industrial scene long before the end of the eighteenth century and in 1794 William Lyttleton patented a screw propeller which would one day, and after much experimentation by others, prove the most efficient way of harnessing steam at sea. In 1802 William Symington had built a canal steamer, the *Charlotte Dundas*, which was followed on the Clyde ten years later by the *Comet*.[2] Two years later, in 1814, Boulton and Watt constructed the first two-cylinder slide-lever steam engine and in the same month in which Napoleon's dreams were shattered on the bloody field of Waterloo, a steam-yacht named the *Thames*, commanded by Captain George Dodd and 'intended to ply between London and Margate', made a passage from her builders on the Clyde to the Thames Estuary 'vomiting forth flame and smoke' and performing 'some extraordinary feats at sea, against wind, waves and tide'.

Among those who would engage with the new-fangled steam-vessel was the young William Pixley. After his release from custody on the Continent he had sailed with his father in his own *Hector*, proudly described as a 'fine corvette', a fashionable turn of phrase for a merchantman. The *Hector* mounted 22 guns and traded to the West Indies, and in a smart action had beaten off a privateer. Pixley rose to become chief mate of the *Rhine* and then of the *Jonah*, ending the war married and in command of Mr Briggs's new ship, the *Orestes*. In the summer of 1815 the man who had danced with the Empress Josephine was homeward-bound under convoy of the 74-gun *Warrior*, Captain Rod, when outbound ships signalled the news of Waterloo. As Napoleon died of stomach cancer on a rock in the South Atlantic, Pixley rose still further in the merchants' service, for this was the dawn of an age of opportunity for men in British shipping.

The clever chicanery adopted in outwitting Napoleon's Continental System had led, in effect if not in law, to the abandonment of the Navigation Acts. Soon the banner which the new United States Navy had flaunted in the face of the Royal Navy – *Free Trade and Sailor's Rights* – would, at least in its first part, replace the old theory of mercantilism and become a driving force of contemporary economics. The ultimate effect this would eventually have on British shipping lay far, far in the future. In the short term there were more immediate concerns to ship-owners and those who served them, not least the fast ships that the damned Yankees built. The Americans were emerging as an increasingly strong commercial competitor at sea: 1816 saw the founding of the Black Ball Line of transatlantic packets and the beginning of half a century of American domination of the North Atlantic.

In 1500 the British mercantile marine had itself formed part of the Navy Royal, summoned to assist the state when necessary in an echo of feudal service, providing men and ships. At the end, with the design and purpose of men-of-war and merchant ships diverging, it was only the men of the merchants' service that the Royal Navy required, and these it helped itself to with almost complete licence. Indeed, one cannot escape the conviction that a state of undeclared but understood social and civil warfare existed between the two sea-services. Moreover, in the absorption of the weaker by the more powerful – aided as it was by the authority of the nation-state – the entire history of the former has been subsumed with the results that Othello articulated: its good name had been filched.

During the Great War with France the mercantile marine had played a vital part, and had suffered for it. The investment of its ship-owners and the activity and skills of its masters, mates and seamen had done nothing less than pump blood into the sinews of war. They had also upon occasion rendered that ancient supplementary support to the armed forces of the nation by fighting alongside them or, in the absence of the state's defences, had fought for their own survival and the assistance of others.

Musing upon trade-protection, one naval officer of the day, Basil Hall, wrote:

> A useful chapter in naval history and tactics could be written, by which it might
> be made manifest, that a determined bearing, accompanied by a certain degree
> of force, and a vigorous resolution to exert that force to the utmost, would, in
> most cases, save the greater part of the convoy, even against powerful odds.

Hall had learned a vital lesson, but did he write these words because he doubted the lesson had sunk in among his peers? Or was his prescience ignored, as was that of a later naval officer who, at the end of the First World War, wrote of the deterrent effect of aircraft upon submarines? Who knows? Convoy worked tolerably well under sail in these years and yet many shades of opinion and many different men opposed it a century later when on the brink of a greater and more catastrophic conflict.

By 1815 the two British sea-services had drifted far from the symbiosis they enjoyed around 1500. By the end of the Napoleonic War all they had in common was a demand for the same limited number of seamen and this ensured that impressment, at least in theory, remained an expedient cudgel of Government. It was, however, never afterwards invoked. Wholesale conscription better became the voracious appetite of twentieth-century warfare, while the increasing specialisation of naval gunnery and the management of men-of-war made the common merchant seaman of no use to the Royal Navy. It was somewhat otherwise with the mercantile officer, as will be examined in a later volume.

By 1816 the dynamics of change were shifting gear. The world stood on the threshold of a new age: that of emigration, social revolution and technology. The British mercantile marine would not merely play its part, but be one of its principal engines.

NOTES

1. The same year, 1796, was also that in which the London Missionary Society sent its first mission ship, the *Duff*, into the Pacific under a Captain Wilson.
2. The Americans had built a commercial steam ship, the *North River*, in 1807 while in 1812 Robert Fulton designed the first harbour defence steamer for the USN, the *Demologos*.

BIBLIOGRAPHY

PUBLISHED MATERIAL

All published in London unless otherwise stated

Armstrong, R., *The Merchantmen* (Vol.3 of *A History of Seafaring*), Ernest Benn, 1969

Barrett, C.R.B. (editor), *The Trinity House*, Lawrence and Bullen, 1893

Barrow, T., *The Whaling Trade of North-East England, 1750-1850*, University of Sunderland Press, Sunderland, 2001

Bateson, C., *The Convict Ships*, Brown, Son and Ferguson, Glasgow, 1969

Beck, J., *Captain John Bull of the Falmouth Packet Service*, South Western Maritime Historical Society, 1995

Blackmore, E., *The British Mercantile Marine: A Short Historical Review*, Charles Griffin, 1897

Biden, C., *Naval Discipline in the Merchant Service*, J.M. Richardson, 1830

Bowditch, N., *American Practical Navigator*, Defense Mapping Agency Hydrographic/ Topographic Center, Washington, 1984

Brooks, L., and Ducé, R.H., (editors), *Seafarers, Ships and Cargoes*, University of London Press, 1951

Brown, C.H., *Nicholls's Seamanship and Nautical Knowledge*, Brown, Son & Ferguson, Glasgow, 1958

Brown, R.D., *The Port of London*, Terence Dalton, Lavenham, 1978

Bulley, A., *The Bombay Country Ships, 1790-1833*, Curzon, Richmond, 2000

Free Mariner, John Adolphus Pope in the East Indies, 1786-1821, British Association for Cemeteries in South East Asia, Putney, 1992

Cameron, A., and Farndon, R., *Scenes from Sea and City, Lloyd's List, 1734-1984*, Lloyd's List, London 1984.

Cameron, V.L., *The Log of a Jack Tar; or, the Life of James Choyce, Master Mariner*, Fisher Unwin, 1891

Charton, B., and Tietjen, J., *Seas and Oceans*, Collins, 1989

Chatterton, E.K., *Valiant Sailormen*, Hurst and Blackett, 1936

    The Mercantile Marine, Heinemann, 1923

    Windjammers and Shellbacks, Fisher Unwin, 1926

    Ventures and Voyages, Rich and Cowan, 1935

    The Old East Indiamen, Conway Maritime, 1971

    Seamen All, Philip Allan & Co. Ltd, 1928

Childers, S. (editor), *A Mariner of England, An Account of the Career of William Richardson...as told by himself*, Conway Maritime, 1970

Clowes, W.L., *The Royal Navy, A History*, AMC Press (Reprint), New York, 1966

Coates, W.H, *The Good Old Days of Shipping*, The 'Times of India' Press, Bombay (Mumbai), 1900

    The Old 'Country Trade' of the East Indies, Imray, Laurie, Norie & Wilson, 1911

Coggeshall, G., *A History of American Privateers and Letters-of-Marque*, C.T. Evans, New York, 1856

Cole, S., *Our Home Ports*, Effingham Wilson, 1923

Colnett, J., *A Voyage to the South Atlantic and Round Cape Horn into the Pacific Ocean*, 1798, Reprinted as Bibliotheca Australiana # 36, De Capo Press, New York, 1968

Compton, H. (editor), *A Master Mariner, Being the Life and Adventures of Captain Robert Willian Eastwick*, T. Fisher Unwin, 1891

Cornewall-Jones, R.J., *The British Merchant Service*, Sampson Low, Marston, 1898

Cotton, Sir E., *East Indiamen*, The Batchworth Press, 1949

Cotton, J., *Memoir on the Origin and Incorporation of the Trinity House of Deptford Strond*, Darling, 1818

Cowen, R.C., *Frontiers of the Sea*, Gollancz, 1960

Crowhurst, P., *The French War on Trade: Privateering, 1793-1815*, Scolar Press, 1989

Damer-Powell, J.W., *Bristol Privateers and Ships of War*, J.W. Arrowsmith, Bristol, 1930

Dann, J.C. (editor), *The Nagle Journal*, Weidenfeld and Nicolson, New York, 1988

Davis, R., *The Rise of the English Shipping Industry in the 17th and 18th Centuries*, David and Charles, 1962

Dearden, S., *A Nest of Corsairs, The Fighting Karamanlis of Tripoli*, John Murray, 1976

Defoe, D., *History of the Union of Great Britain*, Edinburgh, 1709

Ellacott, S.E., *The Seaman*, two volumes, Abelard-Schuman, 1970

Falconer, W., *Marine Dictionary (1780)* (David and Charles Reprints) Newton Abbot, 1970

Farrington, A., *A Biographical Index of East India Company Maritime Service Officers, 1600-1834*, The British Library, 1999

Foreman, S., *Shoes and Ships and Sealing Wax, An Illustrated History of the Board of Trade, 1786 – 1986*, HMSO, 1986

Forester, C.S. (editor), *The Adventures of John Wetherell*, Michael Joseph, 1954

Garstin, C. (editor), *Samuel Kelly: An Eighteenth Century Seaman whose days have been few and evil, to which is added remarks etc. on places he visited during his pilgrimage in this wilderness*, Jonathan Cape, 1925

Gibson, J.F., *Brocklebanks, 1770-1950*, two volumes, Henry Young, Liverpool, 1953

Gibb, D.E.W., *Lloyd's of London, A Study in Individualism*, Lloyd's, 1972

Golding, T. (editor), *Trinity House from Within*, Trinity House, 1929

Gurney, A., *Compass, A Story of Exploration and Innovation*, W.W. Norton, New York, 2004

Hackman, R., *Ships of the East India Company*, World Ship Society, Gravesend, 2001

Hall, C.D., *Wellington's Navy, Sea Power and the Peninsular War, 1807-1814*, Chatham, 2004

Haws, D., and Hurst, A.A, *The Maritime History of the World*, two volumes, Teredo Books, Brighton, 1985

Hayter, A., *The Wreck of the* Abergavenny: *The Wordsworths and Catastrophe*, Pan Books, 2003

HMSO, *The Mariner's Handbook*, Sixth Edition, 1989
  Ocean Passages for the World, Third Edition, 1973
  Seafarers and Their Ships, 1955

Hood, J., *Marked for Misfortune*, Conway, 2003

Hope, R., *A New History of British Shipping*, John Murray, 1990
  Poor Jack, Chatham, 2001
  The Merchant Navy, Stanford Maritime, 1980

Huddart, J., *A Memoir of the Late Captain Joseph Huddart*, W. Phillips, 1821

Huddart, W., *Unpathed Waters, The Life and Times of Joseph Huddart FRS, 1741-1816*, Quiller Press, 1989

James, W., *The Naval History of Great Britain*, Richard Bentley, 1847

Keay, J., *The Honourable Company, A History of the English East India Company*, Harper Collins, 1991

Kemp, P. (editor) *The Oxford Companion to Ships and the Sea*, Oxford University Press, Oxford, 1988

Kendall, C.W. *Private Men-of-War*, Philip Allan, 1931

Kirby, P.R., *The True Story of the* Grosvenor, Oxford University Press, Cape Town, 1960

Knight, R., *The Pursuit of Victory, The Life and Achievement of Horatio Nelson*, Allen Lane, 2005

Lane-Poole, S., *The Barbary Corsairs*, Fisher Unwin, 1890

Lever, D., *The Young Sea Officer's Sheet Anchor*, John Richardson & Others, 1819

MacGregor, D., *Merchant Sailing Ships, 1775-1815*, Argus Books, Watford, 1980
  Fast Sailing Ships, Their Design and Construction, 1775 – 1875, Conway, 1988
  Schooners in Four Centuries, Argus Books, Hemel Hempstead, 1982

Macintyre, D., *The Privateers*, Paul Elek, 1975

Maclay, E.S., *A History of American Privateers*, Sampson Low, Marston & Co., 1900

Marshall, P.J., *East Indian Fortunes, The British in Bengal in the Eighteenth Century*, Oxford University Press, 1976

Mathias, P., and Pearsall, A.W.H., *Shipping: A Survey of Historical Records*, David & Charles, Newton Abbot, 1971

McIntyre-Brown A., *Time and Tide, 200 Years of the Bibby Line Group, 1807-2007*, Capsica Ltd, Liverpool, 2007

Miller, D., *The Wreck of the* Isabella, Leo Cooper, 1995

Milton, G., *White Gold*, Hodder and Stoughton, 2004

Morse, H.B., *The East India Company Trading to China, 1635-1834*, five volumes, Oxford University Press, Undated (*c.*1860)

Moyse-Bartlett, H., *A History of the Merchant Navy*, Harrap, 1937

Naish, G., *The Interwoven Lives of George Vancouver, Archibald Menzies, Joseph Whidbey and Peter Puget, Exploring the Pacific Northwest Coast*, Canadian Studies, Vol.17, The Edward Mellen Press, Lewiston, New York, 1996

Norie, J.W., *A Complete Epitome of Navigation*, Charles Wilson, 1864

Norman, C.B., *The Corsairs of France*, Sampson Low, Marston, Searle & Rivington, 1887

Norway, A.H., *History of the Post Office Packet Service*, Macmillan & Co., 1895

Pares, R., *War and Trade in the West Indies*, Frank Cass, 1963

Parkinson, C.N. *War in the Eastern Seas, 1793-1815*, Geo. Allen and Unwin, 1954
  Trade in the Eastern Seas, 1793-1813, Frank Cass, 1966
  (editor) *The Trade Winds*, Allen and Unwin, 1948

Parry, J.H. and Sherlock, P.M., *A Short History of the West Indies*, Macmillan, 1971

Popham, H., *A Damned Cunning Fellow, The Eventful Life of Rear-Admiral Sir Home Popham, KCB KCH, KM, FRS, 1762 − 1820*, Old Ferry Press, Tywardreath, 1991

Read, A., *The Coastwise Trade of the United Kingdom*, George Thompson, 1925

Rinman, T., and Brodefors, R., *The Commercial History of Shipping*, Rinman & Lindén AB, Gothenburg, 1983

Ritchie, G.S., *The Admiralty Chart, British Naval Hydrography in the Nineteenth Century*, The Pentland Press, 1995

Rodger, N.A.M., *The Safeguard of the Sea*, Harper Collins, 1997
  Command of the Ocean, Penguin/Allen Lane, 2004

Rosser, W.H., *The Law of Storms Considered Practically*, Charles Wilson, 1876

Rutter, O., *Red Ensign, A History of Convoy*, Robert Hale, 1942

Samhaber, E., *Merchants Make History*, Harrap, 1963

Scoresby, W., *Journal of a Voyage to the Northern Whale-Fishery*, Archibald Constable, Edinburgh, 1823
  The 1806 Log-Book, Caedmon Press, Whitby, 1981

Smith, K., Wattes, C.T. and Watts, M.J., *Records of Merchant Shipping and Seamen*, Public Records Office Guide No.20, PRO Publications, 1998

Spavens, W., *The Narrative of William Spavens, A Chatham Pensioner*, Chatham, 1998 (First published in 1796)

Stamp, D., *The World, A General Geography*, Longmans, 1966

Statham, E.P., *Privateers and Privateering*, Hutchinson, 1910

Sutton, J., *Lords of the East, the East India Company and its Ships*, Conway, 1981

Sugden, J., *Nelson, A Dream of Glory*, Jonathan Cape, 2004

Taylor, S., *Storm and Conquest, The Battle for the Indian Ocean, 1809*, Faber and Faber, 2007

Thomas, R.E., *Stowage: The Properties and Stowage of Cargoes*, Revised Edition, Brown, Son and Ferguson Ltd, Glasgow, 1963

Tracy, N., *Attack on Maritime Trade*, University of Toronto Press, Toronto, 1991

Trinder, I., *The Harwich Packets, 1635-1834*, Trinder, Colchester, 1998

Unknown, *Wreck and Loss of the Ship* Fanny, Thomas Tegg, 1803

Villiers, A., *Vanished Fleets*, Geoffrey Bles, 1931

   Monsoon Seas, The Story of the Indian Ocean, McGraw-Hill, New York, 1952

   Voyaging with the Wind, HMSO, 1975

Wareham, T., *Frigate Commander*, Pen & Sword Maritime, Barnsley, 2004

Watson, L., *Heaven's Breath, A Natural History of the Wind*, Coronet, 1985

Wild, A., *The East India Company, Trade and Conquest from 1600*, HarperCollins, 2000

Williams, G., *Voyages of Delusion*, HarperCollins, 2003

Williamson, J.A., *The Ocean in English History*, Clarendon, Oxford, 1941

Wilson, C., *Seamanship; Both in Theory and Practice*, Norie and Wilson, 1841

Whormby, J., *An Account of the Corporation of Trinity House of Deptford Strond and of Sea Marks in General*, Smith and Ebbs, 1746

Woodman, R.M., *The History of the Ship*, Conway, 1997

   ...of Daring Temper, The Marine Society, 2006

   Keepers of the Sea, Revised Edition, Chaffcutter, Ware, 2005

   with Wilson, J., *The Lighthouses of Trinity House*, Thomas Reed, Bradford on Avon, 2002

UNPUBLISHED MATERIAL

Log of the HCS *Walthamstow*, December 1805 to September 1807, 'On a voyage from London's River to Bengal and Ceylon' (with thanks to the Honourable Company of Master Mariners).

Signal Book of Captain Charles Weller, Commander HCSs *Huddart* (1814) and *Albion* (1820), Honourable East India Company's Service. Weller was successively Sixth Mate of the *Princess Charlotte* (1797), Third Mate of the *Earl Howe* (1800) and *Ceres* (1803) and First Mate of the *Sir William Bensley* (1809) and *Huddart* (1814). He was an Elder Brother of Trinity House between 1834 and 1863 when he, unusually, resigned.

OTHER SOURCES

Reference has been made to the *National Dictionary of National Biography* and other information has also been culled over a period of many years from a variety of sources, including the *Naval Chronicle*, the *Mariner's Mirror* and other learned journals and contemporary organs.

Index

Visit our website and discover thousands of other History Press books.
www.thehistorypress.co.uk

The
History
Press